MW00831876

LIFE IMPRISONMENT

LIFE IMPRISONMENT

A Global Human Rights Analysis

DIRK VAN ZYL SMIT

CATHERINE APPLETON

Harvard University Press

Cambridge, Massachusetts
London, England
2019

Copyright © 2019 by the President and Fellows of Harvard College
All rights reserved
Printed in the United States of America

First printing

Library of Congress Cataloging-in-Publication Data
Names: Van Zyl Smit, Dirk, author. | Appleton, Catherine, author.
Title: Life imprisonment : a global human rights analysis /
Dirk van Zyl Smit and Catherine Appleton.
Description: Cambridge, Massachusetts : Harvard University Press, 2019. |
Includes bibliographical references and index.
Identifiers: LCCN 2018012887 | ISBN 9780674980662 (alk. paper)
Subjects: LCSH: Life imprisonment.
Classification: LCC K5105.5 .V36 2018 | DDC 364.6—dc23
LC record available at https://lccn.loc.gov/2018012887

For ROGER HOOD *and* JAMES B. JACOBS,
mentors and friends

Contents

Preface

Life imprisonment is the ultimate penalty for the most serious crimes in most countries worldwide. Yet unlike the death penalty, for which it is often seen as a substitute, relatively little is known about life imprisonment as an international phenomenon. Moreover, the debate about the acceptability of life imprisonment is somewhat parochial, where it exists at all. Our ambition is to address these gaps in knowledge and analysis. We aim to show that life imprisonment, in many of the ways that it is imposed and implemented worldwide, infringes some of the most fundamental norms of human rights.

We start from a low threshold of preexisting knowledge. No one has conducted a global overview of life imprisonment. No one has sought to explain what is meant by life imprisonment in all the 183 countries and territories worldwide that have clear legal provisions allowing its imposition.

No one has tried to quantify how many people are serving life sentences worldwide. Little is known globally about the offenses for which life imprisonment can be, and is actually, imposed. No one has attempted to conduct a meta-analysis of studies of whether the pains of serving life imprisonment are uniquely severe. No one has conducted a worldwide overview of the possibilities of release from life imprisonment or what happens to those released from life imprisonment. The existing knowledge about life imprisonment is largely nationally based and piecemeal.

In this book we begin to answer basic empirical and legal questions about life imprisonment on a global scale. We have carried out the first worldwide survey of persons serving life imprisonment, reviewed legal materials, and consulted secondary research sources. We are conscious that compiling a full and complete picture of life imprisonment worldwide is nearly impossible, because of both the immense difficulties in collecting accurate data, or any data at all in some countries, and the extent to which law and practice are evolving. Nevertheless, this book provides the first critical account of the imposition and implementation of life sentences on a global scale.

Our central question emerges from Chapter 1: Can a sentence to life imprisonment ever be just? Although the question has been posed from time to time as a national issue of criminal justice, the punishment of life imprisonment deserves much more prominence than it has had up to now, as a question of human rights. In the period following the Second World War, the remarkable rise in the prominence of human rights–based critiques of certain types of punishment—the death penalty in particular—has led to the recasting of debates about their acceptability. Punishments are not considered only according to traditional national criteria of criminal justice, but also according to broader human rights standards, and in particular, respect for the human dignity of the persons on whom they are imposed.

The complexity of life imprisonment makes evaluating it against human rights standards far more challenging than evaluating the death penalty against the same standards. The essence of the death penalty is clear. Questions about how capital punishment is carried out are important, but they are secondary to whether killing someone can ever be justified as punishment. The legal basis for the death penalty is also clear. It is relatively easy to identify whether a country has a provision for capital punishment on its statute book, whether it imposes death sentences, and whether it enforces them by execution.

In the case of life sentences, questions of justification are closely tied to what life imprisonment means in law and how it is implemented in practice. Is life imprisonment the incarceration of a prisoner who is subjected to hard labor or other harsh treatment throughout the sentence and an inevitable death in prison, unless the state, which has unlimited power over the prisoner's liberty, decides to be merciful? Or is it a sentence whereby persons may be detained only for a certain minimum period, during which they are offered opportunities of self-improvement, and after which they are set free unless they still pose a serious risk to society? The former is the portrayal of life imprisonment as envisaged by the eighteenth-century penal philosopher Cesare Beccaria, who famously regarded a life sentence as a harsher, and therefore more effective, punishment than the death penalty.

The latter is the only form of life imprisonment that many modern European countries, such as Germany, Sweden, and Finland, regard as just.

At an early stage of our research it became apparent that the complexity of life imprisonment required us to define it and to clearly identify some basic ideal types to describe the different forms it takes. Only then would we be able to portray life imprisonment worldwide in a way that would illustrate the complexity of this form of punishment and allow for a meaningful discussion of its justice. This is the question that we address in Chapter 2: "Describing Life." There we define the sentence of life imprisonment as: *A sentence following a criminal conviction, which gives the state the power to detain a person in prison for life, that is, until they die there.*

Within this definition, we distinguish between two basic types of life imprisonment: The first is *formal life imprisonment,* in which the sentencing authority imposes a sentence of "imprisonment for life," or uses other words indicating explicitly that it intends convicted persons to be held in prison for as long as they live. (Whether the sentencing authority really means these words is a separate question.) The second is *informal life imprisonment;* there, the sentencing authority imposes a sentence that it does not call life imprisonment, but which could actually result in the persons being held in prison until they die there.

As Figure 0.1 shows, both types of life imprisonment, formal and informal, can be further divided into two ideal types. In the case of formal life imprisonment, following US terminology, we distinguish sentences of *life imprisonment without parole (LWOP)* and *life imprisonment with parole (LWP).* At the heart of this distinction is the fact that prisoners serving LWOP sentences are not routinely considered for release, although they may still be granted clemency. In contrast, prisoners serving LWP sentences are entitled to have their release considered after a fixed period of their sentence has been served and regularly thereafter.

In the case of informal life imprisonment, we distinguish between *de facto life* and *post-conviction indefinite detention.* De facto life refers to fixed-term sentences that are so long that they are likely to result in the persons subject to them dying in prison. The focus is on the length of the sentence itself, not the person's ability to survive the term due to age or state of health. Post-conviction indefinite detention refers to sentences and post-sentencing measures that follow from a conviction and provide for the indefinite detention of convicted persons without specifying that they are life sentences.

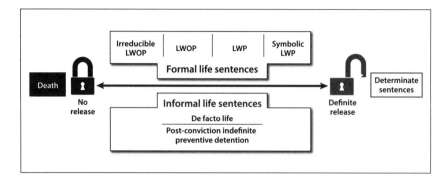

FIGURE 0.1. Defining Life. *Source:* Information collected by authors.

Such sentences are reserved for those individuals who are judged to pose a risk to society, and they generally include provisions for release when the persons so sentenced cease to pose such a risk.

As Figure 0.1 shows, formal life sentences may vary further between those that exclude the possibility of release entirely—LWOP sentences that are not reducible in any way—and LWP sentences in which release is more likely or even, in the case of symbolic life sentences, guaranteed to all prisoners who have had life sentences imposed on them. Informal life sentences, as Figure 0.1 also shows, are not distributed on the same spectrum. In practice, they could amount to LWOP, for example, where a fixed term is for a hundred years, allowing no possibility of release, or they could be the equivalent of LWP, provided they are accompanied by careful provisions for considering the release of the persons who are subject to them.

Following on from the description of life imprisonment, Chapter 3 examines the prevalence of the different types of life imprisonment around the world. The evidence concerning formal life imprisonment sentences in particular is strong enough to indicate what a major punishment life imprisonment is.

- Formal life imprisonment is a statutory penalty in 183 out of a total of 216 countries and territories in the world. In practice, in 2014, life imprisonment was the most severe penalty in 149 of the 216 countries and territories. It is also the most severe penalty in current international criminal courts and tribunals. Far fewer countries have the death penalty as their most severe punishment for crimes committed in peacetime.

- We have information that in 2014, at least 304,814 prisoners were serving formal life sentences worldwide, and we estimate that in fact there were then approximately 479,000 such prisoners. Fewer than 20,000 prisoners were under sentence of death in 2014, with a minority of them likely to be executed eventually.
- In some countries, life imprisonment is regarded as too severe a punishment to be imposed at all. Thirty-three countries do not have life imprisonment or the death penalty as formal statutory sanctions.

Information of this kind is sufficient to establish the bare statistical bones of life imprisonment as a worldwide phenomenon of considerable significance in the penal field, but it is not rich enough to provide the base for a critique of life imprisonment. To remedy that problem, we supplement it with empirical information about the prevalence of the different types of life imprisonment internationally and nationally. We make regional comparisons and note global trends in the use of both formal and informal life imprisonment. This provides a basis for reflection on the forces that contribute to the increased use of life imprisonment in certain regions and countries, and its decline in others. We also estimate global trend data for formal life imprisonment from 2000 to 2014, and we examine LWOP trends in the United States and the rapid rate of growth of this particularly harsh form of life imprisonment over recent decades.

To make judgments informed by human rights norms about life imprisonment worldwide one must go further than description and prevalence. One must also understand why this form of punishment is so often imposed, to the extent that almost half a million people are serving life sentences worldwide. One must know what serving life imprisonment actually entails across different jurisdictions. Finally, one must understand the process by which prisoners are released from life sentences and the conditions and restrictions to which released prisoners are subject to in the community. This is what we set out to do in the further substantive chapters of this book.

Chapter 4 considers persons who are exempt from life sentences, that is, the different groups of people—children, women, and the elderly—on whom life sentences are not imposed in many jurisdictions. Reflection on the human rights justifications for such exclusions, which exist in international treaties such as the Convention on the Rights of the Child, raises wider questions about the reasons for these exclusions to other groups and even about whether to extend them to all individuals facing a possible life sentence.

Chapter 5 presents information on offenses for which life imprisonment may be imposed and is actually imposed. Both are evaluated against the proportionality-based criterion that life imprisonment should only be imposed for the most serious offenses. Attention is paid to how the mandatory use of life imprisonment disturbs this balance. Questions are also asked about how restricting the discretion to impose life sentences by allowing only a limited range of alternatives may risk engendering a distortion that amounts to a fundamental infringement of human rights.

Chapter 6 examines the actual processes for imposing life sentences. To start, it looks at how courts shape individual life sentences to make them more proportionate. They may set minimum terms or make findings about the seriousness of an offense to influence the authorities that will consider the prisoner's release in the future. It also considers briefly the role that other institutions or individuals, such as prosecutors, expert witnesses, and victims, play in the imposition of life sentences.

Chapter 7 assesses what is known about the experiences of prisoners who are serving life terms. It synthesizes existing research on the effects of long-term imprisonment and combines it with accounts from prisoners themselves. This evidence shows that the pains of imprisonment are significantly heightened for individuals serving life sentences, due to the uncertainty of release and the prospect of remaining in prison for the rest of their lives. We also discuss the different regimes to which life-sentenced prisoners are subjected around the world. Evidence from international bodies, such as the European Committee for the Prevention of Torture, and Penal Reform International, shows that in many countries life-sentenced prisoners are singled out for harsh treatment and subjected to increased security measures and impoverished regimes, without any clear justification for doing so.

In Chapter 8 we depart from the largely descriptive pattern and consider what is required in order to implement life sentences well. To this end we examine the international human rights standards that are specifically relevant to the implementation of life imprisonment and the treatment of life-sentenced prisoners. These standards emphasize, not only that no additional restrictions should be inflicted on the basis of the crime that was committed or the sentence that was imposed, but also that prison systems have a duty to recognize and counteract the unique pains of life imprisonment.

All prisoners, including those sentenced to life terms, should be given opportunities for rehabilitation and a clear pathway to release. Furthermore, the chapter focuses on systems around the world that aim to incorporate some of these principles and highlights examples of managing life imprisonment well across different jurisdictions. At a minimum, good practice suggests the need for individualized sentence planning, normalized prison regimes, and purposeful activities for life-sentenced prisoners.

Chapter 9 focuses on the exercise of discretion in releasing persons from life imprisonment. It includes a study of the different bodies with decision-making authority to release life prisoners, such as courts, parole boards, members of the executive authority, and heads of state exercising the power of clemency. We scrutinize the differences in the release procedures for persons formally sentenced to life imprisonment and those subject to post-conviction preventive detention, describe the procedures adopted by the releasing bodies, and evaluate them against standards of due process. This evaluation includes a statistical picture of differing release patterns across jurisdictions.

Chapter 10 analyzes comparative data on life after life imprisonment, focusing particularly on the post-release treatment of life prisoners, including those subject to post-sentence preventive detention. Life prisoners are usually released conditionally, under a wide range of legal restrictions that may remain in force for life and that can, if violated, lead to reincarceration. We assess the reconviction rates of released life-sentenced prisoners and identify key elements of successful reintegration and desistance from crime. Finally, we discuss the fairness of the process for recalling released life-sentenced prisoners, drawing attention to some international recall rates and examining recall practices around the world.

Chapter 11 rethinks life imprisonment against the background of its increasing frequency, while, at the same time, it is increasingly criticized on human rights grounds. We conclude that LWOP can no longer be justified in terms of these developments in human rights. The chapter also considers whether the expansion of a rights-based approach provides arguments, not only for the reduction in the use and penal bite of life imprisonment, but also for its ultimate abolition. We conclude that, while life imprisonment may be outlawed in the future, changes that are incremental and driven by human rights are more realistic in the short run. We then inquire into what a form of life imprisonment that is compliant with human rights would look like, and speculate on whether such a form of life imprisonment would be practically viable. Finally, we consider the role international cooperation can play in propagating such an improved form of life imprisonment and offer guidance to policy makers and practitioners on methods for restricting the use of life imprisonment and implementing it in conformity with standards of human rights.

1

Debating Life

S INCE THE ENLIGHTENMENT at the end of the eighteenth century, the fundamental justice of imposing certain harsh forms of punishment—in particular the death penalty—has been the subject of intensive debate. Nevertheless, ever since then, mainstream penology has generally accepted that fixed-term imprisonment can be imposed and implemented fairly enough to be an acceptable and proportionate form of punishment. The notion of "a just measure of pain"[1] united utilitarian and retributive theorists of punishment, as it united also the ideals of those who imposed sentences of imprisonment and those who carried them out.

Did this approach, with its implicit commitment to proportionate punishment, apply to life imprisonment too? If so, does it still apply? In other words, is it acceptable to impose sentences that deliberately give the state the power to detain convicted offenders in prison until they die there? And can such sentences be implemented justly?

In this chapter we introduce the key debates about the justness of life imprisonment in two related ways, which are designed to provide a framework for the analysis of life imprisonment as it manifests itself worldwide. First, we look briefly at the key justifications for punishment that were put forward for life imprisonment, particularly by criminal justice specialists, as life sentences emerged as a separate form of punishment from the eighteenth century onward.

Second, we focus on the human rights principles that, since the midtwentieth century, have become increasingly important tools for evaluating the implementation of all forms of punishment against wider standards than those that have long been part of debates within criminal justice. In this regard, we pay particular attention to the human rights–based move away from the death penalty. We note that since the last decade of the twentieth century, the anti-death-penalty movement has led to a renewed emphasis on life imprisonment in jurisdictions where previously it had played little or no role. At the same time, we show how it has also led to life imprisonment increasingly being subject to human rights–based challenges that go beyond the critique of it that is advanced from within a purely criminal justice–based approach.

Historical Justifications for Life Imprisonment

Libraries of books have been written about theories of punishment generally. Our modest aim here is simply to introduce the justifications for life imprisonment in terms of the recognized theories of punishment that have emerged from the eighteenth-century Enlightenment onward, in order to reflect in subsequent chapters on what continuing purchase they have on modern life imprisonment. The justifications include both those based squarely in theories of punishment—deterrence, retributivism, and rehabilitation—and concerns about incapacitation and incorrigibility, which are justified in terms of wider social policies.

Deterrence

The notion that punishment should be measured and spelled out clearly, so that the potential offender could know the punishment in advance and could be deterred by it, is usually associated with the work of the eighteenth-century Italian philosopher Cesare Beccaria.[2] But Beccaria also emphasized that, to be just, a punishment ought not to be unnecessarily severe. It should not exceed the degree of intensity that will deter others from crime. Similarly, Enlightenment prison reformers, such as John Howard, were opposed to random cruelty.[3] They demanded that the prisons where the newly prominent prison terms would be served should be regulated by law, which would clearly spell out in advance the rules governing the deterrent regimes they would follow: the implementation of prison sentences had to be firm but fair to achieve its deterrent objectives precisely.

Famously, Beccaria not only wanted to introduce determinate sentences of imprisonment with clear terms set for closely defined offenses but was also opposed to the death penalty as an unnecessary form of cruelty in a well-ordered society. He has remained a hero of death-penalty abolitionists ever since. However, one is immediately struck by the paradox that Beccaria's approach to life imprisonment is very different from that which he adopted toward other forms of imprisonment including, crucially, capital punishment. In an oft-cited passage in support of "perpetual penal servitude" as a viable alternative to the death penalty, Beccaria commented that

> there is no one who, upon reflection, would choose the total and permanent loss of his own liberty, no matter how advantageous a crime might be: therefore, the intensity of perpetual penal servitude, substituted for the death penalty, has all that is necessary to deter even the most determined mind. Indeed, I would say that it has even more: a great many men look upon death with a calm and steady gaze, some out of fanaticism, some out of vanity.... But neither fanaticism nor vanity survives in fetters or chains, under cudgel and the yoke, or in an iron cage, where the desperate man finds that his woes are beginning rather than ending.[4]

Beccaria's opposition to the death penalty but support for life imprisonment was based not on his professed disavowal of the cruelty of capital punishment but on his concern with the maintenance of order.[5] From his perspective, executing murderers would stimulate cruelty among the public, while life imprisonment would make more of an impact as the public would see those subject to the perpetual slavery of a life sentence, and it would therefore be a more effective deterrent.[6] Other early utilitarians reasoned in the same way. Thus Jeremy Bentham remarked in 1841 that "the contemplation of perpetual imprisonment, accompanied with hard labour and occasional solitary confinement, would produce a deeper impression on the minds of persons in whom it is more eminently desirable that the impression should be produced, than even death itself."[7]

Properly understood and enforced, a life-sentence regime for both Beccaria and Bentham should be so harsh that it renders death a mercy. The historical consequence of Beccaria's ideas has been described by Thorsten Sellin, who noted that his "advocacy of penal slavery encouraged [in Austria, Hungary and elsewhere] the invention of horrid forms of imprisonment believed to be more deterrent than death."[8] Many rulers at the time, such as Catherine the Great of Russia and Maria Theresa of Austria, evinced real interest in Beccaria's ideas on life imprisonment and several attempts were made to implement them. Many individuals were thus saved from an immediate execution, but instead were subject to such a harsh form of life imprisonment that their incarceration ended only in early death.[9] In the United States, too, Beccaria's writings influenced debate on life imprisonment in the early eighteenth century and its increasing use in the early nineteenth century.[10]

An important empirical question for this book is the extent to which the utilitarians' bleak vision of life imprisonment and its impact still holds true. A key part of the utilitarian vision of life imprisonment as a deterrent was of life sentences being carried out in full. As we demonstrate in Chapter 3, life sentences from which there is, in law and in fact, no, or almost no, prospect of release continue to play a prominent part in life imprisonment worldwide. Similarly, Chapter 7 shows that the dire prison conditions that Beccaria saw as the norm for persons serving life sentences still exist in many parts of the world. In some jurisdictions, life prisoners are deliberately treated more harshly than prisoners serving fixed terms, arguably to ensure that life sentences are sufficiently dreadful to deter those who contemplate committing the serious crimes for which they are usually imposed.

Retributivism

Retributivism, in the sense that the punishment should fit the crime, has been a staple of penal theory for many centuries. A more nuanced version, that a term of imprisonment could be a fair punishment when imposed in the right proportion to the seriousness of the offense, is fundamental to the Enlightenment penal theory that emerged from the mid-eighteenth century onward. The ideal of proportionate punishment was not limited to the utilitarian objectives associated with Beccaria. It was shared by supporters of deterrence and retribution. It was also reflected in the ideals of those who imposed sentences of imprisonment and those who implemented them with carefully calculated disciplinary harshness.

Life imprisonment was seen not only as a deterrent sentence but also as a retributive punishment that, particularly if implemented harshly and fully, had sufficient penal bite to make it proportionate to the most serious crimes.

For example, in a speech in Parliament in 1868, the English liberal, John Stuart Mill, like Beccaria and Bentham before him, compared the death penalty with life in prison and argued that the former was less cruel:

> What comparison can there really be, in point of severity between consigning a man to the short pang of a rapid death, and immuring him in a living tomb, there to linger out what may be a long life in the hardest and most monotonous toil, without any of its alleviation or rewards—debarred from all pleasant sights and sounds, and cut off from all earthly hope, except a slight mitigation of bodily restraint, or a small improvement in diet?[11]

Mill, went on to argue that "it is not human life only, not human life as such that ought to be sacred to us, but human feelings. The capacity of suffering is what we should cause to be respected, not the mere capacity of existing."[12]

Similarly severe criticisms of life imprisonment were compellingly articulated by Mill's younger contemporary, the British Quaker William Tallack. He noted that few abolitionists "have taken the trouble to make themselves acquainted with the extreme practical difficulties attendant upon the provision of an effectual substitute for that [death] penalty."[13] He highlighted the unmitigated despair and despondency of the prisoner committed for life and commented, "Almost the only possible justification for the horrors of life imprisonment, is that it has been regarded as constituting a substitute for Capital Punishment, which many persons consider to be a still greater evil."[14] According to Tallack, the death penalty "may be mercy itself, compared with the prolonged injury inflicted upon the spiritual and mental powers, extended over many years" under life imprisonment.[15]

There is evidence that some early retributivists were uncomfortable with both the death penalty and life imprisonment, as opposed to fixed-term sentences that could be more easily scaled so that the punishment (the period of the loss of liberty) fitted the severity of the crime. An early example of this unease was reflected in the French Penal Code of 1791. In the form in which it was originally proposed, it would have eliminated both the death penalty and life imprisonment, replacing them by fixed terms of imprisonment for specific offenses. Such sentences would have had to be imposed as legislated, with no judicial discretion to sentence within a range. The statutorily determined fixed terms with no prospect of early release were a way of limiting the power of both the judiciary and the executive. However, the code was not adopted in the form in which it was proposed. In its final form, it included the death penalty and not life imprisonment, but the idea of proportionality as a means of limiting excessive punishments lived on in the fact that the maximum term of imprisonment was twenty-four years.[16]

A similar line of thinking can be found in the writings of the late-eighteenth-century American penal reformer Benjamin Rush. In a pamphlet in 1792, he not only opposed capital punishment for murder (and other crimes), but also argued that all prison sentences imposed instead of the death penalty should be based on a fixed scale of years. He proposed that the length of such fixed-term sentences and the conditions under which they should be served should be proportionate to the seriousness of the offense.[17]

In neither France nor the United States, however, was life imprisonment effectively excluded for long from the palette of punishments. In 1810, a life sentence was added by the Napoleonic French Penal Code, which described it, in terms similar to those of Beccaria, as hard labor in perpetuity.[18] There is also historical evidence that the states that constituted the fledgling United States used life imprisonment regularly in the first decades after independence.[19] At that time, to a large extent, both death sentences and life imprisonment were simply seen as severe but deserved punishments, proportionate to the seriousness of the crimes for which they were imposed. Indeed, early nineteenth-century US commentators remarked critically that life sentences were being undermined because corrupt practices allowed life-sentenced prisoners to serve less than their deserved penalties.[20]

Incapacitation

Punishment that removes offenders from society is sometimes justified simply on the basis that it incapacitates them, thus protecting society from the crimes that they could otherwise commit as they are permanently excluded from normal society. Of course, the death penalty has the same result. However, as concerns about the death penalty's proportionality for crimes other than homicide mounted, and as the public clamor against the imposition of capital punishment on certain classes of offenders grew, life imprisonment became a less controversial alternative. It was seen as a means of expelling those for whom the death penalty might be regarded as a disproportionately severe retributive response for the crimes, but still resulted in their permanent removal. Moreover, this was achieved without the public tumult an execution might entail: out of sight, out of mind.

As an incapacitatory sentence, life imprisonment operated in tandem with transportation for much of the eighteenth and nineteenth centuries. Both were effective ways of excluding unwanted criminals from society. Transportation from the United Kingdom to the colonies, first to North America and, after the independence of the United States, to Australia, could be for a fixed term or for life.[21] Particularly in the case of Australia, it was often very hard for those who had been transported to return to the United Kingdom. This also applies to transportation from France to Guyana, where the assumption was that offenders would die there.[22] That reality was very similar to that of life imprisonment as described by Beccaria. Both life imprisonment and transportation can be seen as means for maintaining social order, arguably with the incapacitatory aspect more significant than the deterrent one.

The close links between transportation and life imprisonment as incapacitatory punishments are perhaps best illustrated by the Indian Penal Code of 1860, which originally made provisions for transportation for life but not imprisonment for life. The code made it clear that a sentencing court did not have to specify the place to which such sentenced prisoners were to be taken. It could also be a prison on Indian territory. Only after some years of independence, in 1955 in India, in 1972 in Pakistan, and in 1985 in Bangladesh, which all still use updated versions of the old colonial Indian Penal Code, was transportation for life formally amended to imprisonment for life.[23]

Rehabilitation

The historical connections between life imprisonment and rehabilitation are of a slightly later vintage than the other theories of punishment that linked life imprisonment and the Enlightenment. The idea that imprisonment could be used positively, not only to deter prisoners and others who were aware of their suffering in prison but also to rehabilitate offenders by improving their skills and their morals, has strong American roots. The idea first developed in the tightly ordered prisons of Pennsylvania and New York, which, in the 1830s, became models for the rest of the world. They were visited by Europeans in particular as blueprints for the ideal prison.

Their regimes were credited with the power of changing inmates into law-abiding citizens.[24] The idea that offenders would respond well to indeterminate sentences, as they encourage rehabilitation, was taken further by Alexander Maconochie on Norfolk Island in Australia in the 1840s and adopted by Sir Walter Crofton in the Irish penal system, with the added incentive of conditional release for those who proved themselves in prison.[25]

These widely admired initiatives were complemented a generation later by the rise of an optimistic "scientific" penology, the practitioners of which claimed that they had the ability to transform most prisoners as long as the sentencing structure allowed them to do so. What these practitioners, such as Enoch Wines and Zebulon Brockway, who from the late 1860s onward were active in Pennsylvania and New York, respectively, sought, were indeterminate sentences, ranging from as little as one year to life imprisonment. This would allow "experts" to decide when someone should be released.[26] On the face of it, such sentences were very different from the harsh whole-life terms that Beccaria had foreseen.

The rhetorical focus was strongly on the ability to prepare most prisoners for release by reforming them long before the full terms of their sentences had been served. Yet, potentially, they remained life sentences. As Wines explained in his address to the trendsetting National Congress on Penitentiary and Reformatory Discipline, which was held in Cincinnati in 1870, "the principle that imprisonment ought to be continued till reformation has been effected, and if that happy consummation is never attained, then during the prisoner's natural life, [has] become a conviction with a large number of American penologists."[27] Failure to reform was seen as the fault of the stubborn prisoner, whose continued detention, beyond what was otherwise justified by the crime he had committed, was the result of his own shortcomings.

The implications for life imprisonment of this new penological movement were profound. It clearly went against the emphasis on offense-based proportionality in retributive penal theory, which operated from the assumption that life sentences were always harsh punishments reserved for the most serious offenses. Sentences with life imprisonment as their maximum could be imposed more freely and for a wider range of offenses, for it was optimistically believed that most, if not all, prisoners had the capacity to reform and thus ensure that they did not stay in prison for excessively long periods. The new movement also placed a great deal of confidence in the ability of experts to judge when a person was ready for release. This meant that they saw life sentences as being reevaluated by expert bodies, that is, the parole boards that were beginning to emerge in the United States and elsewhere.[28]

Incorrigibility

The optimism about treating offenders that arose in the United States in the 1870s was part of a wider international movement that challenged the classical penal theories about the correct relationship between crime and punishment. The basis of this challenge was that scientific study could positively identify the causes of crime. Once this had been done, it was claimed that it would be possible to indicate how individual offenders should be reformed by imposing appropriate sentences and implementing them according to the best scientific principles. It soon became apparent, however, that, while there was agreement that the causes of crime and the methods of treating offenders should be studied, the optimism about the possibility of reforming them through scientific sentencing was not universally shared. Increasing attention began to be paid from the late nineteenth century onward, by European penologists, such as Franz von Liszt, to the notion that some offenders were incorrigible, since they could neither be deterred nor rehabilitated. For von Liszt, considerations of retribution, which he regarded as barbarous, had no place in a system of criminal law that should serve solely to protect the public. To achieve this objective, those who could be deterred should be given sentences, as Beccaria had proposed a century earlier, that were proportionate to the minimum required to dissuade them from committing further crimes. Those who could be rehabilitated should be subject to strict programs designed to achieve just that, and should be released on the successful completion of these programs. However, the truly "incorrigible" should not be treated but simply detained for the rest of their lives with no prospect of release.[29]

It is true that in 1878 the final report of the International Prison Congress held in Stockholm, at which both American and European representatives were present, acknowledged that conditional release was "not contrary to principles of penal law, not harming the judgment, and presenting advantages for society and for the convicted."[30] However, models of parole in Europe were generally characterized by less ambitious goals and by more

limited discretion than their American counterparts. This distinction became prominent during the so-called Progressive era in the United States,
at the beginning of the twentieth century. David Rothman has explained
that the optimistic American reformers of this era were far more trusting
than their European counterparts in accepting that the "experts" of the parole boards would make "scientifically informed" decisions.[31]

The debates in late-nineteenth- and early twentieth-century penology
turned on subtly contrasting responses to the growing body of "scientific"
support on both sides of the Atlantic for individualized treatment for offenders. In the United States, the response was to impose indeterminate
sentences freely. These might range from one year to life, for purposes of
treatment for a wide range of offenses. Parole boards were then, however,
allowed considerable discretion to determine how long the offender would
actually serve.[32]

In Europe, notwithstanding the disdain of von Liszt and his colleagues for
anything in sentencing that smacked of retributive punishment, the protection of individual liberty offered by the classical criminal law, including its
guarantees that sentences should be proportionate to the severity of the offense committed, remained important. Compared to definitions in the United
States, there was a more restricted range of offenses that were regarded as
potentially so serious that a sentence of life imprisonment would be appropriate. In several jurisdictions, however, Europeans departed from
these principles of offense proportionality for a class of "incorrigible" offenders, who could be detained indeterminately, not in order to punish or
reform them but because they could not be reformed. This was done by allowing criminal courts to impose measures that would allow such offenders
to be detained indefinitely, that is, for periods as long as prisoners sentenced
formally to life imprisonment.

In the German-speaking world, this approach was pioneered in the early
twentieth century by Carl Stoos, the author of the first Swiss penal code. Stoos
kept in place the ideal of offense-proportionate sentencing, with life imprisonment at its apex for the most serious offenses. At the same time he established
a second track, which allowed criminal courts to impose measures of indefinite detention on individuals who were regarded either as incorrigible
or as requiring very long terms of detention in order to rehabilitate them.[33]
This form of post-conviction indefinite detention was widened and sometimes abused by being applied beyond its stated purposes, by Fascist governments in the 1930s in particular. In Germany, for example, scholars had

long suggested that post-sentence preventive detention should be introduced
to deal with a small group of dangerous habitual offenders. Provision for
such detention was introduced into the German Penal Code in 1933 but,
with the enthusiastic support of Nazi politicians, it was used for a much
larger group of persons than originally intended.[34] Many of these abuses
were subsequently curtailed.[35] However, as we explain in Chapters 2 and 3,
such indefinite detention, which was often, but not always, called life imprisonment, has remained a feature of many modern penal systems on both
sides of the Atlantic and elsewhere.

The New Framework: Punishment and Human Rights

The theories of punishment mentioned in relation to the historical justifications of life imprisonment continue to shape arguments about its use.
Debates about the deterrent, retributive, and incapacitatory roles of life
imprisonment persist, particularly when life sentences are considered as an
alternative to the death penalty, but also when they are compared to long
fixed terms of imprisonment.

At the same time, although the rehabilitative optimism of the late nineteenth and early twentieth centuries in the United States faded in the 1970s,
ideals of human improvability continue to play a part in life imprisonment
debates around the world. To understand these complex developments, we
need to discuss the impact of the human rights movement on debates about
punishment in general, before considering life imprisonment in particular.

While the theories of punishment directly relevant to life imprisonment
have remained surprisingly stable since the eighteenth century, the same
cannot be said for the wider intellectual climate within which they are articulated and applied to evaluating particular forms of sentencing and punishment. The most dramatic development in this regard since the end of
the Second World War has been the growing attention paid to human rights
standards. Increasingly, they are enshrined in binding international and national legal instruments and are to be applied to all state actions, including
the imposition and implementation of punishment.

This is not to suggest that the major shift in the approach to punishment that took place toward the end of the eighteenth century had not
sought to develop some such guarantees. As Michel Foucault recognized,
the search for appropriate legal standards to support newly articulated ideas

about punishment was driven by an attempt to answer the question: "How are the two elements, which are everywhere present in demands for a more lenient penal system, 'measure' and 'humanity,' to be articulated upon one another, in a single strategy?"[36]

These penal ideals soon found direct reflection in the new constitutional orders that emerged at the end of the eighteenth century in the United States and France. In 1789, the Eighth Amendment to the US Constitution followed the wording of the English Bill of Rights of a century earlier in prohibiting "cruel and unusual punishments," while the French Declaration of the Rights of Man, adopted in the same year, also had the effect of guaranteeing the human dignity of persons subject to penal sanctions.[37] The inclusion of these provisions in the two major constitutional documents of the age increased, not only their legal salience, but also their more general prestige. However, their widespread impact was long delayed. In part, this was because of the sometimes narrow interpretation given to these provisions. It was limited to preventing new and excessively harsh punishments rather than evaluating existing forms of punishment against wider standards.

Although the broad human rights tradition had deep roots in both the ideas of natural law and the Enlightenment, it flourished after the Second World War when, after the defeat of fascism, a determined effort was made to create a new world order in which the human rights of individuals were recognized and given legal force in international law.[38] Civil and political rights in particular were soon reflected in a range of international instruments with clear implications for punishment, to which they tended to refer directly. In 1946, the Universal Declaration of Human Rights recognized the importance of human dignity (Article 1) and a range of other rights, including the prohibition of torture and cruel, inhuman, or degrading treatment or punishment (Article 5). This call was echoed in similar prohibitions on inhuman and degrading treatment or punishment in regional human rights conventions: in Article 3 of the European Convention on Human Rights (1950), in Article 5 of the American Convention on Human Rights (1969), and in Article 3 of the African Charter on Human and Peoples' Rights (1981).

At the international level, the right to human dignity and the related prohibition of torture and cruel, inhuman, and degrading treatment or punishment were given significance as concepts underpinning the regulation of prison conditions by the International Covenant on Civil and Political

Rights (ICCPR), which came into force in 1976. The ICCPR was important both in terms of its careful limitation of the use of the death penalty (Article 6) and in terms of its recognition of prisoners' rights, which could only be achieved if adequate prison conditions existed. Not only did it provide that "all persons deprived of their liberty shall be treated with humanity and with respect for the inherent dignity of the human person" (Article 10[1]), it also provided that "no one should be subjected to torture or to cruel, inhuman or degrading treatment or punishment" (Article 7). This last prohibition is given considerable added weight by the fact that it is the core of the United Nations Convention against Torture and Other Cruel, Inhuman or Degrading Treatment or Punishment, which entered into force in 1987.

The ICCPR contains further provisions that can be interpreted as setting positive requirements concerning prison conditions. Of particular importance is the requirement in Article 10(3) that "the penitentiary system shall comprise treatment of prisoners the essential aim of which shall be their social rehabilitation." This can be seen as an overarching requirement according to which the treatment of all sentenced prisoners and the prison conditions to facilitate it should be judged.[39]

The increasing recognition of the human rights relevant to punishment has been mirrored in a growing number of national constitutions that specified legally binding fundamental rights to be free from torture, and cruel, inhuman, and degrading punishment.[40] Even in the rare modern constitutions in which such a prohibition is not mentioned explicitly in a justiciable bill of rights, it is regarded as implicitly present. In India it has been deduced from the due process clause,[41] while the recognition of human dignity as the fundamental right in the German Basic Law has been held to encompass a prohibition, not only on torture, but also on inhuman and degrading punishment and treatment.[42]

The implications of human rights that are directly applicable to punishment are, however, rarely spelled out in the primary international, regional, or national instruments. In some instances, these instruments are supplemented by protocols on specific penal topics, such as the protocols dealing with the death penalty. Such protocols have the status of binding treaties for the states that have ratified them. In other instances, treaties on a more specific topic, such as the 1989 United Nations Convention on the Rights of the Child (CRC), have a few provisions dealing with penal matters. In the case of the CRC there is a specific prohibition on the imposition of life imprisonment without the possibility of release on children,[43] but such provisions on life imprisonment in the body of the treaty are very rare.

Characteristic of the post–Second World War period is that the general, treaty-level instruments are supplemented by a whole range of secondary material. These include international and regional rules, standards, resolutions, and recommendations. The terminology is somewhat interchangeable.

A further contribution to this body of material is made by interpretations of the primary instruments by international, regional, or national courts. In addition, there are many reports of inspecting and monitoring bodies that appeal to general human rights norms while developing standards that deal with specific manifestations of punishment. Both the United Nations and the Council of Europe publish compendia of these rules that cover virtually every aspect of the penal process.[44] The human rights perspectives that these rules, recommendations, and standards bring to bear on debates about punishment cannot be ignored. They are sometimes described as creating a form of soft law, ostensibly of little legal significance, but that term is misleading. In several instances, bodies of rules may gain additional status by being referred to regularly in the interpretation of binding instruments. An example is the 1955 United Nations Standard Minimum Rules for the Treatment of Prisoners, which, over the years, has grown in status to the point where it is recognized that "some of their specific rules may reflect legal obligations."[45] The argument about the increasing importance of soft law in the field of prisoners' rights was made persuasively recently in the European Court of Human Rights (ECtHR) by Judge Pinto de Albuquerque, who demonstrated that there is a pan-European and worldwide trend toward the hardening of prison soft law. This has important ramifications, Judge Pinto de Albuquerque concluded, asserting that once soft law has "hardened," it has to be followed as a source of binding norms of international law.[46]

The development of international human rights law, both in its hard and soft forms, has led to certain forms of punishment being challenged directly. This has been seen most dramatically in the case of capital punishment where, as Hood and Hoyle noted, "The dynamo for the new wave of abolition [of capital punishment] was the development of international human rights law."[47] They explained that the acceptance of human rights principles in the aftermath of the Second World War "created a climate that advocated, in the name of democracy and freedom, the protection of citizens from the power of the state and the tyranny of the opinions of the masses."[48] In this climate, a political process has emerged that has transformed "consideration of capital punishment from an issue to be decided solely or mainly as an aspect of national criminal justice policy to the status of a fundamental violation of human rights; not only the right to life but the right to be free of excessive, repressive and tortuous punishments."[49]

Similar human rights–based developments can be seen in the case of movements to abolish corporal punishment worldwide. In the case of both corporal and capital punishment there has been considerable interaction between international and national human rights initiatives. A prominent role in incorporating some of this new thinking has been played by major national and regional courts that implicitly or explicitly reflected what the US Supreme Court described as "evolving standards of decency" in its jurisprudence about acceptable punishments.[50] In some instances, this evolution has led to the abolition of both capital punishment and corporal punishment, but even where it has not done so, it has shaped the debate about other forms of punishment, including life imprisonment.

The evolutionary relationship between life imprisonment and human rights norms has been more complex than the relationship with capital or corporal punishment, because life imprisonment is a multifaceted type of punishment that does not offer an easy a target for human rights activism. We do not want to anticipate the overall critique of life imprisonment in Chapter 11 but rather to emphasize that some of the key, human rights–based concepts, which have become prominent in the post–Second World War era, are of particular relevance to the evaluation of life sentences. In this chapter, we refer to the various international standards that are addressed specifically to life imprisonment. The details of what these international standards recommend will be considered in the chapters that follow. What is important for the purposes of this chapter is to note the way in which these standards have been combined with more general human rights principles and have created a new dimension for debates about penal policies that were previously regarded as purely within the ambit of criminal justice.

Human Dignity

First among these general human rights principles is the idea that all persons have human dignity, which must be protected. This includes individuals subject to punishment, even those who have committed the most heinous offenses. While punishment inevitably limits the human rights of those subjected to it, it cannot deny their fundamental dignity. The connection between the protection of the human dignity of all persons and the prohibition of certain forms of punishment, defined variously as "cruel and unusual" or "inhuman and degrading," is close. As the US Supreme Court recognized in 2011: "Prisoners retain the essence of human dignity inherent in all persons. Respect for that dignity animates the Eighth Amendment prohibition against cruel and unusual punishment."[51]

More important than the precise words is the impetus that these prohibitions have given to the critique of certain long-established ideas about specific forms of punishment. Capital punishment has been successfully attacked on the basis that the death penalty is fundamentally contrary to human dignity. This has meant not only that life imprisonment has become increasingly more prominent as a mandatory alternative to the death penalty, but also that the debate has shifted to whether life sentences also infringe the human dignity of those subject to them.[52]

The recent emphasis on life imprisonment is paradoxical. On the one hand, there is renewed interest in ensuring that "life should mean life" so that it will be a "real" alternative to the death penalty. On the other hand, human rights–driven concerns have meant that the analytical tools that a dignity-based analysis offers have been applied to the sentence of life imprisonment, too. The concern is not only whether it is a less harsh sentence than the death penalty, but also whether life imprisonment, at least in its more drastic forms, is not also fundamentally contrary to human dignity. In October 2014, the Pope added his moral authority to this debate by calling for the abolition of all life imprisonment on the explicit grounds that it infringed human dignity.[53]

Proportionality Reconsidered

The idea that a deserved punishment is a punishment that is proportionate to the seriousness of the offense goes back to the long-established penal theory of retribution. However, a concern for human rights has led to the proportionality equation being questioned afresh.[54] A human rights orientation does so: not only by stressing the fundamental cruelty of a punishment such as the sentence of death, which, if it is to be used at all, should be applied only to the most serious offenses, but also by applying the same principle of proportionality to imprisonment in general and to life imprisonment, as the most severe form of imprisonment, in particular.

In the United States the link that was made in the early 1970s between proportionality and life sentences, via the prohibition against cruel and unusual punishments, had as its point of departure an attack on indeterminate penalties for relatively trivial offenses, which could be a sentence of from one year to life. The proportionality argument against such sentences is simple. If persons serve many years or even a life term for such an offense because they are deemed not to be "cured" of their criminal tendency, the length of the punishment would be grossly disproportionate to the crime committed and would therefore infringe their human rights. The essence of the argument was captured in the California case of *Lynch* in 1973. Lynch had been convicted of a second count of indecent exposure and sentenced to a one-year to life term. The Supreme Court of California noted that Lynch had no vested right to release and that he could therefore be imprisoned for the rest of his life for his offense. Viewed in this way, it had no difficulty in holding that his sentence was grossly disproportionate to the crime he had committed and therefore cruel and unusual, thus infringing the Eighth Amendment of the US Constitution.[55]

Lynch's case was much quoted at the time, but the opposition to life sentences that included the possibility of early release was also driven by a wider distrust of state power in general. In the late 1960s and early 1970s in the United States in particular, there were doubts about allowing wide discretionary executive powers over prisoners when seeking to "rehabilitate" them. The argument put forward in this debate was that the success of rehabilitation was, at best, not proven and should therefore not be taken into account when determining sentence. Not doing so, the critics believed, would lead to shorter, fairer sentences. These shorter sentences, the critics argued, should be for fixed terms rather than being indeterminate. Indeterminate sentences would require parole boards to make decisions based on dubious criteria. The critics claimed that parole boards could not judge effectively whether someone had been rehabilitated, and the attempts to do so further distorted the relationship between the punishment and the crime.[56]

The American skepticism about intervention that denied personal liberty in order to rehabilitate was part of a wider critique of institutions of social control in the West during the 1960s and 1970s. In Europe its impact was felt particularly strongly in Nordic countries, where both life imprisonment and other forms of indefinite detention were subject to sustained challenge because of the belief that unjustified rehabilitative claims made for them led to disproportionately severe interventions in the liberty of those upon whom they were imposed.[57] The outcome of this debate differed: in Finland and Denmark it led to a much more restricted use of post-conviction indefinite detention from the 1970s onward, while in Sweden preventive detention following a criminal conviction was abolished outright in 1981. In all three of these countries, formal life imprisonment was subject to a sustained critique and to procedural reforms that would restrict its use and duration. However, only in Norway was life imprisonment abolished outright (in 1981) on the grounds of its indeterminate nature and its socially exclusionary effects.[58] Although deliberate restrictions on the use of life imprisonment on the basis of a denial of its rehabilitative functions have faded somewhat since the 1970s and 1980s in Scandinavia, the importance of proportionality between crime and punishment has continued to be recognized worldwide and is now perceived as a human rights–based restriction on the use of life and other long prison sentences.[59]

Prisoners' Rights

The widespread recognition of a general right to human dignity has also informed the growing emphasis on the rights of prisoners as a subfield of human rights law and practice. In the post–Second World War period, prisoners' rights were developed in several international instruments, of which the pioneering 1955 United Nations Standard Minimum Rules for Treatment of Prisoners (UNSMR) was the most prominent.[60]

In 2015 the UNSMR were finally revised to place more emphasis on the human dignity of prisoners, and renamed the Nelson Mandela Rules.[61] Although these revised rules develop prisoners' rights only in general terms, they have already been applied specifically to the position of life-sentenced prisoners by the Supreme Court of Zimbabwe. The court pointed out that, although the Nelson Mandela Rules are not fully binding on member states of the United Nations, "the general consensus amongst States is that they are highly persuasive in influencing and regulating the treatment of prisoners and the administration of penal institutions generally. They are regarded as being the primary source of standards relating to treatment in detention."[62]

The various United Nations rules have been replicated and elaborated from the 1970s onward at regional and national levels by detailed enactments that spell out the rights and privileges of prisoners much more fully. In Europe a particularly prominent role is played by the 2006 European Prison Rules, which the ECtHR judge Pinto de Albuquerque has described as "the prototype of hardened soft law in the Council of Europe's normative system."[63]

Underlying the movement toward the wider recognition of prisoners' rights worldwide is a fundamental recognition that prisoners are not slaves of the state but rather are entitled to recognition of their rights like any other citizen—indeed, like any other human being.[64] The recognition has grown that people are sent to prison as punishment and not for additional punishment. Moreover, there has been a mounting acceptance worldwide that all this regulation of the treatment of prisoners requires enforcement by a range of formal mechanisms. In many countries, inspectorates, ombudsmen, courts, and other similar bodies oversee, with varying degrees of success, the provision of prisoners' rights. With this has come the recognition of the importance of correct procedures being followed in evaluating whether prisoners' rights are being recognized appropriately. To a growing extent, the rights of prisoners are being extended to procedural rights enabling them to challenge aspects of their treatment.[65]

Insofar as prisoners' rights are recognized, they clearly apply to all prisoners, including individuals serving life sentences. Arguments based on them can be used to challenge claims that life prisoners should, because of their sentence, be subject to extra restrictions for purposes of additional punishment. Indeed, the case can be made that the rights of life prisoners may need increased protection because of the additional vulnerabilities that they face due to the long and indefinite duration of their sentences.[66]

Prisoners' rights relate both to internal prison conditions and regimes, and to external aspects of their treatment, that is, to their release and to restrictions to which they may be subject after release. The internal prison conditions of course matter particularly to prisoners who are going to spend very extended periods, if not their entire lives, in prison. Life prisoners are highly dependent on the prison authorities to keep them in touch with the outside world. Rights to family visits and other forms of contact are aspects of prison law that are of particular salience to life prisoners.[67]

The external aspects are, similarly, very important to life prisoners, for, unlike prisoners serving fixed terms, their eventual release is not assured, but rather depends on a process that involves both the prison authorities and some outside decision makers. Here, too, the right to due process, which is an element of modern human rights–based prison law, provides a useful point of departure for critical analyses of release from life imprisonment.[68] Prisoners' rights relating specifically to life imprisonment are spelled out in an increasing number of national and regional instruments that build on more general standards of prisoners' rights. Thus, for example, a 1994 United Nations report, simply entitled *Life Imprisonment,* takes as its point of departure that states have a duty "to ensure that actual conditions of life-sentence prisoners are compatible with human dignity and accepted minimal standards for all prisoners, in accordance with the Standard Minimum Rules for the Treatment of Prisoners," and then carefully spells out "general considerations" about the use of life imprisonment and the treatment of those who are subject to it.[69] When the report is read closely, it becomes apparent that it gives a great deal of guidance on issues ranging from limiting the use of life imprisonment, through implementing it fairly, to allowing for the consideration of release of all life-sentenced prisoners.

Similarly, the Committee of Ministers of the Council of Europe considered life imprisonment directly in its 2003 recommendation on "the management by prison administrations of life sentence and other long-term prisoners" and also made specific reference to the release of life-sentenced prisoners in other recommendations.[70] In recent years these recommendations have been closely analyzed by the Grand Chamber of the European Court of Human Rights, to decide whether the treatment of life-sentenced prisoners or the arrangements for considering their release are compatible with human rights guaranteed by the European Convention on Human Rights.[71] Likewise, a treaty body, the European Committee for the Prevention of Torture (CPT), which is the key organ of the European Convention for the Prevention of Torture and Inhuman or Degrading Treatment or Punishment, has developed its own comprehensive standards on life imprisonment. The most recent version, which was published in 2016 as part of its annual report on the previous year, elaborates on the 2003 Council of Europe Recommendation in the light of its own empirical reports on the situation of life-sentenced prisoners in various European countries.[72]

Rehabilitation Revisited

A core concern of modern prison law is the question of what positive principles should determine how sentenced prisoners should be treated. While prisoners' rights theory has made it clear that they should not be punished other than by the loss of liberty, is there anything else that has to be done for them? The US approach of the 1970s, with its profound skepticism about rehabilitation, seemed to suggest that not much could be done beyond insisting, on human rights grounds, that all prisoners be contained humanely.

The purpose of imprisonment preoccupied leading European penal theorists, such as Horst Schüler-Springorum and Constantijn Kelk, in the 1960s and 1970s.[73] Their work was based on an expansive view of human rights, which included the recognition of socioeconomic rights that required the state to provide everyone with the means to engage fully in life in a free society. They concluded that the authorities had a duty also to offer prisoners the means eventually to do so. They described this as a right to social rehabilitation, which was the term used in Article 10(3) of the ICCPR, or resocialization, as it is termed in German penology. In 1973, the German Federal Constitutional Court endorsed this view and ruled that the right to resocialization could be found in the human rights principles that are set out in the German Grundgesetz, the Basic Law that forms the bill of rights in the modern German constitution. As that court explained in the groundbreaking *Lebach* case:

> From the point of view of the offender, this interest in resocialization develops out of his constitutional rights in terms of Article 2(1) in conjunction with Article 1 of the Basic Law [i.e., the right to develop one's personality freely in conjunction with the protection of human dignity]. Viewed from the perspective of the community, the constitutional principle of the *Sozialstaat* [social welfare state] requires public care and assistance for those groups in the community who, because of personal weakness or fault, incapacity or social disadvantage were retarded in their social development: prisoners and ex-prisoners also belong to this group.[74]

The application of this logic was to have a profound influence on debates about life imprisonment. In Germany it provided the basis for an argument that life imprisonment could only be constitutional if it provided prisoners with an opportunity to resocialize themselves, which further implied an opportunity to be considered for release. Such an argument was accepted by the German Federal Constitutional Court in 1977.[75]

The same development took place two decades later at the level of the ECtHR, when the court gradually recognized that all prisoners, including those serving life sentences, had a right to social rehabilitation.[76] In turn, this gradually led the Grand Chamber of the ECtHR to accept that, in order for a life sentence not to be inhuman and degrading, a prisoner must have the opportunity in law and in fact to be considered for release.

Many Latin American countries have gone even further, arguing that, since Article 5(6) of the American Convention on Human Rights provides that "[p]unishments consisting of deprivation of liberty shall have as an essential aim the reform and social readaptation of the prisoners," life imprisonment should be outlawed completely on the grounds that it undermines the human rights of offenders by denying them the opportunity to rehabilitate themselves.[77] The dominant idea in Europe, Latin America, and some other countries that have adopted their jurisprudence, as well as in international human rights law, that social rehabilitation is both a right and a progressive concept, also when applied to life imprisonment, is not universal, however. It is certainly the opposite of the ideas in the United States of the 1970s, when rehabilitation was seen negatively, as a device to compel prisoners to do things or to allow things to be done to them against their will. Since then, the ideal of rehabilitation has ceased to be quite as controversial in the United States. However, arguments that all life prisoners should have, as a right, a prospect of rehabilitation, have gained little traction. A major exception has been the recognition, even in the United States, that children have the capacity for positive change and that they should therefore be given an opportunity to rehabilitate themselves and to be released on parole if they do so. The full implications of granting opportunities for rehabilitation as a human right of life prisoners will be explored further in subsequent chapters.

A Human Rights–Based Alternative to the Death Penalty

An overview of the emergence of the ideas that inform debates about life imprisonment worldwide would not be complete without further reflection on the unique relationship of life sentences with the death penalty. As we have seen, life imprisonment has often been debated as an alternative to capital punishment, with the majority of, but not all, participants regarding it as a lesser penalty than death. The demise of the death penalty has been a long process, from its early abolition in the late nineteenth century to its current position as an ultimate penalty used only in a minority of countries. The dramatic acceleration of this process over the last twenty-five years in the light of human rights norms, rather than narrower criminal justice concerns about efficacy, needs particular emphasis, for it provides an important part of the context for the increase in the use of the various types of life imprisonment that now exist around the world.

Before turning to the most recent developments, it is worth noting that the abolition of capital punishment, in Western Europe in particular, preceded the widespread recognition of internationally binding, substantive and procedural human rights norms. Death-penalty abolition was an issue debated largely within nation-states. Although human rights concerns played a part, these debates were cast mostly as matters of how national criminal justice should be developed. Where life imprisonment was brought in to replace the death penalty, be it in Scandinavia from the end of the nineteenth century onward, Germany in the late 1940s, the United Kingdom in the 1960s, or France in the 1980s, little attention was paid to whether its imposition was fair, or whether procedures for release from life imprisonment met human rights standards.[78]

The big increase in the relative importance of international human rights norms in the abolition of the death penalty and the introduction of life imprisonment, or, more unusually, some other alternative to it, came about after the end of the Cold War, in the early 1990s. This shift manifested itself both at the level of international criminal justice and at the level of countries that were compelled by international pressures to adopt changes in their penal systems.

INTERNATIONAL CRIMINAL JUSTICE. In international law, the death penalty was the undisputed ultimate penalty to be applied in the trials conducted at the end of the Second World War.[79] In practice, imprisonment, including life imprisonment, was also a prominent part of the sentencing mix at Nuremberg and at the contemporaneous International Military Tribunal for the Far East. However, all those who were sentenced to life imprisonment by the latter tribunal were released after having served relatively short terms, as were the majority of those sentenced to life imprisonment by the tribunal in Nuremberg.[80]

After the International Military Tribunals of the immediate post–Second World War period had completed their work, the issue of appropriate punishment for crimes against international law was not an item on the international agenda again for the next forty years. Only at the beginning of the 1990s did the International Law Commission (ILC) begin to debate the issue again in the course of developing a draft Code of Crimes against the Peace and Security of Mankind.[81] By then, the somewhat mixed success of life imprisonment as a punishment for these crimes had faded from memory. The ILC was able to look at the whole issue afresh, in a very different climate in which many countries had abolished capital punishment, and international law generally had become more critical of it and much more attentive to norms of international human rights generally.

The debate in the ILC reflected the changes in attitudes inspired by human rights norms. From the outset there was agreement that the principle of legality inherent in the new emphasis on proportionate punishment required any penal provision in a Code of Crimes against the Peace and Security of Mankind to go further than the charter that was used in Nuremberg in specifying penalties. The first attempt in 1990 to draft a clause on penalties for the proposed code included a provision that related to the death penalty, but it was soon clear that there would not be a consensus in favor of it.[82] The draft put forward in 1991 dropped the death penalty entirely and proposed that any defendant found guilty of any of the crimes defined in the code should be sentenced to life imprisonment. If there were extenuating circumstances, the sentence could be reduced to imprisonment for a term of ten to twenty years.[83]

The ILC may have addressed the need for specificity of punishment and the move away from the death penalty, but were the commissioners mindful of the need to test the proposed penalties against the standards of international human rights law? More specifically, was adequate attention paid to these standards in respect to the sentence of life imprisonment, which was the most severe sentence that could be imposed, in the various proposals that refined the ideas put forward in 1991?

There can be no doubt that at an early stage in the debate about which punishments should be allowed, the various experts involved recognized that life imprisonment was potentially problematic.[84] The debate was so vigorous that at the end of it the special rapporteur of the ILC amended the draft penal clause and proposed various options from which life imprisonment could be omitted completely. The substance of this debate is of considerable interest, for it is a rare example of arguments for and against life imprisonment being developed systematically in the context of both international law and human rights. A feature of the debate was that a considerable number of commissioners declared their principled, human rights–based opposition to life imprisonment. Particularly prominent were the views of several commissioners from Latin America, where the domestic law of many countries forbade life imprisonment. As one of them explained:

> Life imprisonment did not seem to be compatible with the Latin American legal system. The criterion adopted in the American Convention on Human Rights that penalties should not only be correctional in nature but should also rehabilitate the convicted person so that he could resume his place in society. A more realistic penalty would be imprisonment for a minimum of 10 years and a maximum of 25 years, which was the longest term of imprisonment in many Latin American countries.[85]

This passage highlights two recurring themes in the opposition to life imprisonment at the international level. The first objection was that it was not a competent penalty for even the most serious crimes in the domestic law of some states.[86] The second objection was that it undermined the human rights of prisoners by denying them the opportunity to rehabilitate themselves so that they could later live in society as free citizens.[87]

Supporters of life imprisonment among the commissioners who were opposed to the death penalty based their advocacy on three traditional criminal justice arguments: the need for an appropriately retributive punishment, general deterrence, and the incapacitation of offenders. The first two of these were given expression by the commissioner from Panama, who argued that "[c]rimes against the peace and security of mankind called above all for the adoption of exemplary penalties which reflected the feeling of condemnation that such acts aroused in the international community and which also had a deterrent effect."[88]

Of particular interest is that this commissioner relied on human rights norms not only for his rejection of the death penalty, but also for his support for life imprisonment in the face of opposition to it from other commissioners from Latin America. The latter penalty was required "in order to prevent [barbarous crimes] from being committed again and to protect human rights and fundamental freedoms."[89] He noted that the international instruments, which made national statutes of limitation inapplicable to war crimes and crimes against humanity and which denied their perpetrators rights of asylum, were based on the same criteria of protecting human rights. Implicit in this argument was the idea that the exceptionally serious crimes that were involved here required life imprisonment as the exemplary penalty, even when it might not be appropriate for "ordinary" crimes.[90] The case for life imprisonment as an instrument of incapacitation was put forward by the commissioner from Italy, who argued that the death penalty was "plainly out of the question."[91] He added, however, that for pragmatic reasons, he would be

> less hesitant than some other members about life imprisonment. . . . he would find it difficult to contemplate the release, even after 20, 25 or 30 years, of a dictator of the type common around 1930, who had been guilty of aggression, genocide and other crimes of similar magnitude, or even the release of a major drug trafficker. Such people could not just be returned to society, as the English had soon realized in the 100 days following Napoleon Bonaparte's exile on the island of Elba. It was a question of fitting the punishment not only to the crime but also to the gravity of the danger, and of preventing a recurrence at all costs.[92]

The 1991 debate of the ILC reveals the extent to which the commissioners felt it necessary to consider human rights principles when arguing both for and against life imprisonment. The opponents of this form of punishment relied on these principles directly. Even the supporters mentioned human rights, both the rights of victims that the life sentence would protect or vindicate and, at a different level, the rights of offenders that could and should be guarded in a system that imposed and implemented life sentences appropriately. In all, the debate went a long way toward confirming that, if the international community wished to take international human rights seriously, it could not simply assume that life imprisonment did not raise issues of human rights principle.

The somewhat leisurely deliberations of the ILC were overtaken by events in Yugoslavia and Rwanda. When, in 1993 and 1994, the UN Security

Council decided to establish ad hoc international tribunals to try individual offenders for crimes against international law that had been committed in those countries, it was directly confronted by the lack of a developed penal framework at the international level. It soon became clear that, whatever penalties these tribunals would be allowed to impose, the death penalty could not be among them, as it would be vetoed by a number of permanent members of the Security Council.[93] However, the issue of life imprisonment as the effective ultimate penalty was avoided by the Security Council when it set up new international criminal tribunals for the former Yugoslavia (ICTY) and for Rwanda (ICTR). The brief sentencing provisions in the founding statutes of these tribunals allowed only for the imposition of imprisonment and provided that in determining the terms of imprisonment, trial chambers "shall have recourse to the general practice regarding prison sentences in the courts of," respectively, the former Yugoslavia and Rwanda.[94]

In the case of Rwanda, legally speaking, the failure to mention life imprisonment in the sentencing provision was unproblematic, as the municipal law of Rwanda did provide for such sentences and the ICTR therefore could clearly impose it, if it chose to do so. The law of the former Yugoslavia, however, provided only for maximum fixed-term sentences of thirty years or the death penalty. The ICTY dealt with this gap in its sentencing framework by effectively ignoring the clear instruction in its statute that it had to have recourse to the general practice that had been followed regarding sentences of imprisonment in Yugoslavia. Not only did it impose prison sentences of longer than thirty years, but it also imposed life imprisonment. In order to enable it to do so, the ICTY added a provision to the rules of procedure and evidence—rules drafted by the judges for their own use. It justified this new rule on the basis that, in the absence of the death penalty, it needed harsher prison sentences than what had been allowed in Yugoslavia to mark the heinousness of the crimes over which it had jurisdiction. The cost of this judicial creation of a life sentence was a loss of legal certainty about the law governing the imposition of sentence by the tribunal.

Similar confusion dogged the provisions governing consideration for release of the persons sentenced by the two tribunals, which varied according to the country to which persons sentenced to life imprisonment were sent to serve their sentences. It too was resolved by judicial fiat, which in 2015 set an effective minimum term of thirty years for all life sentences imposed by the tribunals, no matter where they were being served.[95] While this judicial intervention provided some belated clarity on the release process for persons sentenced to life imprisonment by the two tribunals, the apparent need for drastic judicial legislation of this kind, years after the passage of the original statutes, is a further indication that they are not an ideal model of life imprisonment as the alternative sanction to the death penalty, which international law is increasingly demanding.

The movement away from the death penalty and in favor of a form of life imprisonment that meets the standards of international human rights law was given further momentum by the exclusion of capital punishment as a sentence that can be imposed by the permanent International Criminal Court, which was established by the Rome Statute in 1998. However, in contrast to the statutes of the ICTY and the ICTR, the Rome Statute also deals prominently with life imprisonment in its range of "applicable penalties" for the most serious crimes, thus establishing it clearly as a specific punishment in international law and lending it some legitimacy in the process.[96]

The Rome Statute also clarified the law on release from life imprisonment at the international level that the statutes of the ICTY and the ICTR had left in such confusion. It did so by providing that all life sentences shall be reviewed when the prisoner has served twenty-five years.[97] This twenty-five-year review period has proved to be of wide significance in the debate about an appropriate minimum period for life sentences. It has been interpreted by the European Court of Human Rights and also by the Supreme Court of the Netherlands, as a persuasive, international law based, indication of when, at the latest, such a review of a life sentence should take place.[98]

In all, the recognition at the international level of life imprisonment as the ultimate penalty for the most serious offenses has added significantly to its international profile. Life imprisonment has not only been accepted as the alternative to the death penalty at an international level, but the process of introducing it in international tribunals and courts has made an important contribution to debates about the type of life imprisonment that can be regarded as meeting international human rights standards.

INTERNATIONAL HUMAN RIGHTS AND NATIONAL DEVELOPMENTS. The influence of international human rights on national punishment regimes was felt particularly strongly in countries that, in the early 1990s, debated reforms to their penal systems in the wake of the geopolitical changes brought about by the end of the Cold War. In Europe, countries of the former Eastern bloc were told firmly that, if they wished to join the Council of Europe, they would have to abolish the death penalty and improve the human rights records of their prisons. With the exception of Belarus, they all abolished the death penalty by the end of the 1990s in order to do so. They also largely adopted the two relevant protocols to the European Court of Human Rights: Protocol 6, which outlaws the death penalty in time of peace, and Protocol 13, which outlaws it completely.[99]

The abolition of capital punishment raised the practical problem of alternative ultimate penalties. The Soviet Union was not that different from Yugoslavia in that it did not have provision for life imprisonment as a primary sentence. Similarly, by the early 1990s, Soviet allies such as Poland and Czechoslovakia had provision for capital punishment, but not life imprisonment, in their sentencing systems. By 2000, Russia and all the other European successor states to the Soviet Union except Belarus—that is, Armenia, Azerbaijan, Estonia, Georgia, Latvia, Lithuania, Moldova, and Ukraine—had introduced life imprisonment as their ultimate penalties. The same thing had happened in Poland, the Czech Republic, and Slovakia, as well as in Albania, Bulgaria, and Romania.[100] In Hungary, which already had life imprisonment, the death penalty was simply removed from the statute book and life imprisonment became the ultimate penalty by default.[101]

The successor states to the former Yugoslavia also all abolished capital punishment in the early 1990s. However, only Macedonia initially introduced life imprisonment as a substitute for the death penalty. Bosnia, Croatia, Montenegro, Serbia, and Slovenia all introduced new, longer, fixed terms of years than had hitherto been found in their sanction systems as the new ultimate penalties to replace the death penalty, while leaving in place the relatively short fixed-term sentences that the Yugoslav code had set for serious offenses for which the death penalty was not imposed. The initial changes in the countries that comprised the former Yugoslavia were undertaken in the first flush of human rights–driven idealism, with a conscious attempt being made to reflect what were regarded as desirable "European" standards, while ostensibly keeping in place the relative leniency of the old system.[102]

Outside the Eastern bloc countries, the rise of international human rights also had a growing impact in the 1990s. An example of this was South

Africa, a country that benefited from what Zimring refers to as "virtue by association," with the human rights–driven international movement to abolish the death penalty.[103] The new order in South Africa in the 1990s was indeed very conscious of taking its rightful place in the international community after years of isolation, so much so that the first constitution of democratic South Africa, adopted in 1993, specifically enjoined courts to "have regard to public international law applicable to the protection of the rights" when interpreting the Bill of Rights. In its very first judgment in 1995, the newly created Constitutional Court of South Africa duly abolished the death penalty, with copious reference to international human rights law, and suggested strongly that it could be replaced by life imprisonment. Although at that time South African law made provision for life imprisonment, it had rarely been imposed directly. The immediate result was a massive increase in the number of life sentences imposed after the abolition of the death penalty.[104] This was followed by a review of release procedures, which was designed to make them more compatible with the due process requirements of human rights law.[105]

In sum, developments in Eastern and Central Europe, and in South Africa, in the wake of the abolition of the death penalty, are good indicators of the impact that international human rights norms can have on life imprisonment at the national level and on the form that it will take there.[106]

INTERNATIONAL HUMAN RIGHTS AND US EXCEPTIONALISM. Finally, what role has consideration of life imprisonment against the background of international, human rights–based, death-penalty abolitionism played in the United States? This question is particularly pertinent because of the perceived resistance to the use of international human rights norms in shaping domestic penal policy in the United States.[107]

The long-running debate about the abolition of the death penalty in the United States is a vast topic. For the current purposes of understanding its impact on life imprisonment, a brief sketch will suffice. It is important to note that in the United States, as was the case in Western Europe, the movement to abolish the death penalty was largely a domestic affair, and the abolitionist history of various individual states followed local patterns as diverse as those in Europe.[108] At the national level, the US Supreme Court took the lead. Its 1972 judgment in *Furman v. Georgia*,[109] which culminated in the declaration that the law governing the death penalty in the

United States at that time was unconstitutional, was built on national rather than international understandings of due process and human dignity, and based on the Eighth and Fourteenth Amendments to the US Constitution.

What made the United States different from other countries, such as the United Kingdom and France, that were abolishing the death penalty at roughly the same time, was that in the American federal context, the legislatures of individual states reacted very forcefully against this decision and enacted new death-penalty laws. More than thirty states introduced modified death-penalty laws, and some also added provisions for life imprisonment without parole (LWOP) sentences to their statute books, as they feared that the "improved" death-penalty laws would be found to be unconstitutional again.[110] The death penalty was not the only driver of the rise of LWOP in the United States. From the 1970s onward, the rise of LWOP was compounded by wider law and order concerns, and the American skepticism about rehabilitation and parole generally that emerged at the same time, which also led to calls for longer sentences. The interaction of these factors with questions about the death penalty are crucial to understanding the continued prominence of LWOP in the United States.[111]

The death penalty remained, however, a key factor. In 1976 the US Supreme Court found that some of the laws reintroducing the death penalty, which provided that it had to be a discretionary sentence and could be imposed only if clear criteria with regard to aggravating and mitigating factors were applied, met the procedural standards of the federal Constitution. In the view of the majority of the court, these standards were sufficient to guarantee that the death penalty would be constitutional, as it would only be imposed where it was a proportionate sentence. The practical effect of the decision of the US Supreme Court in 1976 was to shift the debate about the outright abolition of the death penalty to the state level and to limit federal challenges to procedures and to arguments that imposing the death penalty on certain groups would be disproportionately severe.

These changes in the law on the death penalty impacted on the development of life imprisonment in the United States in three ways. The first development was that opponents of the death penalty began to argue at the state level that LWOP sentences were an acceptable alternative to the death penalty. This argument was essentially pragmatic. It was driven by the view that polls suggested that almost half of the general public would support the abolition of the death penalty if the alternative was whole-life imprisonment.[112]

Ironically, support on this basis for LWOP in the United States emerged at the very stage when the principle of irreducible life sentences was beginning to be challenged on human rights grounds in Europe in particular. This pragmatic argument in favor of LWOP has remained a feature of US penal policy. As the American Law Institute explained in 2017:

> The increasing use of whole-life sentences in [the United States] has been driven largely by their role in the death-penalty debate. In many jurisdictions, life without parole serves as the chief alternative to capital punishment for the most aggravated homicides. As a matter of statutory law, sentencing juries in most capital-punishment jurisdictions are instructed whenever life without parole is an alternative to a death sentence in the case before them, and such an instruction is often constitutionally required. In states without capital punishment, legislative authorization of natural-life sentences is sometimes thought essential to public acceptance of a system with no death penalty. In opinion surveys over the past 15 years, public support for capital punishment has been shown to drop markedly when survey respondents are told that life without parole may be substituted for execution. Thus, the political momentum of proposed death-penalty legislation may be offset if the credible alternative of a whole-life tariff is brought forward.[113]

Second, a series of proportionality challenges to different types of life sentences imposed on adults reached the US Supreme Court, but only one of them was successful. In subsequent cases, the proportionality test for the constitutionality of life sentences continued to be recognized in US law, but it was eviscerated to such an extent that it ceased to be an effective way of limiting the use of life imprisonment for adults in the United States.[114]

The third and, for current purposes, most significant development is the increasing emphasis that the US Supreme Court has placed, more recently, on international human rights standards when dealing with aspects of the death penalty. In the case of the death penalty, the new approach emerged in 2002, when the Supreme Court held that executing "mentally retarded" persons offended civilized standards of decency, inter alia, because "within the world community, the imposition of the death penalty for crimes committed by mentally retarded offenders is overwhelmingly disapproved."[115] In *Roper v. Simmons,* which was decided the following year, the majority of the Supreme Court, prompted by briefs from European countries that emphasized the human rights aspects of the case, engaged fully with detailed evidence that capital punishment for juveniles, that is, for children under the age of 18 years, was forbidden by major international human rights instruments, such as the ICCPR and the CRC. The Supreme Court concluded, inter alia on this ground, that no one under the age of eighteen years at the time of the commission of the offense should be sentenced to death. The court held to this conclusion, notwithstanding a scathing dissent from Justice Antonin Scalia, who pointed out that the United States was not a party to the CRC and that it had stipulated in a reservation to the ICCPR that it did not regard itself to be bound by the prohibition on capital punishment for children.[116]

Notwithstanding this criticism, the same form of analysis that was followed in respect to capital punishment for juveniles was adopted also in respect to life imprisonment for juveniles. Close attention was paid to international human rights standards in *Graham v. Florida* in 2010, when the Supreme Court decided that LWOP imposed on a child for a non-homicide offense was unconstitutionally cruel and unusual. Again the court brushed aside concerns about the treaty status of international human rights norms and instead focused on their substance. The court explained:

> The question before us is not whether international law prohibits the United States from imposing the sentence at issue in this case. The question is whether that punishment is cruel and unusual. In that inquiry, "the overwhelming weight of international opinion against" life without parole for non-homicide offenses committed by juveniles "provide[s] respected and significant confirmation for our own conclusions."[117]

This form of analysis is important, not least because it indicates the limits of US exceptionalism in excluding international human rights standards from questions relating to life imprisonment.

The Limits of Human Rights

The renewed emphasis on human rights, both as far as the death penalty is concerned and more widely in respect to other forms of punishment, provides some additional tools for debating life imprisonment and engaging with the theories of punishment that underpin it, but it does not address all the difficult dilemmas that this complex form of punishment raises. Contemporary recognition of human rights norms is widespread internationally, but it is not consistent, either in the substance of the norms recognized or in the extent to which they are applied. Human rights treaties are not necessarily self-executing, and therefore in some legal systems, they do not apply directly. The United States has gone further than other states in making reservations to the human rights treaties it has ratified. It has stated, for example, that it considers itself bound by the prohibition of "cruel, inhuman or degrading treatment or punishment" in Article 7 of the ICCPR only to the (limited) extent that "cruel and unusual" treatment or punishment are prohibited by the Constitution of the United States.[118]

The belief that the most heinous offenses deserve draconian punishment continues to be reflected in the widespread use of highly restrictive forms of life imprisonment. Where the persons who commit these offenses are thought, not only to be highly dangerous, but also to be incorrigible, human rights considerations of the kind we have outlined here are all too easily ignored. It is also to understand limitations such as these that we set out to collect the information reflected in the further chapters of this book, before making any judgements on the potential efficacy of human rights–based constraints on the imposition and implementation of life sentences.

Describing Life

FOR US, *life imprisonment is a sentence, following a criminal conviction, which gives the state the power to detain a person in prison for life, that is, until they die there.*[1] Included in this definition are diverse types of life imprisonment worldwide. They must be examined closely before we can consider the overall significance of life imprisonment and the extent to which life sentences in different countries and jurisdictions meet human rights standards.

This chapter first addresses linguistic and other issues that arise in identifying life imprisonment generally. We then describe the two primary types of formal life imprisonment, namely, life without the possibility of parole (LWOP) and life with the possibility of parole (LWP), as well as some subtypes within these two primary types.

It is also crucial to recognize that sentences that are not expressly designated as life imprisonment may fall within our definition of a life sentence where the state has the power to keep people in prison until they die there. We describe such sentences as informal life sentences. We also identify and elaborate on two types of informal life imprisonment, namely, de facto life and post-conviction indefinite detention.

Understanding these four different types of life imprisonment and the subtypes within them allows one to grasp the sheer complexity of life imprisonment worldwide, and to understand how life imprisonment is used and justified. As with all typologies, these are ideal types, and the boundaries between them can be disputed. Such disputes are not only theoretical, however, for the legal and political acceptability of a particular life sentence may depend on how it is characterized.

Identifying Life Sentences

In identifying life sentences of different types, language may be problematic, even where the translation seems clear. In the same language, several different terms may be used for the same type of life imprisonment. Even in English, one has detention for life, imprisonment for life, or lifelong imprisonment, which do not map precisely onto the types of life imprisonment we develop here. This is relatively unproblematic where a single term is used in a particular legal system. For instance, different Francophone countries use the terms *réclusion à perpétuité* or *réclusion perpétuelle, réclusion à vie, peine privative de liberté à vie, travaux forcés à perpétuité, emprisonnement à vie, servitude à perpétuité* and *servitude pénale à perpétuité*.[2] In the Spanish-speaking world, we come across the terms *presidio perpetuo, cadena perpetua, privación de libertad de por vida, prisión vitalicia,* and *prisión permanente revisable*.[3] Each of these terms is used exclusively in certain countries to designate that country's version of life imprisonment. As a result, the different terminology does not pose any serious problems of interpretation.

The varying terminology becomes problematic, however, when different terms are in one legal system but these expressions do not necessarily reflect substantive differences in the implementation of the sentence imposed. For example, the French Penal Code uses two distinct terms for life imprisonment: *réclusion criminelle à perpétuité* and *détention criminelle à perpétuité*.[4] The former is used for "ordinary" crimes, while the latter is used exclusively for a limited number of political offenses.[5] Belgium adopts the same terminology and the same approach.[6]

In Argentina, there is provision for both *reclusión perpetua* and *prisión perpetua,* which both have dictionary translations as life imprisonment.[7] Is there a difference between the two terms? In the case of Argentina, the Inter-American Court of Human Rights has held that, whatever the historical differences may be, *reclusión perpetua* and *prisión perpetua* are essentially the same indeterminate sentence.[8]

The situation is, however, not always so simple. In the Philippines, both *reclusión perpetua* and life imprisonment (here the English term is used for the alternative) have emerged as substitutes for the death penalty. In the Philippine context, *reclusión perpetua* effectively means a sentence with a minimum term of thirty years and a maximum of forty years, accompanied by a lifelong loss of certain civil rights, while "life imprisonment" means an indeterminate sentence with no minimum period and no subsequent loss of civil rights. Our approach has been to treat all these different terms as formal life sentences and to allocate the different forms in which the sentence presents itself among the types of life imprisonment that we develop in this chapter.

Some terminology may even blur the distinction between formal and informal life imprisonment. The line is particularly difficult to draw when the coy circumlocution, "detention during Her Majesty's [or other head of state's] pleasure," is used in the English-speaking world. When, as in the United Kingdom, it is applied to children under the age of eighteen years who have been convicted of a criminal offense such as murder, the courts have stated bluntly that detention is during Her Majesty's pleasure, and effectively is life imprisonment. For example, in 2014 a judge told a sixteen-year old boy convicted of murdering his high school teacher, "The sentence for murder is automatic: given your age, it is detention during Her Majesty's pleasure. That is an indeterminate sentence; it is, to all intents and purposes, a life sentence."[9] Accordingly, when detention during Her Majesty's pleasure refers to indeterminate sentences imposed on children, we have dealt with it as formal life imprisonment for descriptive and statistical purposes, while remaining sensitive to subtle differences in how it is imposed and implemented. We adopt the same approach to the use of this term in many former British colonies when it is applied to convicted children.[10] However, we note that in a number of these jurisdictions, the term *detention during Her Majesty's pleasure* may be applied to adults, too. Where it is used for adults, we have tried to look behind the term to decide whether it is used as a post-conviction measure, which may be an informal type of life imprisonment, or whether it is a term for the indefinite detention of persons who are not convicted because of their mental condition and therefore should not be regarded as subject to life imprisonment at all.[11]

The distinction between formal and informal life sentences matters for two reasons. The first is essentially pragmatic. The official label is an unavoidable point of departure in order to begin to calculate the number of prisoners worldwide, being sentenced to, and held in prison under formal sentences of life imprisonment. It also enables us to form some picture of the perceived significance of the concept of "life imprisonment." Ideally, one should have similar information about persons serving informal life sentences, but that information is even harder to come by than that for formal life sentences.

The second reason is subtler. As will become apparent, when we consider the imposition of life sentences in Chapter 6, the treatment of life prisoners in Chapter 7, and release from life imprisonment in Chapter 9, there may be important differences in how life prisoners are treated depending on whether they are formally referred to as serving sentences of life imprisonment or not.

Our broad definition of life imprisonment, both formal and informal, does need to be qualified in one important respect. When formulating it, we did not intend to include in it persons who have been sentenced to death. On a literal reading of our definition, they should be included, as of course they too are convicted individuals, being held in prison until they die there. The obvious difference in their status is that, in the case of the death penalty, the state has announced its intention to kill them in prison. This may be why life imprisonment is sometimes referred to as imprisonment for the natural life of the prisoner; as opposed, presumably, to the unnatural ending to a human life brought about by the execution of the death penalty.[12]

In some countries, persons on death row may be kept there for so long that death from natural causes becomes a much stronger likelihood than execution of the initial capital sentence. Alternately, it may be the case that the death penalty is routinely converted to life imprisonment, with the result that death row in any real sense does not exist, for a death sentence in practice always means life imprisonment. In other jurisdictions, some offenders who have been admitted to prison under sentence of death may have their sentences commuted to life imprisonment after a very long period of time. This would suggest a clear distinction drawn between those on death row awaiting execution and others who are then moved to a category of "merely" serving life sentences, but that is not always the case.

The exclusion of prisoners facing execution may significantly understate the overall number of prisoners who may be held in prison indefinitely, that is, until they die there from causes other than being executed. Consider the situation in Sri Lanka, a country that has not executed anyone who has been sentenced to death since 1976 and that has a moratorium on carrying out further executions. A government task force report produced in April 2017 records that in Sri Lanka there were 1,082 persons on death row and 555 life-sentenced prisoners out of a total sentenced prison population of 7,496 persons. As the death- and life-sentenced prisoners already together make up 22 percent of the overall prison population and their numbers are likely to grow further, the task force recommended that the government of Sri Lanka should consider commuting the death sentences to life imprisonment and should release life-sentenced prisoners who have been rehabilitated.[13] It is clear that these two reform strategies go hand in hand to reduce the overcrowding, making a pragmatic case for including both death- and life-sentenced prisoners in an attempt to reduce the number of prisoners who are effectively serving indeterminate sentences. Similarly, in the United States, prisoners can remain on death row for decades while awaiting execution. In 2017, the Human Rights Clinic at the University of Texas reported that one inmate on death row had been there for more than forty years.[14]

In spite of all these caveats, for statistical purposes our definition of life imprisonment should be read as excluding those individuals who are awaiting execution. Accordingly, in countries that retain capital punishment but regularly commute death sentences to life imprisonment, we only count as life-sentenced prisoners those whose sentences have been formally commuted. Although this may lead to an underestimate of the number of persons who can be regarded as life prisoners, the results are probably more accurate than if we included those whose sentences had not been formally commuted as well.

One further matter of terminology: we refer to all persons serving sentences of life imprisonment in the wide way we have defined it as life prisoners, while we call those who are explicitly sentenced to what is formally described as life imprisonment as life-sentenced prisoners, and those who have been released from formal life sentences former or released life-sentenced prisoners. There are instances, in Canada, for example, where the category of individuals sentenced to life imprisonment includes both those who are serving their sentences in prison and those who are on parole in the community, as the two groups are combined in this way in official statistics.[15] However, we do not use *offenders with a life sentence* or a similar term to combine those individuals inside and outside prison, and we treat them separately throughout. These terminological distinctions are not a matter of idle pedantry but rather are needed to make cross-national comparisons.

Finally, we avoid the less precise term *lifer*, which is often used to designate people who are in prison serving terms that fall within the spectrum of what we have described as formal sentences of life imprisonment.

Occasionally the term *lifer* is also used for those who are serving informal life sentences in prison: we avoid this usage too.

Formal Life Sentences

Formal life sentences are those that are designated as life imprisonment and included under that name in official statistics around the world. To illustrate the basic situation worldwide, we have introduced the topic with a map that shows life imprisonment in every country in the world with formal life imprisonment, as well as the countries that have no formal life imprisonment (see Figure 2.1). Where countries or jurisdictions within them have both types of formal life imprisonment that we have identified, LWOP and LWP, we have indicated that too. Indeed, one of the details that emerges most visibly from the map is the high number of countries that have both types of life imprisonment.

Life without Parole (LWOP)

Life imprisonment without the prospect of parole or other form of release, bar exceptional executive intervention, is a type of life imprisonment from which release is not routinely considered. We use the American acronym LWOP for this type of formal life sentence, but it is sometimes also described as a whole-life or true-life sentence, or a sentence for natural life.[16] LWOP is to be distinguished from the other major type of life sentence, LWP, where release on parole or otherwise is routinely considered. As Figure 2.1 shows, LWOP is a widely distributed type of life sentence, which we found in sixty-five countries, and in every continent.

Within the various forms of LWOP worldwide, there is a spectrum of powers of executive intervention that could in theory be used, and in practice are occasionally used, to release prisoners serving LWOP sentences. At the most restricted end of the LWOP spectrum are those jurisdictions where these powers have been eliminated or restricted to an extent that makes them virtually meaningless.

Because persons serving LWOP sentences have, at best, an irregular prospect of release and, at worst, no prospect of release at all, these sentences are often criticized for not providing the prisoners serving them with the hope of returning to society. This is required by modern human rights standards. We return to this aspect when considering release from life imprisonment in detail in Chapter 9 and when rethinking life imprisonment generally in Chapter 11. The focus here is on describing the complexities of LWOP, although some aspects of it can only be understood in the light of developments in human rights law.

FULLY IRREDUCIBLE LWOP.   Where the power to release a prisoner has been fully taken away from even the executive or the head of state, one has an irreducible form of LWOP. This is the type of life imprisonment that was envisaged by theorists, such as Beccaria, who saw the certainty that one would never be returned to society as the harshest punishment imaginable, a punishment that would deter even those who were not frightened by the prospect of the scaffold or the guillotine. In its purest form, irreducible LWOP completely excludes prisoners from being considered for parole or any other form of conditional or unconditional release. Also excluded are powers of clemency of the head of state, or other similarly authorized executive figure, to commute the life sentence by ordering the release of such a person, either directly or by converting their particular life sentence into another sentence from which release will subsequently be possible, thus indirectly providing for their release.

The pure form of irreducible LWOP is found in some parts of the United States and Mexico, and also in Honduras, Haiti, and Israel. In the United States, the federal constitution allows the states to regulate the clemency power over all persons convicted of state crimes, thus restricting the presidential power to exercise clemency to federal crimes. The constitutions of some states specifically allow state legislatures to exclude by statute constitutionally granted gubernatorial powers to exercise clemency, by releasing prisoners convicted of certain offenses. For example, in Wyoming, legislation excludes the constitutionally provided power of executive clemency for individuals sentenced to LWOP with a limited clemency exception in claims of innocence.[17] Other states have similar but far more limited exclusions; only for treason, for example. In the state of Georgia, the constitutional power to commute sentences has been removed from the governor completely, apparently because of lack of trust in the governor being able to exercise this function fairly.[18] Instead, the state constitution vests the "power of executive clemency, including the powers to grant reprieves, pardons, and

FIGURE 2.1. Types of Formal Life Imprisonment Worldwide. *Source:* Data collected by authors.

Types of Formal Life Imprisonment Worldwide

Both Life With Parole and Life Without Parole

Life Without Parole Only

Life With Parole Only

No Life

paroles" in the Board of Pardons and Paroles.[19] However, this power is also qualified drastically by the penal code:

> Notwithstanding any other provision of law, any person who is convicted of an offense for which the death penalty may be imposed and who is sentenced to imprisonment for life without parole shall not be eligible for any form of parole during such person's natural life unless the State Board of Pardons and Paroles or a court of this state shall, after notice and public hearing, determine that such person was innocent of the offense for which the sentence of imprisonment for life without parole was imposed. Such person shall not be eligible for any work release program, leave, or any other program administered by the Department of Corrections the effect of which would be to reduce the term of actual imprisonment to which such person was sentenced.[20]

What one has here is the reinforcement of the irreducibility element of the LWOP sentences that have proliferated in the United States as alternatives to the death penalty.

In Mexico, which is also a federation, only five of the thirty-one states have provision for life imprisonment.[21] However, in at least two of them, Puebla and Quintana Roo, the power to pardon granted to the governor by the state constitution is restricted by the criminal code or by legislation governing the execution of sentences. The Constitution of Quintana Roo allows the governor to pardon offenders convicted of "ordinary crimes" but the Law on the Execution of Criminal Sentences stipulates that pardon is not possible for persons convicted of homicide, kidnapping, or rape or for the offenses with no statute of limitations.[22] This excludes all life-sentenced prisoners, since the only offenses for which life sentences may be imposed in that state are kidnapping and rape.

In Honduras, one of the rare countries where the constitution specifically provides for life imprisonment, the constitution also establishes the president's right to pardon or commute sentences, "in accordance with the law."[23] Honduran law, in the form of the 2013 Act on Pardons, however, contains a list of offenses that can never be pardoned, which overlaps with forms of aggravated murder for which life is a competent sentence. The act explicitly excludes the possibility that these offenders can be pardoned for humanitarian reasons.[24]

In Haiti, where the constitution grants the president the right to pardon or commute sentences, a different provision of the same constitution provides that a sentence of life imprisonment for high treason cannot be commuted.[25] As there is no provision for release from life imprisonment, other than some form of presidential clemency, a life sentence for high treason is irreducible in Haiti.

Israel has an even narrower restriction on the power to commute. Section 30A of the Conditional Release of Prisoners Law of 2001 creates an irrebuttable presumption that in the case of a person sentenced to life imprisonment for the murder of a prime minister for ideological reasons, the Special Release Committee must reject a request to recommend to the president that the sentence be commuted. As a result, the president is effectively prevented from exercising this power. What Israel and Haiti have in common is an irreducible life sentence that is narrowly defined and focused on specific governance problems that these otherwise very different countries have faced.

PRACTICALLY IRREDUCIBLE LWOP. There is the possibility that the legal powers of release applicable to a subgroup of LWOP prisoners may be so restrictive that, even when they are exercised, the sentences will still be irreducible because the best that the head of state or executive branch is empowered in law to do for these prisoners does not amount to "release." The failure to allow for a real prospect of release is, so this human rights–based argument runs, an assault on the human dignity of life-sentenced prisoners. It is therefore a form of inhuman or degrading punishment or treatment.

This argument emerged in the jurisprudence of the European Court of Human Rights (ECtHR), in a series of judgments starting in the late 1990s and raising the possibility that the imposition of irreducible LWOP on an adult could violate the prohibition on inhuman or degrading punishment under Article 3 of the European Convention on Human Rights (ECHR).[26] The argument was directly confronted by the Grand Chamber of the ECtHR in 2008 in *Kafkaris v. Cyprus*. In that case, the court made it clear that a sentence that was irreducible in law or in fact might be inhuman and degrading and therefore infringe Article 3 of the ECHR.[27] The life sentence in *Kafkaris,* however, was found not to be irreducible because Cyprus provided opportunities in law and in fact to consider the release of life-sentenced prisoners.

In 2013, the Grand Chamber of the ECtHR addressed this question again in the landmark case of *Vinter and others v. United Kingdom.*[28] In that case, the court ruled that certain life sentences imposed in England and Wales were to be regarded as irreducible because the action that the executive could legally take in respect of LWOP prisoners in that jurisdiction was so restricted that it did not amount to release at all.

Vinter and his two fellow applicants were part of a small group of English life-sentenced prisoners who were also subject to so-called whole-life orders made at the time of their sentence. These orders meant that their release could not be considered by the parole board, thus placing them firmly in the LWOP category. Only the secretary of state for justice could order their release, but, in terms of the governing statute, even he could only do so where "exceptional circumstances exist which justify the prisoner's release on compassionate grounds."[29] Moreover, the secretary of state had defined exceptional circumstances in the prison service order as referring only to situations where the prisoner is terminally ill or seriously incapacitated.[30] Against this background the Grand Chamber of the ECtHR held that the English legal framework was inadequate. It found that the limited power to allow life-sentenced prisoners to leave prison on compassionate grounds and spend the last few days of their lives in the community was not release in the full sense of the term. Such late "release" would never enable them to engage in society again, as invariably they would be too old and sick to do so in the last days of their lives. In law, therefore, this was not an adequate release procedure. It did not give them any hope of being released at a stage when they could engage fully in society again. Such hope was, in the view of the Grand Chamber, essential to ensure that the human dignity of the prisoner was recognized. In this way the Grand Chamber linked potential reducibility with fundamental principles of human rights.

The decision of the Grand Chamber provoked an angry reaction from the British government and brought it into direct conflict with the English courts, which, prior to the *Vinter* decision, had consistently ruled that English law did not create irreducible life sentences.[31] The judgment in *Vinter* did not lead the British government to amend UK law in any way. Nor were prisoners serving a life sentence pursuant to whole-life orders released. Instead, an enlarged bench of the Court of Appeal, the English court just below the level of the UK Supreme Court, was convened to consider the post-*Vinter* legal landscape. In early 2015 the Court of Appeal ruled that, while it accepted that irreducible life sentences were now illegal, the existing English law could deal with the new situation. The 1997 act should be reinterpreted in the light of the *Vinter* decision to allow release at an earlier stage of the sentence, if necessary, than had been the case hitherto. Furthermore, the Court of Appeal insisted that the ECtHR had misunderstood English law as far as release procedures were concerned. While neither the primary legislation nor the relevant prison service orders had been amended, the Court of Appeal was satisfied that English law, as properly understood, did allow prisoners with whole-life orders to be considered for release before their last days. If necessary, prisoners could ask for a judicial review of any decision taken by the secretary of state to ensure that he or she interpreted his or her powers more widely than had been the case in the past.[32]

Despite *Vinter*, but in the light of the decision of the Court of Appeal, English courts continued to impose life sentences with whole-life orders. No one who was subject to a whole-life order had ever been released. The question was referred to the ECtHR again, and in January 2017, in the case of *Hutchinson*, the Grand Chamber of the ECtHR agreed with the Court of Appeal that English law could be interpreted as allowing release at an earlier stage than the Grand Chamber had previously concluded in *Vinter*.[33]

In our view, such an interpretation is clearly at odds with the English statutory language. As the dissenting opinions in *Hutchinson* point out forcefully, the words, "compassionate" and "exceptional" cannot logically be stretched to include a wider review.[34] However, the legal effect of the *Hutchinson* judgment is limited to England and Wales, as the principle has been maintained that European human rights law requires that all prisoners sentenced to life imprisonment should have a reasonable prospect of release, in the full sense of the term.[35]

In England and Wales, the unfortunate effect of *Hutchinson* is likely to be that whole-life orders will continue to make the life sentences to which they are attached irreducible in practice. The response of the secretary of state for justice to the decision of the Grand Chamber in *Hutchinson* makes that clear. She welcomed the judgment, commenting that it was "right that those who commit the most heinous crimes spend the rest of their lives behind bars." *The Sun* newspaper added gleefully that the "new ruling confirms Britain can continue to keep beasts caged until they die."[36] England and Wales will remain among the few jurisdictions in the world in which the very narrow release provisions ensure that LWOP is practically irreducible.

As far as restricted release powers are concerned, the legal and practical situation in Turkey is very similar to that in England and Wales. In Turkey, different forms of life sentences can be imposed, but aggravated life imprisonment for political offenses carries no minimum period after which release must be considered.[37] Aggravated life imprisonment is effectively a form of LWOP. For those prisoners, one possibility of release remains. The Constitution of Turkey gives the president the power "to remit or commute the sentences imposed on certain individuals, on grounds of chronic illness, disability or old age."[38] This power is applicable to all prisoners, including those serving aggravated life sentences.

The question of whether this power was sufficient to ensure that an aggravated life sentence was a reducible life sentence in fact arose in 2009, when a prisoner challenged his extradition from Germany to Turkey in a German court on the basis that, if extradited, he would face an irreducible sentence, which he argued would be contrary to international law. In order to decide whether extradition should be allowed, the German Federal Constitutional Court had to determine the true status of the aggravated life sentence in Turkey. According to the German court, the answer depended on the meaning of the presidential commutation power. It ruled that having the prospect of only such limited commutation would be cruel and degrading (*grausam und erniedrigend*) and therefore contrary to principles of international law that forbid cruel, inhuman, or degrading punishment or treatment. On this basis, it refused to allow the extradition. The court explained that limiting release to those who are very old or very ill deprived prisoners of "any hope of a self-determined life in freedom. The [Turkish] power to commute that is being considered here does not open even a vague prospect of a life in freedom that makes the implementation of the life sentence bearable in terms of the dignity of the person in any way that would satisfy the German constitutional order: At best it lets the offender hope to die in freedom."[39]

In reaching its decision, the German Federal Constitutional Court did not analyze the procedure for considering a release by the president of Turkey. The Turkish procedures would not have met municipal German constitutional standards, but the court was prepared to accept that international extradition law required the acceptance of different procedural regimes. The sticking point was that Turkish law precluded release that would give the life-sentenced prisoner any possibility of again leading a full life in free society. According to the German Constitutional Court, this was not de facto release at all. From that perspective, it fell within the category of an irreducible life sentence. We too consider such a sentence to be a practically irreducible form of LWOP.

In 2014, in *Öcalan v. Turkey (No. 2)* the Second Section of the ECtHR found, as the German Federal Constitutional Court had before, that in Turkey there was no routine consideration of release from certain aggravated life sentences. The Second Section noted that "it is true that under Turkish law, in the event of the illness or old age of a life prisoner, the President of the Republic may order his immediate or deferred release."[40] Nevertheless, the court considered "that release on humanitarian grounds does not correspond to the concept of 'prospect of release' on legitimate penological grounds," which is what the Grand Chamber had required in *Vinter* in order to constitute a real prospect of release.[41] In spite of this decision, which was followed by two further decisions of the ECtHR on identical grounds in 2015, prisoners subject to irreducible life sentences continue to be detained in Turkey.[42]

In sum, as far as irreducible forms of LWOP are concerned, there are, as reflected in Appendix A, only seven countries—Haiti, Honduras, Israel, Mexico, Turkey, the United Kingdom (England and Wales) and the United States,—that have some life sentences that are in law irreducible or where the powers to intervene are so limited that they may not amount to the power to release at all. Only in some US states, Haiti, Mexico, and Honduras did we find express legal enactments that clearly and unequivocally exclude in law the power of the head of state to commute in the case of certain life sentences.

Turning to LWOP generally, more than 80 percent of all prisoners known to be serving LWOP in the world are in the United States.[43] Accordingly, we begin with LWOP in the United States. We then consider LWOP in Europe, where it is relatively rare and under threat, and end with LWOP in a range of other countries, where it is rarely considered as a matter of principle and is largely the product of unregulated executive powers to intervene in reducing sentences.

LWOP in the United States. Since the 1970s, LWOP has become a prominent sentence in the United States. With the exception of Alaska, every state in the United States, as well as the federal system, has provision for

LWOP. This has been in large part a reaction to the turmoil around the continued use of the death penalty, as described in Chapter 1. The concern in this chapter, however, is with the description of LWOP. In Chapter 5, we discuss the range of offenses for which LWOP may be imposed, which raises serious questions about the proportionality of LWOP as a sentence that is widely implemented in the United States.

How different is the form of LWOP found most widely in the United States from a fully irreducible sentence? It is noteworthy that the US Supreme Court, in the 1974 decision in *Schick v. Reed*, believed that although Schick could never be considered for parole, he was not wholly without remedy. It commented that he could still "apply to the present President or future Presidents for a complete pardon, commutation to time served, or relief from the no-parole condition."[44] In 1987, in *Harmelin v. Michigan*, where the Supreme Court upheld a mandatory LWOP sentence imposed on a first offender for possession of (a large quantity of) drugs as not grossly disproportionate, it adopted a similar approach. In the face of the argument that a mandatory sentence based solely on the amount of drugs in an individual's possession could be particularly disproportionate when imposed on a first offender, the Supreme Court commented that "executive or legislative clemency afterwards provide means for the State to avert or correct unjust sentences."[45]

The point here is not the efficacy of these remedies, which may be vanishingly small, but that, in the understanding of the US Supreme Court, LWOP was not truly irreducible. However, the court has not been consistent in this view. In 2010, in *Graham v. Florida*, when considering the constitutionality of LWOP for children under the age of eighteen years who have been convicted of murder, the Supreme Court discusses LWOP in very general terms and comes very close once again to describing it as irreducible:

> Life without parole sentences share some characteristics with death sentences that are shared by no other sentences. The State does not execute the offender sentenced to life without parole, but the sentence alters the offender's life by a forfeiture that is irrevocable. It deprives the convict of the most basic liberties without giving hope of restoration, except perhaps by executive clemency—the remote possibility of which does not mitigate the harshness of the sentence.[46]

The court goes on to quote with approval the Supreme Court of Nevada, which observed, in overturning an LWOP sentence for a juvenile defendant, that this sentence "means denial of hope; it means that good behavior and character improvement are immaterial; it means that whatever the future might hold in store for the mind and spirit of [the convict], he will remain in prison for the rest of his days."[47]

The conclusion to be drawn from these diverse portrayals of LWOP by the US Supreme Court is that, although the court sometimes mentions an executive power of clemency, when it comes to release, it may be close to an irreducible life sentence. This was the view of American critics of LWOP, who pointed out that in practice, LWOP sentences were seldom commuted. However, the dramatic intervention in 2016 by President Barack Obama to release a significant number of nonviolent drug offenders serving LWOP sentences has served to challenge this blanket presumption.[48] It is clear that, notwithstanding the uncertainties of the extent to why it is fully irreducible, LWOP for adults has not been subject to any systematic legal challenge in the United States.

In contrast, there has been a dramatic shift in the perception in Europe of whether American LWOP sentences amount to an unacceptable form of irreducible life imprisonment. This shift is best understood in the light of changes in Europe on what sentences are to be considered irreducible and contrary to the ECHR. Initially, even in Germany, where any LWOP sentence would now manifestly be unconstitutional, the Federal Constitutional Court in 2005 allowed the extradition to the United States, and specifically to California, of an offender who would have no prospect of parole in the United States but could theoretically receive a gubernatorial pardon. The rationale of the German Constitutional Court was that the necessity of meeting international obligations to deal with serious offenders outweighed detailed procedural safeguards that the German Constitution would require, as long as the foreign legal system, viewed in the round, was fair.[49] In coming to this conclusion, the German court did not consider the fact that California had not pardoned a person convicted of murder and sentenced to LWOP for many years.[50]

In 2008 the House of Lords, which was at that time the apex court in the United Kingdom, adopted a similar approach in *Regina (Wellington) v. Secretary of State for the Home Department.*[51] The focus of the decision was the jurisprudence of the ECtHR. At the time, the leading case was *Kafkaris v. Cyprus,*[52] where the ECtHR was beginning to indicate that life sentences from which there was no prospect of release in law or in fact might be inhuman and degrading and thus infringe Article 3 of the ECHR. However, the House of Lords read *Kafkaris* as saying that the issue of whether life-sentenced prisoners had a reasonable prospect of release would only arise when they sought to challenge their life sentence. They did not have to know at the time of their sentence what their prospects of release were or what they needed to do to have his release considered. Under these circumstances, the House of Lords was prepared to allow Wellington to be extradited to the United States to face a potential LWOP sentence.

For a while, ECtHR case law seemed to support the position of the House of Lords. In two extradition cases in 2012, *Harkins and Edwards v. United Kingdom* and *Babar Ahmad v. United Kingdom,* the ECtHR ruled that LWOP as applied in the United States did not contravene Article 3 and allowed alleged offenders to be extradited to face LWOP sentences.[53]

In 2013, in *Vinter,* the Grand Chamber of ECtHR changed the European position on the acceptability of irreducible life sentences. In the following year, the Fifth Section of the ECtHR, in *Trabelsi v. Belgium,* applied the *Vinter* judgment to the question of extradition to the United States. In a unanimous judgment, it ruled that the same test should be applied to potential contraventions of Article 3, whether they occurred in convention countries or elsewhere.[54] As the *Vinter* judgment had now made clear, all prisoners require a realistic prospect of release. American release procedures should be tested against this standard. If Trabelsi were to be sentenced to LWOP in the United States, his only prospect of release was through presidential pardon or sentence commutation. The ECtHR examined US practice for pardoning persons serving LWOP more closely than it had in the past. Focusing on persons convicted of terrorism and sentenced to LWOP, as Trabelsi could be, it concluded that, while in law the president had the power to commute Trabelsi's sentence, his prospects of release were not "realistic," particularly after the US Department of Justice informed the Belgian authorities that, given the offense for which he might be convicted, there was only "a theoretical possibility" of commutation.[55] Under these conditions, the ECtHR concluded, the life sentence that was liable to be imposed on Trabelsi following his extradition could not, within the meaning of the *Vinter* judgment, be described as reducible for the purposes of Article 3 of the ECHR. As with much else in this fast-changing area, this may not be the last word from the ECtHR on the meaning of irreducibility. The *Trabelsi* case was not taken to the Grand Chamber, which is yet to give a definitive judgment on this matter.

LWOP IN EUROPE.   Can any form of LWOP survive in Europe in light of the developments of the ECHR law on sentences regarded as irreducible LWOP? In addition to England and Wales and to Turkey, both of which have sentences that are deemed to be irreducible by the ECtHR because of the restricted powers of release of the authorities, in Appendix A, based on our 2014 study, we have identified LWOP sentences existing in law in Bulgaria, Hungary, Lithuania, Malta, the Netherlands, and Slovakia. However, the situation in several of these jurisdictions is evolving rapidly.

The continued existence of LWOP in the Netherlands is perhaps most disputed. In the European context it is somewhat surprising that the Netherlands, which abolished the death penalty in 1870 and replaced it by life imprisonment in ordinary criminal matters, still had LWOP in 2014 when our initial survey was undertaken. In the Netherlands, LWOP is in many ways a survival of a much earlier system, where all life sentences could be ended only by royal intervention. In some ways this is still the case. All life sentences in the Netherlands were LWOP until very recently, for there was no mechanism for life-sentenced prisoners to be released, other than by way of a clemency exercised in the name of the monarch. However, life sentences are not mandatory in the Netherlands and the total number of life-sentenced persons is very small, even by European standards.

In terms of formal structure, LWOP in the Netherlands is not the product of a deliberate decision to introduce this type of sentence, but rather the result of not having a parole system for life-sentenced prisoners. Life sentences were not part of Dutch law at all between 1813 and 1870, and were brought back to replace the death penalty. While other European monarchies gradually replaced the exercise of the royal prerogative over the release of life-sentenced prisoners by a system where decisions are taken by the parole board, this did not happen in the Netherlands. The decisions continued to be made by the secretary of state for justice acting on behalf of the king.[56]

This approach was formalized with the enactment of the Clemency Act in 1987. The act established a procedure that has to be followed, including various consultations that must take place, but effectively ensures that decisions about clemency remain with the secretary of state for justice, an elected politician. And such clemency is not granted freely, either. The only commutation since 1987 has been on compassionate grounds: the release of a life-sentenced prisoner who had only a few months to live. As we have seen, there is some dispute about whether this amounts to release at all.

However, if release were allowed, it could take place when the life-sentenced prisoner is still capable of leading a full life in the community. In that sense, it is not irreducible. Therefore, life imprisonment in the Netherlands is a form of LWOP from which release in the full sense is possible in law, although highly unlikely in practice.

A further indication of the status of life imprisonment in the Netherlands may be found in the absence of a rehabilitative purpose with which the sentence has been implemented. In 2012, the Secretary of State for Security and Justice bluntly expounded the logic behind this policy: "Life is life. There is no question of return to society, unless in an exceptional case clemency is extended to a life-sentenced prisoner. Therefore, life-sentenced prisoners do not come into consideration for activities aimed at re-integration into society."[57]

It is against the background of this history and policy that the judgment of the Supreme Court of the Netherlands, the *Hoge Raad,* of July 5, 2016, on the legal position of life-sentenced prisoners in the Netherlands must be understood. The court ruled that the remote possibility of a pardon, which hitherto has been the sole mechanism by which life-sentenced prisoners could be released, was constitutionally inadequate.[58] It held that the current pardon system did not provide life-sentenced prisoners with a clear prospect of being considered for release and was therefore contrary to Article 3 of the ECHR, prohibiting torture and inhuman or degrading treatment or punishment as interpreted and applied in 2013 in *Vinter and others v. United Kingdom* and, in 2016, in *Murray v. the Netherlands.*[59]

The Supreme Court of the Netherlands began cautiously, noting

> that the life sentence is not inherently contrary to the provisions of Article 3 of the ECHR, even if it is fully executed. From the jurisprudence [of the ECtHR] however, it follows that life imprisonment cannot be imposed if it is not already clear at the time of imposition that in due course there will be a real opportunity to reassess the life sentence, which in the appropriate cases can lead to the shortening of the sentence or (conditional) release. This does not mean that providing an opportunity for review of the sentence will always lead to a reduction of the penalty. Reassessment can indeed also lead to a finding that there is no ground for reducing the sentence.[60]

The court then explained the various conditions it regarded as essential prerequisites for a review of a life sentence:

In the review, the question that needs to be addressed is whether there have been such changes on the part of the convicted person and whether he or she has made such progress in their resocialization that the continued implementation of life imprisonment is no longer justified. The criteria used in this context should not be so stringent that release is allowed only when a serious illness or other physical obstacle stands in the way of the further implementation of life imprisonment, or upon reaching an advanced age. The review must be based on information with respect to the convicted person as an individual as well as the opportunities offered for resocialization. Moreover, at the time of the imposition of a life sentence, it must be clear to the convicted person to a sufficiently precise extent what objective criteria will be applied in the review, so that he knows what requirements must be met, if he wants—eventually—to be considered for a reduction of his sentence or for [conditional] release.[61]

The court explained further:

The point of departure in the future must be that the review must take place after no more than 25 years after the imposition of life imprisonment and that after that period the possibility of periodical re-assessment is required. The reassessment shall be surrounded with sufficient procedural safeguards. The case law of the European Court of Human Rights does not require that a provision to curtail a life sentence can only consist of a statutory periodic review of the sentence by a judge. That does not detract from the view of the *Hoge Raad* that assigning the reassessment to a judge in itself represents an important guarantee that the implementation of life imprisonment will take place in accordance with Art. 3 of the ECHR.[62]

The court instructed the government of the Netherlands to reform the law relating to life imprisonment, so that it would meet the standards it had spelled out. The government responded by introducing a complicated and highly restrictive new release procedure. Life-sentenced prisoners will still not receive treatment aimed at their reintegration into society during the first twenty-five years of their sentence. After that, however, they are to be reevaluated by a governmental advisory commission, which will consider their suitability for eventual reintegration. If they are considered suitable, a program to support their reintegration into society will commence. The advisory commission may recommend their release to the Minister of Justice after they have served at least twenty-seven years. In coming to its conclusion the advisory commission will consider not only the risk they may continue to pose to society but also other factors, such as the reaction to their possible release by victims and their families in the context of retribution. The minister cannot release life-sentenced prisoners if the advisory commission does not recommend release. However, the minister may reject a positive recommendation but must give reasons for doing so.

In December 2017, the Supreme Court considered the new procedure and ruled that it is in compliance with European standards, notwithstanding the fact that it did not accept the Court's earlier suggestion that the release process should be a judicial one.[63] Formally, the Netherlands has ceased to be the only country in Europe where all its life-sentenced prisoners are serving LWOP. However, its domestic critics are unconvinced, and question whether the new procedure is really a complete rejection of LWOP.[64]

The next question about Europe generally is whether the ECtHR really expects the abolition of LWOP. Could a modified form of LWOP meet its human rights standards? As the ECtHR has consistently held that the imposition of LWOP sentences is acceptable, it seems that it may still regard it as possible. For that reason, the 2014 decision in *Harakiev and Tolumov v. Bulgaria* is significant. In that case, the ECtHR addressed a system, involving a Clemency Commission introduced in Bulgaria 2012, for reviewing life sentences that do not qualify for routine review. The Clemency Commission reported on requests for clemency to the vice president of Bulgaria who has powers delegated by the president to make decisions on clemency. The court examined the working of the commission, the criteria it took into account in deciding cases, and its relationship to the vice president, who usually agreed with the commission, but gives reasons when he does not. The court concluded that these procedures did give these prisoners a real possibility for release.[65]

This ruling was apparently studied closely in Hungary, which is the only country in Europe with a constitutional provision allowing LWOP. Although the wording is restrictive—"Life imprisonment without parole may only be imposed for a commission of a willful and violent criminal offense"[66]—the intention of this provision appears to be to protect LWOP from outright challenge by the Hungarian Constitutional Court.

In 2014, the ECtHR ruled that the very limited clemency procedures then in force made what in Hungary are regarded as life sentences that merely excluded the routine consideration of parole, unacceptable in European law.[67] The Hungarian government responded in late 2014, and made its release system similar to the one in Bulgaria that had been acceptable to the ECtHR. Hungary strengthened the clemency procedures and provided for an automatic clemency review after forty years. In 2015, these new procedures were upheld by the Hungarian courts as meeting European human rights norms. In October 2016, however, the ECtHR ruled that a forty-year period was too long to give real hope of release and, in addition, that the new clemency procedures still did not meet the requirements of Article 3 of the ECHR.[68] Whether these procedures can be reformed further to meet the requirements of the ECtHR remains to be seen.[69]

In Lithuania, too, life-sentenced prisoners may be released following a presidential pardon, which is available after serving ten years. However, in May 2017, the ECtHR ruled that this did not meet the requirements of Article 3 of the ECHR. In coming to this conclusion, the ECtHR distinguished the Lithuanian procedure from the decision that the Grand Chamber had reached in 2017 in *Hutchinson v. United Kingdom,* on the grounds that the Lithuanian presidential pardon, unlike the decision taken by the secretary of state for justice in England and Wales, was not subject to judicial review.[70]

This latest decision indicates that the ECtHR is likely to remain highly critical of executive release procedures. So are at least some national courts. In March 2018, the press in Malta reported that the Maltese Constitutional Court had ruled that prisoners who had previously been serving LWOP should be considered for parole after having served twenty-five years.[71] One may conclude that the survival of LWOP in Europe is somewhat precarious. There is a real possibility that all variations of LWOP in Europe eventually will be regarded as contrary to fundamental human rights.

LWOP AND HUMAN RIGHTS IN OTHER JURISDICTIONS. Outside Europe there have been few human rights–based critiques of LWOP. In Australia, for example, where most of the states have LWOP, attempts to challenge LWOP have floundered on the lack of an entrenched Bill of Rights in the national constitution, which makes Australian courts very reluctant to challenge primary legislation.[72]

In contrast, in 2016, the Supreme Court of Zimbabwe, in *Makoni v. Commissioner of Prisons,* effectively replaced LWOP with a form of LWP for all life-sentenced prisoners.[73] This decision, which is based on international human rights law and the provisions of the Constitution of Zimbabwe, is so far reaching that it needs further elucidation as an illustration of how far national courts could go, if they were to take a principled stance against LWOP.

In Zimbabwe life-sentenced prisoners, unlike other prisoners serving fixed terms, cannot be considered for parole. The Constitution of Zimbabwe does empower the president to exercise mercy, which includes the power to grant "respite for the execution of any sentence or to substitute or remit the whole or a part of a sentence."[74] Under the Prisons Act, the commissioner of prisons must report to the minister of justice on every life-sentenced prisoner every five years, after the prisoner has served his first ten years. The minister may, but need not, forward such reports to the president. There is thus a rudimentary procedure in place for the president to consider the release of life-sentenced prisoners, but one that may not be effective. The question was whether LWOP Zimbabwean style, with no parole but the possibility of release by executive intervention, meets human rights standards.

The Supreme Court of Zimbabwe was unimpressed with the existing procedure. It began by setting out the rights of prisoners under the Constitution of Zimbabwe and summarizing what it saw as relevant comparative law, including the decision of the ECtHR in *Vinter* and the internationally recognized importance of rehabilitation for all prisoners. The Zimbabwean court found "no reason to depart from the foreign and international jurisprudence that had developed on the subject over the past sixty years."[75] Accordingly, it concluded that irreducible LWOP violated human dignity and amounted to cruel, inhuman, or degrading treatment or punishment, in breach of the Zimbabwean Constitution.

The question remained, however, whether the technically available possibility of release in the Zimbabwean form of LWOP was sufficiently effective to ensure the human dignity of these prisoners in Zimbabwe. The court examined the procedures closely and decided that life-sentenced prisoners were being disadvantaged, compared to other prisoners serving fixed-term sentences, who had access to a parole system, albeit one in which the minister of justice had a final say. This, the court held, infringed against the equal protection clause of the Zimbabwean Constitution, for in its view there was no justifiable basis for limiting the rights of life-sentenced prisoners in this way life. The court concluded:

It is not clear what legitimate public interest is served by depriving life prisoners of the possibility of their release following an appropriate period of reformative and rehabilitative incarceration. In the absence of any such justification, it follows that the impugned provisions are unconstitutional to the extent that they exclude whole life prisoners from the parole process and thereby contravene the right to equal protection and benefit of the law under [the Constitution of Zimbabwe].[76]

The remedy that the Supreme Court of Zimbabwe adopted was equally drastic. It not only declared the provisions of the Prisons Act that had implemented LWOP to be unconstitutional, but also ordered that, until the government of Zimbabwe came up with new legislation, all life-sentenced prisoners should be considered for parole in the same way as other sentenced prisoners.

In other jurisdictions the introduction of LWOP in response to changes in the death penalty has caused great confusion in practice where existing provisions relating to release from life imprisonment have not been taken into account. In Uganda, where LWOP was introduced in 2009 by the Ugandan Supreme Court as an alternative to the death penalty, the court paid no attention to the existing practice of automatic release for life-sentenced prisoners, thus producing not only legal confusion but also a headache for the prison system, which has to distinguish between life-sentenced prisoners who were entitled to release and some who were not.[77]

Similarly, in Kazakhstan, after the de facto abolition of the death penalty in 2003, sentences of death were converted to LWOP. At the same time, life sentences with consideration of parole after a minimum period of twenty-five years were added to the penal code as a new penalty that can be imposed directly. As a result, the Kazakhstan prison service has had to run two parallel systems for life-sentenced prisoners without any logical distinction being drawn between them.[78]

CLASSIFYING LWOP.   The classification of particular forms of life imprisonment is not always simple and required us to make some difficult judgments. For example, consider systems of sharia law that apply in some Muslim countries, where the release of life-sentenced prisoners may depend, not only on the head of state, but also on the consent of the victim's relatives.[79] These forms of release meet the definition of LWOP, but do they belong to the subtype of irreducible LWOP? Our reasons for coming to the conclusion that they do not was that the veto of the relatives does not apply to all crimes that carry life sentences. Moreover, even where the relatives have this power, this additional barrier to release is not absolute and therefore does not make these sentences fully irreducible.

Sometimes it is questionable whether the classification should be LWOP or LWP. In Ghana there is no parole board, and courts do not have the power to order the release of life-sentenced prisoners.[80] However, discussions with the Ghanaian prison authorities revealed that the president of Ghana routinely exercises his power of commutation to convert all life sentences into new fixed-term sentences, after the prisoners who were originally sentenced to imprisonment for life have served ten years.[81] Does the ten-year period make it a case of LWP? In theory, the president does not have to take this step, as it is dependent on the prisoner's good behavior during those first ten years, but in practice he usually does so. Once the sentence has been converted to twenty years, the prisoner qualifies for further remission for good behavior and is usually released before the end of the substituted sentence. Nevertheless, on reflection, given the central role of the president of Ghana and some flexibility about the ten-year period, we classified this as a form of LWOP. The central role of the head of state in Ghana is similar to that in Kenya and Thailand, which are the countries that have the highest numbers of LWOP prisoners outside the United States, and where the authority of the head of state to order release at any time is largely untrammeled.

Life with Parole (LWP)

Life imprisonment with parole is the type of life sentence in which the sentenced prisoners are routinely considered for release by a court, a parole board or similar body. The consideration for release may even be undertaken by the executive. The crucial difference between LWOP and LWP is that the former does not include routine consideration of release, while the latter does. We also include in LWP, life sentences where release is not so much considered but takes place automatically after a set period. This subtype, which we call symbolic LWP, is considered separately at the end of this section.

In 144 of the 183 countries that we identified as having some type of formal life imprisonment, there was provision for release, other than the remote possibility of release by the exercise of a purely executive clemency discretion. LWP is formally the most often used type of life imprisonment in the world. This underlines the importance of routine release consideration as a defining characteristic of most modern formal systems of life imprisonment.

The legal basis for routine consideration of release of life-sentenced prisoners typically takes two forms. Most commonly, legislation provides directly that, after a fixed period following the imposition of the life sentence, routine consideration of release will follow or, at least, the life-sentenced prisoner will have a right to apply for release. Alternatively, the court imposing the life sentence may prescribe the minimum period that the offender has to serve before the first legally mandated review. There are also hybrid versions, where the sentencing court can set a minimum period but it is subject to legislative constraints.[82] A further characteristic of LWP is that, no matter how the timing of the first review is set, there is a provision that prescribes subsequent reviews if the life-sentenced prisoner is not released at the first review.

The description of LWP is deliberately inclusive because of the many forms of routine consideration of release from life imprisonment that are found internationally. The "with parole" part of LWP term may be thought to imply a form of conditional release whereby former life-sentenced prisoners will be subject to supervision in the community after they leave prison, either for the rest of their lives or for a determinate period.[83] However, while the release of life-sentenced prisoners is usually conditional, this is not invariably true. Release following routine consideration may be effected without conditions being set at all. Alternatively, the restrictions on the released life-sentenced prisoner may be so limited—effectively only a requirement not to reoffend—that they do not meet the definition of conditional release (parole) of the Council of Europe, which only regards community measures implemented under individualized post-sentence conditions as conditional release.[84] For our purposes we do not restrict LWP in this way but include all forms of life sentence with routine consideration of release from prison.

In describing sentences as LWP, one should also be aware of the imprecise language courts and even legislatures sometimes use in this regard. A good illustration can be found in the loose language of the International Criminal Tribunal for the former Yugoslavia (ICTY) and the International Criminal Tribunal for Rwanda (ICTR), which use a variety of terms to describe the life sentences they impose. In more recent decisions the usage is remarkably inconsistent, with Trial and Appellate Chambers of the ICTR, in particular, using different formulations to refer to the same sentence in the same case. For example, in 1999 in *Prosecutor v. Kayishema and Ruzindana,* the trial chamber sentenced Kayishema to "imprisonment for the remainder of his life," while in 2001, the appeals chamber in the same case "affirmed the sentence of life imprisonment imposed."[85] Similarly, in 2009 in *Prosecutor v. Renzaho,* the trial chamber uses the expression "life imprisonment," whereas the appeals chamber, in 2011, affirmed "Renzaho's sentence of imprisonment for the remainder of his life."[86] However, scholarly analysis has demonstrated that there is no real basis in the Statute of the ICTR for this distinction.[87] Moreover, the release practices of the ICTY and the ICTR have crystallized recently into a centralized system where the persons sentenced to life imprisonment, no matter how it is described by the tribunals when imposing sentence, are routinely considered for release after they have served thirty years.[88] Thus, all life sentences imposed by the ICTY and the ICTR can fairly be regarded as LWP sentences.

It is sometimes difficult to distinguish between LWP and LWOP when it comes to the decision-making process. This does not arise where the final decision on whether to release a life-sentenced prisoner is made by a court or a fully independent parole board: such decisions, made routinely, are a very clear indication that we are dealing with LWP. However, in some US jurisdictions, the final decision to release must be confirmed by the governor. Where the gubernatorial role is merely confirmatory, we have classified these instances as LWP, as they are taken routinely, even though in practice the governor may intervene regularly to block parole.[89]

Ireland also raises a classification dilemma. Ireland has a parole board that considers the release of life-sentenced prisoners and advises the minister of justice, who tends to follow its advice. However, the Irish parole board has no statutory basis and is appointed by the minister, who is not bound by its decisions.[90] It could be argued that the release mechanism for life-sentenced prisoners in Ireland does not differ that much from situations where heads of state or their surrogates take the final decisions on whether to release such prisoners, perhaps after taking advice from a pardon or clemency board. However, for analytical purposes we regard Ireland as having LWP, albeit of a kind where the minister rather than the parole board has the most powers, because of the routine and regular nature of the decision-making process.

Another example is Indonesia, where the possibility of being released depends in the first instance on a judgment about good behavior. There, a certificate of good behavior must be issued by the prison authorities after the life-sentenced prisoner has served at least one year; and if this is done, the life sentence is converted to a fixed-term of a maximum of fifteen years and treated for purposes of conditional release as such a sentence. Although the requirement for such a certificate gives the executive a means of denying parole, we have included the Indonesian procedure in the LWP category. The reason for this is that, according to our Indonesian source, parole is rarely, if ever, denied by using this device. What this example illustrates is the flexibility of our typology and the need to examine release practices closely.

It is worth pointing out one further potential weakness of the typological distinction between LWP and LWOP. Thus far, we have considered LWP primarily from a legal point of view, as provision for routine consideration of release. However, it is possible to envisage an LWP sentence where LWOP will invariably be the factual outcome, because the minimum period that life-sentenced prisoners have to serve is so long that they have no realistic prospect of ever being considered for release, simply because it is highly unlikely that they will live long enough to be able to do so.

An extreme example of this is legislation in Liberia, where a recent amendment to the penal code provides that someone who commits a rape in the course of armed robbery, terrorism, or hijacking shall be sentenced to "a term of imprisonment for life with possibilities of parole at age 90 (ninety) years."[91] In comparison, life expectancy in Liberia is sixty-one years for men and sixty-three years for women.[92]

Where courts have a power to set minimum periods, they too can produce outcomes that convert what are formally LWP sentences into LWOP. One way of doing this is by setting very long minimum periods, which would take a life-sentenced prisoner of almost any age beyond the average life span. A more subtle way of achieving the same effect is by setting minimum periods that on their face are not excessive but that, given the age of the offender at sentence, rule out any prospect of release, other than an executive commutation.[93] The same result can be achieved by making minimum periods run consecutively. A striking example occurred in 2014 in

Canada. Since 2011, courts in Canada may order statutory minimum periods to be served consecutively. In *R. v. Bourque,* a twenty-four-year-old offender convicted of three counts of first-degree murder, each carrying a life term with a minimum period of twenty-five years, was ordered to serve them consecutively, which will make him ninety-nine years old before he can be considered for release.[94]

The lesson to be drawn from these examples is that claims that a particular life sentence is a form of LWP, and therefore automatically less severe and necessarily more humane than LWOP, have to be examined closely and critically. One should nevertheless not dismiss out of hand the claim inherent in LWP that, as release will be routinely considered, it will somehow make life sentences fairer or more just.

SYMBOLIC LWP.   Consideration of release, of course, does not guarantee release. However, it appears that there is a type of LWP that does seem to guarantee release for those on whom it has been imposed. Somewhat unexpectedly, our research found a sentence that we have termed symbolic life. A symbolic life sentence is called life imprisonment. In practice the judge when pronouncing sentence simply says, something like, "I sentence you to imprisonment for life." Nevertheless, such sentences have a fixed maximum term after which release always takes place. We regard them as a form of LWP, as there is an element of routine to the release. The routine is that release is automatically ordered after a certain period without further consideration. This makes symbolic life sentences a distinct subtype within the LWP type.

Symbolic LWP seems to be found largely in former British territories that adopted versions of colonial criminal codes, criminal procedural codes and prison laws, such as Bangladesh, India, Iraq, Malaysia, Maldives, Myanmar (Burma), Nepal, Pakistan, Sudan, and Uganda.[95] All of these have legal systems shaped to some extent by colonial British law, which, starting with the Indian Penal Code of 1870, seems to reflect a need to standardize how long persons would serve before being released from life sentences.

A clear example of symbolic life can be found in Malaysia, where the large majority of life sentences take this form, and the legislative basis for them is specific: "Where any person is treated as having been sentenced or is hereafter sentenced to imprisonment for life, such sentence shall be deemed for all purposes to be a sentence of imprisonment for thirty years."[96] This particular meaning of life imprisonment is indirectly reinforced in Malaysia by a provision in the 1971 Firearms (Increased Penalties) Act, which gives a different meaning to life imprisonment, but only for the purposes of that particular Act. It provides that "'imprisonment for life' means, notwithstanding section 3 of the Criminal Justice Act 1953 and any other written law to the contrary, imprisonment for the duration of the natural life of the person sentenced." Equating a sentence of life imprisonment with a fixed maximum period is further strengthened by the Malaysian Penal Code, which provides that "[i]n calculating fractions of terms of punishment, imprisonment for life shall be reckoned as equivalent to imprisonment for thirty years."[97]

The legal provisions governing symbolic life sentences in other former British colonies are typically not as clear as those in Malaysia. Thus, there may be a provision on how to calculate fractions of imprisonment, that is, periods of remission, as part of a life sentence, by stipulating a nominal fixed-term of the equivalent of fourteen, twenty, or thirty years, but this may not be backed by any further legislation equivalent to the 1953 Malaysian Criminal Justice Act, spelling out explicitly that release follows after this stated term.

An established routine of releasing all life-sentenced prisoners by this fixed-term equivalent, however, may reinforce the idea that all life sentences have to be of a particular determinate maximum length. A practical example of this can be found in Nigeria, where there are effectively two penal codes: one applied in northern states and the other in southern states. The penal code, applicable in the northern states, sheds light on computation of terms of imprisonment. Section 70 of this Code provides: "In calculating fractions of terms of imprisonment, imprisonment for life shall be reckoned to be imprisonment for twenty years." Although there is no equivalent provision in the penal code that applies in the south, the practice throughout the country is apparently to treat life sentences as fixed terms of twenty years and then to deduct further remission from that.[98]

Maximum terms that are thought to be inherent in symbolic life sentences may prove to be unstable, if not downright confusing, if they are not fully enshrined in law. Typically, such instability is caused when some form of life imprisonment is put forward as an alternative to the death penalty and appellate courts "discover" that in practice "life imprisonment" has long been treated as if it were a fixed-term sentence.

A prime example of such confusion has played itself out in Uganda in recent years. There, the 2006 Prisons Act provides, as did its predecessors, that "for purposes of calculating remission of sentence, imprisonment for life shall be deemed to be twenty years' imprisonment."[99] This provision had formed the basis for a practice treating all life sentences as being sentences of twenty years. However, when the Supreme Court of Uganda declared the mandatory death penalty unconstitutional in 2009, it ordered that persons whose death sentences were not reviewed within three years, should automatically have their sentences commuted to "imprisonment for life without remission."[100] In a subsequent decision, the Ugandan Supreme Court rejected the idea that act could be regarded as having set a twenty-year minimum. It held that "life imprisonment means imprisonment for the natural life term of a convict," but went on to say that "the actual period of imprisonment may stand reduced on account of remissions earned."[101] However, the supreme court did not strike down the provision of the Prisons Act that remission should be calculated as if life sentences were for twenty years. Nor did it give any indication of what should happen where the sentence was one of natural life. Currently therefore, there is a great deal of uncertainty about what life imprisonment means.[102] Courts, other than the supreme court, still seem to regard life imprisonment as being for a maximum of twenty years. Although sometimes they appear to suggest that this applies only to life sentences imposed before the supreme court intervened to "change" the meaning of life imprisonment, in other more recent cases several courts have returned to the position that life sentences have a maximum duration of twenty years.

A similar disjunction exists in Bangladesh, where the penal code, rather than prison legislation, sets a fixed-term that is to be applied when calculating fractions of life imprisonment for purposes of release. The relevant provision is part of the penal code, which was adopted by the British in 1860 for the Indian subcontinent and which is still applicable in Bangladesh. The only significant change is that the fixed-term for calculating fractions was increased from 20 to 30 years in 1985.[103] In 2013, Judge Imman Ali spelled out in the appellate division of the high court what he regarded as the current interpretation of what life imprisonment effectively meant in Bangladesh: it was a fixed-term of 22.5 years in prison. This conclusion had been reached by applying the thirty years mentioned in the penal code and then reducing it in terms of the Jail Code, which entitles all prisoners to automatic remission of one quarter of their sentences. This 22.5-year term could be shortened further by the automatic reduction of the period that the prisoner would have spent in custody prior to conviction, which in Bangladesh could be particularly long, as much as a decade or more.[104] Judge Ali explained that the "sentence of 'imprisonment for life' as used in Bangladesh is utterly a misnomer." He recognized that in "the way it has been interpreted the word 'life' does not bear its normal linguistic meaning" and worried that courts might impose the death penalty rather than life imprisonment because the latter might be perceived as a "lenient sentence" or "not a proper sentence."[105] Nevertheless, this judgment confirmed that, as the law stood in Bangladesh in 2013, all life sentences were symbolic in the sense in which we have used the term: that it is really a fixed-term sentence under another name.

In 2014, however, the Supreme Court of Bangladesh, in upholding an appeal against the death penalty imposed by the International Crimes Tribunal for Bangladesh[106] that had convicted the appellant of crimes against humanity, sentenced him to "imprisonment for life i.e. the rest of his natural life." The court did not explain the sentence, except to indicate that a death sentence would be too severe, "considering the nature of the offenses perpetrated by the accused and his culpability in those crimes." It added that "[a] sentence of imprisonment for the rest of his natural life would be proportionate to the gravity of the crimes."[107] In this instance, the Supreme Court was interpreting the penal provision of the 1973 International Crimes (Tribunals) Act, which provides only for a "sentence of death or such other punishment proportionate to the gravity of the crime as appears to the Tribunal to be just and proper."[108] Arguably, this provision gave the Supreme Court room to define a life sentence differently to what had until then been the case in interpretations of the penal code. Nevertheless, the way has been opened for Bangladesh to have both a life sentence, which is symbolic only, as release is guaranteed after a fixed-term, and a "natural life" sentence, which is really a form of LWOP.

In 2017 the same line of analysis was extended by the Supreme Court of Bangladesh to instances where a court did not impose the death penalty in an "ordinary" murder case but, as an exception to the rule that the death penalty should be imposed, decided to "commute" it to life imprisonment. In such cases, the supreme court ruled, a sentencing or appellate court could direct that the life-sentenced prisoner "shall have to suffer [for the] rest of his natural life."[109] Such a life sentence would be beyond the application of remission. In other words, it would be a form of LWOP, from which release would only be possible by presidential pardon. It is not clear from this judgment whether the purely symbolic life sentence, with an effective maximum of 22.5 years, will continue to survive, but one may assume that that will be the case.

The position in Pakistan is largely the same. On the basis of the old Indian Penal Code and the Prison Rules as amended in that country, an ordinary sentence of life imprisonment has an absolute maximum of twenty-five years and this usually translates into release after fifteen years.[110] However, in practice, courts sometimes make orders for "life imprisonment without the permission for parole." Apparently, these sentences are effectively treated as LWOP.[111]

It is striking that in several countries there is a strong belief that life-sentenced prisoners must automatically be released after a fixed period, even though the legal basis for such release is rather unclear. Until recently the most prominent example of symbolic life was to be found in India, where the belief still persists that the Indian Penal Code requires that life must be treated as a twenty-year term, from which life-sentenced prisoners are entitled to deduct further remission for good behavior, with the result that they should be released after twenty years, and possibly after as little as fourteen years, if they have earned the maximum additional reduction of sentence.[112] The Indian Supreme Court has explained that the reference to twenty years in the penal code is only a means of calculating what reward life-sentenced prisoners should get for good behavior. It has emphasized that such rewards, including a reduction in time served, depend on a decision by the authorities to change the life sentence into a fixed-term of no more than 14 years. If that is not done, life sentences continue to be implemented, as the Supreme Court emphasized in 1961, "for the whole of the remaining period of the convicted person's natural life."[113] In spite of this clear legal ruling the point has persistently been raised, and rejected, in a long line of subsequent cases.[114] As late as 2008, the Indian Supreme Court was still referring to what it regarded as an undesirable form of "standardisation that, in practice, renders the sentence of life imprisonment equal to imprisonment for a period of no more than 14 years."[115] However, the current practice appears to be that, after fourteen years, discretion is now exercised on whether or not to release persons sentenced to life imprisonment. Accordingly, in spite of the importance of the Indian evolution for the history of symbolic life sentences, for statistical purposes we have classified the large number of persons serving life imprisonment in India as serving LWP and not symbolic life.

There are other borderline cases. In Greece, the Criminal Procedure Code provides that all life-sentenced prisoners are to be released when they first qualify for release after having served a minimum period, unless there are specific reasons not to release them.[116] It seems that indeed they are almost all released automatically. Nevertheless, for statistical purposes we regard Greece as having LWP, and the form of legislation as an interesting variation on the release procedure.

Can sentences that are called in law "imprisonment for life," but which are accompanied by provisions that provide a clear, or even an implicit, guarantee of release after a fixed period, be regarded as life imprisonment at all? On their face, they do not meet our basic definition of life imprisonment as a sentence that gives a state the power to keep someone in prison until they die there. On the other hand, in Malaysia, and arguably in other states with similar laws, sentences of "imprisonment for life" are routinely imposed and recorded as such in official statistics, even though they are implemented with fixed maximum periods.

The reality, and even the belief, that some or all life-sentenced prisoners have a legal right to be released after a set period is perhaps the most extreme demonstration of the difficulty of developing an all-embracing definition of life imprisonment. Arguably, the sentences to which symbolic life refers are really not life sentences at all. However, we do not propose to dismiss them as not being fairly labeled. Instead, we keep these symbolic life sentences in our analysis as a separate subtype of LWP, not least because they may reveal important insights into the difficulties of constructing procedurally fair release systems.

The Spectrum of Formal Life Imprisonment

Before concluding the section on formal life sentences, it is worth making two important qualifications about how the typology can be used. First, the real potential for release may not be, and in practice is often not, determined by where a particular life sentence fits on the spectrum of likely release, as reflected in Figure 0.1 in the Preface. A sentence of life imprisonment that routinely allows for some form of consideration of release may be no less punitive than one that does not do so. Even symbolic LWP, where release is guaranteed after, say, thirty years, may in practice be much longer than LWOP, where release depends on the whim of a head of state but the possibility remains that the head of state will order the release of someone relatively early.

Second, although the length of time served in prison, both potentially and in practice, is a key indicator of how punitive a particular life sentence is, that is not the only determinant of its punitivity. There are examples of life sentences where courts may impose conditions, other than restrictions on release, which may deliberately be designed to make those life sentences more punitive than others. In some countries, sentences such as life imprisonment with or without hard labor are possible; while in others particularly harsh regimes, such as semisolitary confinement for a number of years, may be prescribed in the life sentence itself. In countries such as Turkey, courts have a choice between imposing "ordinary" or "aggravated" life imprisonment, and this influences the conditions of implementation directly.[117]

We have not isolated these as separate types of life imprisonment, but we do consider them in Chapter 7, where conditions of confinement are evaluated as elements of serving a life sentence. There is also the possibility that a sentence of life imprisonment may be combined with other sanctions, such as confiscation of property, or a compensation order.[118] This will make it a harsher punishment overall than a life sentence without such an additional requirement. In Singapore, life imprisonment has even been combined with corporal punishment or a fine.[119] Such additional requirements are relatively rare and do not justify being designated as separate types of life imprisonment. They should nevertheless be borne in mind when making comparisons, as should the very different prison conditions that apply in countries across the world.

Informal Life Sentences

Informal life sentences refer to all post-conviction responses to criminal behavior that give the state the power to detain convicted persons until they die in detention. These state interventions have the same impact on the individual serving them as on prisoners sentenced to formal life sentences. There are essentially two types of informal life sentences: (1) the de facto life sentence and (2) the various forms of indefinite post-conviction detention that have no predetermined limit on the time to be served.

De Facto Life

Inordinately long, fixed terms of imprisonment, one hundred years for example, are a type of informal life sentence that we call de facto life. Although prisoners serving these sentences have fixed dates at which release will be considered for the first time, they will inevitably die in prison before that date is reached. If such fixed-term sentences are subject to routine consideration for early release, they become the informal equivalent of LWP. If there is no prospect of release during the long fixed-term sentence, or if consideration of release from such sentences is always delayed until beyond the life expectancy of the prisoner, they may be the informal equivalent of LWOP. Inordinately long, fixed-term sentences may even be the equivalent of irreducible LWOP, if all forms of executive clemency are excluded.

Inordinately long, fixed-term sentences may be imposed in systems where all formal life sentences are potentially subject to parole but the sentencing judge wishes to exclude parole entirely in practice. In the 1999 case of *S v. Silulale and another* in South Africa, the trial court imposed fixed-term cumulative sentences of 155 and 115 years, respectively, on two offenders who had been convicted of multiple counts of murder and robbery. Under the law that was in force at the time, release from fixed-term sentences was not considered before prisoners had served two-thirds of their terms. In *Silulale,* it meant that they had to serve at least seventy years before they could be considered for release. The supreme court of appeal set aside the sentences and replaced them with formal life imprisonment to allow for parole. The court explained that life imprisonment was meant to be the most severe punishment that could be imposed in South Africa, and that there were recognized procedures for considering parole for all life-sentenced prisoners. It added pointedly that "to impose such a long term of imprisonment as to leave the offender with no possible hope of ever being released, no matter what happens, does not fit in a civilised legal system."[120]

De facto life sentences may be simple to describe in the abstract, but in practice it is difficult to identify which fixed-term sentences are so long that they should be regarded as de facto life. For example, in Central and South

America, where most countries without life imprisonment are found, several have provisions for particularly lengthy fixed-term sentences. Colombia and Costa Rica allow for cumulative fifty-year sentences; El Salvador and Guatemala have provisions for sixty-year sentences.[121] Brazil allows sentences of a hundred years, yet provides that no one can serve more than thirty years. In other words, a country may draw a distinction between sentences that can legally be imposed and the maximum time that may actually be served. These examples illustrate the complexity of defining de facto life sentences.

Some guidance on the meaning of de facto life can be found in jurisprudence worldwide. In 2010, the Constitutional Chamber of the Supreme Court of El Salvador faced this issue.[122] Although the Constitution of El Salvador outlawed the death penalty and life imprisonment for all except military offenses, the penal code allowed sentences of up to seventy-five years. The question was whether the seventy-five-year sentence was in effect a life sentence and therefore unconstitutional. The court held that it was and advised the legislature to change it. One basis of the decision was simply factual. Life expectancy in El Salvador was seventy years and as the seventy-five-year sentence could only be imposed on offenders over the age of eighteen, they would not survive it. They would therefore be in the same position as persons subject to life imprisonment. The court noted that, even though persons sentenced to seventy-five years might benefit from early release, pardon or other measures; that was not sufficient. As the court commented: "We have to think of those who might not [be released early], and who will have to suffer the full length of the sentence."[123] They would not have the opportunity to lead a life in free society again, which would undermine the right to a future life of freedom, which should be available to all sentenced prisoners. This is, of course, an argument that chimes with a prohibition of all forms of life imprisonment, including LWP.[124]

Although no jurisdiction in the United States has formally outlawed life imprisonment, US courts have addressed the issue, albeit in different contexts: where diplomatic agreements have prevented the imposition of a life sentence and in the context of the imposition of LWOP on juveniles.[125] In *United States v. Pileggi*,[126] a Canadian citizen and resident of Costa Rica was charged with multiple frauds against elderly US citizens, who suffered enormous losses. The US government sought his extradition on the basis that the effect of his crimes was felt primarily in its jurisdiction. However, the crimes for which he was charged carried a possible sentence of life imprisonment. The Constitution of Costa Rica prohibits both death and life sentences, and the Criminal Code of Costa Rica sets the maximum cumulative prison sentence at fifty years.[127] Accordingly, Costa Rica requested assurances that, upon conviction following extradition to the United States, Pileggi would not be subject to the death penalty or life imprisonment. In response, the US government assured Costa Rica that, if extradited, Pileggi would not receive the death penalty or a sentence that would require him to "spend the rest of [his] natural [life] in prison."[128] Both governments considered themselves bound by the agreement, and Pileggi was extradited to the United States, tried and convicted. At trial, however, the prosecutor incorrectly told the court that the agreement permitted a sentence of no more than fifty years. The trial court found that, because of the agreement, it could not impose life imprisonment and sentenced Pileggi to a fixed-term of fifty years (and an obligation to repay almost $4 million). Pileggi was already fifty years old. The Fourth Circuit Court of Appeals set aside the sentence and the matter was referred back to a different sentencing judge, who imposed a term of twenty-five years.[129] What is particularly impressive about the *Pileggi* case is that the Fourth Circuit sought to give effect to the substance of the agreement with Costa Rica with respect to life imprisonment. It ruled that fifty years was a de facto whole-life sentence when imposed on someone of Pileggi's age.

The Supreme Court of California followed a similar approach in deciding whether a sentence of 110 years to life imposed on a juvenile, a child under 18 years of age, was a de facto LWOP sentence violating its prior ruling prohibiting the imposition of LWOP on juveniles convicted of non-homicide offenses.[130] The question was whether the minimum of 110 years was an effective LWOP sentence. The court held that it was, even though the 110-year period was the aggregate of three consecutive minimum periods following three life sentences for non-murder offenses. The decision was important because it explicitly recognized that a sentence in which the minimum term was longer than the life expectancy of juveniles should be treated in the same way as a formal LWOP sentence.

It is not only courts that acknowledge the existence of functional equivalents of life imprisonment. Governments and researchers have done so also. The government of Columbia faced a similar problem. Despite a constitutional prohibition against life imprisonment, inordinately lengthy fixed-term sentences were quite common. Faced with the question of whether to introduce legislation permitting life sentences for certain offenses, the Colombian minister of justice commented in 2015 that, since sentences of up to 118 years were possible for certain offenses, the question was moot.[131] However, a constitutional challenge to the current law in Colombia may well come to the same conclusion as in El Salvador, namely, that such sentences amount to life imprisonment and are thus unconstitutional.[132]

Similarly, in Brazil, there is constant, although hitherto unsuccessful, political pressure to increase this maximum effective term from thirty years to fifty years. Brazilian law permits the imposition of a term of 100 years, but the maximum term that can actually be served is thirty years. A Brazilian scholar, Giovanna Frisso, has examined whether supporters of the increase were seeking to introduce a (de facto) life imprisonment by the back door. Looking at demographic data of Brazilian prisoners, including their gender, ethnicity and social class, Frisso found that, given these demographics, sentences with an effective fifty-year minimum would result in the majority of them dying in prison. She concluded that the proponents of the longer term deliberately support what would be de facto life imprisonment.[133]

In its 2015 report, *Life Sentences in the Federal System,* the US Sentencing Commission included an entire section on "De Facto Life Imprisonment Sentences." The commission pointed out that, in addition to life imprisonment that is directly imposed, in many cases,

> the length of a sentence imposed is so long that the sentence is, for all practical purposes, a life sentence and likely was intended to be such by the judge who imposed it. In some of these cases, a sentence of life imprisonment was not authorized under any of the statutes of conviction and the court imposed consecutive sentences for multiple counts of conviction in order to achieve the lengthy period of incarceration imposed.[134]

The sentencing commission used a sentence length of 470 months (39 years, 2 months) or longer as a proxy for identifying cases in which a de facto life sentence had been imposed. It explained this proxy by noting that the commission assigned a value of 470 months to sentences of life imprisonment for any statistical analysis in which a term of months was required and therefore it was using the same basis for de facto life sentences.[135] This was based on the commission's estimate that a sentence length of 470 months "is consistent with the average life expectancy of a federal criminal offender, given the average age of federal offenders."[136]

The report *Life Sentences in the Federal System* is unusual in the context of writings on life imprisonment in recognizing and seeking to analyze the category of de facto life sentences, and in providing detailed information about individuals who receive this sentence. However, the 470-month life expectancy measure is fairly rough. No explanation is given of how precisely this was calculated other than by considering the average age of federal offenders, presumably at the time of sentence.

Another difficulty in developing the concept of the de facto life sentence is whether to include prisoners who are likely to die in prison before their imposed fixed-term ends, not because of the sentence itself but because of the prisoner's individual circumstances, such as advanced age or ill health at the time of sentencing. It is interesting that the US Sentencing Commission distinguished such sentences from "de facto life imprisonment sentences" and put them into a category of "Other Sentences Likely to Extend to the Death of the Offender." The commission noted that a characteristic of sentences that fall into this latter category was that "there is less reason to infer that the sentencing judge intended the term of incarceration to extend to the death of the offender."[137] Using its 470-month cut-off for defining de facto life imprisonment, the commission went on to conduct a sophisticated analysis of the life expectancy of each offender sentenced in the federal system in 2013, taking into account gender, race, ethnicity, and age. It then examined the offenders sentenced to less than 470-months—not de facto life—and considered those who were likely to die before serving their imposed fixed-term. The results were surprising. Of all sentenced offenders in the federal system in 2013, 153 prisoners were sentenced to life; 168 prisoners were sentenced to de facto life (over 470 months); and 291 prisoners with sentences shorter than 470 months were likely to die in prison, given their age. In other words, there were more prisoners in this last group than prisoners serving de facto life sentences and actual life sentences.[138]

There is a logical case to be made for including this last group among those who are subject to de facto life sentences. There is a parallel between prisoners serving de facto life sentences and older offenders who are sentenced to life imprisonment with very long minimum periods before their release can be considered, thus effectively converting their sentences of LWP into LWOP. Both groups would fall into what Jessica Henry calls "'death-in-prison' sentences."[139]

For descriptive purposes, we chose to define de facto life sentences as sentences of a fixed-term that could lead to 35 years or more being served in prison. We excluded those instances where the actual terms that prisoners may serve were always less than 35 years. The 35-year figure, like the 470-month cut-off chosen by the US Sentencing Commission, is somewhat arbitrary. However, it allows us to provide a preliminary picture of the pervasiveness of de facto life sentences in the world. The prevalence of such sentences is discussed in Chapter 3.

Post-Conviction Indefinite Detention

Our final type of informal life imprisonment is post-conviction indefinite detention. It encompasses a range of interventions, following a criminal conviction, which may result in the person being detained indefinitely. Post-conviction forms of indefinite detention can also be defined by default by what they are not: they are not fixed terms of imprisonment and they are not formal life imprisonment. Post-conviction indefinite detention is referred to variously as a sentence, sanction, measure or, in some instances, as civil confinement. We deliberately cast a wide net to include indefinite detention in all its forms, undertaken for various objectives, including rehabilitation and even retribution. Its primary use, however, is the prevention of future crime through incapacitation and rehabilitative treatment, but there is a risk that it may be used surreptitiously for retributive purposes.

The inclusion of the word "post-conviction" in the description of this type of informal life sentence is important, as it draws attention to one of the basic boundaries of this study of life imprisonment. We deliberately excluded persons detained indefinitely because of their "insanity," or other mental disorder where there is no criminal responsibility and therefore no criminal conviction.[140] Such a distinction is drawn in every legal system in this study with the exception of Sweden.[141] A distinction based on the absence of criminal responsibility may be difficult to apply comparatively, for legal systems vary in how they deal with those whose responsibility for their actions is diminished by different degrees of mental disorder. A degree of mental disorder is often a criterion for post-conviction indefinite detention. Nevertheless, the definition of mental disorder and its relationship to other concepts, such as unsound mind or mental illness, as alternative, often stricter, criteria, can be highly controversial.

Broadly speaking, legal systems that impose different kinds of post-conviction indefinite detention can be subdivided into two ideal types:

single-track and dual-track systems. In single-track systems, criminal courts are only allowed to impose punishments after a conviction. If a court orders indefinite detention following conviction without calling it life imprisonment, but gives it another name such as an habitual offender sentence or imprisonment for public protection, it remains a criminal sanction and is dealt with under criminal law standards. In the single-track system, if there is a need for a greater indefinite detention, such detention must be ordered outside the criminal justice system, as a form of civil commitment, to be dealt with separately as a civil matter under civil law standards. In contrast, in dual-track systems, criminal courts are allowed to impose punishments for crimes and also measures that are not considered punishment, but are aimed explicitly at preventing convicted offenders from committing further offenses by incapacitating them. This may be done by detaining them, indefinitely if necessary.[142]

SINGLE-TRACK SYSTEMS. Historically, most common-law jurisdictions have had single-track systems, where the formal line between those persons who are unfit to stand trial or insane and those who can be held criminally responsible is supposedly much clearer. Offenders are either criminally responsible or they are not. If they are criminally responsible, the court, following conviction, imposes punishment, including life sentences, often also in circumstances that elicit second-track responses in continental Europe. For example, in the United States, explicitly named mandatory life imprisonment is imposed as a sentence to deal with a wide range of recidivists. Examples are the mandatory life sentences imposed under "three strikes and you're out" legislation or discretionary life sentences to deal with habitual offenders. Such sentences appear within the formal life imprisonment statistics and may be either LWP or LWOP, depending on the release arrangements in place.[143]

Systems that regard themselves as having a single track may provide, however, for sentences that are not called life imprisonment but are clearly punishments formally imposed by the criminal courts. Often such sentences distinguish themselves from life sentences in name only. A good example is the sentence of "imprisonment for public protection," which could be imposed in England and Wales between 2005 and 2012.[144] Imprisonment for public protection was imposed on persons convicted of a violent or sexual offense, found to be dangerous, usually due to at least one previous conviction for a specified serious, violent or sexual offense. A sentence of imprisonment for public protection meant that the convicted person could be kept in prison indefinitely. Although release was possible, after a minimum period (often a very short one) set by the sentencing court was served, the prisoner could only be released if the parole board could be persuaded that their further detention was no longer necessary for the protection of the public. For the many prisoners in England and Wales who were still serving imprisonment for public protection when we undertook our empirical research, their sentence was very similar to life imprisonment, as it was imposed by a sentencing court and served in a prison.[145] Moreover, the standard for release is identical to that applicable to release from a formal LWP sentence after the minimum period has been completed. Like released life-sentenced prisoners, released prisoners initially sentenced to imprisonment for public protection remain subject to license conditions for the rest of their lives. The only difference is that, unlike released life-sentenced prisoners, they can apply for these conditions to be set aside after they have been living in the community for ten years. Even the official status of these sentences is ambiguous. In reporting to the Council of Europe, the English authorities have classified prisoners undergoing imprisonment for public protection as serving a sentence that is a security measure rather than life imprisonment, while the Scottish authorities have included the persons subject to the very similar "order for lifelong restriction" in the figures on life imprisonment reported to the same body.[146]

Some single-track systems can, and do, provide specifically for the indefinite detention of convicted dangerous offenders and do not label these sentences life imprisonment, but rather contrast them to life sentences. For example, in both Canada and South Africa there is provision for courts to declare persons convicted of serious violent offenses as "dangerous," because of their records and psychiatric advice, and then subjecting them to indefinite sentences.[147] In both jurisdictions, the courts have sought to contrast the provisions dealing with dangerous offenders with those relating to life imprisonment. In the leading Canadian case of *Lyons,* the Supreme Court of Canada noted that more evidence was required and more procedural safeguards had to be met before someone could be declared a "dangerous offender" than was the case when formal life imprisonment is imposed.[148]

In South Africa, there are similar evidentiary safeguards and procedural requirements to those in Canada relating to declaring someone a dangerous offender. However, the South African Supreme Court of Appeal warned against a different kind of abuse. The South African law on dangerous offenders allows courts to set a minimum period before the person who has been designated a dangerous offender must be returned to them for consideration of release. In the case of *S v. Bull and another,* a trial judge had ordered that several convicted persons be declared dangerous offenders and returned to court to have their status reconsidered after fifty years.[149] The Supreme Court of Appeal recognized that this was a technique for avoiding the routine consideration of parole after a period of twenty-five years, which is a feature of all formal life sentences in South Africa. It pointed out that life imprisonment was the ultimate penalty in South Africa, and that the dangerous offender statutes should not be used retributively, to impose a sentence effectively more severe than the permissible form of life imprisonment. However, the indefinite detention imposed in such cases is indisputably a penal sanction imposed directly by a sentencing court and served in a prison: it is not a formal second track in the continental European sense.

These British, Canadian and South African criminal sentencing variations that result in indefinite detention in single-track systems are easy to recognize as life sentences, for they often differ from their formal counterparts only in their label. Accordingly, we propose to treat them as informal life sentences, as do some official practices in these countries. Canadian statistics, for example, routinely combine "offenders with life or indeterminate sentences," suggesting that for bureaucratic purposes they are treated similarly.[150]

A more complex single-track variation is what is known in the United States as "civil confinement." Such confinement does not follow directly from the sentencing process but is only imposed, much later, when a prisoner who is due for release from a fixed-term sentence is perceived as dangerous. A modern US example, found in twenty states and the federal system, is the provision for the indefinite detention of so-called sexually violent predators, who have served their full sentences but are still deemed to pose a danger to the public.[151] In many ways this is the classic single-track provision, with the detention falling outside the criminal justice system, as technically it is not imposed in a criminal proceeding but a civil proceeding, based on a recommendation from the prosecuting authorities.[152] However, the civil standard of proof to establish the mental element is significantly less strict than the constitutionally mandated standard necessary to allow the detention of persons who have not been convicted of criminal offenses.

The constitutionality of legislation designed to deal with sexually violent predators was upheld by the US Supreme Court in 1997 in *Kansas v. Hendricks*.[153] In that case the Supreme Court unanimously rejected the argument that the relevant Kansas statute should require evidence of mental illness before indefinite, civil preventive detention could be imposed. It was satisfied with the weaker requirement of "mental abnormality," which meant nothing more than that the offender had a propensity to commit the same offense after release: that is, the offender was dangerous. In spite of powerful academic criticism of the use of civil law in this way for the imposition of what the critics regard as a form of disguised punishment,[154] the US Supreme Court continues to uphold laws of this kind as being merely an acceptable form of civil confinement, and thus not subject to the constraints of the criminal law, which could arguably regard it as a form of double jeopardy.[155]

In two extradition cases arising in the United Kingdom involving alleged sex offenders who, if convicted and sentenced to fixed terms of imprisonment, could be detained indefinitely after having served their sentences, senior English courts have rejected this portrayal of laws governing such detention of sexually violent predators in Minnesota and in California.[156] After careful analysis, including of expert evidence on the procedures and practices followed in these states, the English courts held that the (slightly different) tests applied in the two states would not lead to the potential indefinite detention of the person being sought for extradition, because of their being of "unsound mind" as defined in Article 5(1)(e) of the ECHR. Instead, the English courts concluded that they would run a real risk of being detained indefinitely after they had served their sentences, merely because of their alleged dangerousness revealed by their original offenses. In other words, they faced the risk of being required to serve an informal life sentence that would not have been imposed by the criminal court that sentenced them originally. In both cases, the English courts therefore refused to allow extradition, thus underlining the fundamental differences, even within single-track, common-law systems, about what is to be regarded as punishment and what is not.

Adding new ways of dealing with offenders whose dangerousness is perceived to require interventions that go beyond "normal" sentences often creates difficulties in jurisdictions other than the United States as well. In 2003, the Australian State of Queensland adopted legislation that provided for the indefinite detention of a prisoner who poses a serious danger to the community. Such detention is for purposes of "control, care or treatment."[157] The Australian authorities regarded this as a form of civil confinement even though it could be imposed on a prisoner who was not mentally ill, and it was carried out in a prison. Like the US Supreme Court in *Kansas v Hendricks*, the High Court of Australia, in the case of *Fardon v Attorney General of Queensland*, upheld the constitutionality of the Queensland legislation, even though it had only come into effect shortly before Fardon completed his initial fourteen-year sentence.[158] However, Fardon challenged his indefinite detention before the Human Rights Committee (HRC) of the United Nations. The HRC ruled that his indefinite detention was an additional punishment of indefinite imprisonment.[159] The HRC concluded that it infringed Articles 9 and 15 of the International Covenant on Civil and Political Rights because its retrospective imposition was arbitrary. It also infringed Article 14 because its imposition did not meet the due process standards that should be followed when a penal sentence is imposed.

Australia ignored the decision of the HRC in the *Fardon* case, and did not change its law as a consequence of it. However, the decision is important, for it indicates how post-conviction indefinite detention imposed in a presumably single-track system can infringe international human rights standards.

DUAL-TRACK SYSTEMS. The second-track, or dual-track, system was introduced in continental Europe in the early twentieth century, when the focus was on a subclass of offenders who were considered incorrigible recidivists. These offenders could not be deterred by punishments proportionate to their offenses or to their individual blameworthiness. The second track was designed to stand out from the penal framework, in the sense that it was not conceived of as punishment, even if the particular measure was imposed by the criminal courts and often implemented by detaining the individual in a prison.

The notion that, unlike formal sentences of life imprisonment, such measures are not punishment has persisted in many European countries, even though they are imposed by criminal courts and may result in indefinite detention. Currently, such second-track measures are found in countries with and without formal life imprisonment.

Norway has no provision for a formal sentence of life imprisonment. Nevertheless, a court may order *forvaring*, allowing for the indefinitely renewable preventive detention of someone beyond the maximum fixed-term sentence of twenty-one years (or thirty years in the case of terrorism) if they continue to pose a danger to society.[160]

Other European countries that have formal life imprisonment, such as Denmark, France, Germany, the Netherlands, and Sweden, also have dual-track systems, whereby individuals who commit certain categories of violent or sexual offenses can be detained indefinitely "at the disposal of the state" in specialist institutions, once their initial fixed-term sentences have been served.[161] The details of the law governing the imposition by criminal courts of second-track measures and their implementation in various carceral institutions vary in these countries, but in their modern forms the objective is the same: to protect society from the offenders subject to these measures. Such secure preventive detention is usually combined with treating the underlying mental causes of their dangerousness, in Denmark and the Netherlands in particular, with programs that have a strong psychiatric element.[162] In Switzerland, which also has a dual-track system, it is possible, however, to impose a form of post-conviction indefinite detention during which no treatment is offered on the grounds that the detained person is untreatable.[163]

In 2010, the idea that a second track of secure preventive detention, specifically *Sicherungsverwahrung*, as it was then practiced in Germany, was nonpunitive was rejected by the ECtHR. The court found that it was a penal sanction because it was imposed following a criminal conviction and because it was implemented in a prison with only minimal differences in regime from an ordinary prison sentence.[164] It was therefore subject to all the human rights safeguards related to the imposition of a sentence of imprisonment, including the prohibition against retrospective punishment. This was important in this case, for, when the individual concerned had completed his fixed-term sentence, he had been placed in *Sicherungsverwahrung* for an indefinite period, although at the time of the imposition of his original fixed-term sentence the law had only allowed for *Sicherungsverwahrung* for a maximum of ten years for a prisoner in his category. The German response, orchestrated in a subtle judgment of the German Federal Constitutional Court of May 14, 2011,[165] was not to abandon the second track, but to amend the law in order to include procedural safeguards, akin to those found in criminal law for second-track measures. The German court also required the construction of new institutions to house persons detained in terms of these measures and to introduce regimes that are strongly oriented to treatment and noticeably different from those available in prison. In deciding on whether to impose one of these measures, much more emphasis is now placed on psychiatric evidence of dangerousness.

Before *Sicherungsverwahrung* can be imposed retrospectively, after someone has been sentenced and served the bulk of his or her custodial term, there must be a finding that the offender is not only dangerous but also is suffering from a mental disorder.[166] In 2016 the ECtHR ruled that such detention can be justified under Article 5(1)(e) of the ECHR, which allows detention of persons of "unsound mind."[167] This subclass of German post-conviction preventive detention is not regarded by the ECtHR primarily as an additional criminal penalty anymore. Therefore, it does not have to meet the criteria that apply to the imposition of a criminal sentence, although, of course, the detention still follows from the original criminal conviction. Moreover, the changes introduced to the *Sicherungsverwahrung* regime mean that the ECtHR has recognized that it is now adequate for detaining those who are mentally disordered and dangerous, in a way that the previous regime, where detainees were held in ordinary prisons, was not. The upshot of these changes in Germany is that the second track has been preserved as a separate form of indefinite detention, but only by bringing it increasingly within the framework of a treatment model akin to that operating in a mental institution for persons who have not been involved in the criminal justice process at all.[168]

The same trend is observable also in several other European states, including France, which has added a new treatment-oriented form of preventive detention as an explicitly second-track provision.[169] Nevertheless, for the purposes of this study, we included in our purview of persons subject to informal life sentences those detained indefinitely in institutions of this kind, because it remains the case that they are on the second track as a result of a decision taken after their conviction. This continues to differentiate them from those persons who cannot be convicted because of their mental state, and whose detention is therefore on a different basis.

The detention of criminally convicted and sentenced persons beyond their sentences has been strongly criticized, but that should not obscure the difficulties inherent in drawing distinctions between interventions based on mental disorder for those who are still criminally responsible and criminal sentences worldwide. These difficulties transcend the single-track/dual-track distinction. They are what may have driven the UK legislator to create what have become known as hybrid orders. In terms of such orders, convicted offenders sentenced to imprisonment, including to discretionary life terms, can be referred to a mental hospital immediately, but with the provision that they be returned to prison if they are cured of their mental disorder or if the mental hospital is unable to offer them any further meaningful treatment.[170] The practical effect of such orders in the case of persons with discretionary life sentences is that they will serve the first part of their sentence in a mental institution before going to prison. Their release will be decided by the parole board responsible for the release of life-sentenced prisoners, not by the body determining release of those referred to mental hospitals.

In sum, indefinite post-conviction preventive detention is a difficult category to pin down. It is hard to quantify, even in law, precisely how many countries allow such detention and what form it takes. However, the examples we have given should alert one to the importance of investigating the existence of this type of informal life sentence when attempting to form an overall picture of life imprisonment in a particular jurisdiction.

Summary and Conclusion

The dominant characteristic of the overall picture that emerges from the descriptions of life imprisonment worldwide that were developed in this chapter is its sheer complexity. The isolation of the four ideal types of formal life imprisonment shows that even within the most basic of the four, LWOP and LWP, there are considerable differences in practice in various countries. The use of irreducible LWOP sentences as an extremely severe form of life imprisonment further complicates the picture, as does the existence of symbolic life sentences, that is, formal life sentences that always result in release. Sentences of the last type are particularly unstable, as they can be reinterpreted as LWP, or even LWOP sentences as has happened in Uganda and India.

Informal life imprisonment adds a second level of complexity, for essentially these are life sentences too, even if they are not labeled as such. They fall into two clear types: fixed terms of imprisonment, which are the equivalent of life sentences, and indefinite post-conviction detention, which usually has a strong preventive element. Countries where formal life imprisonment is outlawed by the national constitution, have to decide whether the two types of informal life imprisonment, which, in so far as they are themselves recognized as life sentences, are a challenge to these constitutional prohibitions. This sheds further light on the nature of life imprisonment.

Critical scholars, such as Marie Gottschalk, have recognized that it is the very complexity of life imprisonment, both formal and informal, which makes it so hard to portray clearly, and therefore for a full public debate about its nature and future to take place.[171] This chapter has embraced that complexity and begun to unravel it. However, this description needs to be complemented by an account of how prevalent life imprisonment is. It is to this that we turn in the next chapter.

3

Prevalence of Life

THUS FAR, we have described the different formal and informal types of life imprisonment around the world and attempted to identify the core elements of each type, while pointing out that the distinctions between them may not be as hard and fast as one might have assumed. This chapter takes the next step by asking questions about their use in practice, which is an essential baseline for any discussion of life imprisonment worldwide.

For our research study we initially requested life-sentenced prison population figures for September 1, 2014, or the nearest possible date to that. All the figures we received were within twelve months of that date. For the United States, however, we used life-sentenced prison population data collected mostly in 2016 by The Sentencing Project, rather than our own incomplete figures.[1] National population and prison population data for all countries for 2014 were collated from the United Nations and World Prison Brief, respectively.[2] For the United States, these latter data were from 2015. Figures from these slightly different dates are used throughout this chapter. The relatively small differences in the time when the data were collected should not make a significant difference to understanding the prevalence of life imprisonment worldwide or long-term trends in its use.

In this chapter, we begin by considering the overall prevalence of formal life imprisonment worldwide, based both on the statistical information we collected and careful estimates for the remaining countries. We then turn to prevalence in the United States, the country in which the largest number of life-sentenced prisoners are held. The overall figures for the United States are compared with those in Europe, where it is also possible to form a complete overall picture, but where the numbers are significantly lower than in the

United States. International comparisons follow. The chapter also presents the available information on the prevalence of different types of formal and informal life imprisonment. Finally, the chapter considers trend data for formal life imprisonment. Particular attention is paid to trends in life imprisonment without parole (LWOP) in the United States, which has the largest number of prisoners serving the most severe type of life imprisonment in the world.

Overall Prevalence

Formal life imprisonment is a statutory penalty in 183 out of a total of 216 countries and territories in the world. In practice, in 2014, life imprisonment was the most severe penalty in 149 of the 216 countries and territories. It is also the most severe penalty in all current international criminal courts and tribunals.[3]

The high number of countries and territories in which, in practice, formal life imprisonment is the ultimate penalty can be explained in the reduction of the number of countries that use the death penalty. The 149 countries and territories listed in Appendix A as having life imprisonment as their ultimate sanction include 51 in which, at the end of April 2014, the death penalty was still on the statute book but a moratorium on executions had been declared, or there had in practice been no executions in the last ten years. In six further countries the death penalty had been abolished in law for all ordinary crimes but was still a possibility for other crimes.[4]

The relative decline of the death penalty becomes clearer if one notes that thirty-three countries do not have the death penalty or life imprisonment as formal statutory sanctions.[5] In thirteen of these countries, this is reinforced by a specific constitutional provision outlawing the death penalty and life imprisonment.[6] In addition, the state of Alaska in the United States does not have the death penalty or formal life imprisonment. In Mexico, where the death penalty is outlawed throughout the country, there is no life imprisonment in the federal system or any of the thirty-one individual states except Chihuahua, Quintana Roo, Puebla, State of Mexico, and Veracruz.

We obtained information on the numbers of persons, if any, that were serving formal life imprisonment in 114 countries. They are listed by region in Appendix B, with calculations for each country of the number of life-sentenced prisoners as a percentage of the prison population and per 100,000 of the national population of the country concerned. In these

114 countries, we recorded that there were 304,814 persons who were serving formal life imprisonment at the time when the numbers were obtained. Fifty-one countries, which had 257,372 life-sentenced prisoners between them, provided data on the number of women serving life sentences. The women comprised 3.7 percent (9,648) of these life-sentenced prisoners.

The number of life-sentenced prisoners that we recorded is significantly lower than the true number of such prisoners worldwide, as we were not able to obtain any figures on some of the most populous countries in Asia, such as China, Vietnam, and the Philippines. Information on the Middle East and Africa, particularly from Francophone countries, is patchy, too. In this regard, we faced similar problems to those faced by scholars of the death penalty, when attempting to give an accurate number of individuals who have been sentenced to death and executed worldwide.

We have tried, nevertheless, to estimate the total number of life-sentenced prisoners worldwide. Our best estimate is that there were approximately 479,000 persons serving formal life sentences around the world in 2014. To arrive at this figure, we started with the information that had been collected, and added estimates for countries not included in Appendix B but that we knew have some prisoners serving formal life sentences. Estimates for the latter group of countries were calculated by taking into consideration their general population and their prison populations (sentenced and overall), and then comparing them to countries with similar properties where we did have figures for life imprisonment as well as figures for the prison and national populations.

Assuming that our overall estimate is a reasonable, if conservative, approximation, it is clear that life imprisonment is used far more often the death penalty. Fewer than 20,000 prisoners were under sentence of death in 2014, and only a minority of them were likely to be executed eventually.[7]

National Prevalence: United States

The single most striking finding of the national statistics on formal life imprisonment is that the United States, with 161,957 individuals undergoing formal life imprisonment in 2016, had more life-sentenced prisoners than the other 113 countries on which we had gathered statistical information put together. This does not mean that the United States had more than half the life-sentenced prisoners in the world, for, as indicated, there are some major jurisdictions for which we were unable to obtain numerical information. The United States accounts for about 34 percent of the estimated total of the world's life-sentenced population.

Within the fifty-one jurisdictions of the United States, the prevalence of life imprisonment also varies greatly. In California, there were 39,697 life-sentenced prisoners (including 5,090 serving LWOP) in 2016. If California were a single country, it would have more life-sentenced prisoners than any other country in the world on which we have statistics, with the exception of India. Other state statistics are striking too. In Florida, there were 13,005 prisoners serving life sentences: more than two-thirds of these (8,919 prisoners) were serving LWOP. In other states, this ratio is dramatically different. In New York, for example, where there were 9,535 prisoners serving life sentences in 2016, only 275 were serving LWOP.[8] It is also remarkable how high the ratio of life prisoners to other prisoners is in some states. The study on life imprisonment in the United States by Nellis, which was published in 2017, included for the first time "virtual" (in our terms de facto) life-sentenced prisoners, that is, prisoners serving determinate sentences of fifty years or more. Nellis showed that in California, Louisiana, and Utah, one in three sentenced prisoners was serving either a formal life sentence or a de facto life sentence in 2016.[9]

Comparisons with and within Europe

If one compares the United States with Europe, where we have a complete dataset, it is striking that there were 27,213 life-sentenced prisoners in the whole of Europe, including Turkey and Russia, two countries that in large part fall beyond the geographical boundaries of Europe.[10] The difference becomes even sharper when one realizes that the population of Europe is more than double that of the United States. The number of life-sentenced prisoners as a proportion of the national population of the United States in 2016 was 50.3 per 100,000, whereas in Europe in 2014, it was only 3.3 per 100,000 (see Figure 3.1).

Comparisons within Europe are interesting, too. In Europe, two countries, the United Kingdom (comprising England and Wales, Scotland, and Northern Ireland) and Turkey, with 8,661 and 6,687 life-sentenced prisoners, respectively, accounted for more than half, 56 percent, of the total European life-sentenced prison population. Figure 3.2 reflects the rates of formally

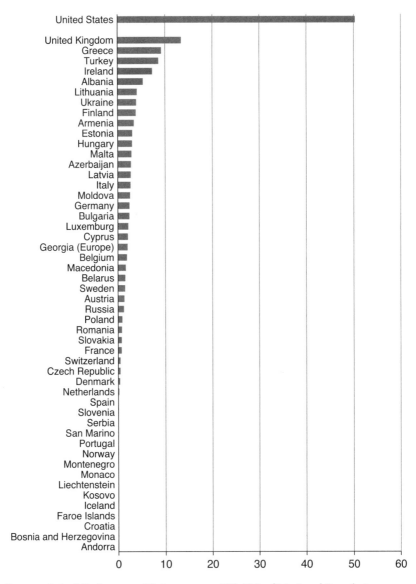

FIGURE 3.1. Life-Sentenced Prisoners per 100,000 of National Populations: United States and Europe. *Data sources:* Ashley Nellis, *Still Life: America's Increasing Use of Life and Long-Term Sentences* (Washington, D.C.: The Sentencing Project, 2017); Marcelo Aebi, Mélanie Tiago, and Christine Burkhardt, *SPACE I—Council of Europe Annual Penal Statistics: Prison Populations, Survey 2014* (Strasbourg, France: Council of Europe, 2016); data collected by authors; United Nations, Department of Economic and Social Affairs, Population Division, *World Population Prospects: The 2015 Revision, DVD Edition* (New York: United Nations, Department of Economic and Social Affairs, Population Division, 2015).

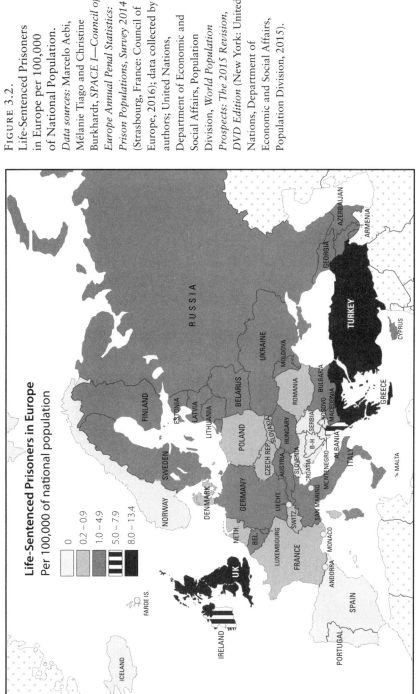

FIGURE 3.2.
Life-Sentenced Prisoners
in Europe per 100,000
of National Population.
Data sources: Marcelo Aebi,
Mélanie Tiago and Christine
Burkhardt, *SPACE I—Council of
Europe Annual Penal Statistics:
Prison Populations, Survey 2014*
(Strasbourg, France: Council of
Europe, 2016); data collected by
authors; United Nations,
Department of Economic and
Social Affairs, Population
Division, *World Population
Prospects: The 2015 Revision,
DVD Edition* (New York: United
Nations, Department of
Economic and Social Affairs,
Population Division, 2015).

Life-Sentenced Prisoners in Europe
Per 100,000 of national population

- 0
- 0.2 – 0.9
- 1.0 – 4.9
- 5.0 – 7.9
- 8.0 – 13.4

life-sentenced prisoners per 100,000 of population in every European country.

High rates of life-sentenced prisoners per 100,000 of national population in 2014 were found in the United Kingdom (13.4) and in Turkey (8.6). Another European outlier was Greece, with 9.2 per 100,000 of population, although the total number of life-sentenced prisoners was relatively small (1,107 prisoners). These rates are significantly lower than the United States, but much higher than for many European countries. The difference between the European countries with highest and lowest rates per 100,000 of population in major countries is striking. At the lower end was Italy (2.7), Germany (2.4), and France (0.7). The difference between France and the United Kingdom is remarkable. As a proportion of the national population, there were 18 times more life-sentenced prisoners in the United Kingdom than in France. These comparisons are particularly significant because both countries have long used life imprisonment as their ultimate penalty. The rates in the former Soviet and the Eastern European countries were also relatively low, but that is because life sentences have only recently become prominent there. Russia and Poland, for example, had 1.2 and 1.0 life-sentenced prisoners per 100,000 of population, respectively.

When one compares these figures with those of the United States, the differences are even more spectacular. Again, as a proportion of national population, there were seventy times more individuals serving life sentences in the United States than in France. Even compared to the United Kingdom, which had the highest rate and number of life-sentenced prisoners in Europe, the United States had almost four times more life-sentenced prisoners per head of population.

Wider Country Comparisons

The country that in 2014 had the second largest number of life-sentenced prisoners (71,632) was India. However, given that the national population of India is more than 1 billion, this amounted to only 5.5 per 100,000 of the population. In other words, relatively speaking, the US life-sentenced prison population was 9.2 times greater than that of India. It is noteworthy, too, that the relative life-sentenced prison population of the United Kingdom was 2.4 times larger than that of India. Another outlier was

TABLE 3.1. Number and ratio of prisoners serving life imprisonment

Country	Life-sentenced prisoners	Percentage of sentenced prisoners	Per 100 000 of national population
France	466	0.8	0.7
Germany	1,953	3.6	2.4
India	71,632	53.7	5.5
Kenya	3,676	11.4	8.2
Russia	1,766	0.4	1.2
South Africa	13,190	10.5	22.7
United Kingdom	8,661	11.0	13.4
United States	161,957	9.5	50.3

Data sources: Institute for Criminal Policy Research, *World Prison Brief,* http://www
.prisonstudies.org/world-prison-brief-data; data collected by authors.

South Africa, which had a total life-sentenced prisoner population of 13,190. This amounted to 22.7 per 100,000, which is slightly less than half that of the United States, but significantly higher than any other country except for some tiny island countries with populations of less than 1 million.[11]

It is also interesting to consider the prevalence of life imprisonment as a percentage of the total prison population and total sentenced prison population of particular countries. Appendix B has these figures for all the countries on which we have statistics. Table 3.1 shows the figures for countries selected to highlight some key significant differences in life-sentenced prison populations around the world.

It is noteworthy that the percentage of sentenced prisoners presents a very different picture to those from other indicators. Russia had the lowest percentage, but this is presumably because life imprisonment was only re-introduced there in the 1990s. The United Kingdom had a higher percentage of sentenced prisoners serving life imprisonment than the United States, which underlines the dominance of life sentences in the United Kingdom. Finally, India was a true outlier in this category, with more than 50 percent of all its sentenced prisoners serving life sentences. One possible explanation may be that trials in India take so long that many prisoners who are serving fixed terms actually serve their sentences while being held as under-trial detainees, thus leaving a majority of life-sentenced prisoners to serve their terms after conviction.[12]

Prevalence by Type of Formal Life Sentences

In respect to LWOP, as detailed in Appendix B, we were able to identify 64,306 persons serving this type of life imprisonment around the world. This is not a complete figure, as a number of countries, including some that provided overall numbers of life-sentenced prisoners, did not provide information on the different types of life imprisonment being served by these prisoners. As far as we can judge, however, it includes all the states that have a large number of prisoners serving LWOP. The striking conclusion from the figures that we do have is the extent to which this sentence is predominantly a US phenomenon: 53,290 of all the prisoners serving LWOP are to be found in the United States. Expressed differently, persons serving LWOP in the United States make up more than 80 percent of all the prisoners serving this sentence that we have been able to identify worldwide. We estimate furthermore that, even if we had complete statistics for all sixty-five countries that impose LWOP sentences, the United States would still comprise significantly more than 50 percent of the total in prison at any one time.

The comparison between the United States and Europe is equally dramatic when one compares numbers of LWOP sentences in the United States with those same sentences in Europe: the respective figures here were 53,290 in the United States and 2,156 in Europe. In other words, there were almost 25 times as many prisoners serving LWOP sentences in the United States as there were in Europe, even though the population of Europe was more than double that of the United States. In most European countries, the numbers were relatively small: at least 24 in Bulgaria, 50 in England and Wales, 41 in Hungary, 118 in Lithuania, 12 in Malta, 32 in the Netherlands, none in Slovakia, and 126 in Turkey, but 1,753 in Ukraine. The difference between the United States and Europe would be even starker if one were to exclude from the European figure the high numbers for Lithuania, where LWOP was declared contrary to the European Convention on Human Rights (ECHR) by the European Court of Human Rights (ECtHR) in 2017, and Ukraine, where that may happen too. In fact, as we explain in Chapter 2, the point may be reached in the not too distant future, where there are no prisoners in Europe serving LWOP anymore.

Prevalence of Informal Life Sentences

It is important to recognize that the figures we have cited include only those individuals who were subject to formal life sentences. When it comes to informal life sentences, we have not been able to draw overall numerical conclusions from the data we collected. This is not to deny the significance of these sentences or the possibility that, when they are considered together with formal life imprisonment data, the total number of life prisoners in any given jurisdiction may be significantly higher.[13]

De Facto Life

With relatively little difficulty, we could identify at least sixty-four countries—there almost certainly are more—that have provision for de facto life sentences, that is, fixed-term sentences of more than thirty-five years before release can be considered.[14] These sixty-four countries include fifteen that do not have formal life imprisonment at all. In some instances, these de facto terms are very long. In the federal jurisdiction in Mexico, where there is no provision for life imprisonment, the maximum fixed-term sentence can go up to 140 years.[15] Similarly, in Alaska, which is the only US state that has no formal life imprisonment, the maximum fixed term is 99 years.[16] This indicates that, in at least fifteen countries with no formal life imprisonment, de facto life terms are a substitute for formal life sentences.

It is noteworthy that forty-six of the sixty-four countries with de facto life imprisonment have formal life imprisonment as well. This means that it is possible that longer fixed-term sentences may take the place of formal life sentences which would otherwise have been imposed. This is an important factor to be considered when comparing long-term imprisonment in ostensibly similar societies. Thus, Dessecker observed that the significantly higher proportion of life sentences in Germany than in France (2.4 per 100,000 of population as opposed to 0.7 per 100,000, respectively) must be understood against the background that German law does not allow a fixed-term sentence of more than twenty years, while in France there are large numbers of prisoners serving such sentences.[17]

We do not have sufficient information on the number of persons serving de facto life sentences worldwide to estimate what role these sentences play in the overall picture of all those who could be regarded as life prisoners.

As noted earlier, however, the 2017 study by Nellis included persons serving de facto life, or "virtual life," for the first time in the work of The Sentencing Project on life imprisonment. Her finding was that in 2016 there were 44,311 persons serving such de facto life sentences in the United States. Including them in the number of life prisoners in the United States would add 27 percent to the overall number, bringing it to 206,628 or one in seven of all sentenced prisoners in the United States.[18]

Indefinite Post-Conviction Preventive Detention.

We were also able to identify at least fifty countries that have provision for indefinite post-conviction detention.[19] We do not have sufficient empirical data on these countries to draw worldwide conclusions on the number of persons in such detention. Nevertheless, there are interesting indications that, in practice, indefinite post-conviction detention may fulfill a preventive function that formal life imprisonment achieves in similar societies. The Nordic countries, Norway, Sweden, Finland, and Denmark, exemplify this possibility. Norway, which has no life imprisonment, uses indefinite post-conviction preventive detention more often than its neighbors, while Sweden and Finland, which have abolished post-conviction preventive detention, make more use of life imprisonment than does Denmark, which has retained both post-conviction preventive detention and life imprisonment.[20] However, there is more to the relationship between these two forms of intervention than a simple "hydraulic" interaction. Careful comparative research in this region by Lappi-Seppälä has shown that, while both forms of intervention are used exclusively to deal with homicide in the countries concerned, there are other ways of adjusting state reactions to homicide and other offenses deemed to be very serious.[21] The use of preventive detention for persons who are deemed not to be criminally responsible may play a role, as may provision for increasing the impact of certain fixed-term sentences by ensuring that those serving them remain in prison for as long as those who are formally sentenced to life imprisonment.

The statistical relationship between post-conviction preventive detention and life imprisonment has also been extensively investigated in Germany, where for many years (until 2012), data on both were collected and published annually in parallel. However, closer investigation shows that here, too, it is hard to identify similar trends in the use being made of the two forms of post-conviction intervention. While the numbers of people sentenced to and serving life imprisonment have grown somewhat over the past fifty years, preventive detention numbers have fluctuated much more dramatically, as legal rules affecting its imposition and release from it have changed significantly since 1965. Indeed, the joint collection of life imprisonment and preventive detention data was suspended after the statistics for 2012 had been gathered, largely because the two institutions were diverging so much, which was the result of the growing complexity of the law governing post-conviction preventive detention.[22]

Trend Data

The figures thus far provide only a snapshot of life imprisonment populations at a certain point in time. What are the overall trends in the use of formal life imprisonment worldwide? Historical data on life imprisonment worldwide is patchy, but we were able to collect trend data for some countries and to calculate some broad international trends.

Figure 3.3 reveals a steady growth in the number of life-sentenced prisoners around the world in recent years, from an estimated 261,000 in 2000 to an estimated 479,000 in 2014.[23] It also demonstrates how a few countries

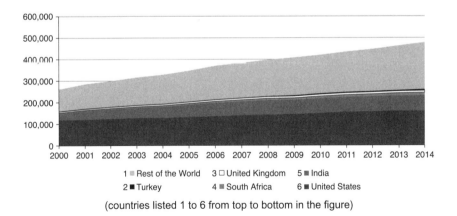

| 1 ■ Rest of the World | 3 □ United Kingdom | 5 ■ India |
| 2 ■ Turkey | 4 ■ South Africa | 6 ■ United States |

(countries listed 1 to 6 from top to bottom in the figure)

FIGURE 3.3. Number of Life-Sentenced Prisoners in the World, 2000–2014.
Data sources: Ashley Nellis, *Still Life: America's Increasing Use of Life and Long-Term Sentences* (Washington, D.C.: The Sentencing Project, 2017); Marcelo Aebi, Mélanie Tiago, and Christine Burkhardt, *SPACE I—Council of Europe Annual Penal Statistics: Prison Populations, Survey 2014* (Strasbourg, France: Council of Europe, 2016); data collected by authors.

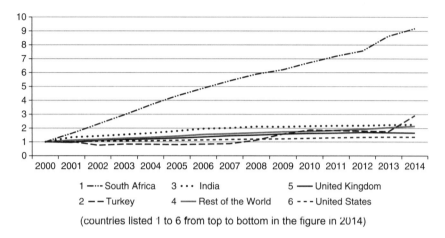

1 — · · South Africa   3 · · · India   5 —— United Kingdom
2 — — Turkey   4 —— Rest of the World 6 - - - United States

(countries listed 1 to 6 from top to bottom in the figure in 2014)

FIGURE 3.4. Annual Rate of Growth of Life-Sentenced Prisoners around the World, 2000–2014. *Data sources:* Ashley Nellis, *Still Life: America's Increasing Use of Life and Long-Term Sentences* (Washington, D.C.: The Sentencing Project, 2017); Marcelo Aebi, Mélanie Tiago, and Christine Burkhardt, *SPACE I—Council of Europe Annual Penal Statistics: Prison Populations, Survey 2014* (Strasbourg, France: Council of Europe, 2016); data collected by authors.

have made a major contribution to the growth of the worldwide life-sentenced prisoner population, namely. the United States, India, South Africa, the United Kingdom. and Turkey. However, the rate of growth, as shown by Figure 3.4, has varied greatly between countries.[24]

In South Africa, the increase in the number of life-sentenced prisoners has been most dramatic of all, with an 818 percent growth since 2000, which is the highest growth that we have recorded anywhere in the world. In Turkey, the increase has been particularly significant more recently, with an increase of 65 percent between 2013 and 2014. In India, the United Kingdom, and the United States, the rates of growth have been much more gradual but the trend is inexorably upward. In global terms, this is significant, as these three countries taken together have a very high percentage of the total number of life-sentenced prisoners worldwide.

In Europe, too, as Figure 3.5 shows, it is clear that two countries have persistently driven the overall growth in the life-sentenced prison population, namely, the United Kingdom and, recently, Turkey. The overall life-sentenced prison population in Europe increased from 15,149 in 2000 to 27,213 in 2014.

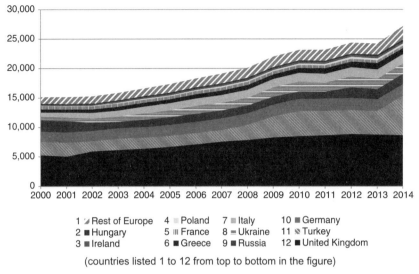

FIGURE 3.5. Number of Life-Sentenced Prisoners in Europe, 2000–2014.
Data sources: Marcelo Aebi, Mélanie Tiago, and Christine Burkhardt, *SPACE I—Council of Europe Annual Penal Statistics: Prison Populations, Survey 2014* (Strasbourg, France: Council of Europe, 2016); data collected by authors.

One further trend deserves to be emphasized, namely, the increase in the use of LWOP. In this regard, we have hard data only for the United States, but they are detailed enough to give us clear indications of trends in a country that houses an estimated 40 percent of all life-sentenced prisoners in the world. In absolute terms, the recent growth in the total US life-sentenced prison population is mainly due to an increase in the LWOP population. The upward trend is remarkable. The number of persons serving LWOP sentences increased from 12,453 in 1992 to 53,290 in 2016, which is an increase of 320 percent. Over the same period, the growth in life imprisonment with parole (LWP) was a more moderate increase of 89 percent, from 57,392 to 108,667, while the number of prisoners under sentence of death has grown marginally from 2,575 to 2,905, an overall increase of 13 percent.

Between 2012 and 2016, the years in which Nellis undertook two major surveys of life-sentenced prisoners in the United States, the number of prisoners serving LWP actually declined, from 110,439 to 108,667, although it is too early to say whether this represented a new trend. However, the increase in prisoners serving LWOP over the same 2012 to 2016 period,

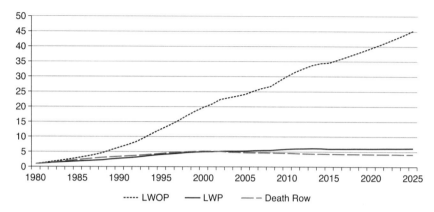

FIGURE 3.6. United States: LWOP, LWP, and Death Row: Rates of Growth, 1980–2025. *Data sources:* Catherine Appleton and Bent Grøver, "The Pros and Cons of Life without Parole," *British Journal of Criminology* 47 (2007): 597–615; Bureau of Justice Statistics, https://www.bjs.gov/; Ashley Nellis, *Still Life: America's Increasing Use of Life and Long-Term Sentences* (Washington, D.C.: The Sentencing Project, 2017); Death Penalty Information Center, https://deathpenaltyinfo.org/death-row-inmates-state-and-size-death -row-year; estimated data derived from actual growth rates by the authors.

from 49,081 to 53,290, was sufficient to ensure that the overall number of life-sentenced prisoners actually increased, from 159,520 in 2012 to 161,957 in 2016.[25] The 2016 position was thus that every third life-sentenced prisoner in the United States was serving LWOP.

The remarkable nature of the growth in the number of prisoners serving LWOP in the United States is best illustrated by Figure 3.6.[26] It compares the rates of growth of LWOP with that of LWP prisoners and inmates of death row since 1980, projected forward until 2025. It shows that the LWOP prison population has increased to such an extent that, in 2016, it was thirty-four times greater than it was in 1980 (increasing from 1,503 to 53,290 individuals serving LWOP). Over the same time period, the LWP prison population increased sixfold (from 18,234 to 108,667), and the death row prison population was four times greater in 2016 than it was in 1980 (increasing from 691 to 2,929 persons on death row). Based on actual growth rates, our predictions suggest that by 2025 the LWOP population will be forty-five times higher than it was in 1980.

Data on LWOP in the United States and its place in the worldwide picture should be read against the background sketched in Chapter 2: although LWOP is being abolished in Europe and in a few other countries, there have been important policy shifts elsewhere, particularly in India and China, in favor of using LWOP.

In India, LWOP is a reasonably recent product of a judge-made exception to a general rule allowing the routine consideration of release in cases of life imprisonment. The Indian Penal Code, when read with the Code of Criminal Procedure, makes clear provision for all life-sentenced prisoners who have served fourteen years to apply to state sentence review boards for what they call remission, a form of unconditional early release.[27] However, in 2015, the Indian Supreme Court ruled definitively that, when a high court is confronted with the appeal of a death sentence imposed by a trial court, it can substitute the death penalty with imprisonment for life and put that life sentence beyond the application of the routine remission available to life-sentenced prisoners. This is effectively a sentence of LWOP rather than a fully irreducible sentence, as the constitutional clemency powers of the Union and State governments of India remain intact, including their power to commute all life sentences even those where the high court excluded routine consideration of early release.[28] The development is, however, so recent that there is no statistical record yet of prisoners in India being sentenced to LWOP.

China has introduced changes even more recently. Since 2015, the law in China provides that where the courts impose suspended death sentences, that is, death sentences that must be reviewed after two years, they may stipulate that if the death sentence is set aside, it may be replaced only by a life sentence from which no release is possible, that is, by LWOP. Sentencing courts have this power only in corruption cases where the death penalty is imposed.[29]

These changes are still too recent to show up in our statistics. However, India and China are the two most populous countries in the world and, if they begin to use LWOP more often, this could lead to a major increase in the number of individuals serving LWOP worldwide.

Conclusion

How successful we have been in translating the information that we had at our disposal into a first picture of life imprisonment worldwide is, of course, for the reader to judge. What is beyond doubt, however, is that more information could have contributed to a more rounded portrayal of life imprisonment worldwide.

Some of what is missing is of a technical nature. As we explain above, we used national population and sentenced prisoner population data as elements in calculations that facilitate estimates of life-sentenced prisoner populations over time. These calculations could have been improved, had we been able to consider other potentially relevant trend data, such as crime reporting, arrest and conviction rates. Also useful for this purpose may have been sentencing, release, death in prison and recall data.

More important, however, is better direct data on life imprisonment. We were surprised to find how many countries told us that the number of persons serving life sentences was an "official secret." In a few cases, we formed the impression that the authorities did not know how many persons were serving life sentences in their prisons. In more instances, there really appeared to be no data kept on how long life-sentenced prisoners had served prior to their release or death in prison. Equally lacking in many countries was information on what happened to life-sentenced prisoners after release. The failure of countries to collect such data, and the reluctance to make data available for research purposes is unacceptable. We hope that, as life imprisonment research matures into a wider study of ultimate penalties, states will realize that they have a duty to make available basic information of this kind.

It is also clear that various aspects of life imprisonment require more research so that their place in the international order can be more fully established. The largest of these is informal life imprisonment, both of the type we define as de facto life and what we define as post-conviction preventive detention.

As far as the former is concerned, studies that combine research into formal life imprisonment with a national overview of informal life imprisonment are very rare. An important exception is Nellis's recent study that effectively combines US data on de facto life imprisonment with data on formal life imprisonment.[30] However, such studies have not been undertaken in other major countries.

The other type of informal life imprisonment, that is, post-conviction preventive detention, has been subject to considerable research in recent years. However, outside Germany and Scandinavia, this research has not always engaged with the parallel development of formal life imprisonment.[31] What is required is research that goes beyond national boundaries and systematically combines studies of both types of informal life imprisonment with studies of formal life imprisonment.

What we can say with confidence is that worldwide, more prisoners are serving life imprisonment than ever before and life sentences are being used increasingly. This is certainly the case for formal life sentences and most probably the case also for informal life sentences. If there are no changes in penal policy, this trend is likely to continue, both as far as life imprisonment generally and LWOP in particular are concerned. Although we did not quantify the overall economic costs of life imprisonment as part of this study, there can be no doubt that this tendency can have major budgetary implications for many countries.[32]

As we have shown, there are major differences, between regions and countries, and even within countries, in the extent to which life sentences generally and of different types are used. These variations indicate that penal policy changes could be made, which would lead to a reduction in the use by the courts of sentences to life imprisonment and by the lowering of the time set before parole can be considered. Before one can suggest what policy changes could be made, one must understand the limits that already exist on the use of life imprisonment, the process by which life sentences are imposed and the justifications that are put forward for its imposition. These are addressed in the next three chapters.

4

Exempt from Life

MOST COUNTRIES in the world accept that some type of life sentence may be imposed on some persons convicted of serious offenses. However, even in countries that allow life imprisonment, there are categories of persons on whom a life sentence may not be imposed under any circumstances. In a small but significant number of countries, this prohibition is applied formally to all persons.

In many legal systems there is an absolute prohibition on all life sentences for children, while in others only certain types of life imprisonment cannot be imposed on children, that is, persons under the age of eighteen years at the time of the committal of the offense. In some systems, the elderly may never be subjected to formal life sentences or, if they are, the life sentences may be restricted in various ways. Perhaps surprisingly, in a number of countries the imposition of life imprisonment on women is also absolutely forbidden.

Analysis of these various prohibitions and restrictions gives an indication of the legal constraints applied to courts that may wish to impose life imprisonment. There may be other restrictions related to particular categories of persons—in Malta and Greece, for example, life imprisonment cannot ever be imposed on deaf-mute offenders.[1] Such restrictions are not widespread, however, and do not raise issues of principle of the kind discussed in relation to children, the elderly, and women, which form the core of this chapter.

Children

The most common prohibition on imposing life imprisonment is the exclusion of children. Indeed, most countries—with the exception of the United States, the United Kingdom, and most Commonwealth countries—prohibit all formal life imprisonment for children. The primary justification for the prohibition is found in international law, in the United Nations Convention on the Rights of the Child (CRC) and related international human rights instruments. The convention will be discussed first. We then consider the justifications for the prohibition developed in regional human rights law, before turning to individual countries.

International Human Rights Law

Some limits on sentencing children to life terms are clearly spelled out in international law. Article 37(a) of the CRC provides that "[n]o child shall be subjected to torture or other cruel, inhuman or degrading treatment or punishment." The article stipulates further, "Neither capital punishment nor life imprisonment without possibility of release shall be imposed for offenses committed by persons below eighteen years of age." This latter prohibition has considerable weight as a principle of international human rights law, for the CRC is a treaty that has been acceded to by all the countries of the world except the United States. Only the United States has legislation specifically providing for irreducible life sentences or for life without parole (LWOP) for children. This has had a dramatic impact on the law regarding the imposition of life imprisonment on children. Although governments may seek to achieve the permanent incarceration of children sentenced to life imprisonment, for example, by manipulating laws formally allowing for consideration of their release, they do so contrary to their international treaty obligations. This significantly reduces their scope to maneuver.

A clear example of the interplay between general international treaty obligations and the more specialized provisions of the CRC, on the one hand, and a government determined to ensure that specific individuals sentenced to life imprisonment remain incarcerated, on the other, is found in the 2014 case of *Blessington and Elliot v. Australia*.[2] In that case, the UN Human Rights Committee (HRC), interpreting the International Covenant on Civil and Political Rights (ICCPR), was asked to determine whether the de facto

LWOP sentences imposed on two prisoners convicted of a murder and rape, committed when they were aged fourteen and fifteen, infringed the ICCPR.[3]

The HRC found that the sentences infringed the ICCPR's provisions prohibiting cruel, inhuman or degrading treatment or punishment in Article 7. It also ignored the duty to orient imprisonment toward "social rehabilitation," together with the requirement that juveniles should be accorded treatment appropriate to their age and status in Article 10(3) and the general children's rights provision in Article 24 of the ICCPR. The key finding of the HRC was that

> the imposition of life sentences on the authors as juveniles can only be compatible with article 7, read together with articles 10, paragraph 3, and 24 of the Covenant if there is a possibility of review and a prospect of release, notwithstanding the gravity of the crime they committed and the circumstances around it. That does not mean that release should necessarily be granted. It rather means that release should not be a mere theoretical possibility and that the review procedure should be a thorough one, allowing the domestic authorities to evaluate the concrete progress made by the authors towards rehabilitation and the justification for continued detention, in a context that takes into consideration [their age], at the time they committed the crime.[4]

On the facts of the case, the HRC held that their prospect of release was "extremely remote" and that "release, if it ever took place, would be based on the impending death or physical incapacitation of the [applicants], rather than on the principles of reformation and social rehabilitation contained in article 10, paragraph 3, of the Covenant."[5] According to the HRC, this was unacceptable, particularly for persons convicted when they were children.

This analysis is very similar to that of the Grand Chamber of the ECtHR in *Vinter and others v. United Kingdom,* which found that offering such limited grounds for setting someone free from life imprisonment may not constitute a true release at all.[6] In coming to its conclusion in the *Elliot and Blessington* case, the HRC explicitly relied on the prohibition on LWOP in Article 37(a) of the CRC as a valuable source informing the interpretation of the ICCPR.[7] Although the Australian government did not respond positively to the conclusion reached by the HRC and Blessington and Elliot continued to serve their life sentences, an important precedent was set, which will develop binding international law and carry weight with courts and governments that take their international legal obligations seriously.[8]

In shaping the law governing life imprisonment for children, international human rights law seeks to go further than merely outlawing LWOP. In 2007, the Committee on the Rights of the Child, which is the UN body formally charged with the interpretation of the eponymous convention, produced a General Comment on "Children's Rights in Juvenile Justice."[9] It includes a lengthy paragraph that ostensibly focuses on the prohibition against LWOP but actually deals much more widely with life imprisonment for children. The main focus of the committee's comment was to emphasize that "[s]tates parties which do sentence children to life imprisonment with the possibility of release or parole that this sanction must fully comply with and strive for the realization of the aims of juvenile justice enshrined in article 40(1) [of the Convention on the Rights of the Child]."[10]

This means, the committee explained, "that the child sentenced to this imprisonment should receive education, treatment, and care aiming at his/her release, reintegration and ability to assume a constructive role in society. This also requires a regular review of the child's development and progress in order to decide on his/her possible release."[11]

The committee was pessimistic about whether this could be done effectively. It therefore strongly recommended the abolition of all forms of life imprisonment for offenses committed by persons under the age of eighteen. This General Comment of the Committee on the Rights of the Child is not binding on states parties in the same way as the narrower prohibition on LWOP in the text of the convention itself. Nevertheless, it is an indication of the extent to which human rights law has become highly critical of all life imprisonment for children.

In 2015, life imprisonment of children was considered in a report to the Human Rights Council of the United Nations by Juan Méndez, the UN special rapporteur on torture and other cruel, inhuman or degrading treatment or punishment, as part of a wider report on children deprived of their liberty.[12] Méndez built on the 2007 recommendation of the Committee on the Rights of the Child and concluded, "Life imprisonment and lengthy sentences, such as consecutive sentencing, are grossly disproportionate and therefore cruel, inhuman or degrading when imposed on a child." He explained, "Life sentences or sentences of an extreme length have a disproportionate impact on children and cause physical and psychological harm that amounts to cruel, inhuman or degrading punishment."[13]

Méndez's recommendation was that "life imprisonment in all its forms" should be prohibited for children worldwide.[14] His recommendation found favor with the Human Rights Council, and in September 2015, the General Assembly of the United Nations urged "[states] to ensure that, under their legislation and practice, neither capital punishment nor life imprisonment are imposed for offenses committed by persons under 18 years of age."[15] Again, it is noteworthy that the prohibition adopted by the General Assembly was of all life sentences for children, not just LWOP.

Regional Human Rights Law

Analyses of life imprisonment for children along the lines adopted by the Committee on the Rights of the Child are found in some regions of the world. An explicitly human rights–based condemnation of *all* life imprisonment for juveniles was developed by the Inter-American Court of Human Rights in *Mendoza and others v. Argentina*.[16] The court also relied on the CRC and the 2007 General Comment of the Committee on the Rights of the Child, placing them in the context of the American Convention on Human Rights.

In the *Mendoza* case, the Inter-American Court reviewed a number of life sentences that had been imposed in Argentina on children who had committed multiple murders when they were under the age of eighteen. They were sentenced to life imprisonment, which at that stage provided that a minimum period of twenty years had to elapse before they could be released. In examining the *Mendoza* case, the Inter-American Court went far beyond the specific facts, and held generally that all life imprisonment for children was contrary to human rights. Therefore, not only could life sentences not continue to be implemented for the individuals whose cases the court was considering, but life imprisonment could also no longer be imposed in Argentina in general, or in any other country within the jurisdiction of the Inter-American Court.

The total rejection of life imprisonment for children by the Inter-American Court of Human Rights was based on three principles of human rights: the prohibition against arbitrary imprisonment; the goal of reintegrating the child into society; and the prohibition against cruel and inhuman treatment. First, the court found that life imprisonment for children was arbitrary. In its view, the prohibition on arbitrary imprisonment generally was found in the American Convention on Human Rights. Focusing on this prohibition, the court noted that the CRC required, not only that imprisonment of children should always be a last resort and for the shortest period possible, but also that it should be reviewed regularly. Furthermore, the CRC specified that children should be released if circumstances changed and their further detention was no longer required, even if they had not yet completed their sentences. A life sentence with a mandatory minimum period—twenty years after conviction in the Argentinian case—precluded such review and release. The Inter-American Court interpreted the prohibition against arbitrariness in criminal sanctions in the context of the best interests of the child. In doing so, it concluded that all life sentences for children were incompatible with the American Convention, because such sentences "are not exceptional punishments, they do not entail the deprivation of liberty for the shortest possible time or for a period specified at the time of sentencing, and they do permit periodic review of the need for the deprivation of liberty of the children."[17]

Second, the Inter-American Court focused on the purpose of a sentence of imprisonment. It noted that Article 5(6) of the American Convention on Human Rights provides that "deprivation of liberty shall have as an essential aim the reform and social readaptation of the prisoners." It bolstered this by a reference to Article 40(1) of the CRC, which provides that:

States Parties recognize the right of every child . . . to be treated in a manner consistent with the promotion of the child's sense of dignity and worth, which reinforces the child's respect for the human rights and fundamental freedoms of others and which takes into account the child's age and the desirability of promoting the child's reintegration and the child's assuming a constructive role in society.

The Inter-American Court explained that it followed that sentences imposed on children should have the "objective of the child's reintegration into society."[18] In the view of the court, "the proportionality of the sentence is closely related to its purpose," and life imprisonment "did not achieve the objective of social reintegration of juveniles."[19] The court explained that a life sentence "entails the maximum exclusion of the child from society, so that it functions in a purely retributive sense, because the expectations of resocialization are annulled to their highest degree. Therefore, such sentences are not proportionate to the objective of the criminal sanction of children."[20]

Third, the Inter-American Court found that life imprisonment was a form of cruel, inhuman, or degrading punishment or treatment, which makes it illegal not only in the American Convention on Human Rights but also in most key regional and international human rights instruments, including the CRC. The court came to this conclusion on the general ground that all life sentences for children are disproportionate to the purpose of sanctioning children and therefore cruel, inhuman and degrading. In this regard, the court relied on extensive empirical evidence of the "extreme psychological impact" that life imprisonment had on the applicants.[21] Although this finding was stated in terms specific to the case, there can be little doubt that the Inter-American Court of Human Rights would come to the same conclusion for other children facing the same sentence.

In Europe, the legal basis for the restrictions on the imposition of life imprisonment on children is not as clear as in countries that accept the jurisdiction of the Inter-American Court of Human Rights. In 1999, in the leading case of *V v. United Kingdom*,[22] the European Court of Human Rights (ECtHR) emphasized that a whole-life sentence for a child would infringe the prohibition on inhuman or degrading treatment in Article 3 of the European Convention on Human Rights (ECHR). The Commentary on the European Rules for Juvenile Offenders Subject to Sanctions and Measures also explains that the emphasis placed on social reintegration in these Rules would "not allow long-term security measures or life sentences that aim solely at protecting society from juvenile offenders and do not give them the prospect of release within a reasonable period."[23] There is also jurisprudence from the ECtHR that young persons under the age of twenty-one should always have a prospect of release.[24] However, although the ECtHR in *V v. United Kingdom* was highly critical of aspects of the way V had been treated during their trial, by a majority of ten to seven votes, it upheld a formal life with a prospect of parole (LWP) sentence—detention during her Majesty's pleasure—that had been imposed on an eleven-year-old boy convicted of murder.

The dissenting opinions were vigorous. One group of five judges condemned the low age of criminal responsibility in England and argued that a life sentence should never be imposed on children as young as ten. Raising the age of criminal responsibility would, of course, be an indirect way of excluding the possibility of a life sentence for many children that might otherwise fall within its net. The same judges commented, "As far as the sentence is concerned . . . the problem lies in the very passing of a sentence of an indefinite nature: the uncertainty and anxiety for persons as vulnerable as children inevitably adds another element of suffering."[25]

Whether the ECtHR would still uphold life imprisonment of any kind for such young children is doubtful. In a 2016 judgment on life imprisonment, the Grand Chamber of the ECtHR seems to leave the question open by limiting to adult offenders its proposition that a proportionate life sentence is not in itself prohibited by or incompatible with Article 3 or any other article of the ECHR.[26]

NATIONAL VARIATIONS IN EUROPE.   In the great majority of European countries, life imprisonment cannot be imposed on children under the age of eighteen years. This is true not only in most Western and Northern European "liberal" constitutional democracies but also in Central and Eastern European countries that introduced life imprisonment for the first time in the 1990s, after the fall of the Soviet Union. Indeed, the only European countries that we could identify with provision for formal life imprisonment for children were the United Kingdom, Cyprus, and France. With the exception of the United Kingdom, no children were serving life sentences in these countries at the time we collected data.[27] In the United Kingdom, life imprisonment is mandatory for children aged ten and above who are convicted of murder.[28] This is the case in Cyprus too, but only for those aged seventeen and above.[29]

Some of the European countries that do not have formal life imprisonment for children do have provision for them to be detained post-conviction under preventive measures that are of indeterminate length. However, such measures are rarely, if ever, used and include many safeguards to restrict their imposition and to monitor their continued use at short intervals so as to ensure that children are not detained for very long.

In Germany, article 7 of the Juvenile Justice Act allows for the imposition of post-conviction indefinite detention (*Sicherungsverwahrung*). The 2007 ECtHR case, *Ilnseher v. Germany*, is a solitary example of the imposition of post-conviction indefinite detention on a young adult tried as a juvenile.[30] In Norway, preventive detention can only be imposed on juveniles in "completely extraordinary circumstances."[31] To date, only one child has been sentenced to indefinite preventive detention, a decision that has been confirmed by the Supreme Court.[32]

Among the European countries that do not allow any type of formal life imprisonment to be imposed on children, several have increased the upper age limit. In Hungary and Bulgaria, offenders have to be at least twenty years old before they can be sentenced to life imprisonment.[33] In Austria and Macedonia, the minimum age for life imprisonment is twenty-one years,[34] while in Serbia, which has no formal life imprisonment but a maximum fixed-term sentence of forty years (which falls within our definition of a de facto life term), offenders also have to be at least twenty-one years old to qualify for such a sentence.[35] In some countries where there is not an outright ban on life imprisonment for young persons who are a few years beyond their childhood, there are provisions that discourage its use. This is the case in Greece, where young adults who are over eighteen but under twenty-one years old may receive a reduced sentence with a ten-year minimum instead of life imprisonment.[36] Similarly in Germany, where the general criminal law is applied to a criminal act committed by young adults between eighteen and twenty years of age, a court may impose a fixed-term sentence of between ten and fifteen years in place of life imprisonment.[37] In practice, however, most young adults are tried under juvenile law rather than general criminal law.[38] This means that the possibility of a young adult being sentenced to life imprisonment does not arise at all.

The absence of the possibility of imposing any formal life imprisonment on children in most of Europe and significant limits on its use for young adults reflect the reality that the dominant objectives in sentencing juveniles in Europe are not primarily retributive. A shift toward a "youth justice" approach has led to increasing concern with procedural safeguards. However, there has been no move away from the focus on the best interests of the child; this is the primary concern of the CRC, and it is widely cited in most European jurisdictions. Indeed, the emphasis on the procedural safeguards has included a concern with proportionality in the sentencing of both children and young adults, as reflected in the influential European Rules for Juvenile Offenders Subject to Sanctions and Measures.[39] Increasing attention is also paid by European policy makers to developments in neurology that recognize that "maturity and psychosocial abilities are fully developed only in the third decade of life."[40] This contributes both to continued moderation in the length of prison sentences for children and young adults and to continued commitment to intensive rehabilitative programs for them.

In England and Wales, in contrast to most other European countries, the use of life imprisonment with parole is a prominent feature of the punishment of children who are convicted of the most serious offenses.[41] Life sentences can be, and are, imposed on children as young as ten. As compared to most of Europe, even relatively young children can get life sentences with long minimum periods before parole can be considered, particularly for murder, where the life sentence is mandatory. While the courts cannot make a whole-life order, the sentence can nevertheless ensure that the release of a person convicted of crimes committed while they were children will not be considered for a very long time. There are a number of recent examples of children in England and Wales who were only fifteen years old at the time of the commission of their offense yet got life sentences with minimum terms of up to twenty years for a single murder.[42] In a 2016 case, a twenty-seven-year minimum period was set for a child who was given a composite life sentence for two murders.[43] What is striking about these judgments is that they are imposed with a strong emphasis on retribution. They make no reference to the CRC, although it binds the United Kingdom in international law and should be used to interpret domestic legislation.

English courts that sentence children who are convicted of murder reason largely as they would about adults and then reduce the minimum period of the life sentence they impose by a few years because of the immaturity of the child. In setting minimum periods that these children must serve, the English courts do not go deeply into what would be in the best interests of the child. They do not consider whether such children's development may be best served by releasing them after a relatively short period rather than leaving them with no prospect of release until they are in their mid-adulthood, when their personalities will have been set long ago and their chances of becoming full members of society are vanishingly small. Moreover, they are prepared to allow the publication of the names of these children for purposes of general deterrence, even where they accept that it may hamper the rehabilitation of the child concerned.[44] Such publication would be illegal in most European countries, where even the names of convicted adult offenders are not published routinely. In all, these sentences of life imprisonment for children seem open to challenge before the ECtHR, which may be expected to apply the ECHR to them in much the same way as the Inter-American Court of Human Rights applied the American Convention on Human Rights in the *Mendoza* case.

Commonwealth Countries

The English approach of allowing life sentences for children is followed in most Commonwealth countries: forty-six of the fifty-three member states of the Commonwealth have life imprisonment for children under age eighteen. As a result, they comprise the majority of the seventy-three countries of the world that punish children in this way. In Oceania the pattern is the most striking: every Commonwealth country in that area has retained life imprisonment for children as a punishment for at least one offense. Typically, life imprisonment is referred to as detention during the pleasure of the head of state.[45]

An interesting and principled exception within the Commonwealth is South Africa. The South African Constitutional Court declared unconstitutional sentencing legislation that made mandatory the imposition of life sentences on children who were convicted of murder, rape, or robbery unless there were "substantial and compelling circumstances" suggesting the opposite.[46] The court relied on a strong constitutional emphasis on the best interests of the child in the post-1994 South African Constitution, combined with overt reliance on the CRC and "soft" international law instruments, to reach its decision. The practical outcome is that the permissible maximum sentence that can be imposed on a child under the age of eighteen in South Africa is twenty-five years.[47]

Other Commonwealth countries that have provision for life imprisonment for children, have limitations on its use and form that do not apply to adults. In Canada, for example, life imprisonment for children can never be mandatory, even for murder. Even to be considered, the Crown has to apply to the court to have the child sentenced as an adult.[48] If the request is granted, the judge has the discretionary power to impose a life sentence or not. If the court decides to impose a life sentence, it must impose a far shorter minimum period before parole can be considered than what would be mandatory for an adult convicted of the same crime. The maximum minimum is ten years for a child aged sixteen or seventeen at the time of the commission of a first degree murder, compared to twenty-five years for an adult.[49]

The United States as an Outlier

When it comes to the imposition of life imprisonment on children, the point of departure in the United States is different to that in the rest of the world. As we have mentioned, the United States is not a party to the CRC, and therefore does not have to follow the peremptory rule that LWOP should not be imposed on children. However, there have been dramatic recent legal developments in a series of judgments of the US Supreme Court, which have identified a significant evolution in standards relating to the death penalty and life imprisonment for children. These have led directly to limits on the power of US courts to impose LWOP. In the process, arguments have been developed that raise some fundamental questions about the imposition of all types of life imprisonment for children generally.

Until 2005, the death penalty could legally be imposed on children above the age of sixteen. In that year, in *Roper v. Simmons*,[50] the US Supreme Court declared the death penalty unconstitutional for all children but noted that, as far as US constitutional law was concerned, children who could previously be sentenced to death for homicide could be punished with LWOP. An important factor in this decision was the holding that the culpability of children was reduced by their "lack of maturity and underdeveloped sense of responsibility," by their being more susceptible than adults to "negative influences and outside pressures" and by their having "less control, or less experience with control over their own environment."[51] For these reasons and others, including, controversially, a consideration of international trends, the court found that the death sentence was disproportionately severe for children under the age of eighteen (juveniles in the US usage) and thus a cruel and unusual punishment, as was prohibited by the Eighth Amendment to the US Constitution.

The effect of *Roper v. Simmons* was paradoxical. On the one hand, it encouraged states that had wanted to execute child offenders convicted of homicide and thus to eliminate them permanently from society, to introduce LWOP, when they did not have it before, and to use LWOP, where they had previously used the death penalty.[52] On the other hand, it seems to have escaped the attention of the majority of the court in *Roper* that the same arguments that had been used to challenge the constitutionality of the death penalty for children could also be used to question LWOP for children. Not only could LWOP be regarded as too severe for juveniles but, like the death penalty, it also excluded the possibility that children could change as they matured and that they should therefore be considered for release when they had become more responsible.

Subsequently, in three closely linked decisions on LWOP for children, the US Supreme Court relied on further medical evidence about the maturation process of children and its implications for the evaluation of blameworthiness for past behavior and predictions about future conduct.[53] In 2010, in *Graham v. Florida*,[54] the Supreme Court held that LWOP was disproportionately severe and therefore unconstitutional when imposed on a child who had committed a crime that was not a homicide.

In 2012, in *Miller v. Alabama*,[55] the court held that the mandatory imposition of LWOP on a child convicted of homicide was unconstitutional, as it could be disproportionately severe. Such a homicide could also be the result of "transient rashness, proclivity for risk, and inability to assess consequences," which sometimes characterizes the conduct of children.[56] What this means is that an adult can be subject to a mandatory sentence of LWOP in circumstances where a child cannot. The potential disproportionality of LWOP for a child resides in the reduced moral blameworthiness of children.

Finally, in 2016, in *Montgomery v. Louisiana*, the court held that the prohibition on mandatory LWOP for children in homicide cases applied retrospectively and that LWOP was barred "for all but the rarest of juvenile offenders, those whose crimes reflect permanent incorrigibility"—also characterized as "irreparable corruption."[57] This last decision meant that children who had been sentenced mandatorily to LWOP in the past had to be either resentenced under new laws in which LWOP was not mandatory or considered for parole without further delay. In *Montgomery*, the proportionality constraint operated slightly differently to the way it had in *Miller*. It could not be assumed that children were irrevocably corrupted. Therefore, for those children who might be corrigible, LWOP could be disproportionately severe from the perspective of what was necessary for purposes of incapacitation.

The rapid development of constitutional jurisprudence has left state legislators in the United States under a great deal of pressure to modify their law on the imposition of LWOP on children. This has elicited some reflection at the state level on the justification for this type of life imprisonment for juveniles. Since *Miller*, in 2012, states have responded in various positive ways by recognizing that children deserve to be treated differently, even when convicted of the most serious offenses. Nine states have abolished LWOP for children entirely since 2012. In other states, the potential imposition of LWOP on children has been substantially reduced by allowing it as an option only in limited circumstances that are highly unlikely to arise in practice.[58]

The supreme courts of individual states have developed further constitutional requirements, based on the same line of reasoning that motivated the judgments of the US Supreme Court. The Supreme Court of California, for example, has extended the practical impact of this jurisprudence by striking down a 118-year fixed-term sentence imposed on a child as an unconstitutional attempt to impose LWOP indirectly.[59] In addition, the provisions for considering the release of children who have been sentenced to life imprisonment, including LWOP, have been considerably improved in California and elsewhere in the United States.

The supreme courts of Iowa and Massachusetts have gone even further than the US Supreme Court. Basing their decisions on state constitutional protections, they have ruled out the possibility of LWOP for children entirely.[60] For example, the Iowa Constitution contains a prohibition against cruel and unusual punishment that mirrors the one in the Eighth Amendment of the federal Constitution. The Iowa legislature, however, enacted legislation giving sentencing courts a limited discretionary power to impose LWOP on children in rare and uncommon cases. The Supreme Court of Iowa held that even this limited possibility would violate the state constitution guarantee against "cruel and unusual punishment." It reasoned that no court, when sentencing a child, could determine whether that child was permanently incapable of reformation. Such a decision could only be taken later by an appropriate body, such as a parole board or a court.[61]

In some respects, the recent and rapid changes in the United States restricting the possibility of the imposition of LWOP for children have much in common with developments in the rest of the world. Many of the arguments used in the United States overlap with those applied elsewhere against the imposition of any type of life imprisonment on children. The decisions of the US Supreme Court and the responses of state legislatures and supreme courts to remove or limit the possibility of LWOP for children have brought the United States closer to the position of the rest of the world prohibiting such sentences.[62]

Differences, nevertheless, remain. Some US states have enacted legislation allowing the continued option of imposing LWOP on children who are deemed incorrigibly violent and who have been convicted of particularly heinous homicides, as the US Supreme Court is still prepared to tolerate such a sentence. Such legislation is unprecedented in the twenty-first century anywhere else in the world. Moreover, little, if any, systematic thought appears to have been given to what forms of discretionary LWP would be acceptable for children. In 2015, the American Civil Liberties Union reported that twelve US states had a total of 8,300 prisoners serving life sentences or sentences longer than forty years for offenses that they had committed while under the age of eighteen.[63]

At best, state courts have struck down life sentences imposed on children that were LWOP in all but name. In May 2016, the Supreme Court of Florida did just that. The case involved a child who had been sentenced to life imprisonment; his sentence had been reconsidered and modified by the parole board to a minimum of 140 years. The Supreme Court of Florida had no difficulty in recognizing this as a (lightly) disguised form of LWOP. At the same time, however, the same court did not hesitate in upholding, without criticism, and applying retrospectively new Florida legislation that sets at forty years the minimum term to be served before consideration of parole by children who previously would have been sentenced to LWOP.[64]

Finally, on the subject of life imprisonment for children worldwide, it should not be forgotten that outcomes may be shaped by aspects of child justice that do not refer directly to the imposition of life sentences on them. Providing that younger children should not be held criminally responsible at all ensures that they cannot be sentenced to life imprisonment. However, international and regional attempts to set a clear uniform minimum age of criminal responsibility have failed, thus limiting the scope of this restriction.

Elderly People

Unlike the restrictions developed on the imposition of life imprisonment on children, international law has had relatively little to say about the imposition of formal or informal life sentences on very old offenders.

At the regional level, the ECtHR takes the position that the advanced age of an offender is not a bar to imposing a prison sentence, even a very long one. However, it has noted that age, in conjunction with other related factors such as the state of health of the offender, should be taken into account when a sentence is imposed and while it is being served, such as when a sentence is suspended or imprisonment is replaced by house arrest.[65] This approach has been applied to life sentences. In 2001, in *Sawoniuk v. United Kingdom*, a seventy-nine-year-old man sentenced to (mandatory) life imprisonment for two murders he had committed more than fifty years earlier argued that in his case his sentence was so severe, because of his advanced age, that it was inherently inhuman and degrading. The ECtHR disagreed.

Because the minimum period that Sawoniuk would be required to serve before possibly being released, if he were no longer dangerous, might be as little as five years, his sentence was not inhuman and degrading. Moreover, if a longer minimum period were to be imposed, Sawoniuk could take the decision to do so on judicial review.[66] This case does not address directly the issue of what would happen if the minimum period were so long that it would amount to a de facto irreducible sentence, as a decision on possible release could not be taken before the person concerned could be expected to die in prison.

Although international law does not require it, there are a number of countries that allow the imposition of life imprisonment in general but specifically prohibit it for the elderly. This is the case in Russia and in several other successor states to the Soviet Union. This prohibition is not found in many countries outside the former Soviet Union, but also exists in Mauritania and Romania. The age limits vary: sixty in Georgia, Kyrgyzstan, Mauritania, and Uzbekistan;[67] sixty-five in Belarus, Kazakhstan, Romania, Russia, and Ukraine.[68]

Recently, the Russian government has sought to explain why treating "seniors"—age sixty-five or older—differently, and prohibiting the imposition of any type of life imprisonment on them, was a reasonably proportionate way of achieving the "principles of justice and humanism." The government argued that seniors, like children, were "vulnerable social groups who had an underdeveloped or weakened capacity to understand the implications of their conduct, to control it and to foresee the consequences of their actions. They were prone to impulsive, unconsidered behaviour that could result in criminally reprehensible conduct." The government explained that, given that all life-sentenced prisoners in Russia must serve twenty-five years before they could be considered for release, "life imprisonment of those aged 65 would make them eligible for early release only at the age of 90, which rendered such a possibility illusory, having regard to the natural life expectancy."[69]

This explanation deserves closer analysis. Many sixty-five-year-olds would be surprised to learn that their capacity to understand the impact of their conduct should be regarded as reduced to such an extent that they should never be punished in the same way as younger adults. They would be equally surprised to learn that invariably they are "prone to impulsive, unconsidered behaviour." While in the case of children, there may be a justification for drawing a bright line designating the reduced moral blameworthiness of all children, there is no justification for doing so for persons aged sixty-five or above. If indeed their capacity to understand fully what they are doing or to control their impulses is reduced, then this is a factor, like many others, that can be taken into account and may justify a court's refusal to impose a life sentence. In Russia, all life sentences are discretionary anyway.

The objection that a life sentence with a twenty-five-year minimum undermines the possibility that offenders will ever be considered for release carries considerably more weight. In Europe, human rights law now requires that all life-sentenced prisoners must have a realistic prospect of release and that what that prospect entails must be made clear to them at sentencing. A hypothetical eighty-year-old who is sentenced to life imprisonment in Russia will not have such a prospect, which is a strong argument for Russia to forbid life imprisonment for persons above the age of sixty-five.

Could this objection be met by imposing a life sentence with a much shorter minimum period? This is a strategy the ECtHR implicitly endorsed in the English case of *Sawoniuk*, where a five-year minimum for a man close to eighty years old seemed to offer the solution.[70] Such an approach would entail a flexible approach to setting minimum periods, which Russian law does not currently allow.

One solution will be to make some changes in the minimum period to be applied. For example, in South Africa, as in Russia, life-sentenced prisoners can normally be considered for release after they have served twenty-five years.[71] If they are over sixty-five and still in prison, their release can be considered after they have served fifteen years. In Tunisia, prisoners over sixty can be paroled earlier than other prisoners sentenced to life imprisonment.[72] Similarly, in France and Spain, life-sentenced prisoners can become eligible for release when they reach the age of seventy,[73] while in Italy, any prisoner over the age of seventy, who was not declared a habitual or professional offender, can be granted home detention.[74] This allows a degree of flexibility but may still not be enough to deal with the position of persons who only begin their sentences at the age of eighty.

A number of countries, mostly in Africa, have adopted a different way of mitigating the impact of life sentences on older prisoners. They allow life sentences to be imposed on them but prohibit any form of hard labor, which might accompany the sentence for younger offenders.[75]

On the face of it, English courts, which now set bespoke minimum periods for all persons sentenced to life imprisonment, are in a position to address this dilemma. However, they show no sign of doing so. On the contrary, they have held bluntly that, while old age may be a general mitigating factor, there is nothing in English law to suggest that a court has to do what it can to ensure that a defendant does not die in prison. The reasoning is as follows:

> If nothing else, no court would be in a position to conduct the necessary actuarial exercise. Even if it were, it would not override the requirement of the sentence to reflect the circumstances of the killing in setting the minimum terms. If those circumstances require a minimum which may result in the offender dying in prison, then that will be the minimum term.[76]

This test was applied in 2014 in the case of *R v. Lowe,* where an eighty-two-year-old man was convicted of deliberately killing his partner and her daughter.[77] In spite of his having no previous criminal record, he was sentenced to a life term with a minimum of twenty-five years before parole could be considered. No actuarial expertise is needed to predict that this sentence amounts essentially to LWOP. The best that someone in Lowe's position can hope for is a discharge from prison on compassionate grounds shortly before death. There appears to be no way in English law in which Lowe could be released, in the full sense of that term as developed by the Grand Chamber of the ECtHR in *Vinter,* to lead a full life in the community before he dies.

The same approach as in *Lowe* was adopted in 2014 in Scotland, in *Her Majesty's Advocate v. Sinclair.* Although Scotland has no formal provision for LWOP, the judge clearly wanted to ensure that Sinclair, a sixty-nine-year-old man who had been convicted of two murders committed many years before, would never be released. In open court, the judge explained that he had to set a minimum period after which the parole board would decide on release. However, the judge added sarcastically that he intended "to make the matter easier" for the parole board. He then imposed a cumulative minimum period of thirty-seven years, effectively ensuring that Sinclair would never be considered for parole, for he would be 106 years old before that would be possible.[78] It remains to be seen whether the ECtHR will be consistent in recognizing the continued imprisonment of the elderly without a reasonable prospect of release as a manifestation of the type of irreducible sentence it has held to be inhuman and degrading in other contexts.

It is possible that the problem of how to deal with elderly life-sentenced prisoners can be ameliorated by factoring in consideration of the age of the prisoner and their prospects for leading a full life in the community into decisions about whether to release them. When it comes to the imposition of life sentences on the elderly, we conclude that national practice has not yet resolved how best to address it.

Women

While imposing life sentences on the elderly clearly raises some complex issues about the relationship between life imprisonment and death in custody, it is not as clear why some countries prohibit the imposition of life imprisonment on women, in circumstances where men could be sentenced to life imprisonment for the same offense. Yet there are such countries. All of those that we could identify, except Albania,—Azerbaijan, Belarus, Kazakhstan, Kyrgyzstan, Moldova, Russia, and Uzbekistan—were part of the former Soviet Union. In addition, Armenia, Bulgaria, Tajikistan, and Ukraine prohibit the imposition of life imprisonment on women who were pregnant at the time of the commission of the offense or of the imposition of sentence.[79]

The reluctance to impose ultimate penalties on women has a long history. In many jurisdictions, women, including those who are not pregnant, were often much less likely to be executed than their male counterparts, even where they were not explicitly excluded from the death sentence.[80] Our empirical research supports the view that women in prison are less likely to have been sentenced to life imprisonment than men. While 6.9 percent of the world's prison population are women, we found that, in the countries for which such information was available, only 3.7 percent of prisoners serving life sentences were women.[81]

The blanket prohibition on the imposition of life imprisonment for women was challenged before the ECtHR as discriminatory by two Russian men who were convicted of murder and given life sentences. In January 2017, in *Khamtokhu and Aksenchik v. Russia*, the Grand Chamber rejected their claim by ten votes to seven.[82]

The arguments of the parties in the admissibility application in this case give an intriguing insight into the underlying reasons for the Russian policy.[83] The human rights arguments of the applicants were straightforward. They contended that giving courts the discretion to impose life imprisonment on men, but not women (or children and older people), infringed against the prohibition on discrimination, in this instance on the basis of sex, in Article 14 of the ECHR. It followed, they argued, that the loss of liberty that their life sentences engendered was not lawful because of its discriminatory basis. In terms of Article 5(1)(e) of the ECHR, loss of liberty following conviction can only be based on a lawful sentence.

In response, the Russian government argued that women differed from men in ways that justified their total exclusion. The differences they listed were "the special role of motherhood in society" and that women were "more psychologically vulnerable than men and were affected to a greater extent by the hardships of detention."[84] They added that, presumably for these reasons, Russian legislation also "provided for more lenient conditions for women held in correctional colonies, while men were detained in harsher prison conditions."[85] The government could not refer to any international human rights standard that specifically excluded women from life sentences. However, it postulated that "international law instruments articulated a more humane attitude towards women, which did not amount to discrimination on account of sex" and that the prohibition on life imprisonment was of a piece with this, as it was designed to achieve substantive rather than formal equality between men and women.[86]

On close reading it is apparent that the Grand Chamber was more divided than its ten-to-seven vote suggests. The majority accepted rather than endorsed the approach adopted by the Russian government toward female offenders, holding that it was "not for the court to reassess the evaluation made by the domestic authorities of the data in their possession [on female prison inmates in Russia and how they were treated] or of the penological rationale which such data purports to demonstrate."[87]

Three judges concurring in the conclusion of the majority, however, disagreed on this point. They all held, with the minority, that there was not sufficient justification, either in human rights law or in criminological knowledge about the differences in the pains of imprisonment between men and women, for reserving the possibility of life sentences for men only. Nevertheless, they did not vote for a finding of an infringement of Article 14, of discrimination on the basis of sex, because in practice the outcome would have been that the Russian government would amend its law to include the women in the ambit of life imprisonment, rather than to exclude men. Such an outcome would be "levelling down," rather than "levelling up."[88] This is not the purpose of human rights intervention.

Conclusion

The human rights–based approach to life imprisonment for women, and the recognition of various categories of persons on whom life imprisonment cannot be imposed, including children and the elderly, may be a way of moving toward the gradual abolition of life imprisonment itself. As Judge Turković explained in his concurring opinion in *Khamtokhu and Aksenchik v. Russia:*

> Although the Court was unable to discern an international trend either in favour of or against abolishing life imprisonment, it has identified exemption from life imprisonment as a progressive evolution of society in penological matters. Life imprisonment as the ultimate sanction gives rise to many of the same objections as the death sentence. Thus I fully agree with Judge Nussberger and Judge Mits [the other two judges who wrote concurring opinions] that it was important for the Court to look at this case from the broader perspective, taking into consideration the spirit of the Convention as a whole as an instrument advancing human rights. The right to human dignity has had an impact in that life imprisonment is now considered acceptable in Europe only under certain conditions. Serious arguments plead in favour of the abolition of life imprisonment. Gradual abolition, targeting groups that are more vulnerable to the harmful impact of life sentences, should be tolerated as a step towards its complete abolition in so far as that difference in treatment does not additionally harm those to whom life imprisonment continues to apply.[89]

When this concurring opinion is taken together with the dissenting opinion in *Khamtokhu and Aksenchik* of Judge Pinto de Albuquerque, who argued the solution to the dilemma was to abolish life imprisonment completely, it becomes clear that restriction of the imposition of life imprisonment on certain categories of persons, is a step toward critiquing the imposition of the penalty on anyone.

We return to arguments for the abolition of life imprisonment in Chapter 11. For now, we must recognize that life imprisonment continues to be imposed in most countries in the world, albeit with restrictions in respect to some groups of people. In the next chapter, we examine the role that a restriction on the offenses for which life imprisonment may be imposed can play in limiting the imposition of life sentences.

5

Offenses That Carry Life

A NOTHER WAY in which the constraints on the imposition of life sentences can be approached is by asking, what are the offenses for which life imprisonment can be, and is, imposed worldwide? The answer matters because it is a first step toward addressing a key question about the legitimacy of life imprisonment, namely, whether its imposition represents a proportionate penal response to the criminal conduct of the offender. It is only a first step, because identifying these offenses and allocating them to typical categories is not enough if we do not know what constraints there may be on imposing such a sentence in practice. Nevertheless, an overview of these offenses does give an indication of what legislatures in different countries consider to be criminal conduct for which life imprisonment of some type would be an appropriate sentence.

This chapter begins by providing such an overview. It then elaborates on the seriousness of the offenses for which formal life imprisonment can be imposed. It also addresses the complexities of how offenses are defined to reflect their relative seriousness. This includes instances where the seriousness of the conduct is claimed on the basis of a pattern of offending that may result in a life sentence for what is still sometimes called habitual offending. The focus in this chapter is primarily on formal life sentences, but an additional section also considers offense-related limitations on the imposition of informal life sentences. Much of the chapter is concerned with legal provisions about offenses that carry life imprisonment, but the chapter also describes for what offenses life imprisonment is imposed in practice.

Overview of Offenses

For which offenses can life imprisonment be imposed? Table 5.1 gives an indication.

The data in Table 5.1 were drawn from 145 countries. In all, 4,820 offenses from the 145 countries were analyzed. These numbers are almost certainly underestimates, given the enormous methodological challenges of identifying all the offenses for which life imprisonment could in law be imposed in a particular country.[1]

In countries with penal codes (the vast majority), extracting the offenses for which life imprisonment may be imposed is relatively straightforward. However, there may be offenses defined in other legislative enactments, including military codes, creating further offenses for which life sentences may be imposed. Where possible, these were also followed up.

In common-law systems, where the criminal law has not been codified, the challenge is even greater. This challenge is illustrated by the position in England and Wales, where the courts retain common-law powers to impose life imprisonment for common-law offenses that do not have a statutory basis. A good example is the English offense of perverting the course of

TABLE 5.1. Categories of offenses for which formal life imprisonment can be imposed*

Crimes against property	Crimes against the person	Crimes against the community	Crimes against public order
Theft (30)	Murder (139)	Incest (8)	Treason/Sedition (120)
Fraud (11)	Manslaughter (49)	Bigamy (1)	Public Violence (41)
Arson (74)	Abortion (11)	Crimes against	Corruption (7)
Burglary (14)	Assault/Torture (49)	Religion (7)	Organized Crime (12)
Extortion (15)	Rape (71)	Drugs—trading,	Terrorism (61)
Other (41)	Other Sexual	manufacturing (38)	Human Trafficking (20)
	Offense (41)	Drugs—possession (8)	Military Offenses (28)
	Kidnapping (78)	Other (18)	Crimes against
	Robbery (62)		Humanity (36)
	Other (75)		War Crimes (40)
			Genocide (53)
			Piracy/Hijacking (53)
			Other (114)

Source: Data collected by authors.

*Figures in parentheses indicate the number of countries in which life imprisonment is imposed for the category of offense.

justice, a common-law offense that theoretically carries life imprisonment. In a headline-grabbing case in 2013, a cabinet minister and his wife were charged with perverting the course of justice by making a false statement to the police about which of them had been driving a car that was found to be speeding. There was much media speculation about the sentence they would face, including the possibility of life imprisonment. However, closer analysis revealed that the normal range for the sentence was between twelve and thirty-six months, and that no one had been given more than ten years for this offense for more than a century. Under these circumstances, the threat of a life sentence seems so remote that it does not justify our listing perverting the course of justice as an offense bearing a life sentence.[2] Instead, for the uncodified common-law systems we included only those offenses for which prisoners were currently serving life sentences.

In order to manage what was still a large body of data, we divided the 4,820 offenses for which some formal type of life imprisonment could be imposed into five broad categories: offenses against property, person, the community, and public order, as well as habitual offenders. These broad categories, in turn, were subdivided into offense categories. These are themselves constructs, because inevitably they do not correspond exactly to the detailed and nuanced offense definitions found in the laws concerned. We therefore had to interpret the law (often with the help of correspondents in the various countries) and place them in the offense categories.[3]

Table 5.1 shows that most of the countries that we examined had provision for life imprisonment for murder. In fact, the number was even higher, for it excludes countries where murder can be punished only by death. For murder, or at least an aggravated form of it, all countries that have life imprisonment, with very minor exceptions,[4] have either life or death sentences.[5] In addition, many death sentences are eventually commuted to life imprisonment, demonstrating that it is the dominant penalty worldwide, even for murder. With minor qualifications, the same can be said about treason.

Clearly, life imprisonment can be imposed for the most serious offenses. Although the list in Table 5.1 includes seemingly less serious crimes, such as theft and arson, many of the non-homicide offenses were only punishable by life imprisonment when they led to death. For example, of the seventy-four countries that allow life imprisonment for arson, at least thirty-six allow it only if it leads to death.[6]

Even if an offense on this list did not lead to death, generally life could only be imposed when the offense was committed under specific aggravating circumstances. For instance, rape was punishable by life imprisonment in seventy-one countries, forty-eight of which allowed life sentences only for aggravated rape. We interpreted "aggravated" to be any additional requirement to the basic definition of the offense. In the case of rape, the aggravating factors include rape of a minor or a vulnerable person,[7] rape by more than one offender,[8] rape with abuse of authority,[9] and rape with torture.[10] Other aggravating factors included the use of death threats, torture, and violence.

Aggravating circumstances are often offense specific. For example, in the case of kidnapping, aggravating circumstances may include the duration for which the person was held,[11] as well as torture and other circumstances. In fact, of the seventy-eight countries that we identified as allowing life imprisonment for kidnapping,[12] sixty-three required a further factor before the life sentence could be imposed: in fifty-four instances the kidnapping had to be aggravated as defined in the relevant statute, while in thirty-eight the kidnapping had to lead to the death of the victim. In twenty-nine countries, life imprisonment was permissible where either of these factors was sufficient to make life imprisonment a competent sentence.[13]

Similarly, thirty-six countries allow sentences of life imprisonment for the some or all of the property-related offenses of theft, robbery and burglary. Of the thirty-six countries, at least twenty-eight require aggravating circumstances in the commission of the offense, such as theft with rape, theft with kidnapping, theft causing grievous bodily harm or severe injury, robbery with the use of violence or torture, or armed robbery, and seven countries limit life imprisonment for robbery to instances when the offense leads to death.

When one connects the offenses specified in the criminal law to individual countries, some interesting political and historical patterns emerge. For example, and not unexpectedly, life imprisonment was a possible sentence for drug-related offenses in all Southeast Asian countries but only in a minority of European countries.[14]

In contrast, kidnapping was recognized almost universally as an offense for which life imprisonment could be imposed in the (relatively few) countries in Latin America that have life imprisonment.[15] Drug offenses were not, however.[16]

Some patterns are more surprising. In francophone African countries, for example, both castration and counterfeiting appeared in almost every code as offenses for which life imprisonment can be imposed.[17] This is presumably a product of the French Penal Code, which served as a model for them.

A key question here is to what extent do the offenses carrying possible life imprisonment provide a constraint that ensures that a life sentence is imposed only for the most serious offenses? The answer is complex and hedged with many caveats. We can assume, however, that a short list, in a particular country, of seemingly serious offenses carrying possible life sentences, provides stricter constraints on the imposition of such sentences than a longer list of ostensibly less serious offenses carrying the same sentence.

The European countries that have recently introduced life sentences tend to have relatively short lists of offenses carrying life imprisonment. For example, Slovenia introduced life imprisonment in 2008 but limited its imposition to genocide, crimes against humanity and war crimes, plus consecutive convictions for crimes drawn from a short list that includes murder and very serious offenses against public order. The unsurprising result is that no one has ever been sentenced to life imprisonment in Slovenia.[18]

In contrast, in the three jurisdictions of the United Kingdom—England and Wales, Scotland, and Northern Ireland—life imprisonment may be imposed for a wide range of offenses, including rape of an adult and burglary, even where no fatal violence is involved. This is different from most European countries, where adult rape and burglary usually do not carry life sentences unless a homicide occurs in the commission of the offense.

In the Americas there are stark differences too. Few countries in Central and Latin America have formal life imprisonment, and those that do have it do not allow such a sentence for nonviolent crimes, including drug offenses. In contrast, in the United States, all states with the exception of Alaska have provisions for formal life sentences for nonviolent offenses and twenty-two US states even have LWOP for nonviolent offenses.[19]

All this matters because the national statutory framework reveals something about a country's approach to life imprisonment. A statutory framework with a short list of offenses carrying life sentences, limited to the most heinous offenses, is an indication that life imprisonment is considered disproportionately severe for less serious offenses. The indication is reinforced where the statutory frameworks also limit the offenses carrying de facto life sentences. In Germany, for example, the maximum fixed term that, in terms of the Penal Code, can be imposed for any offense is fifteen years, which distinguishes it clearly from life imprisonment.[20]

These are no more than indications, however. A country may have a long list of offenses that potentially carry life imprisonment on its statute books, but still only impose it very rarely. A good example is the Netherlands, where there are forty-nine offenses carrying life imprisonment on the statute books, but at the time of our research only thirty-two prisoners were serving life sentences, all except one for homicide. Among countries that have life imprisonment, the Dutch rate is one of the lowest in the world.[21] Clearly, the large number of offenses for which life imprisonment is a potential penalty has not had a determining influence on how often it is imposed.

Definitions of Offenses

The precise definitions of offenses carrying possible life imprisonment in different jurisdictions also provide an indication of the country's approach to life imprisonment. This is a difficult factor to draw out when making international comparisons that depend on generalizations, for it involves looking closely at definitions, which inevitably differ slightly in the detail. Nevertheless, it is important, particularly when there are rules that compel or encourage sentencing courts to impose life imprisonment, or specific types of life imprisonment, following a conviction for a particular offense as precisely defined.

The definition of murder is a good example of the significance of precise definitions. Murder in some form—aggravated murder, first-degree murder, or, simply, murder—was the offense most likely to carry a sentence of life imprisonment that either was mandatory or was strongly encouraged by limiting the choices of the sentencing court. In contrast, for other forms of homicide, such as manslaughter, culpable homicide, or negligent homicide, sentencing courts may be given great discretion not to impose life imprisonment.

A clear illustration of the different impact of small definitional variations can be seen by comparing the definition of murder in England and Wales, on the one hand, and Germany, on the other. Both jurisdictions provide mandatory life sentences for murder and discretionary life for some other forms of homicide. In England and Wales, the definition of murder includes intentional homicide as well as instances where the offender, while intending only grievous bodily harm, causes death.[22]

In contrast, under German law, murder, with its concomitant mandatory life sentence, requires an intentional homicide and additionally the presence of at least one of a list of aggravating circumstances. The German Penal Code lists the aggravating circumstances, focusing on aspects of the conduct of the perpetrator: "the murderer . . . is any person who kills a person for pleasure, for sexual gratification, out of greed or otherwise base motives, by stealth or cruelly or by means that pose a danger to the public or in order to facilitate or to cover up another offense."[23]

In practice, this list of aggravating circumstances is narrowly defined and, as a result, "murder" is found to have been committed far less frequently in Germany than in England and Wales, even though the homicide rates in the two countries are largely similar. Given the definitional differences, it is not surprising that the relative number of persons serving life sentences for "murder" is much higher in England and Wales (9.6 per 100,000 of population) than in Germany (2.4 per 100,000).[24]

Other variations in the legal definition of different classes or degrees of murder within a jurisdiction may also impact life sentences by affecting the minimum term to be served before release can be considered. A good example is Canada, where life imprisonment is mandatory for all murders. However, the law distinguishes between first- and second-degree murder. First-degree murder is defined as a planned or deliberate murder, or is the murder of a peace officer or similar official, or murder with aggravating factors. Second-degree murder is a murder that does not meet the criteria for first-degree murder. The difference is significant because the minimum period to be served before release can be considered is twenty-five years for first-degree murder and ten to twenty-five years for second-degree murder.[25]

For the precise definition of the offense to be directly significant in determining the final outcome, the life sentence need not be fully mandatory. In France, for example, murder (*meurtre*), is defined by the French Penal Code as "[t]he willful causing of the death of another person" and carries a penalty of thirty years.[26] If the murder is premeditated, it becomes an "assassination," for which life imprisonment must be imposed unless widely defined mitigating circumstances are present.[27] In the absence of mitigating circumstances or if there are certain aggravating circumstances, such as the victim being a child under fifteen years of age or a member of the police force, murder that is not "assassination" is punished with life imprisonment.[28]

Depending on the type of aggravating circumstance, the minimum period that a French court must set before release can be considered may also vary.[29] A similar pattern in the use of life imprisonment for murder, as well as the distinction between "murder" and "assassination," is found throughout Francophone Africa, where assassination, parricide, and poisoning are typical forms of murder that carry the severest sentence.[30]

Previous Convictions and Habitual Offenders

Thus far we have focused on the offense as a factor that may limit the imposition of life sentences. In some instances, however, the record of the offender is the determining factor. Jurisdictions that would not allow life imprisonment for a specific offense may allow it if the offender has a prior criminal record. Our indicative survey of 145 countries found examples in 41 countries of formal life sentences that could only be imposed for the current offense on the basis of prior record. The persons concerned were sometimes referred to as persistent or habitual offenders.

The classic modern example is the "three strikes and you're out" legislation in California, where, historically, a relatively minor third conviction of a particular class of offense (albeit a felony) resulted in an automatic life sentence with a minimum term of twenty-five years. Recent amendments to the California law have limited the third strike to serious or violent felonies, thus indirectly introducing an element of offense proportionality into what is still a provision for a mandatory life sentence.[31] In a number of US states, the type of mandatory life imprisonment imposed in such cases is the most severe, that is, LWOP. The offenses that count as strikes, as well as the number of strikes required, vary from state to state.[32] The basis for imposing a life sentence, however, is conceptually different from other LWOP sentences. It is the record of the offender that is used to justify a life sentence to incapacitate the offender, rather than the heinousness of the offense that indicates that a life sentence will be a deserved punishment.

In practice, the distinction may not be that clear. In some instances, the thinking seems to be that a prior offense adds to the heinousness of the committed offense. Although just desert purists challenge this thinking, the notion persists that an offense may be regarded as inherently more serious because it is committed by someone with a relevant previous conviction.[33] Thus, for example, a prisoner who murders someone while already serving a prison sentence for another offense may be thought to deserve a heavier sentence for the homicide than would otherwise apply. This is reflected in some national legislation that specifies life imprisonment for such murder, or even attempted murder, which would not carry such a sentence were it not committed in prison.[34]

In other instances, however, there is no attempt to justify the life sentence on the grounds of the offense alone, for clearly the offense itself is not sufficiently serious to do so. In these instances, the reasoning goes, much as it did historically, that life sentences can be justified on grounds of incapacitation alone for offenders with long criminal records.

The wider question raised by allowing for the imposition of life imprisonment on recidivists is whether the seriousness of the offense should always trump incapacitation. The question arises in cases where the person whose incapacitation is sought is convicted of a relatively minor offense but has a long criminal record. An example of the lack of criteria of offense seriousness, resulting in incapacitatory concerns dominating, arose in the US case of *Solem v. Helm*.[35] In this instance, a court in South Dakota had imposed a discretionary LWOP sentence on Helm for a check fraud of less than $100. The court had been able to do so because Helm's record of six (relatively minor, nonviolent) previous offenses brought him within the purview of the South Dakota recidivist legislation that allowed the sentencing court to impose such a sentence. The South Dakota court had emphasized that Helm was addicted to alcohol and was a habitual offender who committed crimes in order to pay for his addiction.

The US Supreme Court set aside the LWOP sentence. In order to do so, it concentrated on whether the LWOP sentence was disproportionate to the offense for which it was being imposed and thus infringed the prohibition on cruel and unusual punishment in the US Constitution. The focus on the offense led the Supreme Court to develop a tripartite test for judging "objectively" whether an offense is constitutionally disproportionate. Consideration had to be given to:

(a) the gravity of the offense and the harshness of the penalty;
(b) the sentences imposed on other criminals in the same jurisdiction, that is, whether more serious crimes are subject to the same penalty or to less serious penalties; and
(c) the sentences imposed for commission of the same crime in other [US] jurisdictions.[36]

On the facts, the Supreme Court was able to hold that LWOP was a harsh penalty for the offense for which it had been imposed; that other offenders in North Dakota were not punished nearly so harshly for similar offenses; and that the same crime was not punished in the same way in other US jurisdictions. These three holdings allowed the court to find that the life sentence imposed on Helm violated the US Constitution.

The decision of the Supreme Court in *Solem v. Helm* was groundbreaking, not least because it departed from a decision a few months earlier, in which the same court had declined to uphold a claim of unconstitutional disproportionality in a life imprisonment case.[37] The sophisticated tripartite test for offense seriousness developed in *Solem v. Helm* could have provided a framework for wider analysis of proportionality for life offenses generally and in particular for those in which repeated offending was an important factor. It was undermined, however, by subsequent Supreme Court decisions.

In 1991, in *Harmelin v. Michigan*,[38] which involved a first offender who was sentenced to a mandatory LWOP term for possession of a fairly large amount of drugs, a divided court struggled with this test. For four of the nine justices, this was a straightforward case of a sentence being too severe to be imposed on such an offender. The four justices applied the tripartite test and found that the punishment was too harsh for the crime; LWOP was the heaviest possible sentence in Michigan, a state that had long ago abolished the death penalty. Moreover, it was imposed only on drug dealers and murderers in the same jurisdiction; and LWOP was not routinely imposed for first-time possession of drugs in other US jurisdictions. However, their view did not prevail. Two justices rejected the notion that the US Constitution required a proportionality test for offenses other than death. The remaining three, Justice Anthony Kennedy, with whom Justice Sandra Day O'Connor, and Justice David Souter concurred, upheld the constitutional principle of what they called "narrow proportionality," but found that the prescribed sentence was not disproportionate to the offense, thus upholding the LWOP sentence that had been initially imposed.

The reasoning of Justice Kennedy is instructive because it points to the fragility of using offense proportionality as a constitutional test to determine whether or not a prescribed sentence is acceptable. First, he stressed the importance of not second-guessing the legislature in determining what is a serious offense. He was prepared to accept, as the four justices in the minority did not, that possession of a large quantity of drugs may legitimately be regarded as sufficiently grave to justify a sentence as severe as LWOP, even for a first offender. In support of this, he explained that it is for the legislature to determine the purpose of the sentence. He placed great emphasis on the deterrent effect of the LWOP sentence, and thus avoided dealing more narrowly with the question of desert in relation to the offense.

Secondly, having answered the first question in favor of upholding the sentence, Justice Kennedy dispensed with the two other prongs of the test. He argued that they should only be considered if there is doubt about the first prong, that is, the proportionality between the gravity of the offense and the harshness of the sentence. By curtailing the enquiry in this way, he did not consider, as the minority did, the extent to which this penalty was out of line with practice in Michigan and indeed the United States as a whole.

The *Harmelin* case dealt with a first offender, but it led directly to the failure of constitutional proportionality challenges to life sentences in cases involving habitual offenders and incapacitation. In 2003, two cases in the US Supreme Court challenged the "three strikes and you're out" laws in California. Both featured offenders addicted to drugs, whose "third strikes" were relatively petty offenses but who had substantial criminal records. In the case of *Andrade,* the conviction on two counts of stealing nine videotapes was two life sentences, with an effective joint minimum period of fifty years. In the case of *Ewing,* the conviction on a single count of stealing three golf clubs received the mandatory sentence of life imprisonment with a minimum period of twenty-five years.[39] In both cases, the state of California stressed that the purpose of the sentence was incapacitatory. As in the *Harmelin* case, the Supreme Court emphasized that states could determine the penological purpose of the sentence, and it accepted that, for the purposes of incapacitation, the sentences imposed on Andrade and Ewing could reasonably be regarded as proportionate. The facts of these two cases were very similar to the facts in *Solem v. Helm.* Nevertheless, the Supreme Court did not apply the three-pronged proportionality test to establish the outer bounds of what would be acceptable in terms of the relationship between the gravity of the specific offenses committed and the harshness of the penalties. Instead, it focused on the overall record of the offenders, holding explicitly that life imprisonment for habitual offenders, even those convicted of relatively petty offenses, was justifiable. In vain, dissenting justices in both cases applied the full three-pronged test and protested that life imprisonment for the conduct of the triggering offenses was grossly disproportionate, "recidivism notwithstanding."[40]

When one compares the approach adopted by the US Supreme Court to the imposition of life sentences, particularly in these last two cases, to its jurisprudence on offense seriousness and the death penalty, the differences are significant. Although in both instances there is a recognition that certain offenses are insufficiently serious to justify the punishment, the range of offenses for which the death penalty is acceptable is much narrower; it includes only offenses with a homicide element. Internationally, there is a similar and widespread recognition that offenses that carry the death penalty should be strictly limited to certain serious offenses. Although there is room for dispute about what they are, the notion that death could be imposed on petty recidivists is not entertained.

The acceptance, in the United States and elsewhere, that life imprisonment can be used for recidivists whose offenses are not particularly severe, reveals how weak the offense criterion alone can be as a factor preventing its imposition in instances where the punishment does not fit the specific crime of which they are finally convicted. This indicates that, in imposing life sentences, the perceived necessity for incapacitation sometimes trumps offense seriousness in a way that would be inconceivable for capital punishment.

One possible response would be simply to increase the weight given to the criterion of offense severity, even when the offenders are recidivists, and not to allow concerns for incapacitation to sway a decision to impose imprisonment for life on dangerous offenders where the offense alone is not sufficient to justify such imprisonment. This is what is proposed by the new draft Model Penal Code in the United States. It provides for life sentences and generally allows imprisonment "to incapacitate dangerous offenders, provided that a sentence imposed is not disproportionality severe."[41] In the Californian cases discussed, it would be impossible to make the case that the offenses alone were sufficiently serious to justify incapacitation or even for it to be considered as an additional factor.

Further questions need to be asked about when incapacitation can be regarded as a factor even to be considered as an additional justification for a life sentence where the basic criterion of offense seriousness is met. What is meant by limiting incapacitation to "dangerous offenders" in this context? Bottoms and Brownsword have argued that incapacitation should be considered only where there is a "vivid danger" to the public.[42] Von Hirsch and Ashworth have produced an even narrower formulation, arguing that detention beyond what can be justified on grounds of desert alone should only be considered where "harmful consequences of an extraordinary character otherwise would occur."[43] Both Bottoms and Brownsword, and Ashworth and Von Hirsch have developed the philosophical underpinnings of this approach by applying Ronald Dworkin's rights-based philosophy. They note that the key Dworkinian idea is that human dignity requires the right of all people to equal concern and respect. This right must be enforced by the courts, which need to balance rights and, more important, protect individuals against the preferences of the majority.[44]

What these approaches have in common, when applied to considering life imprisonment at the sentencing phase, is that they would limit drastically consideration of the need to incapacitate a particular offender. They do so by focusing not only on the degree of likelihood of reoffending, but also on whether the predicted conduct would constitute grievous harm, such as potentially lethal or very serious violence. In this way, a secondary proportionality test based on the seriousness of the predicted future offense is brought to bear on the justification for incapacitation too.

Offenses for Which Informal Life Imprisonment Can Be Imposed

The pattern of past offenses, the seriousness of the committed offense, and the possible risk posed by future offenses may encourage the courts to impose both types of informal life sentences, that is, post-conviction indefinite detention and de facto life. There are, however, also limitations on their use. In many countries, post-conviction indefinite detention is restricted to individuals convicted of offenses with a violent or sexual element, and, within that class, to specific offenses regarded as sufficiently serious to allow the imposition of informal life imprisonment. Seriousness may be indicated by the fixed term to which an offender is sentenced before the indefinite detention is added. In France, for instance, post-conviction indefinite detention can only apply to persons sentenced to more than fifteen years of imprisonment for assassination, murder, torture, rape, or abduction of a minor, and for aggravated versions of these offenses if the victim is an adult or the offender is a recidivist.[45]

In Germany, the range of offenses potentially subject to post-conviction indefinite detention includes not only violent and sexual offenses, but also offenses under the Drugs Act if they are subject to a fixed term of more than ten years. There are additional criteria: the newly convicted person has to have been convicted twice previously of one of the qualifying offenses and sentenced to a term of imprisonment of no less than one year each time. Most important, there also has to be a comprehensive evaluation of the newly convicted person and his or her offenses. Before post-conviction indefinite detention can be imposed, this evaluation has to show that the newly convicted person has a propensity to commit serious offenses, particularly of a kind resulting in serious emotional trauma or physical injury to the victim, and that the person therefore poses a danger to the general public.[46]

Such restrictions are not universal. In Greece, post-conviction indefinite detention can be imposed following almost any offense, as long as the offender has been convicted three times in the past and appears to be a professional criminal or dangerous. In that case, he or she may receive an indefinite sentence, whose minimum is determined by the sentencing judge, and which cannot be less than two-thirds of the actual sentence accompanying their most recent offense.[47] The Greek post-conviction indefinite detention is therefore, much like the formal US life sentence, based on a wide definition of habitual offending, although in the United States, habitual offenders may receive LWOP or LWP with a long minimum term, while anecdotal evidence for Greece suggests that these informal life sentences are implemented for relatively short periods.

When it comes to the second type of informal life sentences that we have identified, de facto life, there are clear limitations on the offenses for which it can be imposed. Latin American countries that do no not have life imprisonment often have provision for sentences of thirty-five years or more. In El Salvador, for example, the maximum fixed-term sentence for a single offense is sixty years, thus putting it clearly in the de facto life category. However, this lengthy term can only be imposed as a sentence for the murder of a public official, a member of the armed forces, or a penitentiary officer who is on duty, or for aggravated abduction.[48] In this way, offense specification limits the use of a de facto life sentence. This is an analogous approach to that in countries that have a similar closed list of offenses for which formal life imprisonment can be imposed.

De facto life imprisonment can sometimes be created by allowing several fixed-term sentences to run consecutively. The result is that informal life sentences are imposed for offenses that would not justify life imprisonment if considered individually. Some jurisdictions do limit the practical effect of consecutive sentences by setting an overall term that such sentences should not exceed.[49] In other instances, the use of consecutive sentences for multiple offenses committed at more or less the same time is restricted too, although the basis for doing so is not clearly articulated.[50] However, the limits on requiring sentences to be implemented consecutively are not usually based on the type of offenses for which the individual fixed-term sentences were imposed.

In sum, as far as both formal and informal life sentences are concerned, one may conclude that, while the specification of offenses for which life imprisonment may be imposed could, in theory, limit the imposition of life sentences, it often does not do so. The reason is that the range of specified offenses may be very wide, particularly when repeat offenses are concerned. The question, of course, remains whether, in practice, life sentences are imposed for the wide range of offenses for which the law allows their imposition.

Offenses for Which Life Imprisonment Has Been Imposed

Ideally, the overview of the offenses for which life imprisonment can be imposed should be complemented by a factual overview of the offenses for which life sentences have been imposed. In practice, however, collecting such factual information worldwide is very challenging. At the international level, comparable sentencing data specified by offense for which life sentences were imposed proved almost impossible to obtain. Instead, we sought data on the offenses committed by persons serving life sentences on a date as close as possible to September 1, 2014, in particular jurisdictions, as a proxy for what formal life sentences were imposed for. In many countries, the prison authorities, who were the primary source for the data on the use of life imprisonment, did not have data on the offenses for which life-sentenced prisoners were incarcerated. Usable information on numbers of persons serving formal life sentences by offense category was located for forty-two countries.

These data, recorded in Appendix C, reveal certain tendencies that were implicit in the analysis of offenses for which life imprisonment may be imposed. The first of these is the prominence of homicide as the broad category for which by far the most life sentences are imposed. In twelve of the twenty European countries for which we have data on the offenses committed by life-sentenced prisoners, all the life-sentenced prisoners are serving sentences for homicide. To these should be added Finland and the Netherlands, as in both of these countries only a single person is technically not serving a sentence for homicide.[51] However, the predominance of homicide—in fact all these cases are intentional murder—is particularly significant, as it underlies the point that no matter how long the list of offenses, the offenses that are perceived as the most severe are those likely to receive life sentences in practice.

Germany, too, is an interesting example. It has quite a large number of life-sentenced prisoners serving terms for homicide—1,889—but only six for identifiable other offenses (two for sex offenses, three for offenses against the person, and one for a property offense). Closer analysis shows that, of the homicide offenses, 1,866 of the 1,889 were for murder.[52] This is not surprising, for life imprisonment is mandatory for murder, but not for any of the other offenses for which prisoners are serving life sentences. On the other hand, it also shows how reluctant German courts are to impose discretionary life sentences. Out of twenty-four offenses that currently carry life imprisonment in German law, there is no one at all serving a life sentence for fifteen of them.

The statistical evidence on homicide reinforces some other trends that were noticeable when considering offenses for which life imprisonment can be imposed. The relatively low percentage of life-sentenced prisoners in Indonesia can be explained by the fact that a third of persons serving life sentences were doing so for drug offenses, and others are on death row for the same crime.[53] This fits the pattern of drug offenses being regarded as particularly serious in Southeast Asia and being punished, not only by life imprisonment, but also by death. In Australia, too, 8 percent of life-sentenced prisoners had committed drug offenses.

Among the twenty European countries for which figures were available, only Georgia and the United Kingdom had any individuals serving life imprisonment for drug offenses. In the case of the United Kingdom, they were only a relatively small number, 0.1 percent of all life-sentenced prisoners in that country, while the percentage was higher for Georgia (11.7 percent).

It is noteworthy also that life imprisonment has been imposed relatively rarely on sex offenders. This is most noticeable in Europe, where only four of the twenty countries for which we have offense data have any offenders serving life sentences for sex offenses. In Austria and Germany, there are only two offenders in this category in each country. In France there are 32, and in the United Kingdom there are 908, which amount to 6.7 percent and 10.6 percent of the overall life-sentenced population in these two countries, respectively.

The worldwide trend is similar. Most countries do not have prisoners serving life sentences for sex offenses. Only Liberia (32—35.6 percent), Uganda (41—19.7 percent), Kyrgyzstan (29—10.1 percent) and the United States (23,871—15.2 percent) recorded significant numbers and percentages of sex offenders in their total life-sentenced prisoner population. The number of sex offenders in the United States is significant, as it was almost equivalent to the total number of prisoners in Europe serving life sentences for all offenses, and is the largest factor explaining the (relatively low) 63.8 percent serving life sentences for homicide in the United States, as recorded in Appendix C.

South Africa, which had the greatest increase in the number of prisoners serving life sentences,[54] is an interesting example of the role that sex offenses could play in the increasing overall prison numbers. Although rape has long been punishable by life imprisonment in South Africa, that penalty was in practice very rarely imposed for rape and the death sentence, when still applicable, even more rarely. A change in the sentencing law in 1997, coupled with pressure from women's groups for rape to be punished more harshly, brought about a truly dramatic change. In 1995, persons convicted of rape constituted only 4 percent of the 408 prisoners then serving life sentences; by 2006 it had increased to 21 percent of the much larger number, 6,998, of all life-sentenced prisoners.[55]

The South African example is a particularly stark indication of the role that a changed approach to sexual offenses can play. However, international figures must be treated with particular caution in this area. For example, we do not know what number or percentage of life-sentenced sex offenders there are in prison in India, which has the world's second largest life-sentenced prisoner population.

The information collated on life sentences and offenses in Appendix C does not indicate whether the life sentences imposed were with (LWP) or without parole (LWOP). However, as these data were initially recorded by our research instruments for the forty-two countries concerned, we examined the eighteen countries in this group that indicated that LWOP could be imposed. Among these countries, it was noticeable that seven imposed LWOP only for homicide. Further examination of the remaining eleven countries showed that the exceptions to this rule were relatively limited. In Morocco, the twenty-one nonhomicide LWOP sentences were all imposed for terrorism. In the Netherlands there was a single exception for war crimes. Other exceptions were for offenses that fall within our broad categories, other than homicide, but the numbers were very small. In the Cayman Islands, for example, one person was serving LWOP for a sex offense.[56]

There were only two countries in our dataset where LWOP was used on a relatively large scale for offenses other than homicide. One of these was Uganda, where, as we explained in Chapter 2, there is in practice a great deal of uncertainty about whether life sentences are LWOP or symbolic LWP. It may be the case that the judicial creation of an LWOP sentence as an alternative to the death penalty has had the unintended consequence of extending this type of life sentence to a wider range of offenses.

In the United States, there was a significant number of prisoners serving LWOP for offenses other than homicide. In 2016, The Sentencing Project identified 12,736 prisoners serving LWOP for offenses other than murder. This amounted to 23.9 percent of all prisoners serving LWOP. The 12,736 prisoners included 2,451 persons serving LWOP for drug offenses, and 373 for property offenses.[57] These figures may well be an underestimate. Another study undertaken by the American Civil Liberties Union (ACLU) in 2012, identified prisoners serving LWOP for drug offenses (2,578) in just nine states as well as the federal system.[58] In all, the ACLU study identified 3,278 prisoners in these jurisdictions as serving LWOP for nonviolent crimes. Whether all these offenses were "nonviolent" has been questioned: however, it is clear they were not imposed for murder.[59]

Summary and Conclusion

Offense-based limitations on the imposition of life imprisonment vary greatly from one jurisdiction to another, but everyone agrees that restrictions are necessary to ensure that life sentences are imposed as parsimoniously as possible. Limiting life imprisonment to the most serious offenses suggests that life sentences will be imposed in a manner proportionate to the severity of the offense. Having a longer list of offenses, however, does not necessarily indicate the contrary. In systems with long lists of offenses carrying life imprisonment, the sentence is never imposed for many of them.

The possibility of using statutory law to restrict life imprisonment by only allowing it for a restricted number of the most serious offenses is not being exploited to the full. Whatever the law may provide, empirical evidence shows that in many jurisdictions life imprisonment is imposed only for the most serious offenses, often only for homicide. In other jurisdictions, however, life imprisonment, even LWOP, is being imposed for offenses for which it is manifestly a disproportionately severe punishment. This is often the case with recidivists, whose previous convictions may be given undue weight to the danger that they pose to society. Whether life sentences are imposed or not depends greatly on the processes of imposition, which are discussed in the next chapter.

6

Imposing Life

T HE IMPOSITION of life sentences is shaped by various restrictions on the institutions that have the power to impose them. In Chapter 4, we described certain categories of people—children, the elderly, and women—who in some countries are exempt, either fully or partially, from being subject to life sentences. In Chapter 5, we considered the offenses that could be punished by life imprisonment, which constitute a long, but not unrestricted, list. In this chapter we look more closely at how the imposition of life sentences is shaped by the legal framework governing sentencing. We ask what discretion decision-making bodies have to impose life imprisonment, and to shape the life sentences that they do impose by setting minimum terms that have to be served before release can be considered. Our focus is primarily on courts and the framework within which they operate. However, we also consider, more briefly, other institutions and participants. In particular, we discuss the role that commutation of the death penalty plays in the imposition of life sentences. Participants, such as prosecutors, expert witnesses, and victims, who do not make final decisions on imposition, are considered more briefly, but attention is nonetheless paid to how their roles vary, depending on what grounds for imposing life sentences are given primacy.

Chapter 5 has shown that international human rights law gives some recognition to the principle that life imprisonment should be restricted to "the most serious crimes."[1] As in the case of the death penalty, there should also be a framework for considering whether individual cases, on their specific facts, meet the "most serious" standard.[2] In the case of life imprisonment, a further concern in many jurisdictions is whether to impose life sentences on grounds of incapacitation, particularly in cases where the offense is serious, but not necessarily the most serious, and the offender also poses a vivid danger to society.

This chapter asks whether there are adequate procedural frameworks worldwide for deciding on whether to impose life sentences. To assist in understanding whether courts have the power to ensure that life imprisonment is only imposed in the appropriate cases, we have identified four levels of discretion that could operate when life sentences are being considered:

1. Life imprisonment could be *mandatory,* in the sense that a life sentence would have to be imposed if a particular offense were committed.
2. There could be a *mandatory alternative,* with a limited choice between a life sentence and another sentence, such as the death penalty.
3. Imposing a life sentence could be subject to a *qualified mandatory* rule; that is, sentencing law could stipulate that a court shall impose a life sentence but subject that to a qualification, that it should be mandatory unless certain conditions were present.
4. Finally, the sentence of life imprisonment could be *discretionary,* in that the court could choose whether to impose it or not, but even that discretion could be subject to some limitation, for example, a minimum number of years to be imposed in lieu of life.

When analyzing these four levels of discretion in the context of life sentences, there are additional factors that do not apply to the death penalty. Whether to impose a death sentence or not is a simple either/or decision. Life imprisonment is more complex, as there are the two primary types of formal life sentence identified in Chapter 2, namely, life imprisonment without parole (LWOP) and life imprisonment with parole (LWP), and variations within them, as well as possibly also the alternative of an informal life sentence. These further options have constantly to be borne in mind.

Mandatory Life Sentences

A legal rule that would compel a court to impose a life sentence for one or more type of offense, or on an offender who has a specified criminal record, would seem to exclude discretion to the greatest extent. However, within the category of mandatory life sentences, there could be an additional variation that would limit discretion even further. The law could compel the court, following conviction of a particular category of offense, to impose LWOP. Most prominently in the United States, mandatory LWOP for certain forms of homicide is now found in all individual states that have abolished the death penalty, except Alaska, which has only de facto life.[3] In a few countries, such as Turkey, a life sentence that is aggravated in some other way, for example by specifying that the regime be harsher, may also be mandatory for a specific offense.[4]

In the United States, LWOP sentences for adults have not been challenged successfully on the primary basis that they are mandatory. In other parts of the world, however, such challenges have emerged in parallel with the rejection of the mandatory imposition of the death penalty. The leading case is *De Boucherville v. Government of Mauritius,* in which, in 2008, the Privy Council ruled that the mandatory LWOP sentence imposed on conviction for murder was an inhuman and degrading punishment, in breach of the Constitution of Mauritius.[5] The Privy Council came to this conclusion on the explicit basis that serving a life sentence for the whole of an offender's life, in principle amounted to such a breach of human rights and that it was akin to a death sentence.

In this regard, the Privy Council commented that the difference between capital punishment and life imprisonment can be exaggerated, and argued that, like the mandatory death penalty, a mandatory LWOP sentence ran an unacceptable risk of producing grossly disproportionate outcomes. This basis for the conclusion of the Privy Council decision in *De Boucherville* is important, for, as the court of final instance for a number of former British colonies, the Privy Council had led the way in outlawing mandatory death sentences, in the Caribbean in particular. This enabled the Privy Council to draw on its own worldwide jurisprudence on the death penalty and to extend it to LWOP.[6]

In 2016, the impact of the Privy Council jurisprudence was seen in Belize, where the court of appeal struck down a mandatory LWOP sentence for murder.[7] The immediate bases for the decision were the provisions in the Constitution of Belize that guarantee a fair hearing for a person charged with a criminal offense and prohibit inhuman or degrading punishment.[8] The court ruled that the mandatory sentence precluded a fair hearing, after which an appropriate sentence could be imposed, as it did not allow the seriousness of the particular conduct that comprised the offense to be considered. It also found that in this instance—a murder committed by a nineteen-year-old with a clean criminal record—an LWOP sentence would be disproportionately severe, and that under the circumstances, it would be an inhuman and degrading punishment for this particular offender. The court of appeal set aside the life sentence and replaced it with a fixed term of thirty years. In coming to this conclusion, the Belizean court referred with approval to the *De Boucherville* case and also to the parallel with Privy Council decisions in which mandatory death sentences had been found to be disproportionately severe.[9] The government of Belize responded in 2017 by amending the sentencing provisions in the Belizean criminal code relating to murder and by introducing a parole board to consider the release of life-sentenced prisoners. In 2018, the Caribbean Court of Justice ruled on appeal from the Court of Appeal of Belize that the amendment to the criminal code made the life sentences discretionary, and that the new parole system was in conformity with the Constitution of Belize.[10]

In the European context, such decisions are relatively rare, for the focus has been more on the inherent acceptability of LWOP sentences rather than on their mandatory nature. However, in 2002, the House of Lords in the United Kingdom did comment hypothetically that, if "on imposition of a mandatory life sentence for murder the convicted murderer forfeited his liberty to the state for the rest of his days," such a sentence would violate Articles 3 and 5 of the European Convention on Human Rights by "being arbitrary and disproportionate."[11]

There is also the possibility that a mandatory life sentence could allow a sentencing court a choice between types of life sentences or a range of LWP sentences. The court may well retain a second level of discretion to set the minimum period before release can be considered. It may also be able to shape, indirectly in other ways, the eventual release decision through the specific life sentence it imposes. We return to the question of different minimum periods later in this discussion.

Other than that, when a court has given a verdict convicting a person of a crime for which there is a mandatory life sentence prescribed by law, usually in the penal code, there is ostensibly little discretion that it can exercise. This has not excluded attempts to do so by appealing to higher legal norms than those implicit in the criminal statute. One instance in which this was done occurred in 1981, when the Federal Court for Criminal Cases in Germany was confronted by an appeal in the case of a homicide committed by stealth. The facts clearly met the definition of murder, but the homicide had been initiated as a result of gross provocation and threats. The German federal court upheld the conviction for murder, but imposed a lesser sentence than the life imprisonment that, in terms of the German Penal Code, is mandatory for this offense. The federal court did so because it regarded proportionality between punishment and the seriousness of the specific offense as a fundamental constitutional principle, which trumped even the mandatory life sentence prescribed in the penal code. The German federal court held that, in such circumstances, a so-called *Rechtsfolgenlösung* (literally a "legal result solution") should apply. This meant that, where a mandatory life sentence would be disproportionate to the crime committed, a solution had to be found that allowed the sentencing court to come to a more equitable legal result. In this rare instance, the overriding constitutional principle allowed extenuating factors that reduced the seriousness of the offense to be considered, even when there was no specific legislative provision for it to be done.[12] Doctrinal German criminal lawyers have been highly critical of this judgment, seeing it as an "emergency solution" that undermined legal certainty, and even a declaration that the accepted German definition of murder was morally bankrupt.[13] In practice, however, perhaps because of its radical character, it has been applied only rarely.

A similar argument based on the constitutional primacy of proportionate sentencing was put forward in Canada, in the case of *R v. Latimer*.[14] The appellant in this case challenged a mandatory life sentence for second degree murder, on the grounds that the facts of his individual case were so exceptional that the supreme court should find the sentence grossly disproportionate. The facts of the case, a mercy killing, were so unusual that the trial jury, which in Canada did not have the power to sentence, had recommended a very lenient sentence, and the trial judge had granted a constitutional exemption from the mandatory life sentence and imposed a one-year sentence with one year on probation. However, this had been upset on appeal and the mandatory life sentence reinstated, a decision that Latimer in turn challenged before the Supreme Court of Canada.

Latimer may have expected the Supreme Court to be sympathetic, for there was a recent precedent, not involving life imprisonment directly, where the supreme court had indicated that an unusual set of circumstances could result in a constitutional exception.[15] In such circumstances it would not be necessary to argue that the legislation setting the mandatory penalty had to be struck down on the basis that it was grossly disproportionate and therefore an infringement of the prohibition on cruel and unusual punishment in the Canadian Charter of Rights. All that the individual would have to show was that the mandatory sentence was grossly disproportionate to what had happened in his particular circumstances.

The Supreme Court of Canada was unsympathetic, however; and not only on the question of whether the unusual facts of the case justified a lesser sentence. It also emphasized that, for a crime as uniquely serious as murder, parliament was entitled to set mandatory life sentences, and to provide for inflexible minimum periods before release could be considered—ten years in the case of the second degree murder of which Latimer had been convicted. The court found that the vital role that the mandatory minimum sentence plays in denouncing murder trumped otherwise important sentencing considerations, such as rehabilitation, specific deterrence and protection of the public. In the view of the court, for an offense as serious as murder, even in the exceptional mitigating circumstances of the *Latimer* case, these considerations were an insufficient ground for departing from the sentence prescribed in the criminal code.

The outcome of the *Latimer* case indicates how hard courts, even in a relatively liberal jurisdiction like Canada, find it not to impose a mandatory life sentence where the criminal law requires it directly.[16] In contrast, the Court of Appeal in Belize, operating within an almost identical constitutional framework to that in Canada, was prepared to set aside a mandatory life sentence entirely and impose a fixed term. A possible explanation is that in Belize the mandatory sentence was LWOP and that in Canada it was LWP, but that does not fully explain the different approaches.

Mandatory Alternatives

If mandatory life imprisonment for particular offenses has the flaw that it may result in disproportionate sentences, can the problem be resolved by stipulating an alternative to such life sentences? This question is somewhat disingenuous, for it depends on what the alternative is. There are several countries where, in law, for key offenses, the only alternative to life imprisonment is death. Within this larger group, there is an important subgroup where LWOP and death are the only alternatives. Identifying the countries for which life imprisonment of some type and the death penalty are realistically the only options is a complex task. Among the 153 countries for which we were able to collect data on what offenses carry life or death sentences, 29 offered an alternative between these two sentences.[17] Of these, ten were de facto abolitionist in respect of the death penalty, which meant there is no real alternative at all.[18] Of the twenty-five countries remaining, eight countries had an effective choice between death and LWOP.[19] In addition, there were sixteen countries that had alternatives between death and LWP.[20] The United States was the only country in which, in various jurisdictions, both death and LWOP, and death and LWP were options.

When it comes to understanding the decision on whether to impose the death penalty or LWOP, very little is known about what happens outside the United States. In part, this is because, as in India, LWOP has only recently become the mandatory alternative for murder,[21] or, as in Malaysia, the mandatory alternative applies only to a very limited range of offenses.[22] The US experience is significant, however, in that LWOP was widely adopted from the 1970s onwards as an alternative to the death penalty. In some instances, it formally replaced the death penalty and simply became a mandatory sentence, an ultimate penalty for offenses that had previously carried the death sentence, and for more offenses besides. In other instances though, it became the sole alternative to the death penalty for adults who commit homicide.[23] In these instances, after some initial hesitation, the law has developed to the point that juries are now told where there is a provision for LWOP as an alternate sentence that will be imposed automatically if they find that the death penalty should not be imposed.[24]

The impact of this development has to be understood in the light of the unique US requirement that in capital cases, juries, and not trial judges, must not only decide on guilt or innocence. They must also decide whether the aggravating circumstances that are necessary for imposing the death penalty are present and, if they are, whether they are not outweighed by mitigating circumstances.[25] In this context, having LWOP as an alternative has arguably meant that juries are more likely to convict of an offense that potentially carries the death penalty, confident that they will not have to impose a death sentence as the alternative of LWOP will follow if they decline to do so. The paradoxical effect of having LWOP as a mandatory alternative to death is that it ends up being used in cases that would never have led to the death penalty being imposed in the first place. Absent the mandatory LWOP as an alternative, the conviction may have been of a lesser charge, and a less severe sentence than LWOP may have followed. Although it is difficult to demonstrate in practice, this may be one of the reasons for the high number of LWOP sentences in the United States as compared to any other country in the world.[26]

Qualified Mandatory

Where courts do have some discretion on whether to impose life imprisonment or a lesser sentence, which is invariably a fixed term of imprisonment, such discretion can be structured in more or less restrictive ways. The most limited form would be a qualified mandatory sentence. Once a person has been convicted of a particular offense, or combination of offenses, a life sentence could be mandatory, but with the qualification that the sentencing court has a discretion not to do so if certain conditions are met. The extent of the power to depart from a prescribed life sentence depends not only on how the conditions are formulated in law, usually in the penal code or the criminal procedure code of the country concerned, but also on subtler traditions of judicial interpretation of statutory constraints on the judges' power to determine sentence.

Perhaps the most common form that the qualification of the duty takes is that a penal code states simply that particular offenses are to be punished by life imprisonment, but then goes on to provide in general terms that, if "mitigating factors" are present, the sentencing court may impose a lesser sentence. This is most commonly expressed as a general power to mitigate prescribed sentences of all kinds, not just life imprisonment. For example, most Francophone African countries that do allow for mitigating circumstances only have a general provision stating that such factors can be taken into account at the point of sentencing, whatever the offense or the sentence incurred may be.[27] In other instances, the mitigation rules are specific to life imprisonment. Thus, Article 95 of the Criminal Code of Cambodia refers specifically to the mitigation of sentences of life imprisonment, and one finds a similar provision in Article 65 of the Criminal Code of Taiwan.

Sometimes, but not always, the lesser sentence that may be imposed in lieu of life imprisonment may be further qualified. In this respect, we can distinguish between four different approaches.

Absolute Discretion

In certain cases, the sentencing court is granted absolute discretion as to the sentence it can impose in the event of mitigating circumstances. The Penal Code of Burundi, for instance, states that "[i]n the event of mitigating circumstances, prison sentences may be reduced to an extent determined by the judge."[28]

Broad but Not Unlimited Discretion

In other countries, the sentencing judge, when mitigating a sentence, has broad but not unlimited discretion, as the relevant provisions fix a minimum sentence beyond which the judge cannot go. These minimum sentences vary greatly, from "no less than six months" in Iraq[29] to a term of no less than ten years, as is the case, for instance, in Greece, Rwanda, and Cameroon.[30] In one interesting example, Japan limits the sentencing court's discretion in a different way, by setting not a minimum, but a rather a maximum mitigated sentence of thirty years.[31]

A Range of Years

In yet another group of countries, the sentencing court is given a range of years within which a fixed-term alternative to a life sentence must fall. These ranges can be broad—for example, between three and forty years in Belgium, or between five and twenty years in Mali—or limited, such as between twenty and twenty-four years in Somalia, or between fifteen and twenty years in Taiwan. However, most of the examples of fixed-term alternatives that we have been able to identify involve ten- to twenty- or ten- to thirty-year sentences.[32]

A Single Alternative

Finally, in a few rare examples, the sentencing judge has no discretionary power at all as far as the alternative is concerned, for the law prescribes exactly the fixed-term sentence that should replace life imprisonment, should there be mitigating circumstances. An interesting example is Somalia, where, as we mentioned above, the judge may set a sentence between twenty and twenty-four years if there is a single mitigating circumstance; however, if there is more than one such circumstance, the mitigated sentence is fixed at ten years.[33] Similarly, in France, specifically for the case of a crime committed by a person who, at the time, "was suffering from a psychological or neuropsychological disorder which reduced his discernment or impeded his ability to control his actions" (but who retains sufficient criminal capacity and remains punishable), a life sentence is to be reduced to a thirty-year sentence.[34]

Qualified mandatory life sentences are not necessarily introduced to give sentencing courts more discretion. They may also serve to limit the discretion that courts previously had not to impose life imprisonment. A clear example is the 1997 Criminal Law Amendment Act in South Africa, which lists a number of offenses in a schedule and provides that they shall be punished with life imprisonment. However the same act then goes on to provide that the sentencing court may impose a "lesser sentence" if it is satisfied that "substantial and compelling circumstances exist" which justify it in taking this step.[35]

The 1997 act, which also formally removed the death penalty from South African sentencing law, was explicitly designed to encourage courts to impose life imprisonment more often. Sentencing courts did not interpret "substantial and compelling circumstances," which was not a term of art in South African law, consistently; and in 2001 the Supreme Court of Appeal in South Africa was called upon to interpret the phrase. It did so by emphasizing that the new legislation had limited, but not eliminated, sentencing discretion. Nevertheless, ordinarily and in the absence of weighty justification, courts should impose life imprisonment for the listed crimes in the specified circumstances. The Supreme Court of Appeal underlined that "[u]nless there are, and can be seen to be, truly convincing reasons for a different response, the crimes in question are therefore required to elicit a severe, standardised and consistent response from the courts."[36] Departures, could only take place if, in the circumstances of the particular case, the sentencing court was satisfied that the prescribed sentence would be unjust in that it would be disproportionate to the crime, the criminal, and the needs of society. What this interpretation clearly tried to do was to maintain an element of proportionality in sentencing decisions, while giving weight to the intention of the legislature. This balancing exercise was subsequently approved by the South African Constitutional Court.[37] However, the impact of the 1997 legislative change was a dramatic increase in the use of life imprisonment in South Africa, which went far beyond the substitution of life imprisonment for recently abolished death sentences.

Sometimes the mandatory regimes can be very complex and allow sentencing courts a good deal of discretion. An example is the sentence of life imprisonment for a second listed offense, which was introduced in England in 2012 to replace imprisonment for public protection, an informal life sentence that was repealed in that year.[38] On its face, the then new sentence is mandatory for a second offense listed in a schedule of forty-two offenses, for some of which a discretionary life sentence could be imposed in its own right. However, the new life sentence for a second listed offense applies only if it meets two further conditions. These are, first, a sentence condition, that the court would have imposed an effective term of more than ten years for the offense; and second, a previous offense condition, that the previous offense is one that is also on the list of forty-two offenses and that it was punished at the time by a sentence of five years or more. These technical conditions greatly limit the scope of the new "mandatory" sentence. Second, the sentencing court does not have to impose the life sentence for an offense that meets all these quantifications "if it is of the opinion that there are particular circumstances which (a) relate to the offense, to the previous offense . . . or to the offender, and (b) would make it unjust to do so in all the circumstances."[39] The overall result is that a provision that begins by saying that a court "must impose a life sentence" is highly limited in its application, and even where the formal requirements are met, the sentencing court still has very wide scope to depart.[40]

Discretionary Life Imprisonment

Beyond the variations on mandatory life imprisonment come discretionary sentences, where the choice is between some type of life imprisonment and another sentence, usually a fixed term of imprisonment. In some instances, this choice may be formally unrestricted. For example, Article 27(2) of the Penal Code of Malawi provides simply that "[a] person liable to imprisonment for life or any other period may be sentenced for any shorter term." However, the range of choice may be restricted, too, without making the life sentence mandatory. For example, for a specific offense the choice may be life imprisonment or a particular fixed term, say fifteen years, or between ten and fifteen years. We regard all these variations as broadly discretionary, as the court is not pressed by the statute to impose life imprisonment, unlike the situation with the qualified mandatory life sentences discussed above.

Sometimes the discretionary choice can even be between a sentence of death and various forms of life imprisonment. In Uganda, since the death penalty ceased to be mandatory in 2009, the choice of a sentence in a capital case, once it has been decided not to impose the death penalty, is between LWOP and merely symbolic life sentences, where release after twenty years is guaranteed.[41] Similarly in Pakistan, courts that decide not to impose a death sentence impose life imprisonment, which they sometimes accompany with orders that parole should never be considered, while in other cases they do not make such orders, but allow the parole process to run its course.[42]

In addition to providing courts with the authority to exercise their discretion when imposing life sentences, the law may seek to influence how that discretion is exercised in ways other than making life imprisonment a mandatory sentence, and then providing alternatives to it. Indeed, it may do the opposite: that is, it may specify that life sentences should not be the norm. This may be done by allowing for their imposition only if certain general criteria are met. An example is to be found in the Statute of the International Criminal Court (ICC), which sets out the primary penalties that the ICC may impose: "(a) Imprisonment for a specified number of years, which may not exceed a maximum of 30 years; or (b) A term of life imprisonment when justified by the extreme gravity of the crime and the individual circumstances of the convicted person."[43]

This formulation emphasizes the severity of life imprisonment as a punishment, for the crimes of genocide, crimes against humanity and war crimes, over which the ICC has jurisdiction, are usually very grave. The decision by the authors of the Rome Statute to limit its use further in this context points to a proportionality test would require life imprisonment to be imposed sparingly.

This is underlined by the Rules of Procedure and Evidence of the ICC, which explain that evidence of the extreme gravity of the crime and the individual circumstances of the convicted person must be based in the existence of one or more aggravating circumstances. The Rules of Procedure and Evidence provide a list of aggravating circumstances, but, even if one or more of them is present, life imprisonment does not follow automatically, as they must be balanced against mitigating circumstances. Examples of mitigating circumstances are given in the rules, but the ICC may consider other mitigating circumstances too. In the case of aggravating circumstances, the court is bound by the list in the rules, or a specific finding that there are other aggravating circumstances that are similar to those mentioned in the rules.[44]

Shaping Life Imprisonment at Sentencing

Once a life sentence has been imposed, whether mandatory or discretionary, courts are given varying degrees of freedom to set the minimum terms to be served before release can be considered. Where the type of life imprisonment imposed is LWOP, there is no minimum to be set and nothing further the sentencing court can do. Perhaps the sentencing judge may add a note to the file, which the head of state may consider in forthcoming clemency procedures. But that is probably all that can be done, if it may legally be done at all.

LWP sentences all have minimum periods before release can routinely be considered. These can usefully be divided into three subcategories: those where courts have no statutory discretion in setting the minimum but can still influence the outcome: limited discretion provided for by statute; and full discretion.

Indirect Influence on Minimum Periods

It is common practice for life imprisonment statutes to provide a single minimum period that has to be served before release can be considered.[45] In most instances, where the minimum period is a single number of years prescribed by statute, the sentencing court ostensibly has no way of influencing how this minimum period is applied. However, in some countries, as part of its judgment, a sentencing court may still make additional findings that may result in the consideration of release being delayed beyond the fixed minimum period set in legislation. This is the case in Germany where, although the law provides that prisoners serving life sentences may have their detention reviewed after fifteen years, the court that makes the release decision is enjoined to take into account the seriousness of the prisoner's guilt (*die Schwere der Schuld*) when deciding whether to release or to postpone consideration of release to a later date.[46] In 1992, the German Federal Constitutional Court interpreted this provision to place a duty on the sentencing court to consider the seriousness of the guilt, when imposing a life sentence. If the sentencing court did not rule that the guilt was particularly severe, the court considering release would not be allowed to have regard to this factor when making its decision. If, however, the sentencing court made a finding that guilt was particularly severe, then the releasing court would have to take this factor into account.[47]

Did this strategy of influencing the body responsible for release go far enough to ensure that the mandatory life sentences that German courts must impose make them proportionate to the specific offense? In 1992, a majority of the German Federal Constitutional Court believed that it did. The chair of the constitutional court chamber, judge Ernst Mahrenholz, dissented. In his opinion, attempting to meet the requirements of proportionality by laying down how the seriousness of the guilt of the offender should be interpreted at a later stage was likely to be ineffective.[48] Judge Mahrenholz concluded that, although the court had not been asked to consider the question of the mandatory nature of the sentence of life imprisonment for murder, a reconsideration of this aspect of the life sentence was unavoidable. He explained that it had become increasingly clear that the complicated procedure prescribed by the German Penal Code made it impossible to ensure that a punishment that would meet the constitutional standard of proportionality to the guilt of the offender would result. From the recognition that there were degrees of guilt in murder, which was inherent in the seriousness of the guilt test, should follow the simple conclusion that not all instances of murder should be punished with life imprisonment. In his view, there were fundamental constitutional objections to the mandatory life sentences specified in the provisions relating to murder.[49]

This dissenting conclusion found wide support among influential German scholars, who argued that the majority judgment would not succeed in creating uniformity, which had been the primary reason for moving away from the old practice of release by executive commutation. The dissenting opinion was welcomed as an indication that the mandatory life sentence for murder should be reconsidered, even where life-sentenced prisoners did have a prospect of release.[50]

Limited Discretion in Setting the Minimum

A court that imposes a LWP sentence, whether as a matter of discretion or mandatorily as a matter of law, may also have to apply legislation that limits its discretion in setting the minimum term to be served before release may be considered. In some instances, the legislatively prescribed sentence is a term of life imprisonment with a minimum period of between x and y years; or a minimum period of above z years. In the state of New York, for example, persistent felony offenders must be sentenced to life imprisonment, but the minimum term is somewhat flexible: between fifteen and twenty-five years.[51] In such a case, once someone has been found to be a persistent felony offender, all the sentencing court has to do is to set a minimum period to be served before parole can be considered. In considering sentence, a court may exercise its discretion by looking at the nature, not only of the current offense, but also of the earlier offenses. For example, in 2012 in *People v. Smart,* the appellate court ruled that, although the offender was rightly designated a persistent felon, neither his previous convictions, nor his current crime were directly violent. Therefore, his minimum term should be reduced from twenty years, as imposed by the trial court, to fifteen years. The maximum, life imprisonment, remained mandatory and unaltered.[52]

A similar choice exists in New Zealand. There, a court sentencing a person convicted of murder must decide on whether to impose a life sentence or not. (It must impose life unless it would be manifestly unjust to do so: an example of a qualified alternative.)[53] Once having decided to impose a life sentence, it has to make a further choice between LWOP or a life sentence with a minimum period of at least ten years. New Zealand sentencing law structures this last choice by requiring that a court can only impose LWOP if it is satisfied that no minimum term would be sufficient for:

(a) holding the offender accountable for the harm done to the victim and the community by the offending;

(b) denouncing the conduct in which the offender was involved;

(c) deterring the offender or other persons from committing the same or a
      similar offence; [or]

(d) protecting the community from the offender.[54]

In practice, no LWOP sentence has ever been imposed in New Zealand, and the key decision that has to be taken is whether the minimum period will be longer than ten years and if so, how much.

In French law, too, courts have an automatic discretion in all life imprisonment cases to set a minimum period of between eighteen and twenty-two years. If they go beyond the eighteen-year minimum, they have to make a special finding to do so.[55] If life imprisonment is imposed for certain forms of violent assassination, the court may extend the minimum period to up to thirty years, again with the necessary finding.[56]

The power to set minimum periods may also operate in systems where the life sentence itself is discretionary. This power may be used to make the life sentence more, rather than less, severe. In Poland, where courts have a discretion whether or not to impose life imprisonment for murder, the life sentence comes with a minimum term of at least twenty-five years. However, for offenders "with a high degree of moral corruption" courts have a discretion to impose a longer minimum period. A recent study shows that about a third of all Polish prisoners serving life sentences (100 out of 301) face minimum periods ranging from thirty to fifty years, thus ensuring that their sentences will be much longer than the European norm.[57]

Fully Discretionary Minimum Periods

In other instances where primary legislation says little or nothing about minimum periods at all, a separate hearing is held after the imposition of a life sentence to set a minimum period. In the United Kingdom, this has been the case for discretionary life sentences since 1991 and for mandatory life sentences, which effectively are only for murder, since 2002.[58]

The established test in the United Kingdom for determining the minimum period is for trial judges to ask themselves what fixed-term sentence they would have imposed if they had not imposed a life sentence. The minimum period would then be half of that hypothetical sentence, minus any period spent on remand. The underlying thinking is that a person sentenced to a fixed term of, say, twenty years, would be considered for release after ten years, so that a person sentenced to life imprisonment for the same offense, but for which a life sentence was thought to be appropriate, should be sentenced to life imprisonment with a minimum of ten years. The Criminal Justice Act of 2003 modified the position where life imprisonment for murder is concerned, by setting out in a schedule various starting points that are to be adopted in murder of various degrees of seriousness. These range from fifteen years for the least serious, to a whole life order, where there would be no minimum period, for the most serious. The schedule gives examples of crimes that carry various starting points: for example, for murder where a knife was used, the starting point is twenty-five years. Sentencing courts have to give judgments in public to explain why they adopt particular starting points or why they depart from them. However, the courts are free to depart and, in principle, the minimum period is still determined by the courts asking themselves the same hypothetical question about the fixed-term sentence they would otherwise have imposed.[59] Evidence shows that minimum periods set in this way have grown longer since 2003, and there is a strong suggestion that the legislative starting points introduced in 2003 have contributed to this.[60]

Countries that follow in the English procedural tradition grant their sentencing courts similar discretion. For example, the law in the British Virgin Islands also allows judges to set minimum periods.[61] While there is no equivalent to the English schedule of starting points, courts there nevertheless tend to refer to the British schedule for guidance about minimum periods in murder cases.[62] The law in the Cayman Islands is similar. Courts have an unfettered discretion to set minimum periods for life sentences for all offenses except murder. For murder they must normally set a minimum period of thirty years, but they may depart either upward or downward from the minimum, if there are aggravating or extenuating circumstances justifying such a departure. If they do depart from the norm of thirty years, they must give reasons for doing so.[63]

The impact of giving courts this discretion varies. In England and Wales, the courts routinely set minimum periods. Only 50 of the 7,468 persons serving life sentences in 2014 had whole life orders, which exclude minimum periods.[64] In Scotland, where the law is largely similar in other aspects, courts have to set a minimum period in every case, as they are not allowed to make whole-life orders.[65]

Giving courts the discretion to set minimum periods is not always benign. In Malta, where sentencing courts may set minimum periods in cases of life imprisonment, they chose not to do so. As a result, all but one of the twelve life-sentenced prisoners in Malta were serving an LWOP sentence.[66]

The Impact of Minimum Periods

What does the sentencing court envisage when it sets a minimum period, and do limits on minimum sentences constrain the decisions of releasing authorities whether judges, parole boards, or others?

In English law, as well as systems that adopt broadly the same approach, the position is relatively clear. The minimum period in these systems is explicitly the minimum that is necessary for purposes of retribution and deterrence. This means that sentencing courts can expect, as a matter of law, that the parole board will only consider the continued danger that the prisoner poses to society when deciding on release. In other words, the elements of the sentence tied to its proportionality to the offense are dealt with at the sentencing stage by the setting of the minimum period.

In contrast to the position in the United Kingdom, it seems that in some systems the significance of a minimum period determined as part of the sentencing process, for each individual offender on the basis of the offense, can effectively be ignored. That would appear to be the case in New York, where the seriousness of the offense can be used to justify the continued detention of a prisoner beyond the minimum period set by the court, even if every other consideration points in favor of release.[67]

The reality is that no sentencing court can rest assured that setting a minimum period will lead to a proportionate sentence being served, even where there are no grounds, other than those related to the offense, for keeping the life-sentenced prisoner in prison for longer than what the sentencing court intended. This reality reinforces the argument against mandatory life sentences that seek to achieve proportionality by setting minimum periods that a parole board must subsequently consider. As Justice Adrian Saunders explained in 2018 in the Caribbean Court of Justice:

> A commendable Parole Act ameliorates but does not fully compensate for the vice that renders the prescription of mandatory life imprisonment penalties

to be unconstitutional. Every person sentenced under such a regime who, but for the legislature's direction, might have received a judicially determined sentence that was for a duration that was substantially less than life imprisonment is, in a sense, short-changed. The outer extremity of his possible incarceration would not be determined and pronounced by a court upon the conclusion of his trial, as should ideally be the case after every criminal trial.[68]

Commutation and the Imposition of Life Sentences

Courts are not necessarily responsible for imposing life sentences. Thus far, we have focused on the imposition of life sentences by courts within a legislative framework. However, a peculiarity of life sentences is that they may be imposed by the executive, when commuting death sentences. Therefore, in countries that retain capital punishment, we must consider commutation of sentence as a means of imposing life imprisonment and not only as an aspect of the clemency powers that the head of state may exercise to release life prisoners.

China provides a dramatic example of a post-sentence process that may result in the imposition of life imprisonment. In China, a significant number of persons convicted of serious offenses are sentenced to suspended death sentences that may be converted to life imprisonment, or even to a fixed term of years, after two years in prison. The precise number is unknown, but indications are that the number of suspended death sentences imposed has overtaken the number of immediate death sentences. Of those given a suspended death sentence, there are indications that over 95 percent have their sentences converted to imprisonment. Most of them are given life sentences after two years and, as far can be ascertained, all they need to do during those crucial two years is refrain from committing further offenses. To get a suspended death sentence converted immediately into a fixed term, they need to perform "deeds of great merit," something difficult to achieve in prison. The decision on whether to convert a suspended death sentence into life imprisonment (or a lesser term) is taken administratively within the prison system.

Until 2015, such a conversion would always be subject to consideration for release after a minimum period had been served. Since 2015, however, in cases of corruption, the Chinese Penal Code has allowed the court imposing a suspended death sentence after conviction to stipulate that, if the death sentence is converted after two years, it can only be replaced with a life sentence with no release possible. The imposition of LWOP was thus introduced indirectly into the Chinese system.[69]

The Chinese system of converting certain death sentences into life imprisonment with relative ease is unusual. However, the same result of large-scale imposition of life imprisonment through executive intervention can be achieved by the exercise of clemency within a more conventional framework. Kenya provides a dramatic example. In 2014, Kenya had the highest net number of LWOP prisoners (3,676) that we could identify outside the United States. This number is largely the result of two factors: Kenya's answer to the overcrowding problem on death row, and the challenges to the legality of mandatory death sentences has been to use the president's clemency powers to convert death sentences to LWOP. In 2009 and again in 2016, the president commuted all death sentences to LWOP. The numbers were very high, more than 4,000 in 2009 and more than 2,700 in 2016, indicating that these commutations were the legal basis of the life sentences of most prisoners in Kenyan prisons.[70] In December 2017, the Supreme Court of Kenya declared mandatory death sentences unconstitutional. It required parliament to legislate in response to its decision, warning that the mandatory death sentence should not be replaced by mandatory LWOP.[71] It is not yet clear how the Kenyan parliament will respond, or what impact this will have on the number of life-sentenced prisoners in Kenyan prisons.

In India, where there is a more structured clemency process, the great majority of persons facing death sentences end up serving life sentences: "Between 2001 and 2012, nearly 6,000 convicts were awarded the death penalty, of which nearly 1,600 were confirmed while 4,400 were commuted to life imprisonment—and only one was executed."[72]

In the United States, commutation of death sentences is a lesser source of prisoners serving LWOP and other life sentences, but the impact of such commutation is not negligible. The legal basis for LWOP was created by the US Supreme Court in 1974 when it upheld a decision that the president had taken in 1960 to commute a death sentence and substituted LWOP for it.[73]

The Death Penalty Information Center has recorded 280 cases where persons on death row in the United States had their sentences commuted, on humanitarian grounds, between 1977 and 2015. The majority of these had their sentences commuted to LWOP. Although during this period there has been a steady trickle of such commutations, in 2003 the number increased, when 167 death sentences were commuted on a single occasion by the governor of Illinois. Four of these had their sentences commuted to a fixed term of forty years (de facto life sentences), while the remainder had their death sentences commuted to LWOP. In addition to these "humanitarian" commutations, an unknown additional number had their sentences commuted for reasons of judicial expediency, for example where attempting to uphold a death sentence would require a costly and difficult retrial but LWOP imposed in this way was likely to remain unchallenged.[74]

A particular danger of imposing life imprisonment through commutation is that it may result in the imposition of types of life imprisonment that are more severe than the life sentences that the courts would, or even legally could, impose. In Trinidad and Tobago, the president commuted a disputed death sentence to a fixed term of seventy-five years, in a de facto form of LWOP. This minimum term is far longer than that otherwise imposed in that country. Moreover, it was imposed without any indication of how this very long minimum term was arrived at. Nevertheless, the power of the president to do so was upheld by the Court of Appeal of Trinidad and Tobago, and subsequently by the Privy Council.[75]

Other Participants in the Imposition of Life Imprisonment

In addition to courts and the executive that can impose life sentences directly, it is important to recognize that others in the system may play a significant part in determining whether or not life sentences are imposed. Primary among these are the prosecutors. They decide whether to bring charges that carry life sentences. This is particularly important in the case of mandatory sentences and even more so in the case of mandatory LWOP sentences where the courts have no discretion to shape the outcome following a conviction.

If appropriately exercised, prosecutorial discretion is not necessarily a bad thing. The US Supreme Court has recognized that, by not charging a person with relatively less serious offenses, such as possession of a large quantity of drugs, which nonetheless carry mandatory LWOP, prosecutors may avoid the imposition of mandatory LWOP in cases where an LWOP sentence would be disproportionately severe. As justice Anthony Kennedy commented in the US Supreme Court in *Harmelin v. Michigan:* "Prosecutorial discretion . . . provide[s] means for the State to avert . . . unjust sentences."[76] However, the obvious difficulty is that the exercise of such discretion is not subject to judicial control. Therefore, courts cannot ensure a just outcome in the same way as they can when they have the power to decide on the sentence.

In cases involving plea bargaining, prosecutorial discretion can be exercised in a way that would lead to life sentences in circumstances where otherwise they would not have been imposed. In *Bordenkircher v. Hayes*,[77] the accused had refused to plead guilty to a charge with a sentence of five years. He was recharged with an offense carrying life imprisonment and was duly convicted and given a life sentence. The US Supreme Court declined to exercise any judicial supervision of this exercise of prosecutorial discretion, as the accused had refused the offer to plead guilty and would have to accept the consequences of his decision. This is an extreme example of the exercise of prosecutorial power; but even in systems that formally allow prosecutors far less discretion, decisions in borderline cases, on whether to charge with murder rather than manslaughter, for example, may determine whether a life sentence can be imposed or not.

Prosecutorial discretion can also play a key role in determining whether children face the risk of having life sentences imposed on them. In some jurisdictions, life sentences can only be imposed on children if they are tried as adults. Prosecutors may have the discretion to decide whether a child is tried as an adult, or as a child before a juvenile court where the sentencing jurisdiction usually does not include life imprisonment.

In many jurisdictions, two further groups play a key role in whether or not to impose life imprisonment: experts on dangerousness, and victims and victims' families. Experts on dangerousness may be psychiatrists or probation officers who, at the sentencing stage of proceedings, make predictions of the risk that a convicted person may pose to society in the future. At this stage, we have only limited comparative evidence about the role such experts play. We do know that the imposition of informal life sentences aimed specifically at indefinite post-conviction preventive detention depends crucially on psychiatric evidence of dangerousness. This is true both in single-track systems, such as South Africa and Canada, and in dual-track systems, such as Germany, the Netherlands, Belgium, and the Scandinavian countries, which regard these forms of detention as security measures rather than as punishment. Even there, the courts typically have the final say about whether the measure should be imposed or not, although a minimum level of psychiatric evidence is necessary to allow them to go ahead.

When it comes to the imposition of formal life sentences, the role of psychiatrists and other experts varies considerably. Clearly, where the life sentence is mandatory for a particular offense, they have no role related directly to sentence, although their assessment may be relevant to establishing a specific form of intention, which may impact indirectly on the sentence. There is also the possibility that a life sentence may be mandatory if, in addition to the offense requirement, there is evidence of the required level of dangerousness. In this case, the evidence of the psychiatrist may be crucial. Alternatively, a probation officer or other expert may present evidence based on an "objective" risk assessment instrument. Such instruments, which are widely used in the United States, not only in life imprisonment cases, are highly controversial.[78]

Where life sentences are discretionary and future dangerousness is a factor to be taken into consideration, the same expertise comes into play, be it clinical or risk instrument based. Psychiatric experts may also have further functions determining whether additional requirements relating to mental health are met. In England and Wales, for example, historically the common law required that, before a discretionary life sentence could be imposed, it had to be shown, inter alia, that the offender was a person of "unstable character likely to commit an offence in the future."[79] This requirement meant that psychiatric evidence was invariably sought on this point. This requirement was replaced in 2008 by a more conventional assessment of the risk of serious dangerousness posed by the offender, which a court may now find without considering medical evidence, for in the view of the Court of Appeal, "the danger could be represented by a wholly rational individual."[80] Nevertheless, psychiatric evidence on potential dangerousness and its causes is still often sought by English and Welsh courts deciding whether to exercise their discretion to impose life sentences.

In many jurisdictions, victims of crime, or family members of the deceased, who may be indirect victims too, are participating to an increasing extent in the sentencing process. While the rights of victims to participate and to describe the impact of the offense on them are largely undisputed, there has been controversy about whether they should be allowed to propose a life or other sentence.[81] This controversy is not unique to life imprisonment, but given the severity of the sentence, it is of particular salience in this regard.

Summary and Conclusion

Rules governing how life sentences should be imposed play a varying but significant role in determining whether they are imposed. Some of these rules serve the principle of proportionality between the punishment and the crime. In many jurisdictions, the power to impose LWOP is more restricted than for LWP. For LWP sentences, there are also different techniques for ensuring at the imposition stage that, as far as possible, they will be implemented in a way that introduces proportionality considerations by the back door. This may be done by setting an appropriate minimum period after which release must be considered, or by encouraging release after a statutorily fixed, minimum period has been served.

Other rules make it harder to ensure that life sentences are imposed only when they are proportionate to the crime. Mandatory LWOP sentences make it impossible to take account of the seriousness of the particular crime. Mandatory LWP sentences may also be disproportionately severe, as provision for early release is not a failsafe way of ensuring that that will not be implemented for longer than is justified by the offense.

The role of authorities, other than sentencing courts, in determining the imposition of a life sentence should not be underestimated. Prosecutorial discretion during plea bargaining, where life imprisonment can be threatened or can be presented as a softer option in capital cases, and an emphasis on dangerousness brought into the sentencing process by psychiatric and other experts as well as by victims of crime, may all lead to less weight being attached to concerns of offense proportionality.

In all, this chapter presents a picture of courts and other decision makers operating within varying frameworks and attaching different degrees of significance to the human rights shortcomings of life sentences, in particular to their potential disproportionality to the criminal conduct that leads to their imposition. To understand whether those imposing or facilitating the imposition of life sentences have sound assumptions about what life imprisonment means in practice, we must consider not only how it is imposed, but also how it is implemented. That is the subject of the next chapter.

7

Doing Life

W HAT IS LIFE imprisonment like for those who are sentenced to serve it? Our main aim in this chapter is to assess and synthesize what is already known about the effects, experience and implementation of life imprisonment across different jurisdictions. We begin by reviewing briefly the venerable sociological research tradition on the effects of (life) imprisonment and consider the extent to which long-term incarceration may impede or facilitate an individual's transition to the community. We are particularly interested in the question of whether the pains of serving an indeterminate sentence are heightened, or more severe than serving a fixed-term sentence. We proceed therefore to focus on one of the unique pains of doing life imprisonment, that is, the possibility of serving whole-life imprisonment, drawing primarily on first-person accounts and sociological research studies to highlight the subjective experience of serving a life sentence. After this, we assess the treatment of life-sentenced prisoners in different parts of the world and consider two issues that are of particular salience to contemporary life imprisonment: (i) heightened security measures; and (ii) impoverished regimes. Under these headings we synthesize findings from international bodies, such as the European Committee for the Prevention of Torture (CPT) and Penal Reform International (PRI), on the practice of life imprisonment and the treatment of life-sentenced prisoners.

Our conclusion is that life-sentenced prisoners are sometimes, though not invariably, subjected to regimes that are so restrictive and retributive that they are inherently painful, inhuman and degrading, often falling far below international human rights standards, and leaving individuals unprepared for release and for life after release. However, we leave open the possibility that life imprisonment does not necessarily have these characteristics.

The Effects of (Life) Imprisonment

Research on the effects of imprisonment has a long tradition within prison sociology. Much of it has focused on individuals who are subject to life or long-term imprisonment, or on establishments with heightened security measures where the detainees are often serving indefinite prison terms.[1] The results, however, are far from unanimous. Research findings range from no adverse effect, through very mixed evidence, to the argument that imprisonment invariably causes harm.[2] This divergence in the literature is partly due to different research approaches between sociologists, who largely adopt qualitative methodologies, and psychiatrists or psychologists, who generally employ more quantitative methods. Another consideration is whether researchers take account of the so-called climate of a certain institution or focus simply on the individual prisoner.[3] These differences inevitably render any overall assessment of the impact of doing life imprisonment particularly challenging.

Perhaps most important, conditions of confinement for all prisoners, including life-sentenced prisoners, vary greatly across institutions, states, and countries.[4] Correspondingly, prison regimes can, and do, differ greatly in their psychological and sociological impact on different prisoners.[5] The threshold after which a sentence of life imprisonment becomes increasingly harmful (or increasingly routine) may vary between different individuals. Some prisoners, irrespective of the length or conditions of confinement, are able to adjust and develop attitudes and approaches that are better able to withstand the rigors of prison life, some less so. Many of these differences are "a function of prisoners' different backgrounds and preexisting problems or vulnerabilities."[6] Research has shown that throughout the world most prisoners, including those serving life terms, come from socially and economically disadvantaged groups, and have often experienced significant trauma during childhood and adolescence. Their backgrounds often include experiences that increase their vulnerability to adversity and render them less able to cope effectively with, or indeed survive, the turmoil of prison life.[7]

The Pains of Imprisonment

In much of the early literature on the pains of imprisonment, the concept of mental, emotional, and intellectual deterioration of the long-term prisoner was a constantly recurring theme. Early accounts of imprisoned populations found evidence of specific mental disorders. In a report of the psychological impact of confined prisoners of war in 1919, Vischer observed symptoms of "barbed wire disease" or "metapsychosis" among the incarcerated men.[8] Similarly, Grünhut's comparative study of penal reform in 1948 highlighted that most prisoners suffered from mental deterioration, such as dwindling memory, a lack of concentration, obliviousness, and tendency to illusions.[9] In 1961, Taylor wrote that the long-term prisoner "shows a flatness of response which resembles slow, automatic behavior of a very limited kind, and he is humourless and lethargic."[10] And in their classic 1972 work, *Psychological Survival,* Cohen and Taylor, reported the profound fear among long-term prisoners of mental deterioration. They noted that:

> These men felt that all around them were examples of people who had turned into cabbages because they had not been sufficiently vigilant. Every day they encountered an old sex offender who spent hours merely cleaning and filling the teapot, a mindless activity which the old man appeared to be contented with. And this was their problem: at what price would they achieve peace of mind and contentment? Would they start behaving like the old man, as a way of banishing the ghosts of time, the fear of deterioration, and not knowing what was happening to them? In other words, would the cumulative result of years of working at something which looked like adaptation, in fact really be a process of learning how to deteriorate?[11]

In *The Society of Captives,* in 1958, Gresham Sykes argued that the prison environment represented "a social system in which an attempt is made to create or maintain total or almost total social control."[12] This total control of the prisoner is at the core of what Sykes defined as the "pains of imprisonment": the loss of liberty, the deprivation of goods and services, the deprivation of relationships, the deprivation of autonomy, and the deprivation of security. In a similar vein, Goffman's 1961 study of the "social situation of mental patients and other inmates" described the prison regime and similar institutions as comprehensive or "total institutions."[13] He detailed how inmates adapted to prison life following a process of mortification or changing of the self. He defined the total institution as "a place of residence and work where a large number of like-situated individuals, cut off from the wider society for an appreciable period of time, together lead an enclosed, formally administered round of life."[14] In total institutions, all activities are regimented and enforced by the institution's staff. As Goffman stated, "[m]inute segments of a person's line of activity may be subjected to regulations and judgements by staff."[15] The result is a process of self-mortification, which brings about "acute psychological stress," especially in cases of long-term confinement such as life imprisonment.[16]

In essence, many early assessments of the impact of long-term imprisonment were deterministic. In most studies, long-term or life-sentenced prisoners were considered to constitute a unidimensional group and to "react uniformly to the debasing nature of the prison environment."[17] This deprivation perspective was challenged in 1962 by Irwin and Cressey, who criticized the model for being too narrow and ignoring the characteristics of prisoners, which were imported to prison and had some bearing on an individual's experience of prison pain.[18] Many individuals who are convicted of serious crimes enter prison with extensive knowledge of the prison environment. Others, however, may come to prison less prepared for the experience and less able to cope with the potential damage of long periods of confinement.[19] During the latter half of the twentieth century, empirical studies examining the impact of long-term imprisonment did not provide evidence of physical or mental deterioration.[20] Some researchers reported that health concerns among long-term prisoners either decreased or remained stable over time.[21] For example, Rasch's 1981 study of three groups of German life-sentenced prisoners who had served 3, 8.5, and 13.5 years in prison, respectively, reported that as time served in confinement increased, "the state of health did not deteriorate in a serious or constant manner."[22] Reed and Glamser's 1979 study of older US prisoners—prisoners with an average age of sixty, who had served on average twenty-three years—reported that they had fewer problems than their contemporaries in the outside community. The researcher found that, "prison has a number of advantages. Prisoners are reasonably healthy. The availability of regular meals, rest and medical care exceeds that which is available to many adults, and the effects of economic factors are greatly reduced in a prison setting."[23]

Other researchers, such as Goldsmith in 1972, reported no deleterious health effects over time.[24] In their review of the literature reexamining the effects of prison life, Bonta and Gendreau in 1990 concluded that "as far as physical health is concerned, imprisonment may have the fortuitous benefit of isolating the offender from a highly risky lifestyle in the community."[25]

Several investigators have focused on deterioration in cognitive functioning as a result of long-term imprisonment. In England, Banister and colleagues measured cognitive functioning among long-term prisoners, all of whom had been sentenced to at least ten years. Four groups of long-term prisoners were included in their study. The average time served within the different groups was 2.5 years, 4.9 years, 6.9 years, and 11.3 years. They found no differences among the groups with intellectual performance, and that there was no significant deterioration in overall intellectual ability across the different groups.[26] Similarly, Rasch's research also measured the intellectual capacity among his three groups of life-sentenced prisoners. He reported that there was "no evidence found of the development of psychotic symptoms" and "no convincing proof of a constant intellectual deterioration during the course of long imprisonment."[27]

Sapsford's 1978 study of sixty British murderers who were at various stages of their life sentence, also led him to conclude that there was no evidence of deterioration that had been reported. However, he did find some negative effects of life imprisonment among his participants, such as an increase in introversion, a tendency to talk about the past rather than the future, and an increased tendency to be perceived by staff as institutionalized.[28] In a similar vein, other investigators reported "increases in inner-directed hostility, as well as increased introversion, flatness of affect, and dependency upon staff" among long-term prisoners.[29] But generally, empirical studies in the 1970s and 1980s found the overall effects of long-term and life imprisonment were minimal on an individual's well-being. Prisoners seemed to cope and adapt to life in prison surprisingly well, despite an initial period of disorientation and readjustment, and anxieties about losing contact with family and friends.[30]

Similarly ambiguous findings about the effects of life imprisonment played an important role in the 1977 decision of the German Federal Constitutional Court on the overall constitutionality of life imprisonment. The court reviewed the extensive German literature on the effects of life imprisonment, beginning with a large study of more than 2,000 life-sentenced prisoners across Europe that was conducted by Liepmann in 1912. It described in colorful language the "gruesome destructive effect" of life imprisonment, which Liepmann interpreted as providing a "breeding ground for mental disorders."[31] The court emphasized that prison conditions had changed since then, and referred to a number of modern studies that were not as condemnatory. The court also heard four expert witnesses in person and noted that they divided evenly between those who saw life imprisonment as inevitably damaging to the physical and mental health of life prisoners and those who did not. It concluded that the current state of knowledge on the effects of life imprisonment did not enable it to find that (appropriately implemented) life sentences necessarily led to irreparable physical or mental damage that would infringe the human dignity of the prisoners serving them.[32]

More contemporary work has drawn attention to the complexity of the issue. Research highlighting differing responses among prisoners, as well as differences between prison institutions have demonstrated that imprisonment can be extremely, and differentially, painful, depending on an individual's psychosocial resources and personal circumstances.[33] In 1990, Porporino summarized the evidence on prison effects and stated that while long-term imprisonment "is not generally or uniformly devastating," the potential to do harm remains.[34] He conceded that, "relationships with family and friends can be severed . . . particular vulnerabilities and inabilities to cope and adapt can come to the fore in the prison setting, [and] the behavior patterns and attitudes that emerge can take many forms, from deepening social and emotional withdrawal to extremes of aggression and violence."[35]

Even Bonta and Gendreau's 1990 review of the literature, which reached the overall conclusion that imprisonment was not necessarily as damaging as many had previously assumed, qualified their conclusion. They cited a number of studies documenting a range of negative effects, including "physiological and psychological stress responses," "a variety of health problems, injuries and selected symptoms of psychological distress," "increases in hostility and social introversion," "deteriorating community relationships over time," and "increases in dependency upon staff for direction."[36] As Liebling has put it: "Prison is all about pain—the pain of separation and loss, the wrench of restricted contact in the context of often fragile relationships, of human frailties and struggles."[37]

A recent study conducted by Crewe in 2011 to revisit the pains of long-term imprisonment found that contemporary prison practice has created a new range of burdens and frustrations for individuals serving life sentences.[38] These include pains of uncertainty and indeterminacy, pains of psychological assessment, and pains of self-government. Crewe suggested that while pain is no longer "meted out" in prison, and prisoners' lives may have improved in many material respects, these features of modern penal systems have created an additional layer of prison, pain. He argued that the metaphor of "tightness" better describes the experience of contemporary life imprisonment than the ideas of "depth" ("the extent to which a prisoner is embedded into the security and control systems of imprisonment") and "weight" ("the degree to which relationships, rights and privileges, standards and conditions serve to bear down on them").[39] The evidence showed that, while the depth of imprisonment can be moderate and the weight bearable, life-sentenced prisoners felt so tightly entangled in the administration of their sentence that it became virtually impossible for them to wriggle free.

Similarly, Liebling reported in 2011 that a "new and distinctive kind of 'prison pain' had emerged, consisting of a kind of existential and identity crisis brought on not only by the length and uncertainty of contemporary sentences, but also by the restricted facilities available."[40] The combination of lengthy and indeterminate sentences, low levels of trust in prison and high levels of concern about security, as well as the "constant presence of risk assessment as a goal and activity," left prisoners feeling "more trapped, vulnerable and hopeless   and so 'tightly' confined."[41] Furthermore, long-term and life-sentenced prisoners have continued to refer to many of Sykes's pains, identifying such things as the deprivation of liberty, goods, and services, sexual relationships, concern with deterioration, separation from family and friends, unremitting loneliness, the bereavement of oneself, and institutional thoughtlessness as among their primary concerns.[42]

Recent research has also shown that significant percentages of life-sentenced prisoners suffer from a range of psychological disorders. In a 2004 study, Mauer and colleagues drew on data collected by the US Bureau of Justice Statistics to underline the greater prevalence of mental health problems among life-sentenced prisoners in the United States when compared with the general population of prisoners: nearly one in five life-sentenced prisoners (18.4 percent) had a mental illness, compared to one in six in the general prison population.[43] In their 2011 study, Dudeck and colleagues also found that the prevalence of trauma is significantly higher among long-term prisoners when compared with the general population and with short-term prisoners.[44] And Liem and Kunst reported in 2013 that they found a "specific cluster of mental health symptoms" among twenty-five released life-sentenced prisoners, including: "chronic PTSD[,] . . . institutionalised personality traits (distrusting others, difficulty engaging in relationships, hampered decision making), social-sensory disorientation (spatial disorientation, difficulty in social interactions) and social and temporal alienation (the idea of 'not belonging' in a social and temporal setting)."[45] As Irwin and Owen put it: "The official purposes of imprisonment do not include harming prisoners. However, imprisonment invariably does harm."[46] This is certainly true of long-term imprisonment and of life imprisonment in particular.

Prisonization and Adaptation

Not all research has found deterioration in the well-being and adjustment of prisoners doing life imprisonment. Another common proposition is that life-sentenced prisoners are exemplary prisoners, having had time to adapt to the prison environment. For example, in their 1985 comparison of the profiles of short and long-term prisoners, MacKenzie and Goodstein found that prisoners who had recently arrived in the facility and who were anticipating a long sentence were most susceptible to measures of stress—including anxiety, fear, and depression—whereas long-term and life-sentenced prisoners who had already spent several years in prison developed coping mechanisms to adapt to the incarceration experience.[47] Correspondingly, Toch and Adams's 1989 study of prisoner adjustment found that young long-term prisoners had very high rates of disciplinary infractions, but that these rates declined over time. With more time served, many life-sentenced prisoners appeared to develop strategies for adjusting to institutional life and coping with long-term imprisonment.[48] As prison psychologist William Palmer stated: "It is a paradox that the best adjusted residents of our penitentiaries are often those serving the longest terms, whose instant offenses are the most heinous, who are perceived by citizens as presenting the greatest risk, and for whom public approval for leniency is least available."[49]

Research has long recognized that individuals sentenced to extended periods of time may undergo a gradual process of prisonization, or psychosocial transformation, to adapt to the stresses and demands of prison life. In his classic study, *The Prison Community*, first published in 1940, Clemmer defined prisonization as "the taking on in greater or lesser degree of the folkways, mores, customs, and general culture of the penitentiary."[50] In 1950, he outlined several "universal aspects of prisonization," including the "acceptance of an inferior role," "the development of somewhat new habits of eating, dressing, working, sleeping," and "the adoption of local language."[51]

The term *prisonization* is often used by prisoners and institutional staff to describe a prisoner's loss of interest in the outside world, the loss of contact with family and friends, and the loss of ability to make independent decisions. It is a form of coping in response to long-term exposure to regimentation and loss of personal autonomy inherent within the routinized prison world. Johnson and McGunigall-Smith have highlighted the fact that "[p]art and parcel of a repetitive routine is loss of choice."[52] Daily decisions—such as when to get up, where to eat, when to shower and when phone calls and visits are permitted—are made for prisoners. Over extended periods, such routines can become increasingly normal and life-sentenced prisoners can start to define themselves entirely within an institutional context.[53] As John Irwin put it, because "prison life is completely routinized and restricted," over time "prisoners steadily lose their capacity to exert power and control their destiny."[54] He explained, "Months or years of getting up at a certain time to certain signals, going about the day in a routine fashion, responding to certain commands, being among people who speak a certain way, and doing things repetitively inures prisoners to a deeply embedded set of unconscious habits and automatic responses."[55]

The nature and degree of prisonization vary among life-sentenced prisoners, depending, in part, on the length of continuous detention; but also on the monotony of the regime, level of autonomy given to prisoners, contact with the outside world, and personal experiences both prior to prison and during the course of their sentence.[56] Individuals who succumb to prisonization may have difficulty adjusting to life outside of prison following release, which is more unstructured and less predictable.[57] But active and constructive regimes in which the autonomy of the prisoners is enhanced, outside contacts are guaranteed, and prison life approximates as closely as

possible life in the community, will lower levels of prisonization and facilitate a more successful transition to the community on release. While the
effects of prisonization on life-sentenced prisoners may improve compliance and create fewer management problems, these effects may undermine
the process of release.

What seems apparent from the literature is that most long-term and life-
sentenced prisoners appear to make the best of a very difficult situation
and find ways of coping that make the pains of very lengthy imprisonment
more manageable over time. Many prisoners serving very long sentences
not only find strategies for alleviating the difficulties that they encounter,
but often attribute positive meaning of some kind to their experience.[58]
Qualitative studies have identified religion, education, work and vocational
training, a positive attitude, increased maturity, a desire to use time constructively, and a hope of release as some of the factors playing key roles in
negating the detrimental effects of life and long-term imprisonment.[59] In
their recent study on the experiences of men and women serving very long
life sentences, Crewe and colleagues found that over time, prisoners demonstrated a shift from a form of agency that was backward-looking or re-
active to one that was future-oriented and productive, albeit within the
restrictions of a very long prison sentence. While early-stage prisoners appeared to be "stuck in limbo" or "treading water," those further into their
sentences were able to overcome the pains of life imprisonment by learning
to "swim with" rather than against, the tide of their carceral predicament.[60]

Importantly, most research on the effects of life imprisonment has focused
on life-sentenced or long-term prisoners during the period of confinement.
Consideration should also be given to how the effects of imprisonment are
manifested after release.[61] A few small studies have revealed that the problems that life-sentenced prisoners experience in prison have a lasting
impact on ex-prisoners' abilities to cope with the outside world.[62] While prisoners' coping skills may not deteriorate over time, the outside world
increasingly changes as custody lengthens, and there will be significant challenges for released life-sentenced prisoners in coming to terms with a new life
in the community.[63]

The Prospect of No Release

In the light of the different problems and effects of life or long-term imprisonment, arguably the most pertinent or painful aspect for life-sentenced

prisoners is the prospect of doing indeterminate prison time. Being sentenced to life imprisonment, or to an indeterminate period of imprisonment, brings a unique pain to the experience of incarceration, since it removes the certainty of release on a given date in the future. Furthermore, the painfulness of indeterminacy may be more pronounced for individuals sentenced to life imprisonment without parole (LWOP), who have little or no prospect of release. Here, we draw largely on first-person accounts to highlight this distinctive aspect of serving a life sentence.

DOING INDETERMINATE TIME. The prospect of doing indeterminate prison time is at the core of a life sentence. It has previously been said that life-sentenced prisoners experience time differently to other prisoners as they have been given an indeterminate period of time as punishment. As Cohen and Taylor put it, long-term prisoners "have been given someone else's time. Their own time has been abstracted by the courts like a monetary fine and in its place they have been given prison time. This is no longer a resource but a controller. It has to be served rather than used."[64]

The challenge and difficulties of negotiating an indeterminate prison sentence are well documented in the first-person accounts of life-sentenced prisoners. There are numerous references to "doing time," "marking time," "killing time," or being "frozen in time," revealing the monotonous, endless nature of the temporal dimension of indeterminate imprisonment. As Jack Abbott put it in his book, *The Belly of the Beast,* on the realities of life in a maximum security prison: "Time descends in your cell like the lid of a coffin in which you lie and watch it as it slowly closes over you."[65]

Particularly during the early years of a life sentence, the sheer burden of indeterminacy can weigh heavily on the minds of all life prisoners. As one individual has put it: "It's not having a date. The time I can handle. It's not having the numbers at the end of it."[66] Serving an indeterminate life sentence has been described by different individuals as "a tunnel without light at the end," "a black hole of pain and anxiety," "a bad dream, a nightmare," or even, "a slow, torturous death."[67] In Parker's book, *Life after Life: Interviews with Twelve Murderers,* one interviewee convicted of killing a policeman in the United Kingdom, attempts to explain the painfulness of doing indeterminate prison time:

Society's taken its retribution on me like it's entitled to, but it's a whole lot harder than a lot of society's members think, if they ever do think about it.

I took somebody's life away yes, and in return they're doing the same to me. Only their way of doing it is slowly day by day, relentlessly, bit by bit. Eating you away, shrinking you smaller and smaller, inch by inch, depriving you more and more of what's left of your personality and feelings, every shred of your individuality. If society would only say one day, one definite day, they'll take me back, that's all I want, for them to tell me that. Only for Christ's sake while there's still something left of me to take back.[68]

Wright and colleagues suggest that often a sense of "temporal vertigo"[69] is expressed during the early stages of life imprisonment, a sense of dizziness and powerlessness—"like falling out of an airplane"[70]—as life-sentenced prisoners have to learn to adjust to a world that is typically unfamiliar, intimidating, painful and possibly lifelong. Many accounts from prisoners themselves reveal a deep sense of shock and helplessness, faced with the challenge of making sense of doing indefinite prison time. For example: "It's like going deep-sea diving. Going all the way down into the depths and losing your oxygen. You're struggling to get to the top. You don't know if you're going to make it, but you never stop struggling."[71]

For many, an indeterminate life sentence disrupts the life course to such an extent that the experience has been described as a "civil death."[72] The initial shock of receiving the ultimate penalty and the aftershock of serving indefinite detention puts significant strain on an individual's personal identity and many life-sentenced prisoners experience an extraordinary loss of their own sense of self. As one life-sentenced prisoner stated: "A life sentence means that, in effect, you're dead. It's just another form of a death sentence. Instead of having the gall to do it in one fell swoop, you die one day at a time."[73] Another writes that: "My life is ruined for life; there is no redemption, and to some that is a fate worse than death."[74]

Jewkes suggests that the pains of serving indeterminate prison time may be experienced as a bereavement of the self, a lost future and lost identity, and can be likened to being diagnosed with a "chronic or terminal illness."[75] The shock and pain of incarceration are often not dulled until the temporal dimension of life imprisonment has been dealt with. Some prisoners simply avoid discussing or thinking about the enormity of the life punishment: "I wake up and start looking around me and then I just lay there with my eyes closed because I just don't want to look at it. I don't want to see the concrete. I don't want to remember I'm here."[76]

Other life-sentenced prisoners, struggling with the guilt of the offense and the prospect of a lifetime in prison, speak of having considered suicide or indeed a preference for the death penalty:

More than once I've thought if we still had the death penalty and that's what the judge had passed on me as a sentence and I'd thought I'd been hanged, that would've been the end of it. Sometimes I've thought that could never have been as bad as sentencing me to go on living with all this remorse. They don't let you out, you know, it's one of the things they take into account before they do, until they're sure you show contrition for what you've done. . . . I've had treatment of all sorts . . . but none of them has ever cured me. . . . There is no cure, not for me. The end of my life, that'll be the cure.[77]

Some prisoners fight against the pains associated with serving a life sentence: their offense, their indeterminate imprisonment and the correctional system. They resort to violence and bitterness against staff as a way of trying to change or control their environment.[78] John McGrath was a prisoner in Scotland for many years and wrote about his experiences after spending several years in solitary confinement. When staff tried to change his way of dealing with long-term imprisonment, he responded:

You do not touch me. There is nothing you can do to me that you have not already done. I am me and I am stronger and more powerful than you. . . . Move me from cell to cell twice every day. Put another gate in front of my steel door. Surround me with cameras. Be as you are—weak, frightened, powerless. Now there is nothing left you can do to me. You cannot make me any harder, any more dangerous, nor any more loathing.[79]

Pervasive themes in life-sentenced prisoners' accounts are the basic necessity of constantly fighting for survival, and that there is no option but to cope with the deprivations of life imprisonment. As Erwin James, a prisoner who served twenty years of a life sentence before being released, noted in his book, *A Life Inside*: "serving a prison sentence is not something that comes naturally. How to survive once you find yourself 'inside' is something you have to learn to do as you go along."[80]

For many, prison life is mostly a continuous repetition of the same day, week after week, month after month and year after year. There is a sense of time dragging heavily, of knowing that years will follow years of lost freedom and stultifying routine. At the core of the experience is the deprivation of liberty and narrowing of choice. The loss of control or personal autonomy is prevalent in the writings of life-sentenced prisoners. Facing and coming to terms with the circumscribed life that is imprisonment for an indeterminate period of time is a central problem. As one life-sentenced prisoner noted: "The thing I miss the most . . . is the right to choose. I no longer have any choice—when I have a shower, where I go, what I do."[81] Another stated: "Each meal is identical to the last, just as each day is to the one before it: insipid and boring. . . . With every meal on every tray, society reminds us how much it despises us."[82] As Johnson and McGunigall-Smith surmised, "Each day brings mortifications that remind prisoners of their helplessness and the sheer loss of dignity they suffer in a world in which very few recognize their inherent worth as human beings."[83]

References to personal deterioration, the futility of existence and the fear of prisonization (or institutionalization) are reoccurring topics for prisoners doing indeterminate prison time:

> A life sentence is like an insect encased in amber. Amber at one point is a fluid. As it is exposed to air, it becomes more viscous. Sometimes insects may get trapped in it. As it hardens, you see the insect's movements become slower. When it solidifies, he's just there.[84]

> It's too easy to become institutionalized in here—enslaved by the routine that governs our every move. . . . When things are disrupted, I'm always nervous that I am doing something the wrong way, missing some important activity that I need to be part of, or, worst of all, that something really bad is about to happen, and I am powerless to prevent it.[85]

The difficulties of serving indeterminate prison time are not only focused on deterioration of the self but also extend to the loss of family members and friends in the aftermath of the life sentence. Life-sentenced prisoners express profound concerns regarding the well-being of family members, and the fears that close relatives or friends might die during their sentence. Loss of contact with family and friends poses a problem for all prisoners, but for life-sentenced prisoners, it is feared that these relationships will be lost forever. The prospect of maintaining them over a long period is slim. Many life-sentenced prisoners' entire extended families die during the prisoner's long years of prison confinement and there is a nagging sadness of separation from family and friends, and the life once lived. As one life-sentenced prisoner explained: "The longer you are here, the less ties you have to the outside world. Your family begins to die off. And your friends—how long can someone really stand behind you? They eventually just go back to their own lives. That's sad. That really hurts."[86]

Feelings of deep loss may also be experienced by prisoners who are going through a divorce or are deprived of contact with their children. For life-sentenced prisoners with children, a particularly painful aspect of doing life imprisonment is the consideration of the length of time served in custody in relation to the age of their children. Many prisoners talk about how painful life imprisonment is in relation to lost years of parenting:

> The hardest thing about a life sentence is being away from my family. My daughter was two and a half years old when I came to prison. She's now 23. She's grown, and I missed her entire childhood. And my relatives are getting older.[87]

> You watch your family grow up. My son was five years old when I came here. Now he's 28. He has a family. That takes a toll on you.[88]

Arguably for women doing indeterminate prison time, the issues of child-bearing and child-rearing are especially salient. Walker and Worrall highlighted in their study of women life-sentenced offenders in 2000 that women suffer acutely from the pains of indeterminacy, specifically, the loss of control over fertility and losing contact with children.[89] Similarly, Crewe and colleagues have argued in their 2017 study on "the gendered pains of life imprisonment" that women report "an acutely more painful experience"[90] than their male counterparts, mainly in terms of deteriorating relationships with children and the "severe restrictions on fulfilling 'traditional' maternal role obligations imposed by incarceration."[91] As one of their participants stated:

> [T]he hardest thing for me when I came into jail was nobody told me how to not be a mum—I had spent so many years being a mum, I didn't know how to switch that off. . . . And like it never goes away; that missing them, and that kind of ache.[92]

Furthermore, the "biological clock" may have a much greater significance for women than for men. As one respondent in Walker and Worrall's study stated: "men can do a life sentence and come out and still have a family, but a woman can't come out at 40 or 50 and start a family."[93] Nevertheless, missed opportunities to start a family during lengthy prison terms can also impact significantly on male life-sentenced prisoners, who may not be released before their female partners are too old to bear children.[94] Indeed, many life-sentenced prisoners grieve over the loss of hope for the future as well as being no longer able to have or raise children, or provide support for family members.

Over the course of an indeterminate sentence it is not unusual for some prisoners to sever all ties with the outside world, either as a direct consequence of the life sentence or as a means of avoiding the anxiety and despair that comes with being separated from family members. Toch has referred to the strategy of severing external connections as the "de-cathexis of relationships."[95] This involves suppressing thoughts of the outside world and minimizing involvements with families and friends in order to cope with the daily stress and demands of imprisonment. Boyle, for example, wrote in his autobiography, *A Sense of Freedom:* "The only way to pass the time was to do exercises and reading and thinking thoughts of hatred. My former life was far in the distance and I would try not to think of my family as it hurt too much."[96]

As O'Donnell has noted, visits or contact with outside family life have the potential to make time harder to serve "because they refocus time orientation and jolt the prisoner back to an alternative reality that is often an unhappy reminder of their predicament."[97] Going to the prison visiting room can be a very difficult experience, as described by one prisoner: "I don't want to go out there and be reminded of what I'm never going to have again. And then it makes coming back in here twice as bad because when you're out there in an environment where people are halfway normal . . . and I would come back in and it makes this place [prison] seem all that much worse."[98]

Yet, as Toch has suggested, this response is comparatively rare. Most prisoners are deeply aware of the importance of maintaining connections to the outside world. Outside contacts can provide support, distractions and encouragement even if they make doing life much more stressful.[99] While prisoners may report that serving indeterminate prison time would be easier without them, family ties and connections to the outside world give life meaning and a sense of hope for the future, without which confinement becomes more painful still. As one prisoner has put it: "What keeps me going is the realization that sometime, at any age, I am going to get out. I am going to get out. And I hope this is done pretty soon before a lot of my family die off."[100]

DOING LIFELONG IMPRISONMENT. As a subgroup of life-sentenced prisoners, the perspectives of prisoners with no reasonable prospect of release, who are usually, but not exclusively, prisoners serving LWOP sentences, offer further insight into the comparability of life imprisonment to a sentence of death in the suffering that it entails. Such prisoners will usually die in prison and perceive this to be the case, even if in theory and occasionally in practice they may be pardoned or have their life sentences commuted.

The pains of doing indeterminate time identified above are significantly heightened for this subset of life-sentenced prisoners who find themselves having to come to terms with not only doing very long prison time, but dying behind bars. Although the literature base is small, in Hartman's 2013 collection of essays by LWOP prisoners in the United States, for example, descriptions of doing a death sentence pervade. Many of the writers speak of LWOP as "the other death penalty," "a slow death row," and a fate "worse than death," or refer to themselves as "walking dead men."[101] As one prisoner put it: "To subsist under a life without the possibility of parole sentence still classifies one as a dead man walking, only in slow motion."[102]

Other life-sentenced prisoners, who in law may qualify for parole but who believe, often with justification, that they have no realistic prospect of release, have expressed similar sentiments. One such person is Jens Soering, who in 1987 was extradited from the United Kingdom to face a charge of murder for killing the parents of his girlfriend in Virginia in the United States. Soering was duly convicted of the two murders, but the conditions of his extradition prohibited consideration of the death penalty, which the authorities in Virginia would otherwise have sought. Soering was sentenced to life imprisonment with parole (LWP), as LWOP was not an option in Virginia at the time. However, through their statements at the time of his conviction and through the persistent denial of parole to Soering, who has been a model prisoner for thirty years, the authorities in Virginia have made it clear that it is highly unlikely that Soering will ever be released. His parole application has been denied fourteen times. Eventually, Soering reached the point where he declared himself "beyond hope or despair" in much the same way as those serving LWOP.[103]

Unless they receive a sentence commutation or pardon, which rarely occurs, LWOP prisoners, as well as other life-sentenced prisoners who may be in substantively the same position as far as the absence of realistic prospects of release are concerned, must serve their sentences until they die. The uncertainty of when their sentences, and their lives, will expire can significantly contribute to the stressfulness of doing LWOP. That these individuals have no hope of release is perhaps the most difficult aspect of the punishment. Prisoners' descriptions of the sentence clearly draw attention to the inhumanity of whole life imprisonment, a sentence which does not contain within it even the *possibility* of being considered for parole:[104]

> The heart of the other death penalty is the immutable nature of the punishment. Like all forms of execution, there is no possibility for change and growth. . . . At some point, we must all come to terms with this truth. The end of the sentence, the end of the penalty, the end of the daily torment, is the end of our life.[105]

> It's a persistent dashing of hopes as appeal after appeal is arbitrarily denied, as well as a permanent experiment in self-delusion as you strive to convince yourself that there is still hope. It's a compounding of second upon second, minute upon minute, hour upon hour, of wasted existence, and decade upon decade of mental and emotional torture culminating in death. It's a death by incarceration.[106]

It is perhaps not surprising that many LWOP prisoners speak of suicide or a preference for the death penalty, both of which are deemed preferable to a life of endless pain in prison:

> Every night I hope I don't see the morning because there is no life for me. I am depressed 24 hours a day, and I know I'm going to die in prison. I hope I don't wake up—there is no life for me.[107]

> I am alive, and I really don't want to be. I have nothing to live for. I'm serving life without the possibility of parole, and that might as well be a death sentence. I will never leave this place, and the thought of that forces any sliver of hope out of me.[108]

Many believe that the death penalty is the worst of the judicial system, but there is a fate worse than death. It's known as the other death penalty, life without the possibility of parole. How can life be worse than death? Imagine living a life without a point, a reason, or a direction—breathing but never living.[109]

The severing of close relationships and the prospect of being permanently separated from the outside world are also experienced as being akin to death. Research has documented the difficulties that LWOP prisoners have in sustaining meaningful contact with family members from outside prison.[110] LWOP prisoners report that the level of communication, including both the frequency of communication and the number of outside contacts, is often significantly low compared to other prisoners.[111] Many express a profound and growing sense of loss and loneliness over being no longer able to raise children and the realization that family ties will most likely weaken, and relatives will die while they are in prison. These emotional and psychological deprivations can be devastating and can result in intense feelings of sadness, grief, and apathy for life. As one prisoner put it:

> I had to deal with the fact that I was never going home, and all the attendant grief that went along with my time. . . . Most devastating was dealing with the loss of my children. Their absence from my life left me bereft. . . . [I]n the frenzy of my grief, the only solution I could imagine when I contemplated the loss of my children and freedom was death. . . . I fantasized about elaborate plans to kill myself. As an intelligent, creative woman, I knew that I would be able to pull it off without being caught.[112]

The lifelong nature of LWOP also impacts significantly on prisoners' physical health. Like other prisoners, LWOP prisoners have often not had access to proper health care. The effects of medical neglect are compounded and more distressing for this group of prisoners, who expect to be in prison for the rest of their days. Because there is no release date, LWOP prisoners often feel neglected by officials and that it does not really matter to staff whether they live or die.[113] In Leigey's study of older LWOP prisoners in the United States, for example, several participants alleged that prisoners had died of conditions that a person would survive in the community. One prisoner referred to the prison infirmary as "the house of death" because "the people that check into the infirmary, they die."[114]

It has also been well documented from personal accounts and research studies that prisoners are particularly fearful of dying in prison, viewing death in prison as the "ultimate failure."[115] In a recent study of aging prisoners in Switzerland, Handtke and colleagues found that the prison environment was viewed as a "major stressor for older adults," which often escalated the fear and uncertainty of the dying process.[116] While end-of-life care existed in some prisons, it was generally deemed insufficiently compassionate because it was provided in a punitive context. Even if prisons successfully provided this care, concerns remained about the difficulties of coping with the prison environment, regrets about the inability to see family and loved ones, and the perception that dying in prison had a stigma, not only for prisoners, but for their family members as well.[117]

Furthermore, the punishment of LWOP fails to recognize an individual's capacity to reform. Prisoners' accounts reveal that they are often excluded from rehabilitative opportunities:

> We are not members of the regular prison population who are encouraged to take classes, learn new work skills, and rehabilitate themselves in preparation for pending re-emergence into the free world. But we are not on the formal death row either and therefore have no access to their legislated protections. We are not appointed teams of attorneys who diligently work for reversals. We sentenced to life without the possibility of parole are expected to lay low, stay out of the way, and die as soon as possible to free up some much-needed bed space.[118]

> Prospects for rehabilitation are even worse for individuals serving LWOP. The sentence itself contains an unmistakable message that is never lost on offenders serving it. By sentencing offenders to LWOP, society tells them unequivocally that their lives are worthless, they are beyond repair or redemption, and any effort they make to improve themselves is essentially futile.[119]

The loss of hope clearly distinguishes life-sentenced prisoners from other prisoners. In the various editions of his book, *Life without Parole: Living in Prison Today*, Victor Hassine discussed his life sentence beginning in 1981 and reflected on the pains and deprivations associated with doing life.[120] He had hoped that dedicating his life to helping others in prison and to bettering prison conditions for himself and for other prisoners would ultimately lead the board of pardons and parole to consider clemency. After serving twenty-seven years of his life sentence, he sent an appeal to the board, but the members rejected his application without consideration. Shortly after hearing the news that his application had been ignored, Hassine committed suicide.[121]

A similar incident played itself out in New York in the case of John MacKenzie, who was serving a life sentence with a minimum of twenty-five years for the killing of a policeman. Although he eventually served forty-one years and was a model prisoner in all respects, the New York Parole Board persisted in denying release, citing as reason, only the seriousness of his original offense. Finally, the parole board was held in contempt of court for refusing to consider other relevant factors such as MacKenzie's behavior in prison and indications that he had been rehabilitated, but persisted in denying parole. In July 2016, MacKenzie eventually committed suicide.[122]

Of relevance here too is that some LWOP prisoners, as well as those facing LWP with long minimum terms in the United States, are detained in solitary confinement or maximum security facilities at some point during their sentence. Often perceived as "the worst of the worst," they are isolated from other prisoners and held in closed cells for twenty-two to twenty-four hours a day under extensive surveillance, virtually free of human contact and sensory stimulation.[123] Prisoners are isolated from the general population because they are either considered to be dangerous or they are considered to be at risk of violence from others.[124]

Research on so-called "supermax" prisons and segregation units in the United States has shown that this experience often proves to be profoundly painful. The extensive empirical literature in this field has indicated that long-term isolation or solitary confinement in prison can inflict extraordinarily high rates of psychological trauma among segregated prisoners.[125] Haney has pointed out that the complete isolation and sensory deprivation of solitary confinement has been shown to cause a panoply of psychiatric symptoms, including heightened levels of "negative attitudes and affect, insomnia, anxiety, panic, withdrawal, hypersensitivity, ruminations, cognitive dysfunction, hallucinations, loss of control, irritability, aggression and rage, paranoia, hopelessness, depressions, a sense of impending emotional breakdown, self-mutilation and suicidal ideation and behavior."[126]

A growing body of research has shown that in severe cases the effects of solitary confinement can lead to "extremes of self-mutilation," and that "the rates of suicide in solitary far exceed anything found in general prison populations."[127] Around 50 percent of incarcerated people who commit suicide do so while being detained in solitary confinement.[128] Under these circumstances it is unsurprising that survivors of solitary confinement have described the punishment of penal isolation as "the most forbidding aspect of prison life,"[129] akin to being "buried alive"[130] or, as William Blake who was in his twenty-ninth year of solitary confinement in New York's Great Meadow Correctional Facility has recently put it, "torture of a terrible kind" and "a sentence worse than death."[131] O'Donnell reported in his study, *Prisoners, Solitude and Time*, that it is "a deeper, heavier, tighter, experience, in less forgiving surrounds, which is reserved for those who are perceived as too menacing to be handled in any other way."[132]

Significantly, LWOP prisoners are often perceived to be more dangerous than other prisoners. It has sometimes been said that LWOP sentences have the potential to create a "new breed of superinmates, prone to violence and uncontrollable," who have neither hope nor anything to lose.[133] According to Liebling, lifelong imprisonment creates "an environment of no hope, no meaning . . . When you've ruled out the possibility of atonement, most of the ways out are dangerous."[134] This may be so, but empirical research reveals that the majority of individuals serving LWOP, as is the case with other life-sentenced prisoners, are less likely to engage in institutional misconduct or acts of violence in prison than prisoners who are serving parole-eligible sentences.[135] As Johnson and McGunigall-Smith reported, many individuals serving LWOP sentences tend to avoid trouble in prison, knowing how easily any privileges gained can also be lost and are keen to invest in a stable, conflict-free prison environment. Having often served time in maximum or super-maximum security conditions, LWOP prisoners are aware how much more the loss of any privileges they can earn will affect their lives in prison. The researchers explain:

> Any serious rule violation jeopardizes the way of life these inmates have built for themselves; a violent infraction, even one associated with self-defense, unravels the lifers' way of life, landing them in segregation, back to square one, making them start all over again, in a new area, with new neighbors and new staff, with little to go on and a lot to prove. By organizing their routines around avoiding trouble, lifers have taken charge of their lives in the objectively precarious world of the prison and made those lives more secure.[136]

A number of US prison wardens have reported that many individuals serving life sentences are the "best behaved prisoners in their entire system."[137] For example, Leo Lalonde of the Michigan Department of Corrections stated, "After a few years, lifers become your better prisoners. They tend to adjust and just do their time. They tend to be a calming influence on the younger kids, and we have more problems with people serving short terms."[138] Research confirms that most LWOP prisoners can and do adapt to permanent imprisonment, and often find meaning and purpose in their prison lives, although adaptation typically remains "an ongoing and often arduous affair."[139] Leigey's sociological study of twenty-five older LWOP prisoners in the United States found that the participants were able to do more than simply survive decades-long incarceration, largely by depending on their own internal resources, developing new skills and a desire to use their time in prison constructively. While the men acknowledged the deprivations of imprisonment advanced by Sykes, they were able to cope with permanent confinement by confronting personal issues, developing new skills and pursuing activities that they felt were personally meaningful. They attributed their resilience and the ability to withstand the pains of permanent incarceration to "a positive outlook, which for some, was based on a hope of release," despite the very slim possibility of release.[140]

Similarly, O'Donnell's international assessment of prisoners' experience of solitary confinement concluded that some exceptional individuals manage to not only get through the time of social isolation and extreme deprivation, but are able to draw some positive enrichment from the experience. None of this of course offers an argument in support of the acute pains inflicted by permanent imprisonment, or indeed solitary confinement. As O'Donnell surmised, the ability for individuals to flourish under such extreme punishment speaks of the incredible "durability of the individual under even the most arduous of circumstances."[141]

While the majority of research on the experience of LWOP has taken place in the United States, Liem and colleagues' small-scale study of LWOP prisoners in the Netherlands has raised strikingly similar concerns about lifelong detention to those that have been highlighted above.[142] Compared to other long-term prisoners serving time in the Dutch prison system, LWOP prisoners' main concerns included greater levels of uncertainty, the futility of their existence, the fear of mental deterioration and the depressing prison climate. In the Dutch study, many of the LWOP prisoners at the early stage of their sentence expressed disbelief at the permanency of their fate and the uncertainty of their future, often channeling their energy into an appeal pro-cess as a crucial coping mechanism during the early stage of the sentence. The possibility of their sentence being set aside on appeal allowed them to suppress the terminal nature of the punishment:

> They simply [condemned] me unjustly. . . . I hope that soon something will change in the case. . . . Because I'm not going to stay here, I plan to go home and immediately when justice is done to me . . . and perhaps therefore I re-main so strong. I have also had times when I thought to myself: I'm going to kill myself, I don't want [to continue] anymore. . . . The reality is I'm sitting here, I'm fighting to get out."[143]

In addition to the ongoing uncertainty, LWOP prisoners in the Nether-lands highlighted the sheer hopelessness of the sentence and lack of under-standing of the purpose of their punishment, as well as an unsolicited preference for the death penalty over a lifetime in prison. As one prisoner put it dramatically:

> If I could sign up for a bullet now I would sign up. Shoot me down, I'm ready to go. . . . If the state were man enough [they would carry out the death pen-alty]. I get killed every day, therefore just kill me. My next of kin would be happy with it; everyone would be happy. Give me the death penalty. Give me the choice of life or death. . . . But do not do it like in America and leave me for 20 years on death row. Give me a year.[144]

In stark contrast to long-term prisoners with determinate sentences in the Netherlands, many LWOP prisoners there had severed ties with the out-side world because the repeated confrontation of being permanently sepa-rated from family members had become too painful to bear. Both LWOP and long-term prisoners expressed concern about the lack of meaning in their lives and the futility of their existence. Many emphasized a lack of access to education, work or rehabilitation programs and were particularly concerned about mental deterioration and prisonization. Furthermore, many LWOP prisoners reported having often contemplated suicide. The bleak picture that emerges from Liem's study is powerful evidence that LWOP is a particularly harsh form of life imprisonment, even when imple-mented in a country like the Netherlands, which has a reputation for en-lightened penal practices.

Across jurisdictions, a sentence of LWOP is perceived by many prisoners serving it as a sentence of death. Although less coercive and visibly invasive than executions, the inevitability of their death in prison clearly holds a tight grip on prisoners' existence. Taken in totality, accounts from life-sentenced prisoners reveal how painful and problematic the institution of life imprisonment is. It is a world made up of many deprivations, which accumulate to such an extent that many life-sentenced prisoners, and particularly LWOP prisoners, are left without any sense of dignity, meaning, or worth as a human being.

The Treatment of Life-Sentenced Prisoners

While information on the treatment of life-sentenced prisoners is generally difficult, if not impossible, to obtain, there is a small but important body of evidence that suggests that individuals serving life imprisonment are sometimes subjected to more punitive or worse conditions than other prisoners as a direct result of the way that their sentences are implemented. Recent evidence from the CPT in particular, has drawn attention to the fact that in some parts of Europe, life-sentenced prisoners can experience more stringent regimes than other prisoners and be excluded from prison work or rehabilitative opportunities on the basis of their sentence.[145] Correspondingly, recent reports published by PRI on the movement toward the abolition of the death penalty in other regions, including Central Asia, the Middle East and North Africa, and East Africa have revealed that life-sentenced prisoners are often systematically subjected to heightened security and worse conditions than other categories of prisoners.[146] Likewise in the United States and United Kingdom, life-sentenced prisoners often begin their prison sentence in maximum, sometimes super-maximum security establishments with little or no access to rehabilitative opportunities.[147]

Two major themes emerge that distinguish the treatment of life-sentenced prisoners from other prisoners. The first is that life-sentenced prisoners are often systematically allocated to purpose-built high-security institutions, where they are segregated from the general prison population and subjected to heightened security restrictions. The second is that life-sentenced prisoners are frequently subjected to impoverished prison regimes and not provided with appropriate material conditions, human contact, or rehabilitative opportunities. All too often the aim of contemporary life imprisonment is to punish and incapacitate, and rehabilitation plays a minor role, if any.

Segregation and Heightened Security

It has become evident from reports of the CPT over recent years that certain states systematically segregate life-sentenced prisoners from the general prison population and detain them in high-security units on the grounds of the seriousness of the crime of which they have been convicted.[148] In some cases, this may be a condition set by law. In other cases, life-sentenced prisoners are routinely assigned to these units by prison administrations in spite of their not being legally required to do so.

In Russia, for example, special-regime correctional colonies were used following the abolition of the death penalty, specifically to detain former death row prisoners, together with newly convicted murderers, away from the general prison population, under harsh conditions and with heightened security.[149] Individuals sentenced to life imprisonment in Russia are automatically detained under a "strict regime" and must serve their sentences isolated from other prisoners for at least the first ten years of their sentence.[150]

A similar approach to the implementation of life imprisonment has been adopted by a number of former Soviet Union countries, including Armenia, Azerbaijan, Belarus, Georgia, Kazakhstan, Kyrgyzstan, Latvia, Lithuania, Tajikistan, and Ukraine.[151] In 2011, one of us had the opportunity to visit one of these penal colonies—Zhytykary Colony in Kazakhstan—and recalled the following:

> [Life-sentenced prisoners] are held for the first ten years of their sentences in what is a form of semi-isolation where they are not allowed to work and, with the exception of contact with prison officials, effectively are allowed only to communicate with two or three other prisoners in their cells. Time out of the cell is restricted to one and a half hours of exercise a day and even then cellmates are separated from all other prisoners. Exercise is in a small yard and may be further restricted by bad weather. The alternative is a small, cell-sized "gymnasium," which cannot possibly accommodate more than a small number of prisoners, and is inadequate for the numbers involved. I was told that prisoners are able to read and have access to medical and psychological services. Even so, the regime as a whole is clearly not geared to rehabilitation

and is more severe than is necessary merely for maintaining safety and security in an extremely isolated prison colony.[152]

Similarly in Tajikistan, individuals sentenced to life imprisonment must serve their time in penal colonies under "special treatment," segregated from all other prisoners.[153] In Europe, certain countries (including Bulgaria, Moldova, Romania, Slovakia, and Turkey), have implemented a specific regime for life-sentenced prisoners that also systematically segregates them from the remainder of the prison population.[154] In Slovakia, for example, the law provides that "[a] life-sentenced prisoner shall be held in a designated establishment and in a specific cell, in which, as a rule, he/she shall be accommodated and work alone."[155] Likewise in Bulgaria, life sentences are to be served in purpose-built prisons or, failing such prisons, in separate units of other prisons.[156]

To ensure the segregation of life-sentenced prisoners, many of these jurisdictions have implemented both heightened internal security measures as well as increased external security. A common feature is that all life-sentenced prisoners are handcuffed or shackled whenever they leave their cells. This can include wearing handcuffs or shackles during visits to medical and dental services where prison officers may remain present, and sometimes during telephone calls or even outdoor exercise within a secure prison yard.[157]

Life-sentenced prisoners accommodated in high-security prisons can be subjected routinely to rub down searches at all movement times, regular strip searches, cell searches, twenty-four-hour video surveillance, and close restrictions on movement. Liebling and colleagues' study in 2011 on life in a high-security prison in the United Kingdom described how prisoners, the majority of whom (75 percent) were serving life sentences, experienced the deep end of imprisonment and were subject to "very high levels of security including rub down searches at all movement times, regular strip searches, cell searches ('spins'), CCTV camera coverage and close restrictions on movement."[158] Furthermore, during their visits to the prison, the research team was searched and their possessions were x-rayed before "passing through around sixteen locked gates to get to the wings, and a further two to reach the spurs where prisoners lived."[159] In some countries, guard dogs have been used to escort life-sentenced prisoners during movement within prisons.[160] Furthermore, justified on the basis of the personal security and safety of staff and others, individuals serving life sentences have been systematically placed inside cages during meetings with their defense lawyers, prison staff and other professionals.[161]

Often such extreme security measures have been adopted by governments due to the automatic assumption that life-sentenced prisoners are more likely to escape or assault staff or other prisoners. Yet, research evidence confirms that life-sentenced prisoners do not pose more of a risk to the safety and security of the prison than other prisoners and that they can be successfully integrated into the mainstream prison population.[162] Research studies have consistently shown that individuals serving life and long-term prison sentences are often the most compliant prisoners and can even have a calming influence on other groups of prisoners.[163] Indeed, as noted earlier, many of them have a long-term interest in a stable and conflict-free environment.

Of further concern is the routine use of solitary confinement as part of the implementation of a life sentence. Many life-sentenced prisoners are not only segregated from other prisoners in high-security institutions but are routinely confined to their cells (either alone or in pairs) for up to twenty-three or twenty-four hours a day. The life sentence system in Turkey, for example, automatically subjects a subgroup of life-sentenced prisoners to a prison regime of solitary confinement from the beginning of their sentence. Following the abolition of the death penalty, a clear distinction in terms of regime was made in legislation between individuals sentenced to "normal" versus "aggravated" life imprisonment. In Turkey, prisoners who are sentenced to normal life imprisonment are usually not segregated from the general prison population and, in principle, have access to the same regime activities as prisoners who are serving a fixed term. However, prisoners sentenced to aggravated life imprisonment are subject to a special regime which is much more restrictive.[164] These prisoners are accommodated alone in single cells, and the only guaranteed out-of-cell activity is one hour of outdoor exercise a day.

Similarly, in Belarus and Ukraine, life-sentenced prisoners spend at least twenty-three hours a day in their cells with "virtually no out-of-cell, and minimal in-cell activities."[165] Further, sports and exercise facilities are severely limited for life-sentenced prisoners. In Belarus, persons who are sentenced to life imprisonment are entitled to only thirty minutes walking per day, and in Ukraine,[166] the exercise yards to which life-sentenced prisoners have access have been described by the CPT as being "of an oppressive design and too small for real physical exertion."[167]

Such practices can also be found in the United States, where prisoners serving LWOP sentences are routinely held in maximum or super-maximum security units and subject to solitary confinement conditions, often at the beginning of their sentence. While institutions vary across the United States,[168] the essential features of such regimes include "isolation, intense surveillance and elaborate precaution against assault and escape whenever prisoners are out of their cells."[169] Indeed, prisoner movement is severely restricted. Research studies confirm that prisoners are handcuffed and escorted by prison officers to shower or to exercise. Even during exercise or "recreation time," prisoners often remain alone, and kept within caged enclosures.[170] Likewise in Tajikistan, life-sentenced prisoners (all of whom are serving LWOP sentences) must serve their sentences away from other prisoners, confined "under strict isolation" for up to twenty-two hours a day.[171]

In some regions, the level of security to which life-sentenced prisoners are subjected can be reviewed after a number of years. In Bulgaria, for example, all individuals sentenced to life imprisonment with or without commutation must be placed under a "special regime" from the outset of their sentence[172] but that regime can be changed to a less stringent one if the prisoner has served at least five years and has shown good conduct.[173] Persons placed under the "special regime," however, must be kept in constantly locked cells and under heightened supervision.[174] In Romania, life-sentenced prisoners automatically serve their sentence under a maximum security regime with no formal process or structure aimed at integrating life-sentenced prisoners into the general prison population. The regime is reviewed after six and a half years of the sentence.[175] Finally, in Russia (and most of the former Soviet Union countries), individuals sentenced to life imprisonment are automatically placed under a "strict regime" and may be transferred to an "ordinary regime" after serving at least ten years of their sentence. They can then be moved to a "facilitated regime" after a further ten years under the ordinary regime, on an account of improved behavior.[176]

Impoverished Regimes

Concern has also been raised by international bodies that life-sentenced prisoners are frequently subjected to impoverished regimes, including poor and inadequate material conditions, limited human contact, and little or no access to rehabilitative opportunities. In some European countries, living conditions for life-sentenced prisoners have been found to be very poor, or even worse than for the general prison population.[177] In Bulgaria, for example, the conditions for life-sentenced prisoners were criticized recently by the CPT as being characterized by "a more or less advanced state of dilapidation and insalubrity," including mold on the walls, water on the floor, ill-equipped and unclean sanitary annexes, and very poor access to natural light.[178] A similar situation faces many life-sentenced prisoners living in Russia. In 2014, Franchetti reported that prisoners serving life sentences were housed in a "set of decaying Soviet-era buildings" with "no proper sewage system," which means that "prisoners [must] use buckets in their cell, which they slop out only once a day."[179]

Conditions of detention of prisoners subject to life imprisonment in Kyrgyzstan have also come under severe criticism from local and international human rights groups, who have described living conditions as inhumane.[180] According to PRI, life-sentenced prisoners are held in pretrial detention centers in underground cells with inadequate light and ventilation and poor sanitary conditions. Severe problems of overcrowding have meant that cells designed for two persons, house three to five prisoners, with some prisoners having to sleep on the floor. Life-sentenced prisoners receive smaller food rations than the other categories of prisoners.[181] Furthermore, poor living conditions, especially in terms of sanitary facilities, means that health problems, particularly tuberculosis, have been widespread among prisoners.[182] The lack of adequate medical provision in prison facilities led the chairman of the Committee for the Protection of the Dignity and Honour to the Kyrgyz Nation, to conclude that "instead of keeping them in such unacceptable conditions, it would be more humane if they were sent to death."[183]

PRI has also reported on "harsh and discriminatory" prison conditions in the Middle East and North Africa that raise serious concerns about inhuman and degrading punishment for both death row and life-sentenced prisoners: "Serious problems include overcrowding, inadequate living conditions, unsanitary facilities, lack of appropriate medical facilities (including mental health facilities), and inadequate nutrition or clean water, which all constitute a failure to meet international standards."[184]

Likewise, in Kenya and Uganda, death row and life-sentenced prisoners are subject to impoverished and discriminatory regimes, compared to other prisoners. PRI has stated, "Problems of overcrowding, inadequate living conditions, poor access to medical care, and a lack of rehabilitation for those on death row or serving life sentences create serious human rights concerns."[185]

Contact with the outside world can also be highly restrictive for many life-sentenced prisoners, who are often allowed not only far fewer visits than short-term prisoners, but in some cases are also forbidden to have physical contact. In Armenia, for example, while ordinary sentenced prisoners were allowed to receive at least one short-term visit (of up to four hours) per month, and one long-term visit (of up to three days) every two months, life-sentenced prisoners were entitled only to three short-term visits and one long-term visit per year.[186] And in contrast to most other prisoners, life-sentenced prisoners could receive short-term visits only under closed conditions, behind a glass barrier, preventing any physical contact between them and their visitors.[187] Similarly, in Tajikistan, under a daily routine of solitary confinement or "strict isolation," life-sentenced prisoners were eligible for no more than three short-term visits and two long-term visits per year.[188] And in Turkey, prisoners sentenced to aggravated life imprisonment received more restricted visits and telephone calls than other prisoners.[189]

Evidence considered by the Grand Chamber of the European Court of Human Rights (ECtHR), in the 2015 case of *Khoroshenko v Russia,* revealed that restrictions on contact with the outside world for life-sentenced prisoners in Russia were, if anything, even more extreme.[190] Under the strict regime policy, life-sentenced prisoners had the right only to two short-term visits per year, lasting no more than four hours and in the presence of a prison warden. The prisoners and one or more visitors were routinely separated by a glass partition or metal bars.[191] Moreover, telephone calls could take place only in exceptional personal circumstances and might also be monitored by prison staff.[192] These exceptional personal circumstances were limited to "death or serious life-threatening disease of a close relative [and] a natural disaster which inflicted serious pecuniary damage to the prisoner or to his family."[193]

Contact between staff and prisoners, and a positive prison climate are also important. The interests of humane treatment, the maintenance of effective control and security, and the need for staff safety require an emphasis on the development of a good internal atmosphere within prisons through positive relations between staff and prisoners. However, many existing systems, such as the maximum security facilities or solitary confinement regimes in the United States and elsewhere, discourage or even prohibit

staff from getting to know life-sentenced prisoners. Sophisticated technol-
ogies of control, including intensive panoptical surveillance, keep human
contact and sensory stimulation to a minimum. In the United States, even
children serving life sentences have been subjected to solitary confinement,
either as a form of protection or as a disciplinary sanction. A report by
Human Rights Watch in 2012 described the "devastating loneliness" suffered by children serving LWOP sentences. They were often segregated for
twenty-three hours or more a day, "spending their days alone, without any
human contact," the only exceptions being "when a prison guard passes
them a food tray through a slot in the door, or when guards touch their
wrists when handcuffing them through the same slot before taking them to
the exercise room or for a shower once a week."[194]

More generally, many prisoners serving life sentences are subjected to
regimes that exclude and deprive them of rehabilitative opportunities in
prison. A lack of meaningful activities and appropriate sentence planning
is often a feature of life sentence systems where time out of cell, contact
with the outside world and opportunities for interaction with others are
extremely limited. Life-sentenced prisoners are often not allowed to work
outside their cell and are generally excluded from any purposeful activities,
such as educational, vocational or rehabilitative programs. In Kyrgyzstan,
for example, life-sentenced prisoners are not entitled to access education or
work programs that are available to other prisoners and there is no provision for social or psychological assistance.[195] Similarly, in the United States,
many LWOP prisoners, including children, are denied access to educational
and vocational training available to other prisoners on the premise that they
are beyond redemption and should never be released. As one young prisoner serving LWOP in California stated:

> LWOPs cannot participate in many rehabilitative, educational, vocational
> training or other assignments available to other inmates with parole
> dates. . . . The supposed rationality is that LWOPs are beyond salvagability
> [sic] and would just be taking a spot away from someone who will actually
> return to society someday.[196]

Additionally, in some countries life-sentenced prisoners have not been
allowed to work at all, which has the same deleterious effect on any possibility of rehabilitation or reintegration. In their case it is the absence of all

access to work which is the additional punishment. In Ukraine, for example, the CPT has raised concerns that prisoners spend twenty-three hours a day in their cells "in a state of enforced idleness" with no access to educational or work programs.[197] In Belarus too, life-sentenced prisoners spend at least twenty-three hours per day in their cell with no access to education, work, or any other rehabilitative program.[198] And in Russia, PRI has reported that, "very few prisoners sentenced to life imprisonment are able to access employment programmes, and there are no rehabilitation or social reintegration programmes."[199]

Even in institutions with relatively good material conditions and more progressive regimes in Europe, there is evidence from the CPT and elsewhere that life-sentenced prisoners face significant difficulties in terms of accessing rehabilitative opportunities, such as limited access to programs, lack of work opportunities, and little or no individualized sentence planning or preparation for release.[200] In Cyprus, for example, life-sentenced prisoners have been particularly critical of their lack of access to any purposeful activities. In contrast to other prisoners, they have not been provided with individual custody plans and no psychosocial support programs are in place to assist them to come to terms with their period of incarceration, or to prepare them for eventual release.[201] Similarly, in Malta in 2013, the CPT found that most life-sentenced prisoners are excluded from work, education and other purposeful activities. It has therefore called upon the authorities to "take steps as a matter of urgency to draw up and implement specific programmes aimed at supporting life-sentenced and other long-term prisoners."[202] Prison researchers also report that in Poland, with few exceptions, life-sentenced prisoners have routinely been denied access to work or education programs and that "concerns around prison security prevailed over concerns about life prisoners' access to rehabilitative opportunities" among prison staff.[203]

In some parts of the world, penal labor is used as an additional form of punishment to make the life sentence more severe. Rather than an emphasis on work opportunities as a form of rehabilitation, life sentences with a minimum of seventy-five years or even natural life with hard labor have emerged as the new ultimate penalties in Caribbean countries, particularly for those individuals who have had their death sentences commuted to life as a result of several Privy Council decisions.[204] It has frequently been reported that such life-sentenced prisoners would prefer the death penalty given the conditions and severity of the life imprisonment system.[205] Other countries that have included the sanction of life imprisonment with forced or hard labor within their penal arsenal include India, Lebanon, Jordan, and Japan, as well as certain African countries, such as Benin, the Central African Republic, Chad, Côte d'Ivoire, Madagascar, and Mauritania.[206]

In somewhat similar vein, there is evidence that in some countries life-sentenced prisoners are singled out for harsh treatment. In a recent visit to Azerbaijan, for example, a delegation of the CPT received several allegations from life-sentenced prisoners of deliberate physical ill-treatment and excessive force by prison officers, including kicks and blows with truncheons as well as sexual abuse using a truncheon.[207] CPT members also witnessed attempts by prison officers to threaten and intimidate life-sentenced prisoners if they were to complain to the delegation or other international bodies.[208] Further, during the CPT's many visits, it has come to light that life-sentenced prisoners are often singled out from other prisoners and subjected to "anachronistic rules," the sole aim of which are to further punish and humiliate the individuals concerned. These include, for example, rules prohibiting life-sentenced prisoners to lie down on their beds during the day, an obligation to instantly line up and recite the articles of the Criminal Code under which they have been convicted each time an officer opens the cell door, and wearing a distinctly colored uniform. In the CPT's view, such practices clearly have a "dehumanising humiliating effect."[209]

Some steps have been taken by prison authorities, in response to reforms proposed by the CPT, to alleviate the detention conditions of life-sentenced prisoners, in particular, by offering prisoners work and other purposeful activities. Yet, policies regarding the execution of life sentences are still "all too often based on the presumption that life-sentenced prisoners are by definition particularly dangerous and that the regime applied should in one way or another also have a punitive character."[210] In its *25th General Report*, published in 2016, the CPT called on states that are parties to the convention under which it operates to review their treatment of life-sentenced prisoners and significantly improve their regimes.[211] The CPT emphasized that any lengthy term of imprisonment, and particularly a life sentence, can have desocializing effects upon the individuals so sentenced, resulting in many of the deleterious effects set out earlier in the chapter. In the view of the CPT, the regimes which are offered to life-sentenced prisoners should seek to compensate these effects in a positive and proactive way, an issue we pursue in Chapter 8.

Summary and Conclusion

The discussion in this chapter makes it clear that life imprisonment is a particularly harsh sanction. There are two aspects of life imprisonment—its indeterminacy and the differences in the regimes to which life-sentence prisoners are subject—that make it particularly destructive to human dignity.[212] In addition to the pains of imprisonment recognized by Sykes—the loss of liberty, goods and services, relationships, autonomy, and security—life imprisonment brings additional suffering since it removes the certainty of release on a given date in the future. This exacerbates the pains of imprisonment for life-sentenced prisoners who have to deal with a seemingly futile, hopeless existence for an indeterminate period. The depth of the painfulness of life imprisonment in many of the descriptions we have highlighted in this chapter is sobering.

On the treatment of life-sentenced prisoners there is substantial evidence, from the CPT in particular, that in many countries, prison conditions for life-sentenced prisoners are particularly poor and that such prisoners are routinely segregated and not provided with appropriate material conditions, activities, and meaningful human contact. There is also often an absence of sentence planning, programs, or facilities that will enable life-sentenced prisoners to rehabilitate themselves and to progress through their sentence to improved conditions and more open regimes. This is supported by evidence from some countries outside Europe that individuals who are sentenced to life imprisonment can be systematically subjected to special punitive restrictions, likely to exacerbate the painful effects of their long-term (often lifelong) imprisonment, without any clear justification. Such practice closely accords with Beccaria's harsh eighteenth-century vision of life imprisonment that he believed to be more of a deterrent than the penalty of death.[213] Even in countries that do not adopt such measures, there is evidence from life-sentenced prisoners themselves that their prison experience leaves much to be desired and that their requisite needs of rehabilitation and reintegration are not nearly met.

Doubtless, impoverished conditions and restrictive regimes are more likely to discourage life-sentenced prisoners in their efforts to reform, whereas supportive and rehabilitative environments (decent living conditions enriched by sentence planning, relevant programs and committed staff) are more likely to stimulate efforts at change. This important connection between progressive prison regimes and an individual's right to rehabilitation is being recognized increasingly in international human rights law, as well as in certain life sentence systems around the world. In the next chapter, we spell out in more detail the human rights standards that are specifically relevant to the implementation of life imprisonment, and consider examples of implementing life imprisonment well, namely, practice that aims to reduce the human costs of serving a life sentence.

8

Implementing Life Well

G IVEN THE CONTINUING and, in all likelihood, expanding use of life imprisonment, the development of environments that minimize the potential human costs of these sanctions is a critical concern. As we established in Chapter 1, over recent decades, international, regional, and national standards of human rights have emerged as increasingly important means of protecting prisoners against abuse or the types of painfulness and treatment that we discussed in Chapter 7. Our focus here is to make explicit how those human rights, to which all sentenced prisoners are entitled, should apply particularly to life prisoners. We then consider research findings and empirical accounts of where the implementation of life imprisonment comes closest to conforming to international principles and practices of human rights.

Human Rights Standards

The European Court of Human Rights (ECtHR) has led the way in distilling human rights standards relating to life imprisonment in order to develop an analytical framework for evaluating the implementation of life sentences. The 2015 judgment of the Grand Chamber of the ECtHR in *Khoroshenko v. Russia* is now the leading European case on how human rights require life-sentenced prisoners to be treated while serving their sentences.[1]

The case turns on whether Khoroshenko, a life-sentenced prisoner, was given adequate opportunities to maintain links with his family in order to allow an appropriate measure of family contact to continue while he was serving his sentence. In deciding it the Grand Chamber focused on applying Article 8 of the European Convention on Human Rights (ECHR) to the treatment of a life-sentenced prisoner. Article 8 guarantees everyone "the right to respect for his private and family life," but provides also that a public authority may limit the exercise of these rights where it is done in accordance with the law and is necessary in a democratic society for reasons of national security, public safety, and the protection of morals.

To assist with its decision, the court turned first to the 2006 European Prison Rules, the most prominent "soft law" instrument on prisoners' rights in Europe, for guidance on how prisoners' contacts with the outside world should be managed more generally.[2] For more specific guidance on how life-sentenced prisoners should be dealt with in this regard, the court considered the 2003 Recommendation on the Management by Prison Administrations of Life Sentence and Other Long-Term Prisoners,[3] which, like the European Prison Rules, was also a product of the Committee of Ministers of the Council of Europe. A third pan-European source on which the Grand Chamber relied was the standards developed by the Committee for the Prevention of Torture (CPT), a separate treaty-based inspection body that also operates under the broad umbrella of the Council of Europe, and therefore carries particular weight in the European context.[4]

The pan-European material was supplemented by a careful comparative analysis of national practice in Europe relating to visits to life-sentenced prisoners. It demonstrated that most member states allowed, as a matter of principle, life-sentenced prisoners, like other categories of prisoners, to communicate with their families at regular intervals by receiving visits from them. In only a few European states—the judgment listed Azerbaijan, Bulgaria, Lithuania, Poland, Serbia, and Turkey—were certain categories of prisoners, in particular life-sentenced prisoners, subject to special restrictions regarding the frequency and duration of such visits.[5]

The analysis of the Grand Chamber did not stop with Europe. It also turned to United Nations instruments for detailed information on the importance of prisoners' contact with the outside world.[6] In addition, it reviewed the rules governing visitors to prisoners held in the detention facilities of the International Criminal Tribunal for the former Yugoslavia and the jurisprudence of the Inter-American Court of Human Rights dealing with prison visits.[7]

Perhaps the most important contribution that the Grand Chamber made in the *Khoroshenko* case was to integrate these various standards with its own jurisprudence on the importance of ensuring that the implementation of imprisonment facilitates the social rehabilitation of all prisoners, including those serving life sentences. This enabled the Grand Chamber to align itself with the requirement of social rehabilitation in Article 10(3) of the International Covenant on Civil and Political Rights (ICCPR) and to pronounce, after an overview of both the various standards and its own burgeoning jurisprudence on the rehabilitative purpose of (life) imprisonment: "The regime and conditions of a life prisoner's incarceration cannot be regarded as a matter of indifference. . . . They need to be such as to make it possible for the life prisoner to endeavour to reform himself, with a view to being able one day to seek an adjustment of his or her sentence."[8]

The decision in *Khoroshenko* deals with a particular restriction that was unnecessarily imposed on a life-sentenced prisoner, but its application of regional, international and national materials is typical of how the ECtHR uses such materials when the implementation of life sentences is questioned. For the purpose of evaluating the treatment of life prisoners worldwide, we identify three interrelated human rights requirements for the treatment of life prisoners specifically. First, strenuous efforts should be made to ameliorate the unique pains of imprisonment of life prisoners, whether they are serving formal sentences of life imprisonment or not. Second, life prisoners should not be subjected to additional punishment or restrictions merely because they are not serving fixed-term sentences. Third, life prisoners should have a path to release. Taken together, these requirements mean that they should be granted the opportunity to resocialize themselves while in prison, and that prison regimes for them should be structured accordingly. In developing these requirements, we focus on those standards that deal with them most specifically, while acknowledging that there are other, wider standards that underpin them.

Dealing with the Unique Pains of Life Imprisonment

A feature of specialist human rights instruments related to life imprisonment is that they recognize the unique pains of life imprisonment that we described in Chapter 7. Thus the United Nations report, *Life Imprisonment*, notes that "it is essential to recognize the potentially detrimental effects of life imprisonment,"[9] while the 2003 Recommendation of the Council of Europe sees one of its three primary objectives as being "to counteract the damaging effects of life and long-term imprisonment."[10]

How should this be done? The United Nations report pinned its faith on structured treatment programs, while noting that they may be abused and that steps have to be taken to ensure that such programs "are not used as a subtle means of coercion that has the effect of further punishing offenders who have been indeterminately deprived of their liberty."[11]

The 2003 Council of Europe Recommendation took a wider view. It sought to define a set of interlinked principles that should govern the treatment and management of life-sentenced and long-term prisoners. These build on standards embedded in previous, more general, international instruments and provide basic guidance for implementing life sentence prison regimes specifically. The six overarching principles are: individualization; normalization; responsibility; security and safety; nonsegregation; and progression.[12]

The principle of individualization asserts that consideration should be given to the wide diversity of personal characteristics that are found among life-sentenced and long-term prisoners, as with other prisoners. Prison institutions should take account of age, intellectual capacity, education level, social background and circumstances, personality, and typical ways of thinking and behaving to make individual sentence plans according to the needs of, and the risks posed by, each life-sentenced prisoner.[13]

The principle of normalization aims to counteract the risk of institutionalization posed by the effects of lengthy prison terms. It emphasizes that daily prison life often requires prisoners to follow a series of monotonous routines that may render prisoners unfit to readjust to a law-abiding life in the community. Normalization recognizes that "[p]rison life should be arranged so as to approximate as closely as possible to the realities of life in the community."[14]

Closely linked to the principle of normalization, the responsibility principle challenges prison administrations, within the limits of security, to create situations for prisoners to "be given opportunities to exercise personal responsibility in daily prison life."[15] It asserts that prison regimes often deny prisoners the opportunity to make their own decisions and to learn from them. Opportunities should be made available for prisoners to take responsibility for developing attitudes and behavior needed to lead a successful, law-abiding life.

The security and safety principle demands that the nature and level of risk posed by life-sentenced and long-term prisoners be assessed. It highlights the point that life-sentenced prisoners are often wrongly assumed to be dangerous. With regard to the principle of individualization, it states that careful assessment should be made of "any risks posed by life sentence and other long-term prisoners to the external community, to themselves, to other prisoners and to those working in or visiting the prison."[16] Given that risk factors are intrinsically dynamic, assessments should be repeated at intervals.

The nonsegregation principle underlines the security and safety principle. Segregation of life-sentenced or other long-term prisoners cannot be justified "on the sole ground of their sentence."[17] Such prisoners often present little or no risk to themselves or to others. If there is a risk, it may only be present in certain circumstances or for a limited time period. Segregation should only be implemented when a clear and present risk to their own or others' safety exists.

The progression principle emphasizes the significance of "progressive movement through the prison system"[18] for life-sentenced prisoners, from more to less restrictive conditions, to open conditions that allow them to spend as much time in the outside community as possible. Each prisoner's individualized sentence plan should seek to give effect to the progression principle.

In 2016, these six principles were given the powerful endorsement of the CPT, which incorporated them fully into its own empirically based standards, noting that they remained the most pertinent and comprehensive statement of principles on how life prisoners should be treated.[19] The CPT gave detailed guidance on how these principles should be implemented in practice:

> Since being locked up, especially for an unknown period, is inherently damaging for almost all human beings, steps must be taken to minimise the damage. One important method of achieving this for life-sentenced prisoners is to give them a definite date for the first review for possible release, and a tailored individual programme which provides a realistic series of interventions for each prisoner leading towards that date. . . . [S]uch a programme should ensure that all life-sentenced prisoners are given the opportunity to address all aspects of their identified risks and needs before the date of their first review. This should also entail time spent in less secure conditions, especially on leave in the community towards the end of the period, to ensure that the risk and needs management plan will function outside a secure

environment. Continuity of care in the community is crucial to successful reintegration, and a plan for this should be established well before the release date.[20]

The CPT emphasized that "life-sentenced prisoners should have access to as full a regime of activities as possible, and normally in association with other prisoners."[21] It explained that "work, education, sports, cultural activities and hobbies not only help pass the time, but are also crucial in promoting social and mental health well-being and imparting transferable skills which will be useful during and after the custodial part of the sentence."[22] The CPT noted that the involvement of prisoners in these activities also allowed prison staff to assess prisoners' performance, enabling them "to make informed judgments as to when it would be appropriate for the prisoner to progress through the regime and be trusted with lower security conditions."[23] It also emphasized that "[t]he possibility of such progression is crucial, for the management of the prison and for the prisoner. It motivates and rewards the prisoner, providing staging posts in their otherwise indeterminate world, and ensures a deeper relationship between the assessing staff and the prisoner, which contributes to dynamic security."[24]

The CPT explained further that assessments based on the interactions between prisoners and staff that underlie dynamic security made a crucial contribution in deciding when it was safe to allow the individual prisoner access to the community. Such access could initially be in the form of escorted short leave. Ideally, it would then move on to unescorted overnight leave, and finally to conditional release into the community. This would enable staff to develop "an in-depth understanding of the individual, which they can share with decision-making bodies and with those who will take over responsibility for supervision and support in the community."[25]

In 2016, in *Murray v. the Netherlands,* the Grand Chamber of the ECtHR also relied explicitly on the individualization and progression principles to evaluate whether a life-sentenced prisoner had a de facto possibility of release, as ECHR law requires.[26] In this case, which arose in the Netherlands Antilles—that is, not within Europe—the life-sentenced prisoner was not given adequate treatment for his mental illness. This meant that in practice he could not avail himself of any opportunities for self-improvement, which in turn contributed to his not being able to make progress toward becoming less of a danger to society on release. The Grand Chamber ruled that the absence of attention to this individual's needs for treatment for his mental health problems, together with his resultant lack of progress, meant that his life sentence was de facto irreducible. The court therefore found that, taking these two factors together, his treatment had been inhuman and degrading and thus infringed Article 3 of the ECHR.

No Additional Restrictions

Sentenced prisoners should not have their rights restricted more heavily merely because of the particular crimes they committed or because of the particular sentences that were imposed on them. Restrictions on other grounds—safety and security, for example—may be justified if proportionate to the individual risk posed. These should not be used, however, as a way of introducing offense-based restrictions or restrictions based on the length of sentence by the back door. This last point was specifically applied to life imprisonment in the United Nations report, which referred to a guarantee in these cases "that special security measures are applied only on those cases where genuinely dangerous prisoners are held."[27] The CPT too has noted that life-sentenced prisoners are not necessarily more dangerous than other prisoners. It has warned that the false claim that all life-sentenced prisoners are dangerous should not be used as an excuse for placing unnecessary security restrictions on them and thus making the conditions of their detention much harsher than they would otherwise have been.[28]

Additional restrictions on life prisoners may take various forms, some of which have been condemned specifically by the various standards. As noted in Chapter 7, in some countries, life-sentenced prisoners are routinely separated from other prisoners and thus discriminated against. Both the 2003 Council of Europe Recommendation and the 2016 standards of the CPT specify that this should not be done.[29] Similarly, in some parts of the world, life prisoners are not allowed to work while serving their sentences; something that is contrary to several regional and national standards, which require that all prisoners be given the opportunity to work.[30]

Much of the case law of the ECtHR on the treatment of life prisoners deals with additional restrictions of this kind. In many instances, disproportionate restrictions can be challenged by relying on basic human rights treaties and mainstream prison law standards. In *Öcalan v. Turkey (No.2)* for example, the ECtHR found that Turkey's best-known political prisoner was subjected to inhuman and degrading treatment or punishment that infringed Article 3 of the ECHR because of the "social isolation" and other restrictions to which he was subjected as a life-sentenced prisoner. This was in addition to a separate finding that the particular form of life sentence imposed on Öcalan infringed Article 3, because it was irreducible.[31]

In *Harakchiev and Tolumov v. Bulgaria*, the ECtHR also made two separate findings of infringements of Article 3 of the ECHR on almost identical grounds. The unwarranted segregation of these two life-sentenced prisoners from other prisoners for many years on end and their subjection to other forms of ill treatment indicated that this sort of additional punishment was not limited to high-profile individuals but rather may have been part of a wider strategy to punish life-sentenced prisoners particularly harshly. The ECtHR was unequivocal in its rejection, on human rights grounds, of attempts to justify such harsh treatment on vague security grounds.[32]

National courts have adopted a similarly robust approach. Even in the case of the notorious mass murderer, Anders Breivik, whose sentence includes the possibility of indeterminate preventive detention and is a type of informal life imprisonment, a Norwegian court held that his isolation from contact with other prisoners infringed Article 3 of the ECHR. Repeated strip searches were also judged to be degrading by the court. The court ruled that "[t]he prohibition of inhuman and degrading treatment represents a fundamental value in a democratic society. This applies no matter what—also in the treatment of terrorists and killers."[33]

Justification for additional restrictions on life-sentenced prisoners is sometimes sought on explicitly retributive grounds. In the *Khoroshenko* case, which concerned the Russian practice of keeping all life-sentenced prisoners in semi-isolation for the first ten years of their sentence and denying them almost all family visits during that period, the Russian government was frank about the purpose of these restrictions. It was designed to make the life sentence more punitive. The response of the Grand Chamber of the ECtHR was equally clear. This was not an acceptable purpose for implementing a particular way of administering a prison, so it could not, therefore, form the basis for a decision by the prison authorities to limit the Article 8 rights of the prisoner to a reasonable number of family visits. Such visits could be limited, on security grounds, for example, but they would have to be demonstrated in the individual case. Individualized treatment, the

Grand Chamber noted, was the key to social rehabilitation, a goal on which the ECtHR has placed great emphasis.[34]

This approach has been influential in Russia as well. A press report in November 2016 revealed that the Russian Constitutional Court too has accepted that the blanket denial of intimate visits for ten years infringes both the Russian constitution and the ECHR, and has now ruled that every life-sentenced prisoner is entitled to an extended (conjugal) visit each year. In coming to this conclusion the Russian Court has gone further than the ECtHR in one respect. The ECtHR has not been prepared to find that conjugal visits are a fundamental right of married prisoners, although they have spoken in favor of them. In Russia such visits are the norm, and the Russian court appears to have been persuaded that barring them for ten years for life-sentenced prisoners alone was unfair discrimination.[35]

The ECtHR has been prepared, however, to recognize that the right to family life may be asserted in other ways. The case of *Dickson v. United Kingdom* concerned a life-sentenced prisoner and his wife. They wished to start a family, but Dickson was unlikely to qualify for release before his wife became too old to bear children. Nevertheless, the British authorities, which did not permit conjugal visits, had refused to allow artificial insemination either. However, their policy of only allowing artificial insemination in exceptional circumstances was held by the Grand Chamber of the ECtHR to infringe the Dicksons' right to family life as guaranteed by Article 8 of the ECHR, and they were compelled to adopt a more liberal policy.[36]

An interesting aspect of the reasoning of the Grand Chamber in the *Dickson* case was its acceptance that all prisoners had a fundamental right to be given opportunities to rehabilitate themselves, which the court articulated in this much quoted passage:

> [I]n recent years there has been a trend towards placing more emphasis on rehabilitation, as demonstrated notably by the Council of Europe's legal instruments. While rehabilitation was recognised as a means of preventing recidivism, more recently and more positively, it constitutes rather the idea of re-socialisation through the fostering of personal responsibility. This objective is reinforced by the development of the "progression principle": in the course of serving a sentence, a prisoner should move progressively through the prison system thereby moving from the early days of a sentence, when

the emphasis may be on punishment and retribution, to the latter stages, when the emphasis should be on preparation for release.[37]

The ECtHR expressed its belief that Dickson's chances of being rehabilitated would be increased by allowing him and his wife to have a child. The British government was firmly told by the court that, in the face of the Dicksons' rights in this regard, which was derived also from the right specifically recognized by Article 12 of the ECHR of married people to start a family, they were not to take into account either public opinion or the disadvantages that a child born in this way and growing up without a father would face. In all, the ECtHR has emphasized that the human rights of life-sentenced prisoners should not be restricted unnecessarily.

Creating a Path to Release

The duty to allow prisoners to rehabilitate themselves in order to allow them to show that they are no longer dangerous is one of the features of international and European standards of human rights to which we have already drawn attention. For the purpose of understanding how life sentences should be implemented, it is important to reflect on what it means in terms of the specific requirements on how life-sentenced prisoners should be treated.

A prominent example of what is necessarily required is having a sentence plan to guide life prisoners through their prison term and give them a focus for their eventual release. In order to allow such plans to be made, the ECtHR, starting with the decision of the Grand Chamber in 2013 in *Vinter and others v. United Kingdom*,[38] has stressed that all life-sentenced prisoners need to know at the time that they are sentenced when their release will be considered. Indications of the importance of such plans for all prisoners are to be found in the general international and regional standards on how prisoners should be treated. As Judges Pinto de Albuquerque and Turković held in the *Khoroshenko* case:

> The cornerstone of a penal policy aimed at resocialising prisoners is the individualised sentence plan, under which the prisoner's risk and needs in terms of health care, activities, work, exercise, education and contacts with the family and outside world should be assessed. This basic principle

of penological science has been acknowledged and affirmed by statements made at the level of the highest political authorities both in Europe and worldwide.[39]

International penological instruments apply the same approach specifically to life-sentenced prisoners. The United Nations report, *Life Imprisonment,* sets out the requirements for establishing, implementing and reviewing individualized programs for life-sentenced prisoners.[40]

At the European level, the general 2006 European Prison Rules state specifically, in their only direct reference to life-sentenced prisoners, that "particular attention shall be paid to providing appropriate sentence plans and regimes" for them.[41] The more specialist 2003 Recommendation on the Management of Life-Sentenced Prisoners contains a number of detailed provisions on comprehensive sentence plans for each individual prisoner. These include risk and needs assessments; a systematic approach to initial allocation; "progressive movement through the prison system from more to less restrictive conditions with, ideally, a final phase spent under open conditions, preferably in the community"; work, education and training; and, "programmes designed to address risks and needs so as to reduce disruptive behaviour in prison and re-offending after release."[42] The 2016 CPT standards for the implementation of life sentences endorse this approach and emphasize that "the imposition of the detention regime of life-sentenced prisoners should lie with the prison authorities and always be based on an individual risk assessment, and not be the automatic result of the type of sentence imposed."[43]

In the *Murray* case, the Grand Chamber unanimously converted the obligations contained in these various instruments into a binding legal standard that related general principles about social rehabilitation to a specific legal requirement on sentence planning. In his separate concurring opinion in this case, Judge Pinto de Albuquerque summarized the current position of the ECtHR:

[T]he Contracting Parties to the Convention have a positive obligation to promote resocialisation of prisoners namely by providing and implementing an individualised sentence plan. This is the very first time that the Court has acknowledged the crucial importance of an individualised sentence plan for the promotion of resocialisation of prisoners, that importance being reinforced

by a statement of principle of the Grand Chamber. The obligation to promote resocialisation is an Article 3 obligation which imposes on the State a
duty to act or, to use the words of the Grand Chamber, "a duty to make it
possible for such prisoners to rehabilitate themselves." Thus, the Grand
Chamber perceives the State's legal obligations to promote resocialisation and
to provide and implement an individualised sentence plan as two sides of the
same coin.[44]

Even in Europe there is still some resistance to such a strategy. As noted
in Chapter 2, in the Netherlands life imprisonment has long taken the form
of life imprisonment without parole (LWOP), and the Dutch government
has used this as a justification for a policy of not offering any resocialization programs to Dutch life-sentenced prisoners. However, LWOP has been
under sustained attack there too.[45] This has led to the Dutch government
adopting a new policy specifying that, after sentenced prisoners have served
twenty-five years, there should be an investigation into whether they would
benefit from programs that could contribute to their eventual release. However, nothing of that kind should be offered to them before twenty-five
years has elapsed. The new policy is a somewhat half-hearted adoption of
the principle of resocialization, as there are to be no activities preparing
them for release for the first twenty-five years of the sentence. Nevertheless, its adoption does reflect the impact of the European trend toward the
recognition of prisoners' right to given opportunities for resocialization.

Outside Europe, the legal position in respect of a duty to provide rehabilitative programs for all life-sentenced prisoners is much less clear.
As noted in Chapter 2, LWOP sentences remain a prominent feature of life
imprisonment in a significant number of countries worldwide. There is
little recognition that prisoners serving this type of life sentence are entitled to receive the opportunities for treatment that could lead to their eventual reintegration into free society, for example, as a result of their sentences
being commuted. Nor is there evidence of a commitment to ensuring that
they have access to such opportunities in practice.

Finally, to what extent does the requirement of a path to release backed
by an appropriate sentence plan apply also to persons serving informal life
sentences? Governments often claim that they will offer intensive rehabilitative programs to assist persons serving indeterminate sentences, so that
they will to cease to be a danger to society. Courts in various jurisdictions
have been prepared to hold governments to these undertakings.

Thus, when the UK government did not provide the training programs for prisoners serving an indeterminate sentence of imprisonment for public protection (IPP), the national courts found that, in the light of what the government had publically undertaken to do, the failure to do so was a dereliction of a public duty.[46] The question remained what the legal consequence of this failure was, for the practical effect was that IPP prisoners who had not been able to do these courses were not being released, since they could not convince the parole board that they had ceased to pose a risk to society. The English courts initially ruled that this failure did not affect the legality of the detention of these IPP prisoners, since their indeterminate terms could only be terminated when their fitness to return to society had been demonstrated.[47] The ECtHR, however, found that the failure to provide the promised courses jeopardized the legality of the detention of these prisoners. It infringed Article 5 of the ECHR, which allows deprivation of individual liberty only on a narrow list of grounds, one of which is a sentence of imprisonment imposed by a court.[48]

The ECtHR did not order their release. It ruled, however, that they should receive monetary compensation for the period during which the failure to offer them training courses made it impossible for them to apply successfully for release, which meant that they were necessarily detained beyond the minimum period set by their sentence. Subsequently, the UK Supreme Court adopted the same approach. In 2014, it ordered compensation both to persons serving IPP and those serving formal life sentences, who were not able to make a case for their release after having served the minimum period of their sentences because they had been unable to access such courses before their cases were considered by the parole board.[49]

In Germany it has become increasingly clear that prisoners serving indeterminate post-conviction terms of preventive detention (*Sicherungsverwahrung*) must be offered training courses that enable them to apply for conditional release. As we noted in Chapter 2, provision for treatment is the way in which the German Federal Constitutional Court continues to justify a "second track" of indeterminate post-conviction detention. However, at one stage the German authorities did not offer training courses to foreigners in indeterminate post-conviction detention because they planned to deport them. In 2012, the ECtHR ruled that this amounted to discrimination on the basis of nationality, which infringed Article 14 of the ECHR.[50] It held that if a state set up such a system, it had to offer it to all prisoners in the same category. Failure to do so would not only be discriminatory but would infringe Article 5, which guarantees freedom from unlawful detention.

The emphasis on treatment is not universal, even in European countries that adopt a dual-track approach. This is seen clearly in the Swiss system, which has long provided for two categories of potentially indefinite detention of persons convicted of a range of serious offenses and who are found to be dangerous: those who are thought to be incorrigible and therefore untreatable in the long run, and those who suffer from a serious mental illness but who may be treatable. In both these instances, the persons concerned may be released if they are eventually found not to be dangerous, although the latter are not offered any form of treatment. However, in 2004 a popular initiative decided to introduce a third category of lifelong post-sentence detention for highly dangerous and untreatable sex or violent offenders in order to effectively eliminate all possibility of release. A resultant provision, written into the Constitution of Switzerland, provides that such offenders may never be considered for release.[51] The only exception is if new scientific findings allowed for the matter to be reconsidered. If the authorities then grant the release, they must accept liability if the person concerned reoffends.[52] Whether this form of indefinite detention will survive a challenge before the ECtHR remains to be seen.

Outside Europe, a general right to rehabilitative treatment for those who are detained indefinitely because of their perceived dangerousness is not widely recognized. In the leading US case of *Kansas v. Hendricks,* the detainee, Hendricks, objected to his continued detention after he had completed his fixed-term sentence also on the basis that, since he was receiving only minimal treatment, his detention was in fact merely a continuation of the fixed term he had already completed.[53] The Supreme Court, however, rejected this argument on the grounds that, notwithstanding the lack of treatment, Hendricks's detention did not constitute punishment. This approach is in contrast to that of the German Courts, which, unlike the ECtHR, also regard post-sentence preventive detention as being, not a form of punishment, but rather a form of treatment, and insist that such treatment should be given particular prominence to distinguish it from other sentences of (life) imprisonment.[54]

In an important decision in late 2017, in the matter of *Miller and Carroll v New Zealand,* the UN Human Rights Committee adopted the view that the ICCPR "requires that [post-conviction] preventive detention conditions be distinct from the conditions of convicted prisoners serving punitive sentences and be aimed at the detainee's rehabilitation and reintegration into society".[55] A failure to do so contravened Article 9(1) of the ICCPR, as it led to the continued detention of such detainees for an indefinite period being arbitrary. It also contravened the specific requirement of Article 10(3) of the Covenant for prisoners to be given treatment aimed at their "reformation and social rehabilitation".

Doubtless there are some life prisoners who are very dangerous and who pose significant challenges for prisons that have to ensure an appropriate balance between security measures and the treatment of prisoners in line with the human rights principles we have outlined above. However, international standards and norms related to the treatment and conditions of imprisonment of dangerous prisoners recommend that the same approach should be adopted as for other sentenced prisoners who present a risk of escape or a risk to the safety of themselves or others. That is, all persons deprived of their liberty should be treated with humanity and with respect for their human dignity.

More than thirty-five years ago, the 1982 Council of Europe Recommendation concerning custody and treatment of dangerous prisoners stated that prison systems should apply "ordinary prison regulations to dangerous prisoners" and "to apply security measures only to the extent to which they are necessarily required," and "in a way respectful of human dignity and rights."[56] It went on to state that they should aim to "counteract, to the extent feasible, the possible adverse effects of reinforced security conditions," "provide education, vocational training, work and leisure time occupations and other activities to the extent that security permits," as well as "a system for regular review to ensure that time spent in reinforced security custody and level of security applied do not exceed what is required."[57] More recently at the European level, the CPT has also noted that, as with all dangerous prisoners, the overall objective regarding the treatment and management of dangerous life-sentenced prisoners should be to "reduce the level of dangerousness by appropriate interventions and return the prisoners to normal circulation as soon as possible."[58] This includes a progressive system based on detailed individualized assessments of the prisoners concerned, risk management plans to address the individual's needs and to reduce the likelihood of reoffending, as well as regular reviews of their security level. The need to approach the management of dangerous or high-risk prisoners in this positive, progressive manner has been underlined by the United Nations in their 2016 *Handbook on the Management of High-Risk Prisoners*. It stated that:

> Additional security measures required to ensure that such prisoners do not escape and that they do not cause harm to themselves or others should never amount to inhuman treatment. It is important to note in this regard that treating prisoners with humanity does not hinder safeguarding security and order in prisons, but on the contrary, is fundamental to ensuring that prisons are secure and safe. Good practice in prison management has shown that when the human rights and dignity of prisoners are respected and they are treated fairly, they are much less likely to cause disruption and disorder, and more likely to accept the authority of prison staff.[59]

In all, fundamental human rights require the state to provide rehabilitative treatment for all life prisoners, whether they are serving formal or informal life sentences. However, more is required of the authorities to compensate for particular pains of life imprisonment and conversely not to make life sentences harsher than other prison sentences. These further requirements also have a clear foundation in human rights principles. In the following section, we consider examples of where a range of human rights based initiatives have been applied in the implementation of life imprisonment, both in Europe and elsewhere.

Doing Life Imprisonment Well

It is difficult, if not impossible, to present a worldwide evaluation of the extent to which life imprisonment has been implemented well, for not only are the worst practices sometimes deliberately hidden, but prison systems have an interest in presenting accounts of their best practices, while keeping quiet about what they claim, but often fail, to do. On the other hand, in many countries, life-sentenced prisoners are held together with other sentenced prisoners and benefit from the same rights, both in terms of prison regimes and contact with the outside world. Indeed, there are some systems in which life-sentenced prisoners have better material conditions and more progressive regimes than short-term prisoners, due to the long-term nature of their sentence.[60] Here we highlight some examples of practice and initiatives that incorporate, through individualized sentence planning, normalized prison regimes, and the provision of purposeful activities, some of the human rights principles we have summarized above.

Individual Sentence Planning

Ideally, prison regimes for life prisoners should be based on individual sentence plans, which are tailored to the individual risk and needs of each prisoner. The principle of individualization calls for individual sentence planning that is aimed at the process of resocialization and which takes full account of the diversity of personal characteristics found among life prisoners. In addition, the principle of progression calls for opportunities for life prisoners to advance through the system to more open conditions to be taken into consideration in sentence planning.

In many countries, prisoners sentenced to life imprisonment go through an initial assessment and induction process in a high-security prison before being transferred to the main prison system. For example, in Scotland, life-sentenced prisoners are detained initially in the National Induction Centre, which is within a high-security prison. The center aims to help prisoners address any particular problems or issues that arise during the first phase of imprisonment, and to facilitate their entry into the mainstream prison system. Prisoners are then transferred to a prison with a security level based on an individual assessment of dangerousness. The initial assessment process leads to the development of an individual sentence plan that includes an assessment of the prisoner's risk and need, as well as "the various activities and programmes in which the prisoner is likely to be involved throughout his sentence," all of which are primarily aimed at reducing any risk of danger to the public.[61]

Similarly, in New Zealand, all life-sentenced prisoners are subject to a structured induction interview at the start of their sentence, which includes an assessment of the risk they pose and of their immediate needs. Within fourteen days, they are assigned to a security level that is "appropriate to the level of internal and external risk that a prisoner poses."[62] Every security classification is reviewed at least once every six months during the course of a prisoner's sentence and also whenever there is a significant change in the prisoner's personal circumstances. Such a review focuses on "the prisoner's behaviour during sentence, what he has done to address his offending, tempered by historical factors, whether or not the prisoner has any outstanding charges and the time the prisoner has to complete before being eligible for parole, next Parole Board hearing date or release."[63]

In England and Wales, life sentence plans were introduced for all life-sentenced prisoners in 1993. Their purpose is "to plan, monitor and record the means by which each lifer is supported in the process of achieving a reduction in risk during sentence such that he or she may safely be released on licence into the community at tariff expiry."[64] The life sentence plan includes an overall assessment of risk, as well as sentence targets and objectives, and is shared with the prisoner. The overriding concern in the process of risk assessment is the protection of the public, and it therefore focuses on characteristics that might threaten public safety, such as offense history, risk factors, and lifestyle. The plan should be reviewed and revised at regular intervals, with new targets and objectives. Progression to lower security regimes depends largely on the achievement of sentence-planning targets, participation in offending behavior programs, and conformity with the prison regime.[65]

Similar practices are found elsewhere. A 2014 study by Drenkhahn and colleagues, which sought to identify good practice in long-term prison regimes across eleven European Union (EU) countries, found that more than two-thirds of the institutions studied had developed individual sentence plans for life-sentenced and long-term prisoners. Such plans were largely based on information gathered during an initial examination and subsequently revised during the course of the sentence. These examinations were usually carried out by specifically trained prison staff, and were based on an assessment of the person's individual characteristics that were relevant for planning intervention programs. The study found that

> [i]n most institutions where a sentence plan was made, it addressed the allocation of the prisoner to a certain unit; progress to more open conditions (open prison, prison leave); allocation to work, education or vocational training; leisure-time activities; offending behaviour treatment; release preparations; and the risk of self-harm or harm to others.[66]

In the eleven EU countries studied, use was often made of accredited risk and needs instruments, supplemented by professional judgment. The resulting plans became a resource for all persons working with the prisoner, and were revised during the sentence. Drenkhahn and colleagues reported that some countries, including Denmark, England and Wales, Finland,

Germany, and Sweden, had established "a systematic approach to sentence planning" for long-term prisoners, although some problems remained. For example, not all prisoners from the countries in the study with an established approach to sentence planning recognized that they had such a plan or that their plan had been revised at regular intervals.[67]

An important feature of the initial assessment and sentence planning is a progressive system in which life prisoners are given planned opportunities to qualify for increasingly less restrictive conditions and levels of security so that ideally a life prisoner is released from open conditions. Many penal systems acknowledge that life prisoners are not necessarily more dangerous than other prisoners and can quickly proceed to lower levels of security. Equally, life-sentenced prisoners who are assessed as dangerous at the beginning of their sentence may well become significantly less so, not just with the passage of time during their long-term confinement but also with targeted interventions and humane treatment.

Several countries have low-security or open prisons to help prepare life-sentenced prisoners for release at the end of their sentence. The great majority of life-sentenced prisoners in the United Kingdom, for example, are released from open prisons. Over the course of the life sentence, it is recognized that both the security classification and the sentence plan for life-sentenced prisoners require regular review. Most life-sentenced prisoners serve the first part of their sentence under a high-security regime together with other sentenced prisoners, and from there, they proceed to prisons with a medium level of security. A number of years before their anticipated release, life-sentenced prisoners are transferred to a low-security regime or to open prison conditions where they have the opportunity to leave the prison, sometimes for several days at a time, often to become involved with community projects, educational courses, or work experience as part of the final preparation for their return to the community. The importance of the progressive element of the English life sentence system was recently summarized by Stone:

> Because closed prisons provide a protective environment which is not appropriate to the problems facing a lifer on release and prison behaviour in conditions of freedom, it is in the community's interest, as well as that of individual lifers, that they be tested and assessed in a low security environment before release, and that pre-release preparation should be as thorough and varied as possible.[68]

Open institutions are often referred to as "prisons without walls,"[69] meaning that there are usually no secure fences preventing prisoners from escaping. The regime in open institutions is generally more relaxed than in closed prisons, and it serves as a transitional step for life-sentenced prisoners to readjust to life in a free society.

Comparable practices exist elsewhere in Europe, allowing life-sentenced prisoners to leave the institution by day, often to work or pursue educational courses in the community outside, but sometimes also simply to maintain family contacts (for example, in Belgium, Denmark, Finland, Germany, and Sweden).[70] These forms of release are not necessarily linked to open institutions. The philosophy is that regular leave, particularly for the maintenance of family life, should be open to all prisoners who meet the basic criteria of not posing a flight risk and being unlikely to commit further offenses.

In practice, such leave for life-sentenced prisoners is often more restricted than for other prisoners. Thus, German prison law provides that temporary leave for life-sentenced prisoners should normally be granted only after they have served ten years.[71] Moreover, in 1983 the German Federal Constitutional Court ruled, in a majority judgment, that, in exceptional cases, the heinousness of the offense—in this instance, leave for a Nazi convicted of mass murder—could be considered when deciding on the measures to be deployed when implementing a life sentence.[72] This judgment elicited a passionate dissent from the deputy president of the Constitutional court and was widely criticized by German scholars on the grounds that it was introducing a factor that should be irrelevant to the way in which life sentences are implemented.[73] Subsequently, however, the constitutional court retreated somewhat from its restrictive 1983 judgment. It has now emphasized the importance of allowing periods of leave from prison to life-sentenced prisoners when the basic criteria are met, even before the ten-year period has elapsed, as such leave was an essential aspect of their reintegration into normal community life.[74]

Normalized Regimes

All prisoners, including life-sentenced prisoners, should have the same fundamental rights as other citizens and their living conditions should be made to reflect normal life or, as the Council of Europe puts it, "approximate as closely as possible the positive aspects of life in the community."[75] This principle of normalization has not only been included in European Recommendations but has recently been incorporated in the national legislation of many countries, including Germany, the Netherlands, Switzerland, and Scandinavian countries.[76] In most European countries the citizenship of all prisoners, including those serving life sentences, is recognized by allowing them to vote in national elections. European human rights law encourages voting rights for all prisoners but does not currently require it.[77]

Normalized prison regimes are intended to ameliorate the harm caused by the pains of imprisonment and to promote the process of resocialization and reintegration for all prisoners. The Danish Prison and Probation Service Handbook explains, "By establishing conditions which differ as little as possible from those obtaining in daily life outside prison, the grounds for aggression and apathy are reduced and the negative effects of a prison sojourn are limited."[78] On the basis of the normalization principle, life-sentenced prisoners, like other prisoners in Denmark, typically live in units where they are responsible for collectively managing a budget, deciding what they will cook and eat, ordering food from a prison shop, and preparing and cooking their own meals, either individually or in groups. Similarly, in Germany, as in the Scandinavian countries, life-sentenced prisoners have access to communal kitchens, where they can cook food purchased with wages earned in vocational programs. In normalized prison environments, life-sentenced prisoners can also decorate their cells with personal possessions such as family photos, pictures, and plants. They have freedom of movement around their facilities and are expected to exercise judgment about how they spend their time.[79]

In the Netherlands, a prison has recently introduced a pilot wing for life-sentenced and other long-term prisoners that is completely unstaffed so that the residents can live "as autonomously and self-sufficiently as medium-secure conditions allow."[80] By affording life-sentenced prisoners more autonomy and agency, normalized prison regimes can reduce the risk of institutionalization by encouraging prisoners to take responsibility for themselves, their behavior and their surroundings.

Normalized environments clearly incorporate the principle of responsibility, which challenges prison systems, within the limits of security, to create situations for life-sentenced prisoners to learn and exercise personal responsibility. In some countries life-sentenced prisoners are given responsibility as caretakers for the prison grounds and gardens, the visiting area, and for the maintenance of other communal spaces.[81] Taking on these types of responsibilities can then be rewarded, allowing prisoners to experience how positive behavior generates positive outcomes, progression into less secure, open living conditions, and ultimately to release.

In addition, prisons can provide opportunities for life-sentenced prisoners to take responsibility for their own rehabilitation, to find purpose in their lives and to help others in prison or in the community. This can be done even in relatively harsh prison environments. For example, at San Quentin prison in California, some life-sentenced prisoners have found purpose in their lives by assisting other prisoners or members of the community. There are numerous self-help programs that have been established there by life-sentenced prisoners, or that are facilitated by prisoners working closely together with volunteers from the community. Several of them are aimed at educating young people. Others bring together life-sentenced prisoners and victims of crime for counseling, reconciliation, and restorative justice efforts.[82]

Desistance research confirms that these programs often help life-sentenced prisoners, even LWOP prisoners, to take responsibility for their behavior, to make fundamental changes in their lives and develop a new narrative identity, often finding purpose in their lives by offering services to help other people in prison and in the community.[83]

Also important are other forms of prisoner participation through elected representatives, such as the prisoners' councils or committees that are found in some prisons in several European countries.[84] Good communication between prisoners and staff is encouraged, and opportunities are provided for prisoners to express their opinions freely on life in the prison or on certain aspects of it, and also to other forms of free expression of opinion, for example, the production of a prisoners' news bulletin or radio station.[85] In certain jurisdictions (including Denmark, Germany, and the United Kingdom), a number of prisons have been set up as "democratic therapeutic communities," providing long-term offending behavior intervention for prisoners serving lengthy sentences, including life imprisonment.[86] In Grendon prison in England, for example, which was opened in 1962, each wing of the prison, or "therapeutic community," develops its own constitution and all prisoners, who are referred to as residents, have the right to vote on all aspects of prison life. Most prisoners who are admitted to Grendon prison are high-risk prisoners who are serving either long-term or life sentences. The main activities center on a series of regular meetings at which prisoners are invited to give their opinion as to how the community should be run. When internally agreed procedures are breached, the residents have to explain their actions to other members of the community. Such an approach promotes the intrinsic worth of human beings, encouraging prisoners to realize that they are an important part of a community and as such have responsibilities, which is an essential tenet of normal life.[87]

Opportunities to maintain contact with the outside world are also central to a normalized prison regime. As was highlighted in the first-person accounts in Chapter 7, the imposition of a life sentence puts enormous strain on family relationships. While life imprisonment and the concomitant loss of liberty inevitably results in some loss of access to the outside world, there are various positive ways in which prison regimes as a whole can encourage meaningful opportunities to connect with families, friends, and the community. In many countries, life-sentenced prisoners have the same regimes as other prisoners and are entitled to have regular access to visitors, telephone calls, letters, newspapers, radio, television, and even computers, in order to maintain their sense of contact with the outside world.

Most European countries, for example, allow life-sentenced prisoners to have more than one visit per month as a minimum.[88] Prolonged and unsupervised family visits for sentenced prisoners, including life-sentenced prisoners, are a long-standing tradition in several countries, including some in Central and Eastern Europe, Scandinavia, and Central Asia.[89] In Canada, too, a conjugal visit program allows eligible prisoners, including life-sentenced prisoners, to apply every two months to spend three days with either their family, a significant other, or a close personal acquaintance.[90]

Such policies allow prisoners to develop and maintain close relationships in as normal a manner as possible and under conditions where the normal intimacies of family life can be practiced in private. In addition, it helps for other family members, such as spouses, children, and others, who have not committed a crime to maintain regular contact with their family member who is in prison. In some jurisdictions, such as the United States, there are now arrangements to enable prisoners to speak to their families through video links. "Video visits" can be particularly useful for life-sentenced prisoners who are held in custody in remote locations, or where members of the prisoner's family have difficulty in traveling to prison, but only in addition to, rather than as a substitute for, face-to-face contact.[91]

There have also been a number of innovative government initiatives aimed at establishing links between the community outside and life-sentenced prisoners. The LifeLine organization in Canada, for example, recruited released life-sentenced prisoners who had remained crime-free for at least five years to become "in-reach workers" and to establish and maintain contact with life-sentenced prisoners who were still in prison. Their main role was to act as "mentor, motivator and mediator," supporting prisoners through confinement and assisting them in planning for release. Specific activities included "assisting lifers in working toward the objectives listed in their correctional plan, providing escorts and transportation for temporary absences from the penitentiary, helping to address family related needs and concerns, and offering both crisis intervention and general support."[92]

A similar approach has developed in Sweden. An organization known as KRIS (Criminals Return into Society) was established in 1997 and consists mainly of ex-prisoners who have become well-established, law-abiding citizens. Their main aim is to "offer help to incarcerated prisoners to prepare for conditional release and offer to meet and provide lodging to prisoners at the moment of release in order to ensure that they do not drift back into criminal circles."[93] Such initiatives align closely with research on desistance from crime, which emphasizes the importance of strong supportive relationships, whether from professionals, family members, or peers, in helping prisoners to turn their lives around, to construct prosocial roles and a positive identity, and to stop offending.[94]

Purposeful Activities

Prisoners' participation in purposeful activities, such as work, education, sports, and cultural activities, can also contribute to the normalization of prison life as well as to the individual sentence plan and the process of assessing when it is safe for an individual to progress through the prison system and eventually to be released. Access to regular work and to educational, sports, hobbies, and cultural activities for life-sentenced prisoners is not only crucial in terms of reducing their risk of reoffending, but also helps them to adjust to their long prison sentence, provides them with meaningful pastimes, and in due course helps to prepare them for eventual release.

In many parts of the world, life-sentenced prisoners have access to a range of activities, normally in association with other prisoners and often linked to the wider community resources, such as education providers or employment agencies. In Uganda, for example, prisoners serving a life sentence have access to both primary and secondary levels of education. They are also encouraged to join vocational training programs such as carpentry or tailoring on completion of their education courses. Similarly, in Australia, life-sentenced prisoners can work and benefit from educational, recreational, and other life-skills programs during the course of their prison term.[95]

In Europe, Drenkhahn and colleagues found that more than three-quarters of the long-term prisoners in their study took part in work or education or training programs. In several countries a relatively high percentage of prisoners participated in high-level education courses, many of them working on an entrance qualification for university or taking distance university courses.[96] In some Scandinavian countries, prison services are legally obliged to provide all prisoners, including life-sentenced prisoners, with work (for which they are compensated financially) or with the opportunity to participate in education or treatment programs during the entire time of their imprisonment. In Denmark, Sweden and Finland, the principle of normalization is generally understood as meaning that all prisoners are entitled to the same services while in prison, such as health care, work and education, as they would have as civilians in society.[97]

In recent decades there has also been an expansion in the number of offending behavior courses and treatment programs that encourage life-sentenced prisoners to consider the behavior which either led them to commit their offense or at least contributed to it. In Canada, for example, life-sentenced prisoners generally have been encouraged to involve themselves in a variety of programs to help address offending behavior during their incarceration, including sex offender counseling, offender substance abuse programs, anger management, life skills, and problem-solving programs.[98]

Similarly in England and Wales, there is an expectation that life-sentenced prisoners are to make constructive use of their time and particularly to address the causes of their offending behavior through focusing on the areas of risk or concern identified in their life sentence plan. There are a number of standardized programs that have been developed, such as Enhanced Thinking Skills, the Sex Offender Treatment Programme, and the Cognitive Self-Change Programme, and life-sentenced prisoners should be "given every opportunity to attend and complete whichever programmes are relevant to them."[99] However, this does not always happen in practice.[100]

In some jurisdictions, treatment programs have been designed and specifically tailored for long-term and life-sentenced prisoners. For example, Coming to Terms is a fifteen-week group-based program that has been developed by the Osborne Association and implemented in prisons for individuals who have committed homicide-related offenses and are serving long sentences in New York State prisons. The program aims to promote self-assessment, responsibility, remorse, and apology, as well as to encourage individuals to make amends for their past behavior. It draws on group exercises, writing assignments, and various other activities to enable participants to grasp the harm that they have caused to others as a result of their past actions.[101]

Leisure, sports, and religious and cultural activities also play a significant role in many prisons in counteracting the damaging effects of long-term imprisonment and preparing life-sentenced prisoners for release. Research confirms that allowing life-sentenced prisoners access to these activities contributes to improved mental and physical well-being, promotes alternative positive identities, helps to structure time, assists in the development of prosocial life skills, and can encourage the purposeful use of leisure time after release.[102] In the study by Drenkhahn and colleagues, prisons across all eleven European jurisdictions reported a wide variety of leisure and sports activities available to long-term and life-sentenced prisoners, including football, basketball, table tennis, badminton, painting, writing, theater groups, and music groups. The average amount of out-of-cell time that the participants in the survey had was almost nine hours per day, although there were large differences between national samples (three hours in Poland and thirteen hours in Denmark) and it included working hours and time for education or training for prisoners who took part in such activities.[103]

One of us recently witnessed a theater production of the Shakespeare play Hamlet, adapted and performed by eleven life-sentenced prisoners together with professional actors, at Prison No. 17 in Moldova. The "therapy through theater" project was implemented by the Norwegian Mission for the Rule of Law Advisers to Moldova, "to initiate a public discussion . . . about crime and punishment, about the human capacity to change, and about how the state should treat its citizens."[104]

Organized religion can also play a significant role in promoting positive change. In a small-scale study in 2009, John Irwin explained that religion was particularly helpful to life-sentenced prisoners as it offers "meaning and purpose to their unsatisfying past and present lives, a method of expiation, and perhaps a future life after the one they are living now, which has been damaged and diminished profoundly by imprisonment."[105] In Leigey's 2015 study of twenty-five LWOP prisoners in the United States, more than half the respondents cited religion or spirituality as an important coping mechanism. Religion provided a model of good behavior, had a calming effect on their lives, offered purpose and direction in prison, along with "a better existence after their deaths."[106] Developing a deep religious faith or living a "faith-based life sentence" has been highlighted in the writings of life-sentenced prisoners themselves as crucial to instilling values, facilitating change and adding meaning to their many years in prison.[107]

The development of spiritual activities in prison, such as yoga and meaningful meditation, has also been found to have favorable effects. Although research into yoga and meditation programs in prison is still in its early stages, a systematic review and meta-analysis of research studies completed in the United States, United Kingdom, India, and Taiwan, in both minimum- and maximum-security settings, reported significant reductions in perceived stress, depression, and criminal propensity among participants, as well as improvements to psychological well-being and behavioral functioning in prison.[108] It is noteworthy that in the United Kingdom, meditation techniques have recently been introduced in eight high-security prisons, housing some of "Britain's most dangerous prisoners," in order to reduce "stress, anxiety and violent urges" among prisoners.[109] In the United States, too, a number of nonprofit organizations, such as the Prison Yoga Project and Liberation Prison Yoga have worked to "change lives" and confront chronic behavioral issues, such as violence, addiction, and depression in many high-security prisons.[110] In India, the recent growth and success of yoga programs in prison has led the authorities to encourage many life-sentenced prisoners to train and qualify as yoga instructors and to teach yoga techniques to other prisoners.[111] Allowing access to yoga and meditation programs in prison also opens up the opportunity for individuals to continue the practice in the community upon release.

Many open prisons in the United Kingdom seek to prepare life-sentenced prisoners for life outside prison by offering a number of vocational training programs and links to long-term employment. For example, one prison offers work experience to life-sentenced prisoners with a "key cutting and shoe repair company" that can ultimately lead to confirmed employment after release.[112] Such opportunities are seen to be a crucial element of the resocialization process for life-sentenced prisoners, many of whom will have served lengthy minimum terms before facing the transition from prison life to the community.

Another example of practice that aims to help life-sentenced prisoners with the process of release is that of a specialist organization, Café Exit in Denmark, which offers, within an informal environment, tailored services to individuals on leave from prison or who have already been released. These include employment and education guidance, assistance with debt problems, and therapy with trained counselors. Schartmueller writes that the goal of Café Exit "is to help the prisoners or ex-prisoners [to] build up a social network that will help them refrain from a criminal lifestyle . . . to regain control over their own lives and to assist them with becoming responsible members of society upon release."[113]

In sum, while the evidence is patchy, there are some notable examples of implementing life imprisonment well. The good practice and different initiatives highlighted above suggest that there are various positive ways in which prison regimes can ameliorate the painfulness of life imprisonment, and support and encourage the process of rehabilitation and resocialization for life-sentenced prisoners. Penal practice that aims to incorporate individualized sentence planning, normalized prison regimes and purposeful activities in the implementation of life imprisonment closely accords with the standards of human rights and recognizes the right of all prisoners to be treated with humanity and with respect for their human dignity.

Summary and Conclusion

Standards of human rights dictate that prison systems should recognize the unique pains of life imprisonment, and counteract these through the implementation of prison regimes that follow certain key principles, namely, individualization, normalization, responsibility, security and safety, nonsegregation, and progression. Moreover, there should be no additional restrictions imposed on life-sentenced prisoners merely on the basis of the sentence that has been imposed. Dangerous prisoners, too, should be offered opportunities for rehabilitation. Furthermore, contemporary penal systems have a duty to create a clear pathway to release, as well as opportunities to reform.

A number of prison systems have, at least to some extent, adopted human rights–based approaches that aim to counteract the negative effects of life imprisonment and to assist life prisoners to strive for rehabilitation and resocialization. Such systems demonstrate that the implementation of life imprisonment does not necessarily mean that these prisoners must be separated from other prisoners, or even from the community. The use of reintegrative tools, such as individualized sentence plans, normalized regimes, purposeful activities, and open prisons for the purposes of transition to society, means that the links between the life-sentenced prisoner and the community need never be completely severed. The punishment is life imprisonment, but the goal can continue to be to prepare the prisoner for reentry into society.

Central to this approach is the development of good professional staff-prisoner relationships, treating life-sentenced prisoners with respect and dignity according to what they are able to do rather than in the light of what they have done. Allowing staff to develop positive relationships with prisoners within the parameters of a life sentence contributes to the implementation of effective, dynamic security. Good working relationships enable staff to make informed judgments about when life-sentenced prisoners should progress through the regime to more open conditions and ultimately to return to the community. Assessments based on the interactions between prisoners and staff can then be shared with decision-making bodies and individuals who will be responsible for their supervision and support in the community. A reintegrative approach to doing life imprisonment should not be confined only to the prison environment but should also be applied by community agencies and services that may provide support on release, an issue to which we return in Chapter 10.

9

Release from Life

RELEASING PRISONERS who are serving life imprisonment is controversial because the very name of their sentence suggests that the prisoners will remain in prison for the rest of their lives. For this reason perhaps, in many jurisdictions the process, and even the possibility, of release are shrouded in obfuscation and mystery.

In practice, much that will determine when the release process happens is settled long before the actual consideration of release takes place. Life sentences are not all intended to be implemented in prison until the death of the prisoner. On the contrary, as we showed in Chapter 3, the majority of prisoners worldwide are serving life imprisonment with parole (LWP) sentences, which carry with them the prospect that the release of such prisoners will be considered routinely. Even prisoners who are serving life imprisonment sentences without the prospect of parole (LWOP) may have their release considered at some stage, unless there are further restrictions to ensure that their life sentence is entirely irreducible. As demonstrated in Chapter 6, the time when routine release consideration must take place may be determined at the sentencing stage when courts set dates to consider a prisoner's release. Alternatively, release may be considered on a date set by statute. After defining what we mean by release, this chapter sets out to describe and evaluate the way in which the release of life prisoners is considered worldwide. It begins by outlining standards for evaluating decision making on release and then sketches the different mechanisms that are used worldwide for making such decisions and the criteria that they apply. In this regard, our focus is mostly on prisoners considered for release from formal life imprisonment, but we do compare their position with that of prisoners serving informal life sentences. This is followed by an overview of what is known about how long life-sentenced prisoners have to serve as a minimum and how long they actually serve before they are released. The concluding section of the chapter reflects more broadly on the nature of release from life imprisonment.

The Meaning of Release

We define release as the release from prison to the community. This may seem to be stating the obvious. It is necessary, however, because some people regard individuals sentenced to life never to be free from their sentence, since in some jurisdictions they always remain under supervision for the rest of their lives, even when back in the community. Such language is often used by persons seeking to justify limited transparency and restricted procedural safeguards in the release process. We reject this position: the release of life prisoners is release from prison.

From the point of view of life prisoners, release is what gets them out of prison before they die there. Unless their leaving of the prison is temporary, in the sense that they will return to prison automatically after a fixed period, say after a weekend furlough, release does change their position materially. This change is not negated in their minds, or in the minds of the public, by the fact that their freedom is restricted, subject to strict conditions either for a further fixed period or for their rest of their lives. The physical release from prison is accompanied by a fundamental change of status of the persons concerned. An exception to this is the case where life prisoners are transferred from a prison to a psychiatric hospital or other "second-track" institution. While remaining in such institutions, life prisoners do not regain liberty. They should therefore not be regarded as released until they are discharged from such institutions into free society

The decision-making process for release may be a one-step process, or it may involve different stages. The one-step process is the most common. It entails a direct change of status for the prisoner, who goes from serving a life sentence in prison to being conditionally released into the community. A multistage process is one in which the life sentence is first converted into a fixed-term sentence. For example, at the fifteen-year point, prisoners serving a life term may have their sentence converted into a fixed twenty-five-year term. The prisoner can then be released conditionally before the end of the fixed term, or unconditionally at the end of the fixed term. The moment of release remains when the life-sentenced person is finally set free from prison.

As noted in Chapter 8, in the course of serving a life sentence, there ought to be a pathway to release. Precisely how this is implemented may have important implications for the final decision on whether to release a life-sentenced person. In considering the release process as a whole, sight should not be lost of decisions taken during the implementation stage.

Because the final release decision implies a major change to the prisoner's status, it should be subject to important procedural safeguards. But what does release from prison entail? The European objection to irreducible life sentences goes beyond the necessity of appropriate release procedures. It requires more of the "release" itself. In European human rights law, the very notion of release is tied to the idea that human dignity is related to a prisoner's resocialization. This implies that release means life-sentenced prisoners should have the prospect of returning to the community when they have been resocialized and are no longer deemed to be a danger to society, and at a time when they still have the capacity of playing a part in it. Simply allowing the terminally ill to leave prison is not release in the full sense of the term.[1] The European approach to release has much to commend it, but unfortunately it is not universal. In many parts of the world, the idea still holds sway that the release of life-sentenced prisoners is primarily a compassionate gesture made to them during the final days of their lives.

Standards for Evaluating Decision Making on Release

What standards should be applied to evaluate release decisions? As international standards for evaluating decision making on release from life imprisonment have yet to be developed, we consider in the first instance the rigorous standards that derive from European human rights law. We ask whether a particular system for deciding on the release of a life prisoner allows, and ideally requires, the release of life prisoners when the balance of penological justifications for the detention may have shifted while they have served their sentences. The liberty interest at stake for life-sentenced prisoners is profoundly important to them. All release procedures should be judged against their ability to make a fair judgment on whether this overarching standard is met. In setting the scene for this approach to evaluation, it is noteworthy that, in its path-breaking 1977 decision on the constitutionality of life imprisonment, the German Federal Constitutional Court, having determined that all life-sentenced prisoners should have a right to be considered for release, did not stop there. It also specified that, before life imprisonment could be regarded as lawful, there had to be a clear standard for judging when to release a life-sentenced prisoner and a procedure for doing so that met the due process requirements of the German Constitution. It noted that in cases

> in which weighty decisions have to be made involving questions that are of existential significance to the persons concerned, the principle of legal certainty as well as the demands of natural justice require that the preconditions for setting aside a life sentence and the procedure to be followed in making this determination should be regulated by legislation. The detailed form that this should take, should be determined by the legislature, but within the framework laid down by the Constitution.[2]

In the last decade, and particularly since the decision of the Grand Chamber in *Vinter and others v. United Kingdom* in 2013, the European Court of Human Rights (ECtHR) has been developing the standards, both substantive and procedural, that should be met by all mechanisms for releasing life-sentenced prisoners.[3] These standards have crystallized to the point where, in the 2016 decision of the Grand Chamber of the ECtHR in *Murray v Netherlands,* Judge Pinto de Albuquerque could summarize in his concurring opinion the views of the court into five binding principles that should govern release from life imprisonment:

1. The principle of legality ("rules having a sufficient degree of clarity and certainty," "conditions laid down in domestic legislation");
2. The principle of the assessment of penological grounds for continued incarceration, on the basis of "objective, pre-established criteria," which include resocialization (special prevention), deterrence (general prevention), and retribution;

3. The principle of assessment within a pre-established time frame and, in the case of life prisoners, "not later than 25 years after the imposition of the sentence and thereafter a periodic review";
4. The principle of fair procedural guarantees, which include at least the obligation to give reasons for decisions not to release or to recall a prisoner;
5. The principle of judicial review.[4]

The Grand Chamber based these principles on its own earlier decisions, as well as on a careful analysis of international and European requirements for the release of all life-sentenced prisoners. The Grand Chamber explicitly articulated standards that it regarded as applicable to release from all types of life imprisonment, presumably including not only LWP but also LWOP, insofar as it can be regarded as compatible with European human rights standards at all.

The decision in *Murray* is the fullest articulation hitherto of standards to be applied in deciding whether to release a person sentenced to life imprisonment, and we will use the five *Murray* principles to evaluate the different release processes. However, in 2017 in *Hutchinson v. United Kingdom*, the Grand Chamber backed away somewhat from an aspect of the third requirement, that of a "pre-established time frame," and accepted an assurance from the British government that life-sentenced prisoners could apply at any time they chose.[5] This raises some doubts about the commitment of the Grand Chamber to a routine review and therefore seems to allow LWOP sentences to continue to be regarded as compliant with human rights.

The analysis of the Grand Chamber in *Murray* emphasized the importance of creating a path to release for all life-sentenced prisoners, from the point of imposition and throughout the implementation of life sentences. Giving appropriate consideration to release is the next important step on the path that could also subsequently include post-release supervision and other post-release programs. In the European context, this path is signposted by various recommendations adopted by the Committee of Ministers of the Council of Europe. A good example is the 2003 Recommendation on Conditional Release (Parole), which sets out the importance of conditional release in general terms: "Conditional release should aim at assisting prisoners to make a transition from life in prison to a law-abiding life in the community through post-release conditions and supervision that promote this end and contribute to public safety and the reduction of crime in the community."[6] Before spelling out procedures that should be applied to considering conditional release throughout Europe, the same recommendation states categorically that "the law should make conditional release available to all sentenced prisoners, including life-sentence prisoners."[7] The five Murray principles are also supported by non-European international instruments. Many of these assert the need for systems to regulate the release of all sentenced prisoners, albeit without direct reference to those serving life sentences.[8] The 1994 United Nations report, *Life Imprisonment*, goes further. It emphasizes the importance of establishing "a body to review *each* life-sentence prisoner at regular intervals and, if appropriate to recommend or grant release or remission."[9] This report also stresses the importance of the process being independent and nonarbitrary, and also being subject to appeal. The report envisages an evaluation and review process after a specified number of years, and at further regular intervals if necessary, in which the progress to rehabilitation of the life-sentenced prisoner is the primary criterion for release.

Types of Release Mechanisms and the Standards They Apply

What are the mechanisms and processes for releasing life-sentenced prisoners worldwide, and to what extent do they meet the five *Murray* principles? In order to address these basic descriptive questions, we distinguish between four different mechanisms for making routine release decisions: (i) the courts, (ii) parole boards and other expert bodies, and (iii) the executive branch, as well as (iv) the discretionary power of clemency that is used nonroutinely. The mechanisms are ideal types, for, as shall become apparent, in several instances it is not simple to determine by whom the crucial decision on release is made, or even to be sure to what type a particular mechanism is most appropriately allocated.

Release by a Court

The type of release mechanism with the strongest claim to legality and impartiality is a court. Courts can make reasoned, binding decisions about the release of life prisoners. This was the solution adopted by the German legislature in 1981, in its response to the challenge set by its Constitutional Court in 1977. It brought decisions about the release of life-sentenced prisoners under the aegis of the Court for the Execution of Sentences (*Strafvollstreckungskammer*), which already had responsibility for making decisions on the early conditional release of fixed-term sentences.[10] Decisions to release taken by this court are reviewable on appeal, but final in the sense that they require no further approval from any other body or official to be executed.

Courts or judges with similar, if not identical, powers of release to that of German courts exist in a number of Western European countries, including Austria, Belgium, Finland, France, Greece, Germany, Italy, Spain, and Sweden.[11] When Central and Eastern European countries introduced life imprisonment in the 1990s, they tended to adopt similar arrangements: Albania, Armenia, Azerbaijan, Belarus, Bulgaria, Estonia, Latvia, Macedonia, Moldova, Poland, Romania, and Russia all have courts capable of making release decisions after prisoners have served fixed periods prescribed by law and regularly thereafter.[12] This was also followed in some countries in Central Asia that emerged from the former Soviet Union.[13]

Outside Europe and Central Asia, countries in which courts are able to make final release decisions are harder to identify with confidence. In Africa, we can point to only three countries where in law the courts have the final say: Ethiopia, Nigeria, and Tunisia.[14] In South America, in Argentina and Peru, release decisions are taken by the courts too.[15] Release from sentences of life imprisonment imposed by the International Criminal Tribunal for the former Yugoslavia (ICTY) and the International Criminal Tribunal for Rwanda (ICTR) is being decided by a quasi-judicial body, the Mechanism for International Criminal Tribunals (MICT), while in the case of the International Criminal Court (ICC) such decisions will be taken by the Court itself.

The attraction of having a court take the decision on release is obvious in that, by definition, it should be an impartial body. It should be able to make important decisions on the liberty of individuals in a way that meets the principles of legality and procedural fairness. Courts typically give reasons for their decision, and their decisions are subject to judicial review. The release reviews in the jurisdictions listed above are conducted within a preestablished time frame and further reviews take place regularly thereafter. Typically, countries that have courts deciding on the release of life-sentenced prisoners use this mechanism to deal with all the cases of prisoners serving life imprisonment. Only Bulgaria, Hungary, Peru, Slovakia, and Turkey have special provisions for a subset of life-sentenced prisoners serving LWOP. Their release is dealt with differently from the majority of life-sentenced prisoners, whose release is decided by the courts.

In practice, court procedures may suffer from a number of shortcomings. Perhaps the most basic concern is whether cases for which release has to be considered reach the courts at all. This clearly depends on what the procedure is for bringing cases before them. Ideally, courts should review cases once life-sentenced prisoners have served their minimum terms, and at regular intervals thereafter. However, in many, if not most, systems, that does not happen automatically. Another step may need to be taken. This could be that prisoners have to apply to the court to have their release considered. Where prisoners have access to lawyers and confidence in the system, they may do so routinely, but this may not be the case in all systems. There could be barriers placed on their applications: either informally by making the application process practically very hard to access, or even, as is the case in China, formally forbidding them to apply in certain circumstances.[16]

A further example of a formal prohibition is the law in Russia that, after the minimum period has been served, allows applications only from prisoners who have a clean disciplinary record for three years before they apply.[17] This means that they can effectively be blocked from ever approaching the court that has the power to make the final release decision. In other countries, the barriers may be even higher.

In Bulgaria, the application is brought by a prosecutor, and the court can convert the sentence to a fixed-term sentence of fifteen years to run from the moment when this release decision is taken.[18] In Ethiopia and Nigeria, applications for release have to be brought to the court by the prison authorities. Although theoretically the court has the last word, this gives the prison authorities immense power.[19]

In law, a similar situation applies in the federal system in the United States where, on application from the director of the Federal Bureau of Prisons, a court may order the release of a prisoner who is at least seventy years of age and who has served at least thirty years in prison, if the director has determined that the prisoner is not a danger to the safety of any other person or the community.[20] However, as this provision was first adopted in 1994, it will not come into force until 2024. In addition, the inspector general of the US Department of Justice has reported that the US Bureau of Prisons is highly reluctant to use provisions of this kind, thus establishing a formidable barrier to a court ever being asked to consider release on this basis.[21] In such instances, one may query whether the officials of the US Bureau of Prisons rather than the court are the crucial decision makers.

Assuming that a court has the power to make the crucial and final decision on release of life-sentenced prisoners and that these prisoners have relatively easy access to it, the ability of a court to make appropriate release decisions will be influenced by a number of factors, including the composition of the court and the range of its powers. In this regard, it is useful to consider in more detail the structure and operation of some of the specialist European courts that make these decisions.

In Belgium, parole boards responsible for the release of life-sentenced prisoners were replaced in 2007 by sentencing implementation courts as part of a wider reform of the release system. This was designed to increase the independence and expertise of the decision-making body. A positive feature of this new court is its multidisciplinary nature: it is comprised of a judge and two assessors with penological expertise, thus putting it in a strong position to assess the different penological grounds for continual incarceration. The process provides the prisoner the right to be heard and represented. The right to appeal is limited to questions of law. Recent amendments have meant that in cases involving both life imprisonment and post-conviction indefinite detention, the bench of the Sentencing Implementation courts is enlarged to three judges and two experts. Periods before the first hearing have been lengthened but remain under twenty-five years. Decisions to release conditionally have to be unanimous, which in the case of the enlarged court means that a single dissenter out of five can block the release. Since the amendment, review is not automatic but must be activated by an application from the prisoner. A prisoner who is turned down may apply again within a year.[22]

The system in France is very similar. A specialized court, the *tribunal d'application des peines*, of three judges hears applications from prisoners for conditional release. They are all professional judges. Appeals against a decision to deny conditional release are possible, both on the substance and the law, to a five-member court of appeal consisting of three professional judges, one representative of a rehabilitation association and one representative of a victims' association. There are set periods before the first review. Although they may be as high as thirty years, the ECtHR has held that this is not so far beyond its preferred period of a maximum of twenty-five years as to be unacceptable.[23] As in Belgium, prisoners must apply and if their applications fail, they can apply again within a year.[24]

In Germany, the Court for the Execution of sentences (*Strafvollstreckunskammer*) consists of a single judge. Life-sentenced prisoners have to apply for their cases to be considered, but it can also be done ex officio by the prosecution bringing the case to the attention of the courts. The prisoners always have the option of refusing to accept conditional release, although this is less common with life-sentenced prisoners than with those serving a fixed term, who may prefer to remain in prison rather than accept onerous release conditions that may extend beyond the end of their sentences. The parallels with the other specialist Western European release courts are strong. The decisions of a German court for the execution of sentences can be fully reviewed by a higher court. If release is denied the prisoner may reapply, although the court that rejects the initial application may order that no further application may be made for a period of up to two years.[25]

The German release mechanism is particularly interesting for its sophisticated way of dealing with the assessment of the different penological grounds for continued incarceration. A German sentencing court is required to make a decision on how severe the guilt of the offender is and this is used by the court for the execution of sentences.[26] If the sentencing court does not find the prisoner's guilt to be particularly severe, the fifteen-year minimum cannot be changed by the court for the execution of sentences; it becomes the maximum that can be served for the purpose of punishment. The sole function of the court for the execution of sentences is then to find whether the release is justifiable, taking into account the security interests of the public. If it finds that the release is justifiable on this basis, the court for the execution of sentences is under a legal duty to order the release of the prisoner. In practice, expert prognoses are sought a year or more before the fifteen-year point is reached so that the prisoner may be permitted periods of leave, which will allow the Court for the Execution of Sentences to observe whether the prisoner is capable of operating in a free society. This will allow the court to order the release of the prisoner promptly at the fifteen-year mark if their final conclusion is positive.[27]

Even in such a system, however, the process may go wrong. There is at least one reported instance where German prison authorities had not prepared a life-sentenced prisoner for release by granting him temporary leave before he had served fifteen years of a life sentence, even though there was no legal basis for not doing so. At sentence, his guilt had not been found to be particularly severe and the psychiatric prognosis was that he posed no further danger to society. In this instance the Federal Constitutional Court ruled that the permanent release would have to be delayed until the prisoner's behavior in the community while on temporary leave could be evaluated by the court for the execution of sentences. However, the Federal Constitutional Court was very concerned that the actual period of imprisonment would be disproportionately long and suggested that the risk criterion should be treated less strictly under the circumstances.[28]

Where the sentencing court does make a finding of particular severity, the court for the execution of sentences must decide how much further imprisonment beyond the fifteen-year minimum is required on punishment grounds. What happens in practice is that, around the fifteen-year point, the court for the execution of sentences rules what extra period the life-sentenced prisoners will have to serve, thus effectively setting a new minimum term. When that period beyond fifteen years is reached, the court for the execution of sentences decides on the basis of risk to the public whether it is now justified to release the prisoner. If at that stage the court for the execution of sentences finds the level of risk justifies release, it has to order the release of the prisoner. It cannot consider the seriousness of the original offense.[29] This procedure may be seen as a sophisticated way of dealing with two potentially competing purposes of continued detention: punishment and the protection of the public. Since the German Federal Constitutional Court has accepted that the longer a life-sentenced prisoner has served, the greater the justification for accepting a higher risk to the security of the public, the German system effectively balances the liberty interest of prisoner against the security interest of the public. On the other hand, including consideration of the severity of the guilt of the prisoner again at the release stage could be seen as a form of double jeopardy.[30]

The same issues of reevaluating the seriousness of the initial offense arise at the international level: When the MICT, in the first such case to arise, *Prosecutor v. Galić,* had to create criteria for considering the release of prisoners sentenced to life terms by the ICTY and the ICTR, it underlined that it took into account, not only the treatment of similarly situated prisoners, but also "the gravity of the crime or crimes for which the prisoner was convicted, the prisoner's demonstration of rehabilitation, and any substantial cooperation of the prisoner with the Prosecution."[31] In this instance, the MICT ruled that, although there was strong evidence that the applicant was fully rehabilitated, he could not be released as he had not served the thirty-year minimum period the MICT set, somewhat arbitrarily, before release would from now on normally be considered.

The ICC has yet to sentence anyone to life imprisonment, let alone consider their release. However, the ICC Statute provides for release to be considered by the court itself after a life-sentenced prisoner has served twenty-five years, and regularly thereafter. Article 110 of the Statute of the ICC provides further that "in reviewing the question of reduction of sentence" it shall take into account:

(a) The early and continuing willingness of the person to cooperate with the Court in its investigations and prosecutions;
(b) The voluntary assistance of the person in enabling the enforcement of the judgements and orders of the Court in other cases, and in particular providing assistance in locating assets subject to orders of fine, forfeiture or reparation which may be used for the benefit of victims; or
(c) Other factors establishing a clear and significant change of circumstances sufficient to justify the reduction of sentence, as provided in the Rules of Procedure and Evidence.

The Rules of Procedure and Evidence of the ICC in turn list the following factors:

(a) The conduct of the sentenced person while in detention, which shows a genuine dissociation from his or her crime;
(b) The prospect of the resocialization and successful resettlement of the sentenced person;
(c) Whether the early release of the sentenced person would give rise to significant social instability;
(d) Any significant action taken by the sentenced person for the benefit of the victims as well as any impact on the victims and their families as a result of the early release;
(e) Individual circumstances of the sentenced person, including a worsening state of physical or mental health or advanced age.[32]

As the ICC is often seen as establishing international standards, it is noteworthy that the criteria set in the statute do not refer to either of the widely recognized key penological criteria: the seriousness of the offense or the risk that the offender may pose following release. The factors given the most prominence are those that would further the goals of international criminal justice and not necessarily what is most appropriate for the life-sentenced individual concerned. In the further factors set out in the Rules of Procedure and Evidence, there is reference to the resocialization and the issue of whether the sentenced person has disassociated themselves from the crime. However, there is no reference to the seriousness of the offense or degree of culpability of the person concerned. Furthermore, considering whether "the early release of the sentenced person would give rise to significant social instability" would be an illegitimate consideration in many national systems, where judicial independence is designed to insulate the release decisions from the vagaries of public opinion. Finally, consideration of the worsening state of health or advanced age of a person serving life imprisonment is not really part of a penological analysis, except in as far as it may point to diminution of the danger posed to society by releasing the persons concerned. Such a consideration is more relevant to clemency. Of course, it is the case that the ICC has no sovereign or head of state with that power, which may explain why it is included in the list of factors for the routine consideration of release by the court. Nevertheless, one cannot ignore that, in structuring release decisions, the ICC Statute gives prominence to factors that in national jurisdictions would not be considered penological, as they do not relate to the traditional justifications for punishment.

How close do courts generally come to meeting the five *Murray* principles? (1) Courts typically meet the principle of legality as the rules in terms of which they operate are laid down clearly and precisely in domestic legislation. (2) Courts assess the penological grounds that would justify release on the basis of objective preestablished criteria. However, there may be some differences regarding what these criteria should be and how they should relate to each other. The Belgian, French and German systems all manage a substantive reevaluation of the shifting primary justifications for continued detention, that is, the weight to be given to punishing the underlying offense and the continued risk that the prisoner poses to the public. However, other court systems use criteria that are not narrowly penological but relate to wider policy criteria. As we have seen, the ICC is an example of such a system. A further example is that of Italy, where persons sentenced to life imprisonment for offenses related to organized crime cannot even be considered for release by the judicial supervision tribunal unless they break their links with organized crime and cooperate with the authorities.[33] The latter requirement, in particular, may lead to imprisonment for far longer periods than could be justified by the heinousness of the original offense, or by the risk the prisoner poses to society and may be unfair because of the risk a prisoner may face by cooperating with the authorities against the mafia.[34]

(3) Courts do conduct their assessments within a specified time frame, but in some instances the specified period before the first review may be longer than twenty-five years. For example, in both Argentina and Peru, where courts decide on the release of life-sentenced prisoners, the minimum time to be served before that review can take place is thirty-five years.[35] Further consideration of cases where release is not granted initially also takes place within a reasonable period. (4) Finally, courts are geared to acting in a procedurally fair way, and (5) having their decisions subject to further judicial review.

In conclusion, as far as the use of courts to make release decisions are concerned, the verdict must be cautiously positive. While court-based systems have individual peculiarities and shortcomings, overall they can be regarded as meeting the five principles set out in the *Murray* case. Although the ECtHR has never insisted absolutely on having release decisions made by courts, its Grand Chamber has made it clear that it regards courts as the best mechanisms for making this fundamental decision, and has assembled as much international evidence as it can to nudge European countries in this direction.[36]

Release by a Parole Board

The second main type of body deciding on the release of life-sentenced prisoners—excluding those serving LWOP—is a parole board or an equivalent body. Australia, Bermuda, Canada, Chile, Cyprus, Jamaica, Kosovo, Israel, Liberia, Papua New Guinea, New Zealand, and the United Kingdom all have versions of parole boards that have the power to make key release decisions.[37] Parole boards with such powers are also found in many states in the United States.[38] In certain jurisdictions, the decision of the parole board is subject to approval by a head of state or minister acting on behalf of the head of state, who may have a power of veto, but the primary decision remains that of the board.[39]

A critical question about parole boards is whether or not they have sufficient independence to apply set criteria in reaching a release decision. The question does not arise to the same extent where the release decision is made by courts, for judicial independence tends to be assumed, even if legal framework within which courts operate and the standards they apply are less than ideal. The independence of parole boards may be questioned, not only at the level of their procedures and standards but also that of the members of the parole board, who must be sufficiently independent to take decisions that reflect their own judgment. Other questions concern the criteria that parole boards apply, and whether they meet the further *Murray* principles.[40]

As far as the question of independence is concerned, the Parole Board for England and Wales (which considers the release of all English and Welsh life-sentenced prisoners except for those who are subject to whole-life orders) is broadly regarded as an example of a board that is independent. Although the procedures for the appointment and tenure of its members do not meet the standards of those applied to the judiciary, in practice decisions on parole for life prisoners are taken by a panel consisting of a judge, a psychiatrist, and a lay member. In entrenching its independence, the Parole Board for England and Wales was assisted by the ECtHR ruling that deemed such a parole board to be a court-like body able to make release decisions independently and impartially.[41]

The procedures adopted by the Parole Board for England and Wales have also been challenged, and in 2008 the English courts even doubted the independence of the parole board.[42] Today, however, these procedures are much improved. Although funding shortages may cause delays, life prisoners whose release is considered by the parole board may expect a hearing that broadly meets due process standards, such as access to all documents, a personal hearing, legal representation, and reasons for refusal to grant parole.[43] The current rules of the parole board forbid it, however, from giving reasons for its decisions. In March 2018 the High Court held that, given the importance of open justice in the functioning of the parole board, this rule should be struck down and replaced with a provision that allowed reasons for parole board decisions to be made public.[44]

At a substantive level, the powers of release of the Parole Board for England and Wales have evolved differently from the release powers of courts and indeed of many other parole boards in other countries. The parole board considers only risk to the public, not punishment. This was prompted by a series of interventions by both English and European courts concerned with due process on human rights' grounds.[45] Under English law, courts imposing life sentences—other than whole-life orders—also set a bespoke minimum term, a fixed number of years. That term (previously known as the *tariff*) is deemed to be sufficient to meet the requirements of punishment: that is, of retribution and deterrence. Once this fixed minimum period has been served, the only decision for the parole board is to determine whether it is "satisfied that it is no longer necessary for the protection of the public that the prisoner should be confined."[46] This practice has led to the recognition by both European and English courts that the parole release decision is a new sentencing decision that directly affects the liberty of the individual subject to it. As a result, its decision must meet not only the standards of Article 3 of the European Convention on Human Rights (ECHR), the prohibition on inhuman and degrading punishment that forms the basis for the *Murray* principles. The parole board must also meet the further procedural standards of Articles 5 and 6 of the ECHR and the procedural requirements of the English common law, all of which are more stringent when liberty interests are directly at stake.[47]

Even in European countries that have courts that are directly responsible for the release of life-sentenced prisoners, such high procedural standards are not necessarily required. The reason is that the ECtHR has distinguished the release of life-sentenced prisoners in the United Kingdom from release of such prisoners in other European countries, where there is not as clear a distinction between the criteria applied at the sentencing stage and those applicable when release is considered. In the view of the ECtHR, where punishment for the initial offense remains a factor to be considered at the release stage, as is the case in Germany, the decision on whether to release someone is qualitatively different from that which has to be taken in the United Kingdom. In such cases, so the argument runs, the original decision to impose life imprisonment is what also allows the continued detention. It is not necessary to have a fresh decision for continued detention to meet the requirements of Article 5, the habeas corpus provision in ECHR law. Accordingly, the procedural guarantees associated with habeas corpus decisions and spelled out in Article 5(4) of the ECHR do not have to be applied to release from life imprisonment, as least as far as the ECtHR is concerned. The practical result has been that the ECtHR has ruled that not all release procedures have to operate in the way expected of parole boards in the United Kingdom.[48]

The Parole Board for England and Wales has demonstrated its independence. A prominent example is the case of Harry Roberts, who was released in 2014 after having served forty-eight years of a life sentence for murdering three policemen. This decision elicited widespread criticism, largely because of public sentiment that his crimes were deemed to be so heinous that he should never be released. However, the parole board was able to justify its decision on the basis that Roberts had served more than his original thirty-year minimum term and that at the age of seventy-eight he no long posed a risk to the public. The board did not, indeed could not, take into account the nature of his original crime. Subsequent (hostile) tabloid accounts have shown Roberts leading a full life as a retired member of society.[49]

One weakness of the English system is that, while the parole board has an absolute power to order release, it has no power to compel the prison authorities to take specific steps that are necessary to prepare the prisoner for potential release. (This is a weakness that the English parole system shares with some court-based systems, like that in Belgium, where the sentencing implementation court also cannot intervene in a decision of this kind.)[50] In England and Wales, the prison authorities retain the power to decide whether life-sentenced prisoners should be transferred to a minimum-security (open) prison. In practice, the parole board will not release someone until this has been done, as it would want to see whether the prisoner can cope with a degree of freedom without posing a risk to society. On occasion, the parole board has requested the authorities to transfer a prisoner to such a facility. However, when the authorities have failed to do so, the board has not been able to compel them, with the result that the particular prisoner is effectively prevented from being released.[51]

Worldwide, the same broad claims of procedural probity as in the United Kingdom can be made for a few other parole systems. In Canada, for example, the parole board enjoys similar powers to release after the minimum period has been served and is subject to similar procedural safeguards to those in England.[52] However, as in England, there is now the possibility that minimum periods before release is considered may be significantly longer than the twenty-five years, which the ECtHR has stipulated should be the effective maximum for such terms.[53]

Claims about the independence of parole boards need to be closely examined. In a recent opinion, the UN Human Rights Committee, which had previously held that the parole board in New Zealand was a court-like body, ruled that its status was compromised by the lack of an adequate system of appeals against its decisions in cases of indeterminate post-conviction preventive detention. Judicial review of the decisions of a parole board that focused only on procedure, but not on fundamental questions of law and fact that determined how long persons subject to such sentences would serve, was insufficient to meet the requirements of Article 9(4) of the International Covenant on Civil and Political Rights with respect to access to a court on questions relating to the deprivation of liberty.[54]

In contrast to the parole boards found in many Commonwealth countries, the different parole mechanisms in the United States have striking shortcomings at all levels: the independence of their members, their procedures, and their substantive criteria. There has been a tendency in the United States to move away from the discretionary release of sentenced prisoners generally, which is one of the factors contributing to the rise in the number of LWOP prisoners. Nevertheless, the majority of prisoners sentenced to life imprisonment in the United States still have a legal prospect of release. Parole boards or similar bodies in the United States have the power to consider the release of the more than 100,000 persons currently serving LWP sentences in that country.[55] The movement toward determinate sentences does not apply to all states.[56] Moreover, even where parole for life-sentenced prisoners has been abolished, as it has in the US federal system, similar bodies still operate to consider the release of prisoners sentenced before the change in the law.[57]

Recent studies seriously question the independence of parole boards in the United States. Inspired in part by the duties imposed by the US Supreme Court on states to review life sentences imposed on juveniles, major evaluations have recently been conducted of how parole mechanisms across the US deal with LWP generally—in 2016 by the American Civil Liberties Union and in 2017 by The Sentencing Project. Their overall findings, building on scholarly research on parole more generally, have been damning on a number of important fronts. The independence of US parole boards is open to challenge. Members of parole boards are typically appointed by the governor of the state in which they operate and they serve at the governor's pleasure. There is considerable anecdotal evidence, including statements from serving parole board members, that they feel pressured to make decisions that will be regarded as politically acceptable. In a minority of states the governor can, and regularly does, veto decisions of the parole board to grant parole, but even where, in law, there is no such power, there is considerable room for the political authorities to exert influence on decisions ostensibly taken independently by parole boards.[58]

Procedurally too, the systems in the United States for deciding on whether to grant parole to life-sentenced prisoners tend to be very weak. This reflects the view expressed by the US Supreme Court that parole is a privilege and that therefore parole decision-making is not bound by constitutional due process rights.[59] Prisoners seeking parole have only the procedural rights granted to them by state parole legislation. These rights may be very limited. In many states the participation by life-sentenced prisoners seeking parole is restricted: they are cursorily interviewed only by a member of the parole board and cannot appear before the boards themselves or if they can, must do so without counsel. Only in a minority of cases are full hearings conducted, and even then they are often cursory. Victims of the crime often have a more prominent place in the hearings than the individuals seeking parole. US parole boards make extensive use of risk assessment instruments, but they are shrouded in secrecy. In many instances the instruments developed by private companies are not freely available and the methods of using them are not open to scrutiny: even the "risk scores" of prisoners seeking parole may not be revealed to them. US parole boards often do not give reasons for their decisions to deny parole, and, if they do give reasons, these are often brief and general. Finally, there is a growing tendency for US parole boards to deny parole and set long periods, as long as fifteen years, before reconsideration can be sought, thus effectively undermining the efficacy of periodic review.[60]

Perhaps the biggest weakness of the US parole systems is widespread confusion about the criteria that they should apply when assessing whether the incarceration of life-sentenced prisoners should continue. Although in most instances in the United States the minimum period for consideration of release following a conviction for a particular offense is set by statute, or determined by the sentencing court deciding within a range set by the penal code, parole boards can and do give overriding prominence to the initial offense. In many instances they rule that this is the sole relevant criterion for further detention and resist attempts to force them to take a more inclusive view. There is little guidance on how different criteria for release should be balanced against one another.

An example of the problems that can arise when lack of attention to impartiality and due process are combined with uncertain criteria has emerged in the case of Jens Soering, a German national serving an LWP sentence in Virginia for murder. Soering's case has become something of a *cause célèbre* in Germany. In 2012, he applied for the eleventh time to be considered for parole. Shortly before his parole hearing, Christoph Strassen, the parliamentary spokesman on human rights for the German Social Democratic Party, wrote in his official capacity to William Muse, the then chairman of the Parole Board in Virginia, asking that Soering be granted parole, as ostensibly he was fully rehabilitated. In his response, Muse acknowledged that Soering was a well-behaved prisoner who had sought to improve himself, and that his release did not appear to pose a risk to the public. However, Muse explained, "While the risk to public safety is of paramount importance, a low risk to re-offend and the offender's efforts at rehabilitation are off [sic] times offset by the serious nature of the crime and the sentence imposed. Simply stated, that balance has not yet tipped in Mr. Soering's favor."[61]

On the face of it, this analysis is a typical example of the difficult weighing exercise that many bodies considering the release of life-sentenced prisoners around the world are required to undertake. However, what makes it problematic was that it was expressed 11 days *before* the parole board that Muse chaired was due to consider Soering's application. That Soering would not have a realistic hope of release from a parole board that had so blatantly prejudged his case, is apparent, as is the lack of clarity about the relative importance of the different criteria.

Soering's treatment is not an isolated example. In April 2017, the Board of Parole in New York refused parole in the case of Judith Clark, the driver of a getaway car, who had played a role, albeit not the central one, in the killing of a civilian and two police officers and had served more than thirty years of her life sentence. As in Soering's case, there could have been no doubt in the mind of the parole board that Clark had become rehabilitated and posed no further threat to society. In Clark's case it was also clear that she had served the term necessary for purposes of punishment, as earlier in 2017 the governor of New York had intervened and exercised his clemency powers to set a bespoke minimum term of thirty-five years for her, which, by the time her parole was considered by the board, she had already served. The parole board was bound by this new minimum term but nevertheless refused to grant her parole. The basis for its refusal was not that Clark as an individual required further punishment or that she posed a risk to society. Instead the board emphasized that releasing her would undermine the welfare of society and the rule of law, two further criteria that the New York parole regulations allow the board to apply. There was no evidence before the board to support that conclusion but there were a number of representations from the police, politicians and the families of the victims of Clark's crimes, who wanted further punishment for her. In part, the refusal to grant Clark bail may be due to the very broad criteria that the New York Parole Board was asked to apply. It is more likely, however, that this major US parole board, unlike its English counterpart, was not sufficiently independent and thus susceptible to public pressure where a police homicide was involved.[62]

There are more positive developments in some US states. In 2008, a court of appeals in California ruled that the parole board should not consider the seriousness of the original offense as a factor in its own right when deciding on the release of life-sentenced prisoners who had served the minimum period applicable in their cases. Instead, it should focus on the danger the prisoners would pose to society if they were to be released. Although the initial offense could be relevant indirectly, as an indicator of risk, some further evidence of risk was required.[63] This positive element is offset by the legal requirement that the governor of California has to approve any release recommended by the parole board. In recent years the governor has been accepting far more recommendations of the parole board than in the past. However, the very existence of this gubernatorial veto power undermines the parole board as an independent decision-making body.

When one evaluates parole systems generally against the *Murray* standards, the picture is mixed. Broadly speaking, the parole system in England and Wales, like the other UK parole systems in Scotland and Northern

Ireland, as well as that of Canada, meet the *Murray* standards for the consideration of release of all life-sentenced prisoners. The only exception is that the minimum periods, which are set by the sentencing courts in individual cases before the parole board can intervene, may be far longer than the twenty-five years referred to in the *Murray* standards. For the rest, in law at least, some of the standards to which the English Parole Board are held may be higher than those developed in the *Murray* case, for they are derived from Articles 5 and 6 of the ECHR, the key provisions of the convention that guarantee due process before the liberty of an individual may be curtailed. In contrast, the procedural guarantees that reached their full flowering in the *Murray* decision are the product of a more indirect reasoning related to what is required to ensure that a life sentence is not inhuman or degrading because of it being implemented in prison for an excessive period.

The picture that emerges from the analyses of the different parole systems that consider the release of life-sentenced prisoners in the United States is that they do not come close to meeting the standards set in *Murray:* the legislative framework under which they operate is unclear and uncertain; objective preestablished criteria for assessing continued incarceration are often absent or framed very widely; the time frame for assessing release is sometimes longer than twenty-five years, and periodic reviews can be delayed for many years; procedural guarantees are limited; and, judicial review of parole board decisions is very restricted, if available at all. Outside the United States, parole boards that meet high procedural standards appear also to be the exception rather than the rule.

Our overall conclusion from these contrasting accounts is that, in principle, parole boards with the power to make primary decisions on whether to grant the release of life-sentenced prisoners can be structured in ways that enable them to meet the standards set in *Murray.* At its best, as the US Supreme Court pointed out in 1972 in *Morrissey v. Brewer,* "Rather than being an ad hoc exercise of clemency, parole is an established variation on imprisonment of convicted criminals."[64] However, parole boards are more likely to meet the *Murray* standards if they are court-like bodies, and if their decisions are subject to appeal to the courts, than if the discretionary powers they exercise are left unchecked. Judicial review of the decisions of parole boards is particularly important if the criteria that they are supposed to apply are not stated clearly.

Release by the Executive

It is also possible that the final decision on release on parole of a life prisoner could be made routinely by the executive. This can be done without the life sentence being LWOP, from which release is only possible by the exercise of executive clemency (which, as we explain in the next section, is qualitatively different). Release by the executive is a further ideal type, as the primary decision-maker is not a specialist (parole) board, but often, although not always, the minister of justice, who may be advised by some other administrative body. Can such decision-making meet at least some minimum human rights standards? The examples that come the closest to doing so, at least on paper, are to be found in African countries with roots in the French or Belgian administrative traditions. Benin, Burkina Faso, Burundi, Central African Republic, Chad, Côte d'Ivoire, the Democratic Republic of Congo, Madagascar, Mali, Mauritania, Niger, the Republic of Guinea, and Rwanda are all examples of countries where primary statutory law provides for the construction of a dossier that must be referred to the minister of justice after a fixed period.[65] The dossiers typically contain reports from the prison authorities and the prosecution, and sometimes also from a judge or the police. National variations are relatively minor; for example, in Côte d'Ivoire and Niger, the minister of justice must also consult the minister of the interior, while in Mauritania the dossier must also include the opinion of the administrative authorities of the area where the crime was committed.

Arguably, these mechanisms meet the principle of legality, in the sense that they are spelled out in legislation, and have the requirement of assessing release within a preestablished time frame. There are also, typically, relatively strict provisions, specifying when reassessment of failures to grant release should take place: for instance, in Benin and in the Central African Republic, they specify that prisoners may reapply after one year. It may even be possible for the decision of the minister to be subject to judicial review, though this is only rarely the case. In some instances, review or appeal is specifically excluded. In Rwanda, for example, Article 247 of the Criminal Procedure Code states explicitly that "[t]he decision granting release on parole shall not be subject to appeal."

There are, however, major shortcomings in allowing the decision on release to be made by the executive, that is, usually by a government minister, in this way. One difficulty is that the prisoner may be completely isolated from the eventual decision-maker, and that the lack of direct participation will undermine the procedural fairness of any process conducted in this way.

Perhaps more important is that a member of the political executive is unlikely to undertake a careful weighing of the "penological grounds" for release on the particular facts of an individual case. A dramatic example is the case of *Kafkaris,* where the Grand Chamber of the ECtHR established the principle that, in Europe, life sentences had to be reducible in law and in fact, although the majority found on the facts that Kafkaris had had a reasonable prospect of release. One of the dissenting justices, Judge Borrego, accused his colleagues of ignoring reality. In his dissenting opinion, he noted that, shortly after his conviction and sentence, Kafkaris, a hired killer, had been visited in his cell by the president and the attorney-general of Cyprus, who would have to decide on his release after a number of years had elapsed. There the president offered to have him moved out of Cyprus with a new identity if he agreed to reveal who had hired him. Kafkaris refused. Under these circumstances, Judge Borrego regarded it as inconceivable that the attorney-general and president would subsequently exercise their discretion impartially, when deciding on whether Kafkaris should be released.[66]

It is conceivable, nevertheless, that executive decisions could be constrained by procedural checks and balances that would allow a relatively objective assessment of release. It was this aspect that in 2016 attracted the Supreme Court of Zimbabwe, when, having set aside release depending solely on presidential clemency as unconstitutional on grounds that it violated human dignity and the prohibition on inhuman and degrading punishment, it accepted as an alternative a form of release where the decision would be made by the minister of justice. The court noted that, in Zimbabwe, the minister and the authorities who advise him, including an advisory board and the commissioner of prisons, were "administrative authorities *stricto sensu.* Accordingly, the exercise of their functions and powers under the provisions [of the Prisons Act], unlike the presidential prerogative of mercy, is ordinarily reviewable on the established grounds of irrationality, illegality or procedural irregularity, either under the common law or in terms of . . . the Administrative Justice Act."[67]

Other systems exist in which the minister of justice operates in close cooperation with an advisory board, which may not be as independent as a parole board that can make binding decisions, but which nevertheless can make a measured input into the release process. An example would be Singapore, where, after a person has served twenty years, the minister may make a decision to release someone. Such decisions are made following the advice of a special statutory Life Imprisonment Release Board, but the minister is not bound to follow the advice of this board.[68]

Mixed systems of this kind, where the minister has the final say but where he or she is advised by another body, abound. A complex example is that of Ireland, where there is a "parole board" involved. However, the Irish Parole Board is not only appointed by the minister of justice, but there is also no formal statutory basis for the minister of justice to do so. Technically, only the minister of justice has the power to order the release of life-sentenced prisoners and the board is merely an administrative device to assist the executive on reaching a decision. However, in practice, the minister routinely considers the findings of the parole board, and in more than 80 percent of cases follows them. In a case involving two life-sentenced prisoners, Lynch and Whelan, the Irish procedure was challenged on the basis that the minister is effectively making sentencing decisions that would be contrary to the strict division of powers in the Irish Constitution, and doing so with minimum procedural safeguards, which would infringe the ECHR.[69] Before both the Supreme Court of Ireland and the ECtHR, however, the challenge was unsuccessful.[70]

The ECtHR was not even prepared to consider a challenge brought on the basis that the procedure followed for considering life imprisonment in Ireland was inherently inhuman and degrading. At a preliminary hearing, decided after the decision of the Grand Chamber of the ECtHR in *Vinter,* it found that even the procedurally challenged system that exists there gives Irish life-sentenced prisoners a prospect of release in law and in fact, and that therefore it did not infringe Article 3 of the ECHR.[71] At a further hearing, the ECtHR followed the Irish Supreme Court in rejecting the remaining, essentially procedural, challenges on the basis that the life sentence in Ireland was of "a wholly punitive nature and does not incorporate any element of preventative detention."[72] This meant, both courts reasoned, that the clear distinction, recognized in English law, between the punishment part of the life sentence and the part designed to incapacitate the life-sentenced prisoner in order to reduce risk to society, simply did not apply to life imprisonment in Ireland. Once all avenues of appeal against conviction and initial sentence had been exhausted, the life sentence was final and not subject to challenge.

In our view, this reasoning is flawed. It ignores what both the Irish Parole Board and the minister say that they do. Both insist that they pay a great deal of attention to establishing whether the life-sentenced prisoners whose release they consider after certain set periods still pose a danger to society. There is no reason to doubt their word. On the contrary, Irish empirical research supports the view that, when the Irish Parole Board makes recommendations or the minister finally decides on release, danger to the public is perhaps the most important consideration in determining whether to release someone or not.[73]

Another cause of the flawed analysis is that it misrepresents the nature of the sentence of life imprisonment. The Irish courts in particular insisted that a life sentence was indivisible as a punishment because the released person remains subject to recall for the rest of their lives. That is the case in many, although not all, countries.[74] Nevertheless, it does not follow that therefore release from prison is not a profound change in the penal element of the sentence. The conditionally released person ceases to be a prisoner with all that that entails. This is true in England and Wales too, but it does not mean that for that reason life sentences in that country are regarded as serving the punishment part of the sentence only. On the contrary, return to the community, even under constraints, changes the nature of the penal relationship. The Irish attempt to underplay this by emphasizing that the mechanism is temporary release, even though it can remain in place for the rest of the life of the individual concerned, simply disguises this reality.

A third weakness is that the Irish court confuses the powers of the minister to release life-sentenced prisoners on parole (by using the temporary release mechanism) with "'special remission', [that] is the power of commutation or remission vested in the Executive (formerly known as the 'royal prerogative')."[75] As the ECtHR recognized, but did not analyze further, these are two very different powers. The latter, as we explain more fully below, operates independently of any routine process for considering release. The former, the Ministerial power coupled with a parole board opinion, could have been portrayed as a legal process that should be expected to meet all the fundamental procedural standards spelled out in *Murray*. However, the Irish Supreme Court simply regarded the Irish release process as being "in the form of an exercise of clemency or commutation," and therefore free of procedural constraints, and the ECtHR in the end went along with this.[76]

We conclude that release directly by a political executive, even if it is part of the routine consideration of release from life imprisonment, is less likely to meet the *Murray* standards than release by either a court or a parole board striving for impartiality. The reason is that executive release often lacks a clear legal basis; that the criteria to be considered for assessing the penological grounds for continued incarceration tend to be confused; that time frames are not clear; and that procedural guarantees may be very limited. It is possible that a well-run administration backed by a rigorous system of administrative law, including judicial review, could avoid some of these pitfalls. However, from what we know about worldwide practice, this is unlikely when routine release decisions are taken by the executive alone. We would also underline that routine consideration of release by the executive should not be confused with clemency release, to which we now turn.

Clemency Release

Thus far, we have considered mechanisms for release that apply only to prisoners serving LWP sentences, as the routine consideration of release is the key characteristic that distinguishes LWP from LWOP. However, there is a further type of release mechanism that can be applied to all types of life sentences, except for those few extreme examples of LWOP that are specifically designated in law as fully irreducible. We refer here to the clemency powers of heads of state to intervene in all punishments imposed by the courts. Such powers are linked to a notion of a power of mercy, which heads of state traditionally have used to go beyond the formal framework of the criminal law in order to reduce the harshness of its outcomes. Terminology varies across legal systems, but for us clemency is a wide term that includes both a pardon that annuls conviction and sentence, and commutation that reduces sentences, usually conditionally. In addition, there is an amnesty, which applies not to individuals but to classes of prisoners in much the same way as commutation, but is rarely used specifically for the release of life-sentenced prisoners.

Clemency powers are usually regarded as the prerogative of the head of state, although, in practice, they may be delegated to a government minister, who acts on behalf of the head of state.[77] Such clemency differs in crucial ways from the routine consideration of release by a parole board, or indeed by the executive, in that it is not a regular exercise of release discretion after a fixed period, but part of an ad hoc exercise of the power of mercy. In 1983 the US Supreme Court explained this distinction in the context of life imprisonment:

> [P]arole and commutation are different concepts, despite some surface similarities. Parole is a regular part of the rehabilitative process. Assuming good behavior, it is the normal expectation in the vast majority of cases. The law generally specifies when a prisoner will be eligible to be considered for parole, and details the standards and procedures applicable at that time. Thus it is possible to predict, at least to some extent, when parole might be granted. Commutation, on the other hand, is an ad hoc exercise of executive clemency. A Governor may commute a sentence at any time for any reason without reference to any standards.[78]

In federal countries, such as the United States or Germany, clemency powers rest with governors of the individual states or their functional equivalents.[79] In the United States the president retains the clemency power for prisoners convicted of crimes at the federal level.

Clemency powers may sometimes also be exercised by the legislative branch, particularly where the clemency is in the form of an amnesty that reduces the sentences of all prisoners, or of a class of prisoners. However, in the case of life-sentenced prisoners, parliaments rarely intervene to grant clemency. A rare historical example of parliamentary intervention occurred in the Netherlands in the 1970s when the Dutch parliament persuaded the minister of justice, who exercised the clemency power on behalf of the Queen, not to commute the sentences of three prisoners who were serving life imprisonment for war crimes during the Second World War.[80]

Life-sentenced prisoners can benefit from any form of clemency, including a full pardon. However, of these various forms of clemency intervention, commutation is of the most specific relevance to life imprisonment, as, once exercised, it essentially changes the indeterminacy of the life sentence. Commutation may be used to release prisoners immediately without pardoning them but releasing them based on time served. Commutation can also be the first part of a two-step process in which the life sentence is commuted to a fixed term, from which the prisoner can then be released following the procedures ordinarily applied to a fixed-term sentence. Where someone is serving LWOP—assuming the initial conviction is sound, which usually makes heads of state reluctant to grant life-sentenced prisoners a full pardon—commutation becomes effectively the only mechanism for clemency release.

The great majority of the sixty-five countries that had provision for LWOP in 2014 had some provision for their heads of state to commute sentences. We could identify only some individual states in the United States and in Mexico, as well as Honduras, Haiti, and Israel that in law had removed the power of the head of state to commute life sentences or excluded it for a few categories of offenses that carry life sentences.[81]

Powers of commutation can also be exercised when someone is ill or dying. Such medical commutation can be applied to both LWOP and LWP sentences—in the case of the latter, both before and after the minimum period has been served. As explained in Chapter 2, there is some doubt about whether this form of commutation should be regarded as release at all as it does not enable the life-sentenced person to lead a full life as a member of society again. When describing clemency powers, however, it cannot be ignored, as the release of the ill and the aged is an exercise of mercy par excellence and the form of release most often regarded as typical of clemency.

The key difference between the ideal type of clemency, in its various forms of commutation, pardon or amnesty, and the three other types of release mechanism discussed so far is that clemency does not happen routinely. Instead, it is triggered by some special event or circumstance that, in the judgment of the head of state, requires an intervention in the further implementation of a life sentence. This means that, even in its ideal typical form, commutation does not meet the third *Murray* principle of assessment within a fixed time frame.

Historically, clemency powers would also have failed most if not all the other standards set in *Murray*, as the powers are not clearly described in domestic law, thus not meeting the principle of legality. Nor would a clemency release decision based on clear penological grounds have succeeded. Instead, the much more amorphous concept of mercy would be used. Procedural guarantees, the fourth *Murray* standard, would be missing; as would any form of judicial review, the final *Murray* standard.

Modern clemency procedures do not always fail to meet all the *Murray* standards. In his path-breaking study of executive clemency in the common law world, Andrew Novak has shown how in many countries, minimum due process standards have emerged to prevent arbitrariness and discrimination in the exercise of this power.[82] In part, this movement is underpinned by the international law requirement that anyone sentenced to death has a right to seek pardon or commutation of their sentence.[83] However, the evolution goes further than that and may apply to commutation of other sentences, including life imprisonment.

In many instances, the driver may be the need to have a bureaucracy in place to assist the head of state in making decisions about the release of life-sentenced prisoners. There may, for example, be standard forms that give an indication of the factors that a head of state will consider and therefore what information a prisoner should submit to improve his chances of clemency. With this may come a degree of due process.

There may now also be a clemency committee that advises the head of state or the government minister acting on their behalf. Examples of such committees can be found in several countries, ranging from Hungary to Malawi, the Netherlands, Vietnam, and the federal system in the United States. Such procedural safeguards may, however, still fail to meet the *Murray* standards. Hungary, for example, has sought to protect its constitutionally sanctioned LWOP sentences by providing for a clemency board to reconsider the position of LWOP prisoners after they have served forty years. The clemency board must examine whether "there are reasonable grounds to believe that the goal of the punishment will be achieved without further deprivation of liberty" of the prisoner concerned.[84] The clemency board must make a reasoned recommendation, via the minister of justice, to the president of Hungary on whether the prisoner should be granted clemency. On the face of it, this procedure followed by the clemency board meets the standard set in *Murray* of an assessment on penological grounds of whether the prisoner should be detained further. However, in October 2016, the Fourth Section of the ECtHR ruled that a forty-year period was much longer than the twenty-five years suggested in *Murray* to give a realistic prospect of release. Applying *Murray* directly, the Fourth Section also held that the new clemency process still did not meet the requirements of Article 3 of the ECHR, as the president of Hungary, who was the final decision maker, was not bound by law to consider the same criteria as the Clemency Board or to follow any set procedure.[85]

In the 2014 case of *Trabelsi v Belgium,* where the applicant faced extradition to the United States, the ECtHR was also highly critical of the procedures followed by the President of the United States for considering granting clemency to a prisoner serving LWOP:

None of the procedures provided for amounts to a review mechanism
requiring the [US] national authorities to ascertain, on the basis of objective,
pre-established criteria of which the prisoner had precise cognisance at the
time of imposition of the life sentence, whether, while serving his sentence,
the prisoner has changed and progressed to such an extent that continued
detention can no longer be justified on legitimate penological grounds.[86]

This ECtHR decision, which predates *Murray* but adopts the same standards, can be contrasted with President Obama's own account of how in
the post-2014 period he personally reinvigorated the US presidential
clemency power as a tool for advancing criminal justice reform.[87] For
Obama, the main purpose of using his powers to commute sentences was to
reduce overly harsh mandatory sentences. Many of these were LWOP sentences mandated for drug crimes. In some instances, these sentences had
been imposed under a sentencing framework that had changed, in that
LWOP was not mandatory any more for the same offenses committed now,
or the life terms required previously had been replaced by determinate
sentences.

According to Obama, there was also a second criterion in his decision
making: "Each of the [commutation recipients] had earned a second chance"
by taking advantage of opportunities offered to them in prison to rehabilitate themselves.[88] This second criterion illustrates the complexity of the
practice of commuting LWOP sentences. Concern with rehabilitation as a
means of avoiding the release of life-sentenced prisoners who pose a danger
to society was a primary reason for having the routine evaluation of fitness
for release, which LWP requires after a minimum period has been served.
It has even been argued that, for prisoners serving LWOP, rehabilitation
should be regarded as a prohibited ground for commutation, for by
choosing this type of life imprisonment the legislature has foresworn the
rehabilitative ideal entirely.[89] On this view, commutation should focus on
mercy alone. However, this analysis misses the point that the very open-
ness of the commuting power allows the head of state or other person exercising it to include criteria that the legislature may seek to exclude.

What this debate shows is that commutation also fails to meet the second
Murray principle of having "objective pre-established criteria" for evaluating release. When this weakness is taken together with its other procedural shortcomings, it is clear the commutation cannot be regarded as a

release mechanism for life-sentenced prisoners that can meet basic human rights requirements. This does not mean, however, that clemency should be excluded entirely from the release process. It can be used as a complement to routine release procedures. For example, where procedural rules exclude other release processes before a minimum period has been served but a prisoner needs to be released on compassionate grounds, say a terminal illness, it may be useful to have the possibility of clemency as a backup mechanism. However, even such intervention, sometimes referred to as medical parole, does not necessarily have to come from the head of state. It can be undertaken by a court, a parole board or even by an official with delegated powers.

Release from Informal Life Imprisonment

In most jurisdictions, release from informal life imprisonment is considered by similar, if not identical, mechanisms to those that decide on release from formal life imprisonment. While we do not have as full an overview of these mechanisms as for formal life sentences, we have enough examples to form an impressionistic picture.

In the case of de facto life sentences, the mechanisms are generally not different to those that are ordinarily used to consider parole for fixed-term sentences. These may, however, not be the same as those that apply to formally life-sentenced prisoners. The differences may be quite subtle. In South Africa, for example, all prisoners serving terms of more than twenty-five years are considered for release by a parole board after they have served this minimum term. Such prisoners would include de facto life prisoners, who may have consecutive sentences of thirty-five years or more. Persons sentenced to life imprisonment are also considered for release after twenty-five years, but in their case the release is subject to consideration by a further board and the ultimate approval of the minister of correctional services.[90] The upshot is that, in law, it would appear to be slightly easier for a prisoner serving de facto life to be released than one serving LWP.

When it comes to post-conviction indefinite detention the picture is more mixed. Procedurally, there may be more safeguards for such prisoners. Thus, in Canada, their release is considered by the parole board that also decides on the release of life-sentenced persons.[91] However, the Canadian parole board must consider their cases at a much earlier stage and review them much more regularly than is required when formally life-sentenced prisoners are involved.

In South Africa, the release of dangerous persons is considered by the sentencing court and not by the parole board. This procedure is spelled out in primary legislation and is subject to more procedural guarantees than is the case with release on parole.[92] In continental European countries, such as Belgium, France, and Germany, release from post-conviction indefinite detention is also considered by specialist courts for the executions of sentences, and is subject to the same procedural safeguards we have discussed for formal life imprisonment in these countries.[93]

In the United States, the release of "sexually dangerous persons," who are committed civilly for indefinite terms after they have served their criminal sentences, is controversial. This is particularly so in Minnesota, where between 1994 and 2015, not one of the 714 persons committed to the Minnesota Sex Offender program was released.[94] The controversy there was not so much about the procedure, which was based on psychiatric evaluations that were subject to judicial review, as about the criteria for release, which were stricter than those applicable to being detained in the first place. In 2015 a federal district court judge found that the strict statutory requirements for release were an unconstitutional denial of liberty, both on their face and as applied in practice. The judge also ordered practical changes to the program, including a restructuring of the treatment offered so as to make the eventual prospect of release more realistic. In January 2017, however, the Eighth Circuit of the US Court of Appeals overturned this judgment, holding that a court could only intervene if it could be found that the conduct of the state was "conscience-shocking," which was not the case here. It also reiterated that the provision of treatment was not essential, as the state was entitled to detain those for whom treatment was not available.[95]

The true difference is that in many instances the substantive criteria for release from post-conviction indefinite detention are different from those for life imprisonment. Such persons are only being held because of the danger they pose to society and therefore, once they have served a minimum period sufficient for purposes of punishment, they should be released, unless it is clear that continue to be dangerous. Moreover, the UN Human Rights Committee explained, in a case involving continued indefinite preventive detention of a convicted rapist, which continued far beyond the minimum non parole period set by the initial sentence, that, "as the length of preventive detention increases, the State party bears an increasingly heavy burden to justify continued detention and to show that the threat posed by the individual cannot be addressed by alternative measures. As a result, a level of risk which might reasonably justify a short-term preventive detention, may not necessarily justify a longer period of preventive detention."[96]

Time Served before Release

Across the different release mechanisms, decisions about release are influenced by one crucial factor, namely a minimum period before release can be considered. The purpose of such a period is to ensure that, as implemented, life sentences have an appropriate penal element. As we explained in Chapter 6, in some countries this minimum period can be determined individually at the stage of sentencing. In British and British-influenced jurisdictions, in particular, sentencing courts have the power to set any minimum period that they deem appropriate. Conversely, if the sentence is LWOP, there should logically be no minimum period because release is never considered routinely. However, even countries that have LWOP sometimes have legislation that sets minimum periods before powers of commutation can be exercised.

There are however, many countries, probably the majority in the world, where minimum periods to be served before release can be considered are set in legislation and that applies to all life sentences. Table 9.1 below lists the ninety-eight countries that we have been able to identify as having statutory minimum periods. It includes countries, marked with an asterisk (*) where the same minimum period does not apply in all cases, or where some life-sentenced prisoners are subject to LWOP (marked with °) while others have a standard fixed minimum. Deliberately excluded are federal countries—the United States, Australia, and Mexico—where there are examples of statutory minimum periods, but differing state laws make it difficult to get a national picture.

The figures reflected in Table 9.1 show that the average minimum period in all the countries listed there is 18.3 years, the median is 18 years, and the mode is 15 years. All three are significantly shorter than the 25-year minimum set by the Statute of the International Criminal Court, which has

TABLE 9.1. Minimum time before consideration of release

Years	Countries
40	Kosovo
35	Argentina, Peru
30	Benin, Cuba, Estonia, Gabon, Kyrgyzstan, Philippines°
27	Israel*°
26	Italy*
25	Albania, Antigua and Barbuda, Azerbaijan, Georgia, Hungary, Latvia, Macedonia, Mongolia, Namibia, Poland,* Russia, Senegal, Slovakia, Slovenia, Somalia, South Africa, Spain, Taiwan.
24	Turkey
20	Armenia, Aruba, Bahrain, Bangladesh, Belarus, Bulgaria, Cambodia, Chile, Curaçao, Czech Republic, Egypt, Eritrea, Ethiopia, Jordan, Romania, Rwanda, Singapore, Ukraine
18	Central African Republic, France,* Lebanon, Swaziland
16	Iceland
15	Algeria, Austria, Belgium, Burkina Faso, Chad, Côte d'Ivoire, Djibouti, Germany, Greece, Republic of Guinea, Kazakhstan, Laos, Luxemburg, Madagascar, Mali, Mauritania, Monaco, Montserrat, Niger, Pakistan,° South Sudan, Switzerland, Tunisia, Vietnam
13	China,° Uganda°
12	Cyprus, Denmark, Finland, Sweden
10	Belize, Burundi, Canada,* Jamaica, Japan, Liberia, Papua New Guinea, South Korea (Republic of Korea)
7	Botswana, Ireland,
≤5	DRC (5), Barbados (4), Trinidad and Tobago (4), Guyana (3), Gambia (1)

Source: Data collected by authors.
*Indicates countries where the same minimum period does not apply in all cases.
°Indicates countries where some but not all life-sentenced prisoners are subject to LWOP.

been strongly endorsed by the ECtHR. However, it should be borne in mind that some of the very short minimum periods set in countries are not applied in practice. In Trinidad and Tobago, for example, the minimum period is nominally four years, with follow-up periodic reviews every four years if the first one is unsuccessful. In practice, however, release is not seriously contemplated after as little as four years. As a 2012 report by the Trinidad and Tobago Inspector of Prisons notes, "[s]tatistics from prison administration show that more than half of the scheduled reviews are not being conducted and the expectation and hope of the prisoners for a review is normally misplaced, often shattered and usually lowered into a crypt of despair."[97] Similarly, in Ireland the parole board in practice simply ignores the statutory minimum period and does not consider release until a life-sentenced prisoner has served at least fifteen years.[98]

In most countries, the minimum is relatively straightforward, as it applies to all life-sentenced prisoners (though whether it is respected is an entirely different question). In others, the matter is more complicated. For example, the 2004 Turkish Law on the Execution of Penalties and Security Measures lays out an intricate pattern of more than ten different minima for various categories of life-sentenced prisoners, ranging from twenty-four years for a simple life sentence, to thirty years for a single sentence of aggravated life imprisonment and up to forty years for prisoners with multiple sentences of aggravated life imprisonment.[99]

How long do persons formally sentenced to life imprisonment actually serve before they are released? From the point of view of life-sentenced prisoners and, perhaps to a lesser extent, of the public, this is one of the most important questions that can be asked about life imprisonment. This aspect has proved surprisingly hard to research on a comparative basis. Our requests for information addressed to every country in the world on the average time served by life-sentenced prisoners released in the calendar year 2014 produced usable data from only seventeen countries. These ranged from 163 months in Finland, through 233 months in Germany and 290 months in Chile, to 380 months in Japan. We do not have equivalent figures for the United States, but Mauer, King, and Young estimated that in 1997 the average time served before release was 348 months.[100]

Even these figures must be treated with caution, however, as the numbers released in the statistical year were very small; six and eight in in Finland and Japan respectively. Further factors to be borne in mind are that these figures do not include those who die in custody or those who are not released in the year under review. The latter, in particular, may end up serving longer than what these average release times suggest. On the other hand, the average (the mean) may itself be misleadingly high as, given the small numbers involved, a few persons serving very long terms before being released may distort these figures. This has been demonstrated by Dessecker, who showed that between 2002 and 2010 the median term served by persons released from life imprisonment in Germany was 204 months, while the mean average was 223 months over that nine-year period.[101]

Our primary research did not gather data on changes in length of time served before release. However, there are indications from some jurisdictions that it has increased. One dramatic example of an increase is England

and Wales, where the average sentence served by life-sentenced prisoners prior to release in 1979 was 108 months, while by 1997 it was 168 months. By 2013, the average time served by life-sentenced prisoners prior to release was 221 months.[102] In England and Wales, Hood and colleagues' study in 2000 of released sex offenders provided a detailed examination of the decision-making processes of the parole board. They found that there has been a "dramatic decline in the use of parole" and that parole board members tended to "overestimate the degree of risk posed by many prisoners" emerging from life and long-term imprisonment.[103]

Another explanation is that where sentencing courts set minimum periods before release can be considered, these periods are becoming much longer. Recent data from the Ministry of Justice for England and Wales reveal that the minimum term imposed by the courts for mandatory life-sentenced prisoners has almost doubled in recent years, from 150 months in 2003 to 253 months in 2013.[104] This means that the minimum period now being imposed is longer than the current average time served before release, which will almost certainly lead to longer average times before release in the future than is currently the case.[105]

There are similar developments in other jurisdictions. In Sweden, the growth in the number of life-sentenced prisoners has been explained as being the result of an increase in the time that these prisoners spend in prison.[106] This appears to be related to changes in the release practice, which were formalized and placed under judicial control in 2006.

The English and Swedish experiences alert us to the uncomfortable possibility that developments in due process may not be related directly to earlier release. The country on which the most data of this kind are available is Germany. Comparisons there between the period when release depended exclusively on clemency and the current system where specialist courts take most decisions on release, suggest that the difference in time served before release is fairly marginal.[107]

This possibility is heightened by the radical reform proposal that was put forward in 2017 by the American Law Institute (ALI) in its draft revision of the US Model Penal Code (MPC). The ALI has proposed that parole should be abolished completely in the United States. Instead, all long prison sentences should be subject to resentencing by a judicial panel or other judicial decision-maker after the prisoner has served fifteen years. The commentary on the relevant provisions of the MPC makes it clear that the proposed judicial procedure is not to be a substitute for a parole hearing, but that there should be a new sentencing hearing in which the decision-maker would be asked whether the original sentence was still appropriate. The practical effect of this intervention will be that LWP sentences would be subject to review but that the outcome could well be that the original sentence is confirmed. Indeed, the ALI warns that its proposals could result in fewer rather than more life-sentenced prisoners being released.[108]

It is clear that the driving forces in this reform are the perceived need for procedural clarity and the rejection of the current US parole system because of the weaknesses that we have outlined above, rather than reducing the use of life imprisonment. The strategy of the ALI is to warn that LWP is a very severe sentence and to attempt to limit its imposition, rather than to ensure the earliest possible release of life-sentenced prisoners.

Participation in Deciding on the Release of Life Prisoners

Understanding the release of life prisoners requires more than an analysis of those institutions that formally have the power to make binding decisions in this regard. In 1994 Lord Mustill commented perceptively in the UK case of *Doody*, that "nobody knows what [life sentences] do mean, since the duration of the prisoner's detention depends on a series of recommendations . . . and executive decisions . . . some made at an early stage and others much later, none of which can be accurately forecast at the time when the offender is sent to prison."[109]

This insight into the release process in the United Kingdom can be applied more widely, as it conveys much about the important role that "recommendations" play. As is the case with the imposition of life sentences, key roles are played in release decisions by experts on dangerousness, and by victims and victims' families. However, their relative significance is different. Experts on dangerousness tend to be more influential at the release stage, as the decision about future risk to society is the primary, and in some instances the only, criterion for deciding whether release should be granted. As discussed in Chapter 6, the probative value of expert recommendations is controversial, whether they are based on clinical findings or actuarial calculations. Nevertheless, it is appropriate for the releasing authority to consider such recommendations, as long as it remains aware of their strengths and weaknesses and takes the responsibility for the final decision itself.[110]

The role of victims should logically be less important at the release stage than at sentencing, as the seriousness of the initial offense, as revealed in information of its impact on the victim, should not be in dispute any more. Victims may, however, be able to present cogent evidence about the risk that a prisoner may pose to them on release. Nevertheless, in the United States and several other common-law jurisdictions, victims are allowed to present evidence without restriction at parole hearings.[111] This raises a real danger that parole boards, which may lack the independence of courts, will be heavily influenced by emotional accounts of the harm to the victim. This may undermine their ability to evaluate whether the prisoner has been rehabilitated and still poses a risk to society. There is therefore a strong case to be made for not allowing victims to testify on the offense or express an opinion on whether prisoners should be released on parole, but only give information that is directly relevant to what the releasing authority has to decide.[112]

Summary and Conclusion

Much of the mystery surrounding release from life imprisonment can be dispelled by examining the different types of mechanisms that are deployed worldwide. This examination has revealed that release by a court provides the most effective way of ensuring procedural fairness, although this is not necessarily the case. Parole boards and even release by the executive can meet this standard too, although it is less likely that they will do so.

Release as a result of the exercise of clemency tends not to meet basic procedural standards, although in recent years it too has become subject to some constraints. Clemency is also not a suitable mechanism for dealing with the routine consideration of release, which is required by LWP. However, it can be used as a complement to routine release in order to deal with release on compassionate grounds when routine procedures would not apply. It is also an appropriate vehicle for exercising a degree of mercy that more rigorous procedures may exclude.

All parties involved in making decisions about the release of life prisoners should recognize that, as the decision affects the liberty of the person concerned, procedural safeguards are very important. Once the penological grounds for their continued detention are found to be insufficient, further detention becomes unlawful and release should follow immediately. This means that, ideally, all life prisoners should be entitled to have their release decisions approached in the same way as a habeas corpus application. Like anyone else deprived of their liberty, life prisoners should be able to rely on the rights enshrined in Article 5(4) of the ECHR; that is, they should be entitled to take proceedings by which the continued lawfulness of their detention is decided speedily by a court, and their release ordered if their detention has ceased to be lawful.[113]

Whatever release mechanism is used, the key question is: What should be the substantive criteria when deciding on whether there is still sufficient penological justification for the continued detention of a life prisoner? Once the minimum period that is required for purposes of punishment has been served, the primary other concern is dangerousness. Such danger should be extreme for it to justify delaying release beyond the minimum period. All parties involved in making decisions about the release of life prisoners should recognize that standard, as the decision affects the liberty of the person concerned.

In release decisions, concerns about just deserts and danger should not be entirely independent of one another. It is possible that, with the wisdom of hindsight, an offense may not be seen to be as heinous as it was thought to be when the initial sentence was imposed. Moreover, there is nothing immutable about the degree of risk that society should tolerate. It needs to be weighed against the suffering induced in the life-sentenced prisoner by serving very many years in prison. Arguably, therefore, society should be prepared to tolerate a bit more risk when a life prisoner has served very many years, thus bringing proportionality into the release calculation in a slightly different way. The extent to which society is willing to tolerate risk is also a factor in how former life prisoners are dealt with after release. That is the subject of the next chapter.

10

Life after Life

W HAT HAPPENS to individuals who are released after life imprisonment? What release conditions are imposed? What are the chances
of a successful, crime-free, resettlement? Although most life-sentenced prisoners will be released into the community at some point during their sentence, little is known about the processes shaping life after life imprisonment.[1] In this chapter, we analyze international standards and comparative
data on conditions of release for life-sentenced prisoners across different
jurisdictions, and assess what is known about levels of recidivism and the
factors that impact on their chances of resettlement and desistance from crime.
We also examine briefly the process of recall to prison. In so doing we
consider the procedural fairness of recall processes and their compatibility
with international human rights.

Release Conditions

When life-sentenced prisoners return to society, they are often bound by a
number of conditions of release.[2] The different release mechanisms discussed in Chapter 9 can, and usually do, set the conditions that are to be
met by persons who are released from life imprisonment. In addition to
these conditions, a number of further restrictions may be applied to life-
sentenced prisoners on their release, including, for example, civil disabilities,
violent and sex offender registration, notification schemes, and multi-agency
public protection arrangements.

A primary question is: What should the conditions of release for life-sentenced prisoners encompass? In this regard the United Nations guidelines are of very little direct use. The major UN report on *Life Imprisonment* speaks simply of the gradual "diminishing level of police and court control over the conditionally released [life-sentenced] prisoners," but gives no indication of what conditions should be set for such prisoners.[3] It does, however, establish that post-release intervention should not only be regarded as a means of further monitoring and control, but should also provide "after-release assistance that offers adequate social support to all former life-sentence prisoners."[4] It emphasizes that in order for life-sentenced prisoners to "begin afresh" following release, their social relations and after-care are of crucial importance.[5]

At the European level, little further guidance can be gleaned either from the General Reports of the European Committee for the Prevention of Torture (CPT) or from the judgments of the European Court of Human Rights (ECtHR) on what such release conditions or aftercare should entail. However, the 2003 Recommendation of the Council of Europe on the management by prison administrations of life-sentence and other long-term prisoners has two provisions specifically on managing their reintegration into society. The first of these speaks in general terms of the importance of post-release plans that address the risks posed by persons released from a life sentence, and the needs that they may have in the community.[6] The second provision stipulates that conditional release for life-sentenced prisoners should be guided by the more general 2003 Recommendation on Conditional Release (Parole), which are more detailed and informative, offering a set of general principles that should inform the process of release. These principles emphasize that the overarching aim of conditional release should be to assist prisoners to make "a transition from life in prison to a law-abiding life in the community" through post-release conditions and supervision that promote the resettlement of prisoners and contribute to public safety and the reduction of crime in society.[7]

More specifically, the Recommendation on Conditional Release (Parole) promotes the imposition of individualized conditions, including reparation and the payment of compensation to victims, drug and alcohol treatment, participation in personal development programs, work, education or vocational training as well as a prohibition on residing in, or visiting certain places where necessary for public safety. It emphasizes that conditional release should be accompanied by supervision consisting of both care and control measures and that the nature, duration and intensity of supervision should be tailored to the individual, allowing for the possibility of making adjustments during the parole period. It stipulates that conditions or supervision measures should be imposed for a proportionate period of time, and that indeterminate supervision measures should only be applied "when this is absolutely necessary for the protection of society," and with the appropriate procedural safeguards.[8] Furthermore, they should meet the substantive standards set by the 2017 European Rules on Community Sanctions and Measures.[9]

To what conditions may life-sentenced prisoners be subject at the national level? Our empirical research produced data on the conditions of release from a total of eighty-three countries.[10] The responses showed some variation in practice, and that released life-sentenced prisoners may be subject to a broad range of legal restrictions and control measures. For countries from which we received no parole information, we were sometimes told informally that there were no formal parole structures in place, or that it was the role of the police to keep an eye on released life-sentenced prisoners in the community, the latter sometimes coupled with a formal obligation for the ex-prisoner to report to the police. In addition, in some relatively newly developed life sentence systems, parole information was not provided because the procedures for release had not been set, as no one had been released yet.

In most of the eighty-three countries on which we received parole information, life-sentenced prisoners were required to place themselves under supervision, and to report to the appropriate authorities soon after release and at regular intervals thereafter. Most life-sentenced prisoners were supervised on release by parole or probation agencies. In general, released life-sentenced prisoners had to report, at regular intervals, to parole or probation officers, for as long as the conditions of their release remain in force. This was not always the case, however. In Bangladesh, for example, no conditions were imposed on released life-sentenced prisoners. As we were informed, "once you are freed, you are free."[11]

In the majority of countries, life-sentenced prisoners were bound by several standard parole conditions, together with any additional conditions that the authorities tailored toward individuals' risk profiles or specific circumstances. Standard conditions generally related to regular supervision attendance, approved residence, home visits by the supervising officer, approved employment, and travel and behavior restrictions. In England and Wales, for example, all life-sentenced prisoners were bound by a "life license," which specified seven standard parole conditions as a minimum. A released life-sentenced prisoner is required:

1. To place himself or herself under the supervision of whichever supervising officer is nominated for this purpose from time to time;
2. To report to the supervision officer so nominated, and to keep in touch with that officer in accordance with that officer's instructions;
3. To receive visits from that officer where the licence holder is living;
4. To reside only where approved by his or her supervising officer;
5. To undertake work, including voluntary work, only where approved by his or her supervising officer;
6. Not to travel outside the United Kingdom without the prior permission of his or her supervising officer;
7. To be well-behaved and not to do anything which could undermine the purposes of supervision on licence, which are to protect the public, by ensuring that their safety would not be placed at risk, and to secure his or her successful reintegration into the community.[12]

Similar restrictions applied in many other countries. In addition, there could be individualized restrictions on residence, movements, possessions, and alcohol and substance use, as well as released life-sentenced prisoners being required to undertake further offending behavior programs in the community, or participate in psychological, psychiatric or medical treatment. In Romania, for example, the court may require a released life-sentenced prisoner to attend vocational training courses and not to attend certain sports events, cultural events or public gatherings, or drive certain vehicles. Where deemed necessary, released life-sentenced prisoners in many of the jurisdictions in Australia must comply with random drug or alcohol testing and urinalysis; they must participate in relevant offending behavior programs and medical treatment. They may also be subject to an accommodation curfew.[13]

In most states in the United States, released life-sentenced prisoners were subject to standard conditions of parole and also special conditions that were tailored to their offending behavior.[14] These might include, for example, restrictions on movement, periodic drug or alcohol testing, participation in offending behavior programs or counseling, a curfew, driving restrictions, and prohibitions against associating with, or contacting, specific individuals. Similarly in the United Kingdom, additional conditions might include psychological counseling, medical treatment, and restrictions on accommodation, employment, and movement (particularly in cases of sex offending). In a small number of countries, including Switzerland, Monaco, and Peru, released life-sentenced prisoners could be required to make reparation to victims and called to repair any damage that was caused by the offense.[15]

When we considered the length of time that release conditions remained in force, we found wide variation across jurisdictions. Some systems were far less stringent and regulatory than others, though data were limited. Of the eighty-three countries for which we have data on the conditions of release, fifty-three provided information on the length of time for which conditions remained in force: 26 percent of the fifty-three countries imposed conditions that lasted until death, and in 64 percent of these countries, release conditions remained in force for a set period of time, ranging from three to eighteen years after release from prison. As shown in Table 10.1 below, in the vast majority of those countries (85 percent), release conditions remained in force for between five and ten years. In four countries, the duration of release conditions was determined at the time of the decision to release. There was also the possibility that, where a life sentence was commuted to a fixed term, parole conditions remained in place until the end of the full term to which the sentence was commuted.

In addition to the restrictions set out in the conditions of release, released life-sentenced prisoners were particularly likely to be subjected to a growing number of civil disabilities. For example, in several states in the United States, many released felons, including all life-sentenced prisoners, lose several rights of citizenship. As Petersilia noted in her 2003 study on parole and reentry in the United States, convicted felons may lose "the right to vote and to hold public office, and are often restricted in their ability to obtain occupational and professional licenses. Their criminal record may also preclude their receiving government benefits and retaining parental rights, be grounds for divorce, prevent their serving on a jury and nearly always limits firearm ownership."[16] Such civil disabilities serve as punishments in addition to the conviction and sentence imposed by the court.[17]

TABLE 10.1. Duration of conditions

Country	Duration of conditions
Finland, Monserrat, Lebanon (3)	3 years
Algeria, Bahrain, Côte d'Ivoire, Denmark, Eritrea, Estonia, Germany, Italy, Kosovo, Kyrgyzstan, Switzerland (11)	5 years
France (1)	5–10 years
Czech Republic (1)	7 years
Argentina, Austria, Belgium, Benin, Burkina Faso, Central African Republic, Chad, China, Djibouti, Greece, Guinea, Luxemburg, Monaco, Poland, Romania, Spain (16)	10 years
Hungary (1)	15 years
Turkey (1)	18 years
Armenia, Australia,* Bahamas, Cuba, Cyprus, Georgia, Kazakhstan, Ireland, Latvia, Macedonia, New Zealand, Rwanda, Slovenia, United Kingdom (14)	Lifelong
Cambodia, Madagascar, Mauritania, Niger (4)	Release decision determines duration
Israel (1)	Until the end of the full term to which the sentence was commuted

Source: Data collected by authors.

*In Australia, life-sentenced prisoners who are released are subject to lifelong parole in the Australian Capital Territory, New South Wales, the Northern Territory, Queensland, Tasmania and Victoria. In Western Australia, conditions remain in force for the duration of the parole period, as specified by the Prisoners Review Board (Sentence Administration Act 2003, s 28(1)(b)). In South Australia, a life-sentenced prisoner will remain on parole "for the period recommended by the [Parole] Board and approved by the Governor" (Correctional Services Act 1982, s 70(1)(b)).

Furthermore, in a small but growing number of countries, life-sentenced prisoners may be required to register with the police or public protection agencies on release. Registration of violent and sex offenders, notification systems, and multi-agency public protection arrangements have proliferated around the world over recent decades, starting in the United States, which introduced sex offender registration legislation in 1994. At least twenty-nine additional jurisdictions have developed laws governing sex offender registration and notification systems.[18] These registration schemes are not exclusively for released life-sentenced prisoners, but many are subject to them.

Other public protection measures that can be applied to released life-sentenced prisoners include, for example, the multi-agency public protection arrangements (MAPPA) that have recently been developed in the United Kingdom. MAPPA were first established in England and Wales under the Criminal Justice Act 2003 to manage released sex and violent offenders who pose a risk to public safety. MAPPA are set out under sections 325–327 of the 2003 Act, which require the "Responsible Authority"—consisting of the police, the probation service, and prison service—to work together to make arrangements for assessing and managing risks posed by: registered sex offenders (Category 1); violent and/or sex offenders (Category 2) who have received a custodial sentence of twelve months or more; and, "other dangerous offenders" (Category 3) who pose a risk of serious harm to the public.

Life-sentenced prisoners may become eligible for MAPPA in various ways. MAPPA guidance states that, "where an offender is serving life or an indeterminate public protection sentence, he or she will be a MAPPA offender under Category 1 or Category 2," with active multi-agency involvement.[19] For other released life-sentenced prisoners, the nature of their offense and the risk they pose to the public must be considered in order to assess whether they qualify as a Category 3 offender, requiring active conferencing and senior representation from the lead agency and partners. Multi-agency meetings are first held six months prior to the expected release of a life-sentenced prisoner and a risk management plan is devised, taking into account a number of actuarial risk assessment tools, such as the Offender Assessment System, the Offender Group Reconviction Scale, and intelligence gathered from the Violent and Sexual Offenders Register. The decision to apply individualized parole conditions is also negotiated at the initial MAPPA meeting as part of the risk management plan, but enforced by the probation service. The length of time a released life-sentenced prisoner remains supervised by MAPPA varies significantly, ranging from less than six months to life, and again depends on the seriousness of the offense committed.[20]

The development of such control measures and restrictions to protect the public, which are often applied to life-sentenced prisoners on parole, can be seen as manifestations of what has been called the "new penology." In many countries, the conditional release process for life-sentenced prisoners points toward a marked shift in modes of crime control, away from an old penology concerned with normalization and rehabilitation, to a relatively "new" penology, linked to what has become known as actuarial justice and illustrating the prominence of risk-based approaches to crime control.[21] Extended parole conditions, civil disabilities, sex and violent offender registrations, notification schemes, and entities like MAPPA are characteristic of the new penology. Feeley and Simon have argued, in the US context, that such an approach to risk or danger management has come to dominate parole and that it has evolved into a "waste management" system, rather than a normalizing or rehabilitative one.[22]

Supporting this contention, Petersilia reported in her 2003 study that parole supervision in the United States has been transformed ideologically from a social service agency to a law enforcement system of surveillance and control: "The traditional correctional objectives of rehabilitation and the reduction of recidivism have given way to the rational and efficient deployment of control strategies for managing (and confining) high-risk criminals. Surveillance and control have replaced treatment as the main goals of parole."[23]

Some scholars have argued that the proliferation of managerialist penal policies, which are constructed around incapacitation and targeted surveillance, have not completely eradicated or overtaken traditional resettlement practice. While countries such as the United Kingdom and the United States have opted for more punitive regulatory policies for managing released individuals convicted of violent and sex offenses, many of whom are released life-sentenced prisoners, the majority of continental European countries have opted for more inclusionary therapeutic interventions in their approaches to dealing with so-called dangerous offenders, and particularly sex offenders.[24] Even in England and Wales, recent research suggests that, while protecting the public is at the center of parole and resettlement practice, many of the traditional rehabilitative aims continue to underpin the release and resettlement process for life-sentenced prisoners.[25]

Recidivism and Resettlement

Support for lengthy, intrusive and protective conditions of release is often based on the assumption that released life-sentenced prisoners will continue to be a danger to the public, and commit further offenses in the community. A small but growing body of evidence from across different jurisdictions suggests that recidivism among paroled life-sentenced prisoners is rare, in the sense that they are unlikely to commit further serious offenses. It follows that life-sentenced prisoners do not pose a greater threat to the community than other prisoners.[26] For example, a 2004 report by The Sentencing Project revealed that, in Michigan, 175 individuals who had been convicted of murder were paroled between 1937 and 1961; none committed a further homicide, and only four were returned to prison for other offenses.[27] More recently, a 2013 California-based study found that "the reconviction rate of lifers was approximately one-tenth the rate of those who served determinate sentences."[28] Of eighty-three life-sentenced prisoners who were released in California during 2006–2007, only four were reconvicted within three years of release. Similarly, in 2011, Weisberg and colleagues found the recidivism rate of a cohort of convicted murderers released since 1995 in California to be "miniscule." The researchers stated that

> among the 860 murderers released by the Board since 1995, only five individuals have returned to jail or returned to the California Department of Corrections and Rehabilitations for new felonies since being released, and none of them recidivated for life-term crimes. This figure represents a lower than one percent recidivism rate, as compared to the state's overall inmate population recommitment rate to state prison for new crimes of 48.7 percent.[29]

Drawing on release data between 1985 and 2011 from the state of New York, and using a three-year follow-up period, Keyser reported in 2013 that "[w]hile offenders with crimes such as burglary, stolen property offenses, and robbery had the highest return rates, offenders released after serving time for murder and manslaughter returned at the lowest rates."[30] Moreover, most returns to custody among individuals convicted of murder occurred as a result of technical parole violations. Using data from the Pennsylvania Department of Corrections in 2014, Liem and colleagues found that of the ninety-two homicide offenders who were paroled between 1977 and 1983, "very few homicide offenders re-offended by committing another homicide."[31] In a similar vein, Bjørkly and Waage concluded in their review of studies conducted in the English language on recidivistic single-victim homicide in 2005, that "killing again" was very rare among released life-sentenced prisoners, ranging from 1 to 3.5 percent of all homicides, although they conceded that more research is needed.[32]

In Canada, between 1920 and 1967, 199 individuals who had had their death sentences commuted to life were eventually released on parole, and one person was convicted of another homicide. An additional thirty-two persons were released between 1959 and 1967, and by 1967 only one had been convicted of a new offense, which was not a murder.[33] In 2002, the National Parole Board of Canada reported that 11,783 prisoners, convicted of murder (4,131) or manslaughter (7,752), were released between 1975 and 1999. Of these, 37 (0.3 percent) were subsequently convicted for further homicide offenses.[34] In 2015, the board stated that over the last twenty-one years, individuals serving indeterminate sentences on full parole were 1.8 times more likely to have died than to have had their supervision periods revoked for having committed a new offense; and they were 4.7 times more likely to have died than to have had their supervision periods revoked because of a violent offense. The ratio almost doubled for those offenders who were on full parole for over five years.[35] The report stated:

> Between 1994/95 and 2014/15, 2,598 offenders serving indeterminate sentences had completed 3,024 federal full parole supervision periods. As of April 19, 2015, 54% of the supervision periods were still active (supervised), 20% had ended because the offender had died while on parole, 15% were revoked for a breach of condition, 7% were revoked as the result of a non-violent offence, and 4% were revoked as the result of a violent offence.[36]

In England and Wales, the vast majority of released life-sentenced prisoners are successfully integrated into the community, with recent research showing that "only 2.2% of those sentenced to a mandatory life sentence and 4.8% of those serving other life sentences reoffend[ed] in any way, compared to 46.9% of the overall prison population."[37] In their assessment of dangerousness and the risk posed to the public by persons convicted of murder in England and Wales, Mitchell and Roberts highlight that "during the period 2000–01 and 2010–11, there were 6,053 convictions for murder or manslaughter, and only 30 cases (< 0.5 percent) of persons who had previously been convicted of such an offense.[38]

In a 2011 study on the relationship between the length of time served in prison and recidivism in the Netherlands, Snodgrass and colleagues found that, on average, "offenders serving longer sentences are reconvicted at a lower rate and have a lower probability of ever being reconvicted" compared to short-term prisoners.[39] Similarly, in Australia, studies have consistently found that "prisoners with homicide and sex offences have considerably lower recidivism rates than average."[40] Highlighting how rare repeat homicide convictions are, a recent study by Broadhurst and colleagues in 2017 found that within a twenty-two-year follow-up period (from 1984 to 2005), 3 out of 1,088 released homicide offenders in Western Australia were subsequently arrested and charged with a further homicide. They reported that "[t]wo in five offenders (40.2%) had been re-arrested for any offence and 18.6 per cent for a serious offence."[41] And in Scandinavia, researchers have found low rates of serious violent offending among released homicide offenders. In Sweden in 2014, for example, Sturup and Lindqvist followed up 153 homicide offenders more than 30 years after release and found that 10 percent of the cohort had been reconvicted, five of whom (3 percent) had committed a further homicide, of whom two were reconvicted of murder.[42]

Broader measures of recidivism, such as rearrest rates, reveal that life-sentenced prisoners also constitute a category that would be least likely to be rearrested. For example, in 2004, Mauer and colleagues found that individuals released from life sentences in the United States were less than one-third as likely to be rearrested within three years compared to all released persons, and were more likely to be charged with a property than violent offense.[43] Similarly, a large-scale US Bureau of Justice Statistics study, carried out by Durose and colleagues in 2014, based on over 400,000 released US prisoners, found that prisoners who had committed homicide had the lowest five-year rearrest rates compared to all other groups of released prisoners.[44]

Many commentators in the United States have noted the difficulties in predicting future dangerousness on the basis of a past offense.[45] For example, in their follow-up study of 239 released life prisoners who had their death sentences commuted to life imprisonment after the *Furman* decision in 1997, Marquart and Sorensen reported that "these prisoners did not represent a significant threat to society" and found that that they could not "conclude from these data that their execution would have protected or benefited society."[46] The data showed that, overall, nearly 80 percent of this group did not commit additional crimes, having spent an average of five years in the community,[47] and that a small percentage (less than 1 percent) of released murderers were returned to prison for committing a subsequent homicide.[48]

In all, contrary to the popular perception that risk levels associated with released life-sentenced prisoners are high, there is a small but growing body of evidence that suggests the reviewable life sentence is a relatively effective penal measure with lower reconviction rates for life-sentenced prisoners released under supervision in the community than any other sanction.[49] While it would seem to be the case that released life-sentenced prisoners rarely repeat their original crime, much more systematic research is needed on reoffending and recidivism rates of this group. More than thirty years ago, Hugo Bedau commented insightfully on the same issue:

> While not complete, these data are encouraging. Although they prove that the popular belief is true, that murderers do sometimes kill again even after years of imprisonment, the data also show that the number of such repeaters is very small. Both with regard to the commission of felonies generally and the crime of homicide, no other class of offender has such a low rate of recidivism. So we are left to choose among clear alternatives. If we cannot improve release and parole procedures so as to turn loose no one who will commit a further murder or other felony, we have three choices. Either we can undertake to *execute every* convicted murderer; or we can undertake to *release none* of them; or we can reconcile ourselves to the fact that release procedures, like all other human practices, are not infallible, and continue to improve rehabilitation and prediction during incarceration.[50]

Even though research shows that rates of recidivism and rearrest are low among released life-sentenced prisoners, particularly in comparison with other prisoners, our understanding of why this is the case remains limited. Mainstream theories of desistance offer some insight on this point. Over recent decades there has been an upsurge of interest among criminologists in how and why some people stop, or desist, from offending, and two related bodies of research have emerged. The first encompasses largely quantitative studies that focus on life-course transitions, such as aging, and changes in structural factors, such as employment, marriage and parenthood, as significant turning points that can redirect a person's life path away from crime.[51] The second consists primarily of qualitative research studies, which emphasize the subjective evaluations, internal motivations or other cognitive transformations that frequently occur as an integral part of the reform process.[52]

Despite the increase in research on post-release resettlement and the process of desistance, the main focus has been on released short-term prisoners, while the factors that specifically concern released life-sentenced prisoners have been relatively neglected. Very little is known about how such individuals successfully resettle after release from life imprisonment. Is it a result of aging and maturation, improved social bonds, or more subjective changes, such as internal shifts in self-identity, or processes of special deterrence? Exploratory research has started to address these questions by examining the release of life-sentenced prisoners within the framework of resettlement and reintegration.

In a pioneering study in 1985, Coker and Martin investigated the supervision and resettlement of 239 life-sentenced men who were released into the community across England and Wales during the 1960s and 1970s. In-depth interviews were carried out with thirty-three of these men and their supervising officers, which provided an important account of the supervision and resettlement process as seen from both sides. The researchers found that most of the released life-sentenced prisoners were generally successful in achieving social reintegration. They attributed their success to a combination of subjective and social factors. These included a determination to succeed on release, opportunities for further education provided by prison authorities, fear of recall to prison, the natural consequences of aging and, for some participants, the effects of a good supervision relationship.[53]

A more recent study carried out by one of us in 2010, in the same jurisdiction, examined life after life imprisonment for 138 released discretionary life-sentenced prisoners, all of whom were released between 1992 and 1997. Interviews were carried out with over 100 supervising officers and 37 life-sentenced prisoners, 9 of whom had been recalled to prison following their initial release. Among the successfully released life-sentenced prisoners, there was strong evidence of subjective change, and a fundamental shift in their narrative identity. In general terms, their life sentence or the enormity of their situation led them to hit rock bottom, triggering a reevaluation of life priorities, a shifting sense of self, and a determination to change and succeed, despite the difficulties that they faced. With the help of external influences, usually involving a dedicated individual within the criminal justice system or rehabilitative intervention, life-sentenced prisoners were able to recast their life direction, develop a prosocial sense of self, formulate clear and tangible goals, and rebuild their lives. By comparison, the small number of recalled interviewees lacked a strong sense of personal agency, self-efficacy, and purpose and planning for the future. Equally important to successful reintegration was a respectful and committed probation officer who provided support and guidance, as well as a positive prosocial relationship in the community.[54]

A small-scale Canadian study carried out by Munn and Bruckert in 2013 offers further insight into life on the outside for twenty former long-term prisoners, including sixteen life-sentenced prisoners, all of whom had remained crime free for at least five years.[55] Many of the participants struggled to negotiate the lasting effects of life and long-term imprisonment, and what the researchers refer to as "fragile freedom."[56] They were often fearful of returning to prison for violating parole conditions, carried emotional and psychological scars from their lengthy prison terms, and had "a profound sense of being abnormal, of being outside, of not belonging."[57] Munn reported that the participants developed "multiple strategies to cope with the implications of incarceration," including building a support network, taking time to gain perspective, finding a balance between dreams and reality, psychological help, smoking cannabis, and relying on a higher power or spiritual belief. Although the participants wanted to achieve more than "not recidivate," their ability to contribute to their communities, to start employment or become active citizens was often hampered by the magnitude and stigma of their life sentences.[58]

In the United States, Liem recently carried out a follow-up study of sixty-eight released life-sentenced prisoners in the state of Massachusetts.[59] A high proportion of the sample (more than two-thirds) was re-incarcerated at least once following their initial release. The majority of these returned to prison for violating parole conditions, not for committing a new offense. Liem highlighted the significant impact of disenfranchisement, social stigma, a lack of support programs and, employment, and accommodation difficulties on adjusting to life after release for this group of paroled prisoners. Moreover, these adversities were often compounded by the challenges they faced in maintaining personal relationships, due to the long period spent imprisoned, as well as the hardship of negotiating stringent parole conditions. Despite these significant obstacles to resettlement, the majority of the participants desisted from crime. Liem revealed that for some, aging out of crime determined their success, while for others it was a "healthy fear" of recall to prison.[60] However, what most distinguished the interviewees who succeeded in staying out of prison from the re-incarcerated participants was a strong sense of control over their lives, or sense of individual self-efficacy. Conversely, those who were reincarcerated lacked a sense of self-efficacy or control over their lives, gave way to impulsivity, and often attributed their failure to external factors.

These studies differ significantly in many respects, but they potentially have far-reaching consequences for the resettlement process of life-sentenced prisoners and the development of theories of criminal desistance. The findings lend some support for an integrated theory of desistance, involving both structural processes as well as the internal subjective changes, although the internal change process was by far the most significant.[61] Most prominently, the capacity to embrace a new noncriminal identity, a strong sense of self-efficacy, and a determination to succeed were found to be integral to successful resettlement.

Often these important changes occurred during the prisoners' long periods of incarceration, a factor that has been largely ignored by the desistance literature.[62] As Irwin established in his study of seventeen incarcerated individuals (*Lifers*) in 2009, participation in prison programs and prisoner-led groups can contribute greatly to the transformation process of life-sentenced prisoners because they not only teach skills but can also facilitate personal transformation.[63] Interventions targeting life-sentenced prisoners should ideally assist individuals as they make the difficult transition from long-term imprisonment to life in the community. Since desistance is in part about discovering self-efficacy or agency, prison interventions are most likely to be effective where they support the development of a new, prosocial identity, encourage a sense of self-responsibility, respect self-determination, and focus on prisoner motivation and achievement.[64]

These studies also reveal some differences between the resettlement process for life-sentenced prisoners and other types of prisoners. Life-sentenced prisoners are confronted with a unique set of challenges in the community due to the long period of time spent behind bars. These relate in particular to the residual effects of long-term imprisonment, forming new relationships, barriers to employment, social stigma, the threat of recall, and the refusal of the community to accept that someone has changed. Preparation for the release of prisoners who have spent a large part of their lives in prison is therefore likely to be quite different from the release of short-term prisoners.[65]

Furthermore, parole and probation agencies, as well as community organizations, become even more important as an alternative network to assist life-sentenced prisoners facing a new world. The type of supervisory relationship identified as most helpful to released life-sentenced prisoners is one built on trust and dignity, within the legal framework of the life sentence. This depends on a system that recognizes the importance of enabling life-sentenced prisoners, both inside and outside prison, "to take responsibility, to strike out independently, to look beyond the prison label, and to recognize their own potential and strengths as human beings."[66]

Perhaps most importantly, the small but growing body of resettlement and recidivism studies further challenge support for the imposition of LWOP sentences. They show that most released life-sentenced prisoners are able to overcome adversity and resettle successfully without committing further homicide or other serious crimes.

Recall to Prison

In most jurisdictions, released life-sentenced prisoners remain at risk of being recalled to prison at any point during the parole period if they commit a further offense or if they violate their conditions of release. The 1994 UN report, *Life Imprisonment,* asserted that "[n]o assessment procedure can guarantee that a released prisoner will not relapse into crime" and that "[a]ny failure to observe release conditions may result in a recall to prison."[67] In some jurisdictions, the power to recall a released like-sentenced prisoner remains in place for the rest of the individual's lifetime.[68] Doubtless the decision to recall is a sanction of considerable gravity, as it may result in released life-sentenced prisoners returning to custody for a lengthy or even indefinite period. Such a process "[r]equires the most stringent application of the principles of fairness. Those to whom it applies have already served the period of imprisonment deemed sufficient as punishment, and have been assessed as posing no further risk to society. There should therefore be powerful, and challengeable reasons for re-detention."[69]

The UN *Life Imprisonment* report provides very limited guidance regarding the principles of fairness that should apply to the process of recall. It states simply that "recall procedures be governed by law," and that "[a] person faced with the risk of being recalled to prison should be given an opportunity to present his or her case."[70] At the European level, however, a significant aspect of the 2003 Recommendation on Conditional Release (Parole) is the procedural guidance it offers for the revocation of parole.

It recommends that recall procedures should not be invoked for minor infringements. Where such procedures are instituted, the possibility of a warning, stricter conditions, or temporary revocation should be considered.[71] In decisions relating to the granting, postponing or the revocation of conditional release, there should be a range of procedural safeguards:

a. Convicted persons should have the right to be heard in person and to be assisted according to the law.
b. The decision-making authority should give careful consideration to any elements, including statements, presented by convicted persons in support of their case.
c. Convicted persons should have adequate access to their file.
d. Decisions should state the underlying reasons and be notified in writing.[72]

In addition, "convicted persons should be able to complain to a higher independent and impartial decision-making authority established by law about the substance of the decision as well as against non-respect of the procedural guarantees."[73] The 2003 Recommendation on the Management of Life-Sentenced Prisoners specifically makes the requirements of the Recommendation on Conditional Release applicable to life prisoners.[74] Other recommendations of the Council of Europe reiterate that imprisonment should be used only as a last resort.[75]

As far as the ECtHR is concerned, the test for whether recall should be considered derives from the 2002 Grand Chamber decision in *Stafford v. United Kingdom*.[76] Stafford had been released conditionally in 1979 from a mandatory sentence of life imprisonment imposed following a conviction for murder. In 1994, however, he was convicted of fraud and sentenced to a six-year term. When he had served that term, the secretary of state wished to continue to detain him under his original life sentence. However, the ECtHR ruled that a crime of dishonesty did not justify the reinstatement of a life sentence for a crime of violence.

Technically, the *Stafford* case did not deal with recall, as Stafford was already in prison when the arbitrariness of his further detention under his original life sentence was successfully challenged. However, it did establish the important principle that recall should only be allowed when it is necessary to re-detain the individual concerned to protect the public from the danger posed by the sort of conduct for which the life sentence was imposed.

Released prisoners who are living in free society have important liberty interests that must be considered when decisions are made about their recall to prison. This principle of human rights was recognized by the US Supreme Court, which has accepted that all released prisoners have constitutionally recognized due process rights that they may exercise in recall procedures.[77] Similarly, the UN Human Rights Committee has recently held that persons facing recall to prison in order to continue serving an indeterminate sentence of preventive detention have a right to have their case determined by a court, and to the procedural protections that go with judicial decision-making. This right flows from Article 9 of the International Covenant on Civil and Political Rights that guarantees access to a court in all matters relating to the deprivation of liberty.[78]

To what extent does contemporary recall practice align with human rights standards, as developed in the Council of Europe recommendations, by the US Supreme Court and by the UN Human Rights Committee? We were able to collate some information on recall procedures from a total of seventy-nine countries, although the data provided varied greatly in scope.[79] Several respondents noted that recall data were often not included in official statistics, and that the frequency of recall remained unclear. Furthermore, in a minority of countries, recall procedures for life-sentenced prisoners had not yet been established. For example, respondents from both Kyrgyzstan and St. Christopher and Nevis highlighted the fact that there was no provision in their criminal legislation on recall procedures. Similarly, the Czech Republic stated that there had been "no experience of recall during the last 25 years," and our Belarus respondent stated simply: "No one has been released. It is not necessary to talk about recall processes." And in Bangladesh, released life-sentenced prisoners cannot be recalled. Those who commit further offenses "will be sentenced anew."[80]

While recall procedures varied significantly across different jurisdictions, it was possible to identify some common themes across the data. Of the seventy-nine countries on which we collected information, sixty-eight (86 percent) reported that recall procedures could be initiated for released life-sentenced prisoners following the commission of a further offense, the violation of parole conditions, or both.[81] For example, in Slovenia, a court must recall released life-sentenced prisoners, "if the parolee commits one or more criminal offences, for which a prison sentence of more than one year may be imposed" during the parole period.[82] It may revoke parole if the parolee commits at least one criminal offense for which a sentence of up to one year may only be imposed. The court may also revoke parole if the parolee does not obey the release conditions stipulated in the decision to grant parole.[83] Similarly, in Germany, conditional release can be revoked by a court if the released life-sentenced prisoner:

1. Commits an offence during the operational period showing that the expectation on which the suspension was based, has been disappointed;
2. Grossly or persistently violates directions or persistently evades the supervision and guidance of the probation officer, thereby causing reason to fear that he will reoffend; or,
3. Grossly or persistently violates conditions.[84]

Of the sixty-eight countries, twenty-three (34 percent) could initiate recall on much broader, more arbitrary grounds than these.[85] These included, for example, "the event of misconduct," "antisocial behavior," "cause for concern," "notorious bad behaviour," or "to protect society"—grounds that go beyond specific parole conditions.[86] In Cuba, for example, the penal code states that released life-sentenced prisoners can be recalled to prison if "the parolee commits another offence, or displays antisocial behavior, or if the organisation vouching for him/her has withdrawn its support."[87]

In eight of the total seventy-nine countries (10 percent), the threshold for recall was significantly higher than for the majority. Conditional release could only be revoked following the commission of a new offense.[88] In Finland, for example, a mere breach of release conditions did not constitute grounds for parole revocation, and if parole was revoked because of a new offense, the period of re-detention would be for a maximum of three years.[89]

A common theme to emerge from the data was the role of the executive in the decision to recall. It seems clear from the international standards that there should be judicial oversight of the recall process, but this was often not the case. In many African countries, the decision to recall a life-sentenced prisoner is typically made not by a judge, but by the minister of justice.[90] The Criminal Code of Burundi, for example, clearly states:

Conditional release is ordered by the Minister in charge of Justice, following an opinion by the Public Prosecutor and the prison Governor. It is revoked by the same Minister upon the initiative of the Public Prosecutor. The preventive detention of a person on conditional release can be ordered by the

Prosecutor General or one of his/her General Deputies, on condition that they immediately notify the Minister in charge of Justice.[91]

In some European countries, such as Ireland, Luxemburg, and the United Kingdom, the initial decision to recall released life-sentenced prisoners remains largely in the hands of the executive. The secretary of state in England and Wales is able to recall a life-sentenced prisoner to prison without prior consultation with the parole board, but the case must be referred to the parole board thereafter.[92] Similar procedures exist in Scotland and Northern Ireland, too.

Research has shown that, even within judicialized systems, courts are often influenced by decisions made earlier in the process, and depend on correctional authorities to provide them with the information on which the recall decision must be based. In several countries, such as Austria, Germany, and the United Kingdom, parole or probation officers play a prominent role in the procedures of recall for life-sentenced prisoners, either as initiators of concern or in providing information, advice, or a recommendation.[93] In other countries, such as France, while recall decisions are made by the judicial authority, the prison administration may, in some cases, revoke parole for a short period until a judicial authority has examined the case.[94] In the United States, research on the release of life-sentenced prisoners has also shown that recall procedures or so-called "back-end sentencing" are usually determined by correctional officials rather than the judiciary.[95]

While the most common reason for recall, identified by our data, was the commission of a further offense, it was not always clear from the data whether a further conviction was required. In several countries, released life-sentenced prisoners could be recalled to prison on the basis of unproven allegations rather than firsthand evidence. Previous research confirms that life-sentenced prisoners can be recalled to prison merely on allegations of the commission of an offense, which were never substantiated and for which the prisoners were never prosecuted, or if prosecuted, the prosecution resulted in an acquittal.[96]

Good practice requires that re-detention can only be justified when there is a sufficient link between the original life sentence and the risk of reoffending. In our study there were several countries in which a graded response to revocation was possible. In Switzerland, for example, a court can re-detain life-sentenced prisoners if they commit a further offense. However, despite

the commission of a new offense, if there is no reason to fear that the parolee will offend again, the judge may decide not to recall, but rather issue
a warning and prolong the parole period by half.[97] In Austria, too, if conditional release is not revoked because of a reconviction, the supervisory
period can be extended to a maximum of fifteen years for life-sentenced
prisoners.[98] Other jurisdictions were far more stringent. In the Australian
Capital Territory, for example, parole is automatically cancelled when a
released life-sentenced prisoner is convicted or found guilty of an offense
that is punishable by imprisonment.[99] And in South Australia, released life-
sentenced prisoners will automatically be recalled following the breach of
any designated conditions of parole.[100]

Of significance here too is the very high number of recalled life-sentenced
prisoners in some jurisdictions. For example, Liem's study of sixty-eight released life-sentenced prisoners in Massachusetts, reported a "relatively
high" rate of reincarceration. More than two-thirds of the interviewees were
re-incarcerated at least once, the majority of whom had been recalled for a
technical violation, including the use of alcohol or drugs.[101] There is also
evidence that the number of life-sentenced prisoners recalled to prison has
grown dramatically in some jurisdictions. Appleton's study in 2010 revealed
that the number of released life-sentenced prisoners recalled to prison in
England and Wales had risen by almost 500 percent between 2002 and
2007.[102] Moreover, in 2006, "the number of life-sentenced prisoners recalled to prison exceeded, for the first time, the number of those released
into the community by the Parole Board": there were 154 recalled life-
sentenced prisoners compared to 135 released by the Parole Board.[103] Figures from our research revealed that this number reached 236 in 2014.[104]
Further evidence shows that prisoners subject to informal life sentences
in England and Wales have been recalled at an even faster rate than
formal life-sentenced prisoners during recent years. In March 2012, there
were fewer than 100 recalled prisoners serving imprisonment for public protection. By June 2017, this number had risen to 760.[105]

Summary and Conclusion

This chapter has demonstrated that a life sentence has consequences that
continue long after a term of imprisonment has been served. In most coun-

tries, released life-sentenced prisoners are bound, not only by standard parole conditions, but also by additional restrictions or public protection measures. In the majority of countries, release conditions remain in place for a set period of time, but in several countries parole conditions remain in force until death. Without transformative goals such as rehabilitation or reintegration, many characteristics of the conditional release process could be seen as indicative of the new penology, with the main emphasis on protection of the public.

International standards, however, emphasize that the overriding aim of conditional release should be to help released prisoners make a successful transition from prison to the community. It should consist of both care and control measures, it should be tailored to the individual, and it should be imposed for a proportionate period of time.

Studies of recidivism by released life-sentenced prisoners have shown that very few of them commit offenses similar to those for which they were convicted. The evidence suggests that rates of recidivism and re-arrest among individuals who have been released from life imprisonment are significantly lower than for other released prisoners. Desistance studies have revealed that released life-sentenced prisoners are faced with significant challenges in the community, including the effects of long-term imprisonment, barriers to employment and accommodation, social stigma, the threat of recall, and a lack of acceptance in the community. Crucial to overcoming these obstacles are resettlement programs and supervision that helps to support new noncriminal, prosocial identities, a strong sense of self-efficacy and responsibility, and a determination to succeed.

International standards recommend that there should be procedural safeguards governing the revocation of parole and that the decision to recall (or not to recall) should be open and transparent. This chapter has shown that recall systems are often procedurally unfair. Given that recall may involve returning someone to prison for something they have not yet done but might do, it is important that the power to recall should be exercised with caution. Consideration should be given to a graded response to infringements of release conditions. A warning letter or increased support and intervention in the community should be among the first options. Those who are recalled to prison should be considered for re-release by a court, or a court-like body, as soon as possible.

In some jurisdictions there has been a rapid increase in the number of life prisoners being recalled, coupled with closer surveillance of such prisoners. These developments may reflect a growing preoccupation with public protection and risk avoidance. In the long run, they could lead to life imprisonment becoming an ever more repressive instrument of social control. In the final chapter, we will consider how this can be avoided.

11

Rethinking Life

O UR FINDINGS on life imprisonment challenge us to rethink its place as a penal sanction, in light of its many shortcomings when judged against standards of human rights. In this chapter, we confront life imprisonment without parole (LWOP), the harshest from of life imprisonment, and argue that it can never meet fundamental standards of human rights. We then ask whether the abolition of life imprisonment would not be a simple solution to all the criticism that can be brought, not only against LWOP, but also against life imprisonment generally. We describe what a system of life imprisonment that was compliant with human rights could look like. Finally, we consider how a renewed emphasis on the recognition of human rights standards internationally could lead to the abolition of LWOP, the reduction in the overall use of life imprisonment, and even its eventual abolition.

The Human Rights Case against LWOP

The primary case for prohibiting LWOP (a term that refers to any life sentence from which there is no routine or realistic prospect of release) is based on fundamental human rights. At the same time, abolishing LWOP will reduce the overall use of imprisonment.

If LWOP is not rejected completely, its recent introduction in both India and China, as well as its increasing use in the United States, poses the danger that, rather than being phased out gradually, it will be used ever more frequently. The danger should not be underestimated. As Jacques Derrida and others have noted, LWOP was not only an attractive ultimate penalty to Beccaria. The unrestricted authority to exclude offenders from society for the rest of their lives remains an attractive option for modern states that are concerned with having some absolute power as an effective means of maintaining order.[1]

Human rights law challenges states to eschew this power. The human rights basis for prohibiting LWOP is simply stated in a brief proposition in the German Federal Constitutional Court's 1977 life imprisonment judgment, which we have referred to throughout this book: "The essence of human dignity is attacked if the prisoner, notwithstanding his personal development, must abandon any hope of ever regaining his freedom."[2] In Chapter 1 we explained that human dignity has become a core organizing principle of modern human rights law. The implication is that any punishment that fundamentally infringes human dignity is unacceptable, no matter what virtues it may be perceived to have within a criminal justice context. Human dignity has increasingly become the basis for rejecting capital punishment, since it destroys human life, on which all dignity is based. The question of specific relevance to LWOP is whether having to abandon the hope of living in free society is a fundamental denial of human dignity. The answer is that the negative effects of a specific form of punishment do not have to be as drastic as the deliberate extinction of human life to qualify as a fundamental infringement of human dignity. There must, however, be damage to the essence of the humanity of the person concerned.

The link between hope and human dignity is to be found in the concept of the right to personal development. This has led to increasing worldwide recognition of a right of all prisoners to be provided with an opportunity to rehabilitate themselves. This reflects an advance in human rights arguments about how prisoners should be treated, which goes beyond the negative right not to be subject to unacceptable punishment, to the positive recognition that prisoners have a social right to public care and assistance. In the European context, prisoners' right to opportunities to rehabilitate, which is generally described as a right to social rehabilitation, resocialization, or even reeducation, has become a mainstay of thinking about the implementation of all sentences, including life imprisonment. In 1977, when the constitutionality of all life sentences was challenged directly on the ground that inherently they offended human dignity, the German Federal Constitutional Court, in perhaps the most influential judgment ever given on life imprisonment in general, held that some life sentences could be constitutional. These were life sentences that provided opportunities for resocialization in prison, as well as the possibility of eventual release and an appropriate mechanism for considering such release.

In recent years the European Court of Human Rights (ECtHR), while confirming the legitimacy of life sentences per se, has moved toward recognizing a right to social rehabilitation specifically for life-sentenced prisoners.[3] In 2013, in *Vinter and others v. United Kingdom,* the Grand Chamber of the ECtHR, after summarizing its own jurisprudence on social rehabilitation as well as a wide range of international and comparative sources, concluded that "there is also now clear support in European and international law for the principle that all prisoners, *including those serving life sentences,* be offered the possibility of rehabilitation and the prospect of release if that rehabilitation is achieved."[4] Coupled with this was the "right to hope," which was seen as closely related to an inherent human capacity to change, to develop positively and thus to rehabilitate. In a brief concurring opinion, Judge Power-Forde explained the essence of the *Vinter* judgment as follows:

> The judgment recognises, implicitly, that hope is an important and constitutive aspect of the human person. Those who commit the most abhorrent and egregious of acts and who inflict untold suffering upon others, nevertheless retain their fundamental humanity and carry within themselves the capacity to change. Long and deserved though their prison sentences may be, they retain the right to hope that, someday, they may have atoned for the wrongs which they have committed. They ought not to be deprived entirely of such hope. To deny them the experience of hope would be to deny a fundamental aspect of their humanity and, to do that, would be degrading.[5]

This approach has had far-reaching consequences for the debate about what could be regarded as a form of life imprisonment that was compliant with human rights. The impact of the recent European jurisprudence is being felt far beyond the continent, leading to a reconsideration of the type of life sentences that may legitimately be imposed. In jurisdictions as diverse as Belize, Namibia, Mauritius, and Zimbabwe, national norms of human rights have been reinterpreted, in the light of the emerging European notions of rehabilitation, to reject LWOP sentences because they do not allow for the prospect of rehabilitation, because they make it effectively impossible for life-sentenced prisoners ever to be released.[6]

This approach has also been reflected in an important judgment of Judge Theodor Meron, president of the Mechanism for International Criminal Tribunals, which is responsible for finalizing the work of the International Criminal Tribunals for the Former Yugoslavia and for Rwanda. In 2015, Judge Meron had to decide for the first time whether someone who was sentenced to life imprisonment by those tribunals could be released. In coming to the conclusion that "the relevant international legal standards strongly suggest that those sentenced to life imprisonment are not barred from being considered for early release," Judge Meron noted the importance attached to the rehabilitation of all prisoners in the International Convention on Civil and Political Rights and the United Nations Standard Minimum Rules for the Treatment of Prisoners. He also quoted with approval the judgment of the ECtHR in *Vinter,* which he summarized as ruling that "the rehabilitative principle and respect for human dignity, *inter alia,* require that all prisoners, including those serving life sentences, be afforded both a possibility of review of their sentences and a prospect of release."[7] We agree with Judge Meron's conclusion, not only as a matter of international law, but also as a statement of human rights principle. Because we accept as a fundamental point of departure the proposition that society cannot write off a human being as irredeemable, society cannot impose an LWOP sentence, as its stated objective is the intention to keep someone in prison until they die.[8]

The dignity-based arguments against LWOP are not universally accepted. Thus, Michael Tonry has maintained that in the contemporary United States there is no live legal or constitutional doctrine of human dignity. It follows, according to Tonry, that, because of the effective absence of equality and human dignity norms from penal policy in the United States, restrictions on various forms of harsh punishment, including LWOP, have no firm basis in US law.[9] Other scholars are not as pessimistic, however. Jonathan Simon has made a case for arguing against LWOP in the United States on the basis that it is contrary to human dignity. However, he also recognizes that the absence of a strong conception of dignity in US public law is an obstacle to such arguments.[10]

Whatever the practical reality, there is no reason to think that human dignity necessarily has no place in the US debates. In a recent article, Joshua Kleinfeld noted that that there is no deep or intrinsic reason why the prohibition on cruel and unusual punishment in the Eighth Amendment to the US Constitution could not be applied to LWOP in the same way as the ECtHR has applied Article 3 of the European Convention on Human Rights (ECHR).[11] Kleinfeld explains the underlying thinking:

> Seen in comparative perspective, parole in general and LWOP in particular turn out to be chock-full of symbolic meaning. They do not attract the kind of political or scholarly attention in the United States that, for example, capital punishment and three-strikes laws do, but they should. The cultural and moral stakes at issue with parole and LWOP are as high as almost anything else in the criminal justice system. The insistence on parole and the elimination of LWOP stand for the belief (or better, the commitment to believing—the faith) that all offenders are capable of leaving their criminality behind, nothing is unforgiveable, no one past saving, and no one forever excluded from the social world—that, in a word, criminality is mutable. The elimination of parole and insistence on LWOP stand for the belief or faith that some offenders are permanent criminals, that some wrongs are unforgiveable, and that some people who cannot be saved must be banished from the social world—that, in a word, criminality is potentially immutable. These organizing faiths reach even into the constitutions of both Europe and America.[12]

Given a clear rejection of LWOP on dignity-based, human rights grounds, can LWOP sentences be defended at all? Two arguments can be made in favor of LWOP. They relate to the severity of the crime and the dangerousness of the offender. There is also a third, more pragmatic, argument; that preserving LWOP for a narrow group of offenders may still be justified if its absence as an alternative would result in their being sentenced to death.

LWOP and Retribution

The simplistic defense of LWOP is to argue that some crimes are so heinous that no sentence, other than one guaranteeing the incarceration of the life-sentenced persons until they die in prison, is sufficiently severe. In other words, the need for a retributive sentence—a well-established, traditional criminal justice ground—trumps whatever human rights concerns there may be with this form of punishment.

The same reasoning could, of course, be applied to capital punishment, and some US scholars that support LWOP do just that. Craig Lerner, for example, argues that, as pure punishment for the most heinous crimes, the death penalty can be justified. LWOP in contrast, he contends, is a "conflicted punishment," a compromise that is supported by those who, no matter what human rights standards may require, are prepared, in principle, to punish as harshly as would be justified by the crime, but are still somewhat squeamish about the death penalty.[13]

In any event, in Lerner's view, modern LWOP is not as severe a punishment as Beccaria suggested. Prisoners serving LWOP in the United States are not necessarily subjected to harsh prison conditions, and they do have opportunities for rehabilitation and some (limited) prospects of release: appeal, executive clemency, and even a change in the law may give them hope. According to Lerner, the true function of the LWOP sentence is to bind future generations by making release very difficult but not impossible:

> The lure of compassion is powerful, and the present generation, fired with indignation and a sense of vengeance and confident in its judgment, seeks to protect future generations from their own weakness. If there were a simple legal mechanism for release, it would be difficult to resist the temptation to indulge in mercy. In that sense, LWOP in its harshness is nonetheless an acknowledgement of the softness of the men and women who will be compelled to administer it, legally constrained against tender human inclinations to imprison a human being until his death.[14]

Lerner contrasts what the LWOP sentence purports to do, that is, ensure detention for the natural life of the prisoner, with what it in fact does: "At the time of sentencing, LWOP purports to brand a defendant with the mark of Cain, but as administered, the sentence neither withholds the possibility of reform nor denies hope to the convicted defendant."[15]

Lerner's conclusion is not an explicit endorsement of LWOP. However, one is left with the sense that, precisely because it is an ambiguous punishment, LWOP is a type of life imprisonment that is acceptable both to those who are in favor of the death penalty and to those who are squeamish about death but want a harsh and effective punishment. The sometimes extreme rhetoric of US supporters of LWOP, and their acceptance of whole-life sentences on retributive grounds, should not blind us to the fact that they sometimes speak in terms of opportunities for rehabilitation and hope of release, the denial of which are the very grounds on which LWOP is rejected by the ECtHR and others adopting a human rights–based approach. The crucial difference between the supporters of LWOP and those opponents who reject it outright on human rights grounds is that the latter approach deals with enforceable rights to the rehabilitative opportunities and prospects of release. In contrast, even in the most benign view of LWOP, there are no rights to these opportunities and prospects. Their availability depends on the compassion of administrators. In any society governed by the rule of law, that is not good enough. An inalienable right must be enforceable and LWOP rejects that. It follows that LWOP should never be imposed and that all life sentences must include a reasonable prospect of release.

LWOP and Dangerousness

The second argument that is brought in favor of LWOP is that some offenders are so dangerous that they should be given a sentence that ensures that they never be set free. It follows, so this argument goes, that therefore there should be no mechanism for routinely considering their release, and ideally no such mechanism at all. Sometimes, LWOP supporters argue, if a person convicted of a very serious offense should not be executed in order to protect society, the only other sentence that can guarantee public safety is LWOP.

In reality, however, arguments for LWOP based on the dangerousness of the offender are seldom presented in a pure form. The assumption is often made that someone who commits a particularly heinous offense is inherently so dangerous that they should not be set free. The death penalty is sometimes supported on the same basis. Where capital punishment is not available, LWOP may be put forward as an alternative that will achieve the same objective.

In some instances, however, clear distinctions will be drawn between even the most heinous offenses and the detention of offenders who are found to be incorrigible. In Switzerland, for example, a sentence of LWOP is excluded as all formal sentences of life imprisonment have to be reconsidered after fifteen years. However, if a person who is convicted of a serious offense is found after conviction to be untreatable, such a person can be detained under dual-track preventive measures, from which release is effectively impossible. In such cases there is no regular review of such informal LWOP. Review only takes place if a psychiatrist is prepared to testify that developments in psychiatry now make treatment possible, which, if successful, would reduce the risk that such a person poses to the community. This controversial provision was introduced into Swiss law as a result of a referendum, following a heinous crime committed by a released person, and it reflects public distrust in professional judgments of whether someone should be returned to the community.[16]

What all arguments in support of LWOP have in common is public wariness of institutions making subsequent decisions about the liberty of persons who have been sentenced to life imprisonment. They do not trust "specialist" courts or parole boards assisted by "experts," to evaluate whether prisoners serving life sentences should be released on grounds of dangerousness. They do not accept the truism that age diminishes a propensity to commit crime. Nor do they trust the authorities not to become "soft" with the passage of years and allow release on nonspecific considerations of mercy which, in the view of supporters of LWOP, would undermine the original sentence.

The human rights–based rebuttal of the argument that LWOP should be used to deal with dangerous offenders can take two forms. Both are based on a commitment to the view that all offenders are in principle open to reform. The first of these would posit that a release procedure could be set up to determine when a person is so reformed that he or she should be released. It would accept, though, that some offenders might in practice not meet this criterion and that they might have to remain in prison for a very long time, if necessary until the end of their lives, in order to protect the public. In order to prevent abuses, this rebuttal of LWOP would insist on various safeguards: limiting the imposition of life sentences, ensuring that they are implemented in a way that allows prisoners to improve themselves, providing for fair release procedures, and giving former life prisoners the post-release support that will enable them to lead useful and crime-free lives in the community.

The second rebuttal argument takes its belief in the possibility of reform further. It argues that all forms of life imprisonment—and therefore LWOP—should be abolished. We will examine this latter rebuttal closely before reflecting in more detail on the possibilities of implementing a form of life imprisonment that would offer a realistic prospect of release. However, we must first consider the more pragmatic argument that acknowledges the shortcomings of LWOP but nevertheless accepts it as a necessary evil in the fight against the death penalty.

LWOP and the Threat of the Death Penalty

In the United States, and elsewhere, it is sometimes argued that LWOP should be retained because of the role it plays as an alternative to the death penalty where capital punishment still exists, and as an ultimate penalty that is perceived as severe enough to prevent the reintroduction of capital punishment where it no longer exists.[17] This case is often made by those who profess to be opposed to LWOP. A sophisticated recent example is the 2017 draft by the American Law Institute (ALI) of the new sentencing provisions of the Model Penal Code, which notes that the Institute's position in favor of LWOP "has been forged with reluctance."[18] The ALI explains:

> Viewed as an independent policy question, that is, if capital punishment were not part of the nation's legal landscape, the Institute would not endorse penalties of life imprisonment with no chance of release. Natural-life sentences rest on the premise that an offender's blameworthiness cannot change substantially over time—even very long periods of time. The sanction denies the possibility of dramatically altered circumstances, spanning a prisoner's acts of heroism to the pathos of disease or disability that might alter the moral calculus of permanent incarceration. It also assumes that rehabilitation is not possible or will never be detectable in individual cases. Such compound certainties, reaching into a far-distant future, are not supportable.[19]

Nevertheless, the ALI "recognizes the advisability of the penalty of life imprisonment with no chance of release when it is the only alternative to the death penalty. In this circumstance, it is defensible for a legislature to authorize a life prison term that is not subject to later sentence modification."[20]

As the ALI explains almost apologetically:

> The Institute's position on this score should be understood as a concession to the broader landscape that includes capital sentences, not as a freestanding endorsement of natural-life prison sentences. Because of the death penalty's unmatched severity, it exerts a gravitational pull on other sanctions, both in specific cases and in the legislative process.[21]

In these circumstances the ALI would support LWOP only if it were never mandatory and could be imposed only for the relatively narrow range of offenses that could be punished by death in the United States.

Rethinking LWOP requires confronting this difficult case. We would caution, however, against such a concession on grounds both of practice and principle. The difficulty is that the exception may not remain as narrow as the ALI envisages. Once one accepts that individuals may be detained for the rest of their lives without prospect of release, the temptation is to extend this penalty to offenders whose offenses, though serious, would not qualify for the death penalty. This is what has happened in the United States, where LWOP can be imposed for a wide range of offenses for which the death penalty would not be constitutional.

The principled argument is simple enough. If we accept that standards of human dignity condemn LWOP as an affront to human rights, we should not support the preservation of LWOP on grounds that it prevents another form of punishment that, arguably, is a greater affront to an individual's rights. One cannot avoid the conclusion that both the death penalty and LWOP offend fundamental human rights. This argument was well expressed by Lord Justice Laws in the English Court of Appeal:

> The abolition of the death penalty has been lauded, and justified, in many ways; but it must have been founded at least on the premise that the life of every person, however depraved, has an inalienable value. The destruction of a life may be accepted in some special circumstances, such as self-defense or just war; but retributive punishment is never enough to justify it. Yet a prisoner's incarceration without hope of release is in many respects in like case to a sentence of death. He can never atone for his offense. However, he may use his incarceration as time for amendment of life, his punishment is only exhausted by his last breath. Like the death sentence the whole-life tariff is *lex talionis*. But its notional or actual symmetry with the crime for which it is visited on the prisoner (the only virtue of the *lex talionis*) is a poor guarantee of proportionate punishment, for the whole-life tariff is arbitrary: it may be measured in days or decades according to how long the prisoner has to live. It is therefore liable to be disproportionate—the very vice that is condemned on Article 3 grounds—unless, of course, the death penalty's logic applies: the crime is so heinous it can never be atoned for. But in that case the supposed inalienable value of the prisoner's life is reduced, merely, to his survival: to nothing more than his drawing breath and being kept, no doubt, confined in decent circumstances. That is to pay lip-service to the value of life; not to vouchsafe it.[22]

Instead of supporting LWOP as a limited antidote to capital punishment, a rethink should look at whether another ultimate penalty, be it a fixed-term sentence instead of a life sentence, or a form of life imprisonment other than LWOP, can be put forward that would meet the legitimate concerns about how best to deal with the most serious offenders.

Prohibiting LWOP in Practice

In order to ensure that LWOP is prohibited, a number of practical steps need to be taken. The simplest way to prevent human rights abuse by LWOP sentences is not to allow them to be imposed. Yet this step has not been taken; not even by the ECtHR, which has focused on release from whole life orders. The practical result in England has been that judges have continued not only to impose whole life orders but also to tell offenders on whom they impose these orders with brutal frankness that they will die in prison, without mentioning any prospect of release.[23] This is hardly conducive to giving these offenders the hope of release, to which they have a human right, or an indication, which they are supposed to have from the beginning of their sentences, of what they will need to do in order to be released.

Practical steps also need to be taken to ensure that LWOP is not imposed indirectly by sentencing an offender to life imprisonment with parole (LWP) but setting such a high minimum period that the offender would have no realistic prospect of release. One way of preventing this would be to have a clear understanding of what the maximum minimum period should be: in other words, what time should be allowed to elapse before release is considered. In this regard the twenty-five-year maximum that the ECtHR, following the International Criminal Court and other international pointers, has recognized, has much to commend it.

The acceptance of the twenty-five-year maximum for the purposes of distinguishing LWOP from LWP should not be understood as an endorsement of twenty-five years as a universal maximum minimum period. As we shall see when discussing LWP below, a shorter period before release is first considered may be desirable, either as a general rule, or in particular cases where proportionality concerns may require it. A shorter maximum minimum period may be a human rights imperative in order to avoid making a LWP sentence into a de facto LWOP in the case of older offenders who are unlikely to live for a further twenty-five years. In Chapter 4 we discuss various solutions that have been suggested. These range from excluding older offenders completely from life imprisonment to setting prescribed or bespoke shorter minimum periods for them.

Further practical steps are needed to prohibit fixed-term de facto life sentences that amount to LWOP because the fixed term is so long that it gives the offender no prospect of release. The extreme cases are easy to recognize and forbid. A fixed term of 100 years with no prospect of being considered for early release is clearly a form of de facto LWOP and should be treated as infringing human rights.

Borderline cases are harder to identify. One way of doing so is to ask whether a prisoner serving a very long fixed term will be considered for release after having served twenty-five years or less. Thus, for example, a fifty-year sentence, where the offender would be considered for release after half the sentence, twenty-five years, would pass muster, but a fifty-year sentence where release will be considered after two-thirds would not. Where a person is subject to a number of consecutive fixed-term sentences, particular care needs to be taken to ensure that release is considered by the time twenty-five years has elapsed.[24]

The effective prohibition of LWOP requires constant attention to release practices. The "platitude of hope" can easily be expressed, but the practice may be very different.[25] Life prisoners may be put in the position that, no matter what they do, or how much they change for the better, they are never likely to be considered for release fairly. This may be so either because those making release decisions are not minded ever to regard life prisoners as having been sufficiently punished, or because they are not prepared to take even the most minimal risk that they will reoffend after release.

Finally, we must emphasize that if the objective is to eliminate LWOP, it requires its consistent rejection in principle and in practice. Arguing that LWOP should not be imposed for particular offenses, non-violent drug offenses for example, because they are insufficiently serious, may, paradoxically, actually reinforce LWOP. Rejecting LWOP for lesser offenses implies that it is appropriate for the most serious offenses, when it is not.[26]

Abolishing Life Imprisonment?

The simplest way of ensuring that LWOP is never imposed is to abolish all types of life imprisonment, which would of course address many of the problems with life sentences generally. What can we learn from the thirty-three countries that have abolished life imprisonment, or from jurisdictions where there have been serious debates about doing so?

One can begin by contrasting the position of those in favor of abolishing life imprisonment completely, with those at the opposite end of the spectrum, who support LWOP, or who oppose LWOP but who are not opposed to all forms of life imprisonment. Life imprisonment abolitionists and opponents of LWOP share the belief that all prisoners have a right to be able to rehabilitate themselves. However, life imprisonment abolitionists also share with the supporters of LWOP the belief that the organs of the state cannot be trusted with the ultimate decision on when life prisoners have been rehabilitated to pose no further risk to the public and should therefore be released. The difference is that, while supporters of LWOP fear excessive leniency, life imprisonment abolitionists fear excessive caution, which may result in life prisoners being detained for longer than is justified, not only because of the offenses they have committed but also because of any danger they may pose to society.

Portugal, a country that effectively abolished the death penalty in 1854, provides an early example of how nineteenth-century ideas about rehabilitation could provide the justification for the total abolition of life imprisonment. In 1884 the minister of justice explained to the Portuguese parliament, when proposing abolition of life imprisonment, that life imprisonment was "opposed to the laws of man's moral nature according to which the improvement of evil tendencies and the regeneration of spirits, even the most perverted ones, are always presumptively possible."[27]

What is striking about this formulation is that, language aside, it is not very different in substance from the modern twenty-first century insistence of the ECtHR on the centrality of the provision for rehabilitation in order to legitimate life imprisonment. In the same speech however, the Minister commented that life imprisonment was always "unfair as punishment, excessive as a means of intimidation."[28]

Life imprisonment has never returned to Portugal.[29] It is one of the thirteen countries in the world where the constitution specifically prohibits life imprisonment.[30] These constitutions are all to be found in countries with a Portuguese or Spanish heritage and reflect a longstanding distrust of the exercise of state power.

Countries with constitutional prohibitions on life imprisonment are particularly interesting, because such provisions have to be interpreted in order to determine whether sentences that are not formally labeled as life imprisonment still infringe the prohibition, whether they are lifelong security measures or excessively long fixed-term prison sentences. These wider

considerations depend on the wording of the constitutions; they may prohibit formal sentences of life imprisonment as well as informal types of lifelong detention or excessive fixed-term prison sentences. The Constitution
of Portugal, for example, provides that "[n]o sentence or security measure
that deprives or restricts freedom shall be perpetual in nature or possess an
unlimited or undefined duration."[31] Notably, the reference to security measures means that it applies also to informal life sentences, such as post-
conviction indefinite detention.

The constitutions of Bolivia, Nicaragua, and Venezuela specifically limit
criminal sanctions to a maximum of thirty years' imprisonment,[32] that is,
less than the thirty-five years that we have adopted as the minimum fixed
term to be regarded as de facto life imprisonment. As we explained in
Chapter 2, constitutional prohibitions on formal life imprisonment have
been used effectively in a number of countries to identify long determinate
sentences as informal life imprisonment, and to prohibit them.

Although the existence of an explicit constitutional prohibition prevents
life sentences from being introduced by ordinary legislation, constitutional
provisions are not immune to challenge. From time to time, attempts have
been made to amend a constitutional text in order to allow for the introduction (or reintroduction) of a sentence of imprisonment for life. In 2009 in
Colombia, for example, there was an initiative to amend Article 34 of the
constitution, which expressly prohibits life sentences. The proposal was to
allow life sentences for crimes against minors, specifically rape. However,
the attempt to submit the proposal in a referendum was blocked by the constitutional court, although its decision was based on a technicality and did
not enter into the substance of the arguments on life imprisonment.[33] Further attempts to amend the constitution were rejected without the courts
being asked to intervene.[34] Although there appears to be mounting pressure from public opinion to introduce a sentence of life imprisonment, specifically for violent sexual offenses against children, there is still significant
resistance, best summed up using the words of the Colombian Advisory
Board on Criminal Policy. The board, when asked to advise the government
on one of these proposed amendments, concluded, in a scathing report, that
"[t]he initiative in question is not . . . the expression of a good criminal
policy, in accordance with the principles of democracy, but a form of pop-
ulism or punitive demagoguery."[35] Overall, the situation in countries with
constitutional prohibitions on life imprisonment is relatively stable, in the

sense that there have been no successful attempts to amend constitutions to allow the reintroduction of life imprisonment in recent decades.

The same cannot be said, however, about countries where there was no explicit constitutional prohibition but the penal code simply did not provide for life imprisonment. Mexico is an example of a country where change has occurred against the background of constitutional uncertainty. Though the Mexican Federal Constitution does not explicitly prohibit life sentences, it does prohibit any punishment that is cruel and unusual (*"penas inusitadas y trascendentales"*).[36] In 2001, the Supreme Court of Justice, following the South and Central American model, had confirmed that life imprisonment was unconstitutionally severe.[37] This meant that, at least until 2005, the possibility that a suspect might face a life sentence was seen as a potential barrier to extradition of suspects from Mexico to the United States in particular.[38] Subsequently however, the Supreme Court of Justice has repeatedly ruled that life imprisonment is not unconstitutional.[39] The practical outcome has been that there is now provision for life imprisonment, indeed for LWOP, in five Mexican states, Chihuahua, Puebla, Quintana Roo, the State of Mexico, and Veracruz.[40] However, the remaining twenty-six Mexican states and the Mexican federal system have no such provision. The legal situation in the country as a whole is somewhat unstable, however, as single rulings of the Supreme Court of Justice of Mexico are not automatically binding on all states unless they have been approved by a majority of eight justices, which has not, so far, been the case with the decisions declaring life imprisonment compatible with the federal constitution.[41]

On the other hand, some Latin American states that do not have life imprisonment but also have no constitutional prohibition on its introduction have been more resistant to change. In Ecuador, an initiative to introduce life imprisonment was grandly brushed aside by President Rafael Correa, who remarked that "in their narrow minds and souls, [the authors of this proposal] do not understand that we do not need more repression but more justice, more equality, more opportunities, more kindness, more solidarity."[42]

In both Slovenia, in 2008, and in Spain, in 2014, penal codes have recently been amended to provide for life imprisonment. Interestingly, by late 2016 the sentence had not been imposed in either country. In Slovenia, the reason given was that the grounds for its imposition were so narrow that an occasion for its imposition had not yet arisen. In Spain, continued disputes about its constitutionality and political disagreement about its implementation have ensured that it has not yet been used.[43]

In recent years there have also been a variety of initiatives to abolish life imprisonment that have not come to fruition but yielded valuable arguments about the nature of life imprisonment. Attempts by courts to abolish all forms of life imprisonment on the grounds that they are incompatible with human rights norms expressed in national constitutions have been rare and relatively unsuccessful. In the 1970s, a judgment of a German higher regional court in Verden declared all life imprisonment a fundamental affront to human dignity, and therefore unconstitutional. The German Federal Constitutional Court overruled that decision, holding that a life sentence that provided opportunities for resocialization in prison, a realistic possibility of release and an appropriate mechanism for considering such release would pass constitutional muster.[44] With appropriate amendments following this judgment, life imprisonment has survived in Germany. Although academic critics continue to doubt its constitutionality, abolition of life imprisonment is not seriously considered in official circles.[45]

A similar situation arose in Namibia, where the constitution explicitly outlaws the death penalty and protects human dignity. A single trial judge argued that life imprisonment was a delayed death sentence, which destroyed all hope and dignity of persons subject to it, and therefore unconstitutional. However, the Supreme Court of Namibia overruled that decision. It found that a close reading of the Namibian prison law on the treatment of prisoners and their possible release, in light of the constitution, demonstrated that life imprisonment could be applied consistently with constitutional standards, thus allowing its continued use.[46]

This form of human rights based judicial intervention has not disappeared. On the contrary, it has now been taken up at the higher level of the ECtHR. In 2014 in *Öcalan v. Turkey (no. 2),* Judge Pinto de Albuquerque agreed with the majority that the LWOP sentence imposed on Öcalan should be struck down, but, dissenting in part, questioned the compatibility of all life imprisonment with the principles of the ECHR and with international law generally. Judge Pinto de Albuquerque did not mince his words, and argued: "Life imprisonment may work, and indeed has worked in the past, as a privileged instrument of abuse of civil liberties." He went on to suggest that life sentences could not be proportionate as they are "an unrestrained, unnecessary and disproportionate State reaction to crime," and that the principle of resocialization demanded "a categorical rule against life imprisonment."[47] Although these views are expressed as a minority opinion of a single judge, it is significant that the abolitionist arguments were spelled out judicially at this very high level. In future this intervention may come to be seen as the equivalent of those of Justices William Brennan and Thurgood Marshal in the US Supreme Court in the development of the law on the death penalty in the 1970s.

Three years after *Öcalan*, in 2017, Judge Pinto de Albuquerque returned to the fray in the Grand Chamber of the ECtHR with a minority opinion in the case of *Khamtokhu and Aksenchik v Russia*.[48] And again he made a forceful case for the abolition of life imprisonment as a punishment. In this opinion he came to the challenging conclusion that life imprisonment, like the death penalty, is inherently too severe ever to be imposed.

The pioneering arguments Judge Pinto de Albuquerque made in favor of abolition, however, are not equally strong. He saw an international trend toward abolition that he identified as a factor supporting the demise of life imprisonment.[49] Our worldwide study has not identified such a trend. In Europe, both Slovenia and Spain have reintroduced life imprisonment in recent years. The same has happened in individual states in Mexico. And our worldwide life imprisonment population figures suggest significant growth in the use of life imprisonment, including in the use of life imprisonment without parole sentences.

Recently, the Pope took a principled position against all life imprisonment, which led to its abolition in the Vatican. Although the Vatican follows Italian law in criminal matters, it has the power to amend it. In 2014 it did just that, by removing life imprisonment as a permissible punishment in the Vatican. It did so because of the view expressed by the Pope that all life imprisonment was an affront to human dignity. This is largely symbolic, however, as the Vatican does not normally try persons charged with offenses that could be subject to life imprisonment.[50]

Our conclusion is that the number of states that have abolished life imprisonment worldwide is largely static. The strongest support for abolition is found in historical patterns, such as the continued absence of life imprisonment in former Portuguese colonies, rather than in a contemporary international movement.

Judge Pinto de Albuquerque is undoubtedly correct in stating that rights to opportunities for resocialization and realistic prospects of release are

powerful factors in the contemporary evolution of life imprisonment worldwide. We agree that these rights should shape thinking about the future of
life imprisonment. However, Judge Pinto de Albuquerque makes a logical
leap when he argues that recognition of these rights necessarily implies the
abolition of all life imprisonment. Indeed, life imprisonment does not necessarily destroy any prospect of social reintegration. Notwithstanding all
the weaknesses in the processes of implementing life sentences that we have
identified, there is evidence of life sentences sometimes working as planned;
of some prisoners grasping opportunities for self-improvement while serving
life sentences; and of release decisions taken correctly on grounds that, after
having served a number of years, the prisoner concerned has been punished
sufficiently and no longer poses a significant risk to society.[51]

While, as discussed in Chapter 10, some life prisoners do return successfully to society, this does not mean that life imprisonment is a desirable
form of punishment. We agree with Judge Pinto de Albuquerque that, as
with the death penalty, there is no convincing evidence of the unique deterrent value of life sentences. Systematic studies that compare the deterrent
effect of life sentences to fixed-term sentences that are long, but not so long
that they amount to de facto life imprisonment, have not been undertaken.
However, there is little reason to believe that clear evidence can be found
that the deterrent effect of life sentences is greater than that of long fixed-
term sentences.

Judge Pinto de Albuquerque is also correct that the recognition of prisoners' rehabilitation-related rights means that these rights cannot be over-
ridden by the need for retribution alone. That is why LWOP sentences are
unacceptable. It is also why retributionists have had to accept that the punishment element of life sentences has to be limited in some way or another to
allow for a prospect of release.

Once this has been recognized, the legitimate question arises: Why not
set the maximum sentence, even for the most serious offenses, at a fixed
term from the outset? This option has attracted the attention of penal reformers because of its legal certainty. It was the underpinning of Norway's
decision in 1981 to set the maximum penal term at twenty-one years.[52] It
is also the basis for a recent reform proposal by Tonio Walter in Germany
that would abolish formal life sentences for murder—the only offense for
which life imprisonment is mandatory and the offense for which almost all
life sentences are currently imposed in that country—and replace it by a

fixed-term sentence of between fifteen and thirty years, which would re-flect the heinousness of the particular murder within a fixed range.[53] In the American context, a similar proposal has been made by Marc Mauer, who has argued that sentences in the US federal system should be limited to a maximum of twenty years, "unless a court has determined that the individual presents an undue risk to public safety".[54]

Both Norway and Germany retain the second-track, post-sentence indefinite detention as a means of ensuring that persons convicted of serious offenses who remain dangerous can be incapacitated by continuing to detain them, potentially for the rest of their lives. For that reason Judge Pinto de Albuquerque refuses to recognize Norway as a country that has abolished life imprisonment.[55] For the same reason, he would presumably not regard the proposed German reform as abolition either. In the case of Mauer's proposal for the United States, it is not clear what form detention beyond twenty years on public safety grounds would take, but it is likely to be a type of informal life imprisonment that would be open to the same critique.

Judge Pinto de Albuquerque does recognize that life sentences, including presumably post-sentence indefinite detention, could serve the purpose of incapacitation (negative special prevention). Incapacitation would require that life prisoners (both those subject to formal life sentences and those serving post-sentence indefinite detention) would be detained until a decision could be made that they were no longer a risk to society. However, he is highly skeptical about a presumption that such a decision could be made fairly. In Judge Pinto de Albuquerque's words:

> [T]his presumption is based on a faith in highly problematic prediction scales that are closer to a form of divinatory anticipation of the future than to a scientific exercise, as the experience of many 'false positives' has shown. Moreover, the net-widening effect of the concept of dangerousness of the offender, which has gone so far as to include "personality disorder," "mental abnormality" or "unstable character," blurs the borderline between responsible mentally fit offenders and irresponsible mentally unfit offenders, with the serious risk of mislabelling offenders.[56]

In any case, Judge Pinto de Albuquerque would not regard the need for incapacitation as a sufficient ground for either a formal or an informal life sentence; not only because of the difficulties in assessing when it should be set aside but also because of the power it gives the state over the individual. Indeed, he points to historical abuses of power, such as the life sentence imposed on Nelson Mandela or the use of *Sicherungsverwahrung* by the Nazis. Ultimately though, his reasoning comes down to a form of limiting retributivism. No one should serve a sentence or measure for longer than they deserve, in order to protect the public, or for any other reason. Because human rights standards forbid a life sentence on purely retributive grounds, it should never be imposed. The only permissible sentence is the minimum number of years necessary to reflect the purposes of punishment. Judge Pinto de Albuquerque argues that individualized sentencing based on the parsimony of state intervention requires no less.[57]

Supporters of limited life imprisonment abolitionism, that is, supporters of the Norwegian model and the German model put forward by Walter, would argue for an exception to this general rule. They would agree that formal life sentences should not be imposed and accept fixed-term sentences set on the lines suggested by Judge Pinto de Albuquerque. They would, however, carve out an exception for further detention on a second track, to be strictly limited to a few individuals who commit very severe offenses and continue to pose a very high risk to society. Safeguards would be built in, to ensure that these individuals have access to the best possible treatment while in prison and for the constant review of their suitability for release into the community. In their view, the incapacitation of the individuals whose conduct would have "harmful consequences of an extraordinary character" for society can be justified if it is restricted accordingly.[58]

Limited abolitionism lays itself open to a claim that a properly constituted LWP sentence could achieve the same limited ends within the framework of a life sentence. If it is accepted that for each life sentence an appropriate minimum period should be set on a parsimonious and individualized basis, and that the life-sentenced prisoners should only be detained beyond the minimum where there is clear evidence that they continue to pose a vivid danger to society, their situation is not substantially different from that of a Norwegian prisoner.

By way of illustration, on July 22, 2011, Anders Behring Breivik massacred 77 people and was sentenced to Norway's maximum sentence: a fixed term of twenty-one years. But his sentence also provided that, after he has served the fixed term, he will be subject to *forvaring,* that is, the Norwegian form of post-sentence preventive detention, which can be repeatedly extended for up to five years, as long as he is still considered a danger to society.[59] If, in another country, he had been given a life sentence with a minimum period of twenty-one years, after which he was to be released when no longer a danger to society, his position would not be significantly different.

Human Rights–Compliant Life Imprisonment?

Assuming that LWOP is prohibited, but some type of life imprisonment remains, how should it be applied to comply with human rights standards? The detailed answer to this question is implicit in the substantive analyses of the different aspects of imposition and implementation of life imprisonment, set out in Chapters 4 to 10. Here we highlight the minimum steps that we believe need to be taken. We do so in the light of the overarching principle of human dignity and its requirement that punishment must not be disproportionate or infringe human rights in any other way.

Rethinking life imprisonment must be undertaken against the background of the worldwide increase in its use. This trend is likely to continue unless there are changes in the penal policies and practices of the countries that use it most frequently or are contemplating using it more often. Such a trend is highly problematic. Life sentences are not necessarily more effective in preventing crime than other alternatives. Moreover, they are costly to implement. On these pragmatic grounds alone, reducing the use of life imprisonment should be a goal of penal reform and of any strategy for combating mass incarceration.[60] Reduction of the use of life sentences may not be the only, or even primary, reason why life imprisonment needs to be rethought fundamentally, but it remains a worthy goal in its own right.

For the reasons explained in Chapter 5, the imposition of life imprisonment should always be governed by the principles of parsimony and offense proportionality. The parsimonious imposition of life imprisonment is the most important way of ensuring a long-term reduction in the number of life prisoners. The recognition of the proportionality principle will ensure that life imprisonment is only imposed for the most serious offenses, an approach also adopted in international death penalty jurisprudence. In the words of Judge Ackermann of the South African Constitutional Court:

> The concept of proportionality goes to the heart of the inquiry as to whether punishment is cruel, inhuman or degrading, particularly where [it is] the

length of time for which an offender is sentenced that is in issue. . . . To attempt to justify any period of penal incarceration, let alone imprisonment for
life . . . without inquiring into the proportionality between the offense and
the period of imprisonment, is to ignore, if not to deny, that which lies at the
very heart of human dignity.[61]

More difficult is the question, also raised in Chapter 5, of life sentences
for the serial commission of offenses that are serious but do not necessarily
meet the most serious criterion, and where, in addition, the offender is de-
monstrably dangerous. In such cases, life imprisonment should only be
considered where the danger is a vivid threat of severe physical harm to
others, and the offenses committed are of a high level of seriousness. Such
life imprisonment need not necessarily take the form of a life sentence; instead, it could be post-conviction indefinite detention following a fixed-term
sentence.

For the imposition of life imprisonment to meet human rights standards,
as noted in Chapter 6, it has to fulfill the basic requirements of due process
to which every person facing a long period of incarceration is entitled. Most
important, the procedure must enable the sentencing authority to decide
whether the specific offense or offenses committed are serious enough to
justify its imposition. Mandatory life sentences of any kind are unacceptable for the simple reason that they make it impossible for the court to determine whether the sentence is proportionate to the specific offense for
which it is being imposed. It is desirable, however, that discretion concerning
whether to impose life sentences be guided by further rules that will assist
the sentencing authority in determining the appropriateness of a life sentence in a particular case.

Life imprisonment should always be imposed on the basis that persons sentenced to life may be required to spend the rest of their lives in
prison. If that outcome would be disproportionate to the crime, a life
sentence should never be imposed. Moreover, given how daunting the
prospect of lifelong loss of liberty is, there is no justification for adding
to the penal bite of life sentences, for example, by making them subject
to hard labor.

Courts can, however, often influence the length of time for which these
sentences are likely to be implemented. They do so by giving an indication
of the minimum period an individual should serve for purposes of punish-

ment alone. Where the courts have the flexibility to set a specific mandatory period before release is considered, the principles of parsimony and
proportionality should be applied to make the punishment fit the crime
more closely, although that cannot fully remove the danger that the life
sentence may be still be inappropriately severe.

Where courts do not have this power because the minimum period is
prescribed by law, they can still give an indication of the seriousness of the
offense to the body that will eventually consider release. What the sentencing courts should not seek to do is to bind the releasing body with regard to assessments of dangerousness or risk to society, as these decisions
are better made at a later stage.

As we saw in Chapter 7, life imprisonment is a particularly harsh punishment with a potentially deleterious and destructive impact on the individuals who serve it. The principles of human rights require that these
negative effects be combated as far as possible. They also require, as was
highlighted in Chapter 8, that the state has a duty to offer prisoners opportunities for rehabilitation and preparation for release from prison. Failure to
do so may lead to implementation of the sentence in a way that is inhuman
and degrading. Prison authorities should not segregate life-sentenced prisoners from others, nor should they impose additional restrictions on the
basis that life-sentenced prisoners should be treated more harshly. On the
contrary, they should implement individualized sentence planning, normalized prison regimes, and purposeful activities for all life prisoners.

Decisions about release from life imprisonment should meet the highest
procedural standards. This is particularly important as life prisoners do not
have the guarantee, which other sentenced prisoners have, that they will
be released at the end of fixed, court-imposed terms. For life prisoners the
release decision determines for how long they will be deprived of liberty.
In Chapter 9, we analyzed the different release procedures and concluded
that a court is more likely to meet these standards. The release decision requires balancing the minimum time that prisoners should serve to meet the
requirements of punishment with the assessment of the danger that they
may pose to the public. To ensure a proportionate outcome, minimum terms
should be as short as possible. Our research shows that where minimum
terms are fixed in legislation, the most common period is fifteen years and the
average is eighteen years. These are shorter than the twenty-five-year maximum minimum that has been used by international bodies to distinguish

LWOP from LWP. We recommend that minimum periods should be tailored to the specific offense committed, and that where there is a statutory minimum, it should be no longer than fifteen years. Once the requirements of punishment have been met, the focus should be exclusively on future dangerousness. The presumption should be in favor of release unless there is a vivid and continuing danger. If release is not granted, there must be regular reviews thereafter.

An important part of the life sentence is post-release supervision in the community. As explained in Chapter 10, such supervision should be focused on enabling released life-sentenced prisoners to integrate into the community and desist from crime. Supervision may be used to reduce the risk that the released life-sentenced prisoner may pose, but it should not be an additional form of punishment. There is no reason for released life-sentenced prisoners to remain subject to release conditions and the possibility of recall until death. In many countries, release becomes unconditional after a fixed period. Where this is not the case, we recommend a procedure for formally removing the conditions. Released life-sentenced prisoners who are subject to recall should only be returned to prison if they pose a danger to society. The procedure for doing so should recognize that these former prisoners are already at liberty. Accordingly, recall should only be ordered or reviewed by a court. Such recall should be for the minimum period necessary to deal with any renewed danger that the life-sentenced prisoner may pose, and be subject to regular review.

Propagating Ultimate Penalties That Are Human Rights Compliant

Our worldwide overview shows that reform of life imprisonment inevitably proceeds from different starting points, depending on what other ultimate penalties are contemplated. We have not approached life imprisonment primarily as an alternative to the death penalty, but it must be recognized that in a number of countries capital punishment still looms large, if not in practice, then as a policy option. In this regard, it is worth emphasizing that sophisticated opponents of capital punishment have engaged simultaneously with the shortcomings of different forms of life imprisonment. They range from scholars who supported the abolition of capital punishment, such as

Hugo Adam Bedau, who explained why LWOP too had to be opposed, albeit on different grounds than for the death penalty, to international non-governmental organizations, such as Penal Reform International, which have critiqued many aspects of life imprisonment while consistently opposing all capital punishment.[62]

In thinking about reform, one must accept that for many people, life imprisonment has an important symbolic value as a way to formally recognize the severity of the crime and prove the determination of the state to protect the public from serious harm. Furthermore, it may ensure that for crimes that are not subject to life imprisonment, the punishment will be less severe. For example, in Germany, as a person convicted of armed robbery cannot be sentenced to life imprisonment, the maximum sentence for armed robbery is fifteen years, thus ensuring a clear, proportionality-based distinction from a life sentence for murder, which is the most serious crime.

The desire to preserve life imprisonment can be harnessed to justify compliance with human rights. Proponents of life imprisonment may be open to accepting that its use should be limited to the most heinous crimes and that it should be implemented humanely. A country that is asked to extradite criminal suspects to be tried on serious criminal charges and possibly sentenced to life imprisonment can make extradition contingent on the receiving country satisfying conditions as to when it imposes and how it implements life imprisonment.

At the international level the growing importance of mutual assistance in criminal matters provides an opportunity for pushing for the reform or even the abolition of life imprisonment, as well as the abolition of the death penalty worldwide. The current position in international law is that most extradition agreements allow a country to refuse to extradite someone to stand trial in another country on the grounds that he or she would face the death penalty, and in Europe, human rights law requires that countries do so. What this means in practice is that where a retentionist state, such as the United States, wishes to try someone who faces the death penalty if extradited, it must give an undertaking that it will not impose a sentence of death on the person.

Less well known is the fact that extradition agreements may also provide that countries can refuse to extradite someone who may face life imprisonment, or life imprisonment of a kind that does not meet fundamental human rights standards. The possibility of not allowing extradition at all of someone facing life imprisonment is raised in the UN Model Treaty on Extradition.[63]

Life imprisonment is dealt with more directly in the Americas, where the majority of countries do not have provision for life sentences in their national laws: Thus, the Inter-American Convention on Extradition provides:

> The States Parties shall not grant extradition when the offense in question is punishable in the requesting State by the death penalty, *by life imprisonment,* or by degrading punishment, unless the requested State has previously obtained from the requesting State, through the diplomatic channel, sufficient assurances that none of the above-mentioned penalties will be imposed on the person sought or that, if such penalties are imposed, they will not be enforced.[64]

The 1998 Extradition Agreement of Rio de Janeiro goes further, prohibiting, without qualification the requesting member state from imposing a sentence of death or life imprisonment and limiting it to imposing the maximum sentence that could be imposed in the requested state.[65] In the case of *Alejandro Saúl Schayman Klein,* Chile sought the extradition of Schayman from Bolivia. Bolivia does not have life imprisonment; Chile does. A Chilean court had convicted Schayman of parricide and sentenced him to "qualified life imprisonment," but he had fled to Bolivia before the sentence could be implemented. In Chile, he would have become eligible for release only after forty years, which would not be acceptable in Bolivia. Under the Agreement of Rio de Janeiro, extradition was authorized but conditional on the LWP sentence being commuted to a sentence of fixed-term imprisonment with a maximum of thirty years.[66] In this way, the extradition could go ahead without the agreement being violated.

Other treaties enable countries that do not allow life imprisonment to be imposed to influence how suspects that they extradite will be treated in countries that do have life imprisonment. For example, when Portugal, a country that prohibits all life imprisonment, acceded to the 1996 European Convention on Extradition, it declared that it would grant extradition

> for an offence punishable by a life sentence or detention order only if it regards as sufficient the assurances given by the requesting Member State that it will encourage, in accordance with its law and practice regarding the carrying out of sentences, the application of any measures of clemency to which the person whose extradition is requested might be entitled.[67]

On this basis, Portugal can refuse to extradite someone if, in terms of its own understanding of what human rights standards require, it finds the release procedures in the requesting state to be unacceptable.[68]

Similar influence can be exercised where any European Union member state is asked to execute a European Arrest Warrant (EAW). Although the EAW is a form of mandatory extradition, the framework decision that created the EAW makes a partial exception for persons who may face life imprisonment. The requested state can refuse to execute a warrant if the person who is to be transferred in terms of it would face a life sentence without a prospect of release for longer than twenty years, thus indirectly asserting pressure on the requesting state to reform a specific aspect of its life imprisonment regime.[69]

The decisions of the ECtHR have placed European states under a human rights duty to ensure a realistic prospect of release for persons sentenced to life imprisonment. Moreover, since its decision in the 2014 case of *Trabelsi v. Belgium*, the ECtHR expects all European states to ensure that such prospects exist in all states to which they extradite persons who may end up facing life sentences.[70] This means that, whenever someone objects to being extradited on these grounds, the courts of the requested state (or other human rights tribunal with jurisdiction) will have to consider whether the requesting state is implementing its life sentences in a way that offers all potential life prisoners sufficient opportunities for rehabilitation and realistic prospects of release.

This will have the effect of exposing the implementation of life imprisonment to close judicial scrutiny. In January 2017, one had the spectacle of the United Kingdom defending the way life imprisonment is implemented in Florida, including a commitment to rehabilitation, before a skeptical Grand Chamber of the ECtHR, in order to justify extraditing a prisoner to face trial in the United States. Although this case was eventually dismissed on a technicality, it raises the possibility that the implementation of life imprisonment will be analyzed closely in international fora for many years to come.[71]

The developments should not be limited to courts. Other recent European initiatives are promising too. In 2016, the European Committee for the Prevention of Torture, which has a treaty-based duty to prevent all forms of inhuman or degrading treatment and punishment in all European countries, not only condemned LWOP outright but provided detailed guidance on how life imprisonment should be implemented.[72] It can be expected that this guidance will find its way into European human rights law and eventually shape mutual cooperation with countries worldwide.

At the international level, more work is urgently required. The key United Nations document on life imprisonment was published in 1994 and has not been updated.[73] Its conclusions, while still valid, are phrased very tentatively. The recent revival of interest in international prison standards, as embodied in the 2015 Nelson Mandela Rules, that is, the revised Standard Minimum Rules on the Treatment of Prisoners, may provide a basis for pressing for a stronger statement from the United Nations on what needs to be done to make life imprisonment human rights complaint.[74]

Many specific aspects of life imprisonment that we have covered in this book should also be studied further to provide further emphasis for reform. These include the experience of women, children, and older people serving life sentences. More work is needed on the problem of institutionalization and other potentially deleterious effects of life imprisonment, as well as the impact of life sentences on prisoners' families and wider communities.[75] Some issues, such as the treatment of terrorist prisoners subject to life sentences and the use of de facto life sentences, are likely to be more salient in the future. Above all, as pointed out in Chapter 3, we need better statistics to demonstrate the extent to which life imprisonment, both formal and informal, is a global problem.

Other areas that require further investigation are not necessarily unique to life imprisonment, but arguably are more controversial when they arise in the context of life sentences. These include the role of victims in sentencing and release decisions, public opinion, predicting dangerousness and recidivism, racial bias, economic costs, and recall procedures, as well as the deterrent effects of life imprisonment when compared to other forms of punishment.

At both the international and national levels, reformers should continue to press for reduction in the use of life imprisonment and improvements in the way in which it is implemented. At the same time, they should bear in mind the more radical alternative of abolition, be it of all types of life imprisonment or only of formal life imprisonment, while leaving the possibility of post-conviction indefinite detention to deal with cases of vivid danger. As overall knowledge about the practice of life imprisonment increases, we predict that there will be more human rights–based challenges to various aspects of its imposition and implementation in fora around the world. These may proceed much like challenges to the death penalty in the United States, which have reduced its scope without being able to have it outlawed completely, or they may lead to the eventual abolition of life imprisonment too.

In this book we have sought to clarify, on the basis of existing knowledge, what life imprisonment entails worldwide, and we have demonstrated its many shortcomings. What life imprisonment means is confusing and often misunderstood. Life sentences are too easily and too often imposed, including on children and for crimes that are not the most serious. They result in excessive detention, and they often encompass appalling treatment, unjust release procedures and inadequate support in the community. If our work assists others in challenging life imprisonment on human rights grounds, we will have achieved what we set out do.

Appendix A

Formal Sentences of Life Imprisonment

TABLE A.1. Formal Sentences of Life Imprisonment

Country by region	Life sentences	Irreducible LWOP	LWOP	LWP	Symbolic LWP	No life	Life as ultimate penalty*
Africa							
Algeria	•			•			•*
Angola						•	•
Benin	•			•			
Botswana	•			•			•
Burkina Faso	•			•			•*
Burundi	•			•			•
Cameroon	•		•	•			•*
Cape Verde						•	
Central African Republic	•			•			•*
Chad	•			•			•*
Comoros	•			•			•*
Congo	•		•	•			•*
Côte d'Ivoire	•			•			•*
Democratic Republic of Congo	•			•			•*
Djibouti	•			•			•
Egypt	•			•			
Equatorial Guinea	•		•	•			
Eritrea	•			•			•*
Ethiopia	•			•			
Gabon	•		•	•			•
Gambia	•			•			
Ghana	•						•*
Guinea (Republic of)	•			•			•*

328

Country						
Guinea Bissau	•			•		•
Kenya	*				•	•
Lesotho	*			•		•
Liberia	*			•	•	•
Libya				•	•	•
Madagascar	*			•		•
Malawi	*			•	•	•
Mali	*			•		•
Mauritania	*					•
Mauritius	*			•	•	•
Morocco	•					•
Mozambique	•	•				
Namibia	•			•		•
Niger	*			•		•
Nigeria				•		•
Rwanda						•
Sao Tome e Principe	•	•		•		
Senegal					•	•
Seychelles	•			•	•	•
Sierra Leone				•		•
Somalia	•					•
South Africa	•			•		•
South Sudan	•		•			•
Sudan			•	•	•	•
Swaziland	*				•	•
Tanzania	*					•
Togo	•					•

(continued)

329

TABLE A.1. Continued

Country by region	Life sentences	Irreducible LWOP	LWOP	LWP	Symbolic LWP	No life	Life as ultimate penalty*
Africa Continued							
Tunisia	●						●*
Uganda	●			●			
Western Sahara	●		●		●		●
Zambia	●		●				●*
Zimbabwe	●			●			
Total: 55	**51**	**0**	**18 (17)**	**34**	**3**	**4**	**40 (25*)**
Asia							
Afghanistan	●		●			●	
Bangladesh	●			●	●		
Bhutan	●						●*
Brunei Darussalam	●		●	●			●
Cambodia	●			●			
China	●		●	●			
DPR Korea	●			●			
Hong Kong (China)	●		●	●			
India	●		●	●			
Indonesia	●			●			
Iran	●		●	●			●
Japan	●			●			
Kazakhstan	●		●				
Kyrgyzstan	●		●	●			●*
Laos	●						
Macao (China)						●	

	(29)	(0)	(14)	(17)	(6)	(3)	(17, 7*)
Malaysia	•		•		•		*
Maldives	•				•		•
Mongolia	•						*
Myanmar (Burma)	•			•			•
Nepal	•		•				
Pakistan	•			•	•		
Philippines	•			•	•		
Singapore	•			•	•		•
South Korea (Republic of Korea)	•			•			* •
Sri Lanka	•		•				*
Taiwan	•			•			
Tajikistan	•		•				*
Thailand	•		• •				
Turkmenistan				•		•	*
Uzbekistan	•						• •
Vietnam	•		•	•			
Total: 32	**29**	**0**	**14**	**17**	**6**	**3**	**17(7*)**

Caribbean

Anguilla (UK)	•			•			*
Antigua and Barbuda	•			•			•
Aruba (Neth.)	•			•			
Bahamas	•		•				*
Barbados	•		•				*
Cayman Islands (UK)	•			•			•
Cuba	•			•			*
Curaçao (Neth.)	•			•			•

(continued)

TABLE A.1. Continued

Country by region	Life sentences	Irreducible LWOP	LWOP	LWP	Symbolic LWP	No life	Life as ultimate penalty*
Caribbean Continued							
Dominica	•		•				•*
Dominican Republic						•	
Grenada	•			•			•*
Haiti	•	•	•				•*
Jamaica	•			•			•
Montserrat	•			•			•*
Puerto Rico						•	
Sint Maarten (Neth.)	•			•			•
St. Christopher and Nevis	•			•			
St. Lucia	•		•				•*
St. Vincent and the Grenadines	•			•			•*
Trinidad and Tobago	•			•			•*
Virgin Islands (UK)	•			•			•
Virgin Islands (US)	•		•	•			•
Total: 22	20	1	6	15	0	2	19(10*)
Central America							
Belize	•		•	•			•*
Costa Rica						•	
El Salvador						•	
Guatemala		•	•			•	
Honduras	•	•				•	•
Mexico†	•	•	•			•	•
Nicaragua						•	
Panama						•	
Total: 8	3	2	3	1	0	6	3(1*)

Albania	•		•	•
Andorra	•	•	•	•
Armenia	•		•	•
Austria	•		•	•
Azerbaijan			•	•
Belarus	•		•	•
Belgium	•		•	•
Bosnia and Herzegovina	•	•	•	•
Bulgaria			•	•
Croatia	•		•	•
Cyprus	•	•	•	•
Czech Republic	•		•	•
Denmark	•		•	•
Estonia	•		•	•
Faroe Islands		•		•
Finland	•		•	•
France	•		•	•
Georgia (Europe)	•		•	•
Germany	•		•	•
Greece	•		•	•
Hungary	•		•	•
Iceland	•		•	•
Ireland	•		•	•
Italy	•		•	•
Kosovo	•		•	•
Latvia	•		•	•
Liechtenstein	•		•	•

(continued)

TABLE A.1. *Continued*

Country by region	Life sentences	Irreducible LWOP	LWOP	LWP	Symbolic LWP	No life	Life as ultimate penalty*
Europe Continued							
Lithuania	•		•				•
Luxemburg	•			•			•
Macedonia (Former Yugoslav Republic of)	•			•			•
Malta	•		•				•
Moldova	•			•			•
Monaco	•			•			•
Montenegro						•	
Netherlands	•		•				•
Norway						•	
Poland	•			•			•
Portugal						•	
Romania	•			•			•
Russia	•			•			•*
San Marino						•	
Serbia						•	
Slovakia	•		•	•			•
Slovenia	•			•			•
Spain	•			•			•
Sweden	•			•			•
Switzerland	•			•			•
Turkey	•	•		•			•
UK†	•	•		•			•
Ukraine	•		•				•
Vatican City						•	
Total: 51	41	2	7	37	0	10	40(1*)

Middle East

Bahrain	•						
Iraq	•						•
Israel	•			•	•		
Jordan	•						
Kuwait	•			•			•*
Lebanon	•		•	•			
Oman	•		•	•			
Palestine	•						
Qatar	•		•	•			•*
Saudi Arabia	•		•	•			
Syria	•		•	•			
United Arab Emirates	•	•	•				
Yemen	•		•				
Total: 13	13	1	7	7	1	0	3(2*)

North America

Bermuda	•		•	•			•
Canada	•		•	•			•
Greenland						•	
United States†	•	•	•	•		•	•
Total: 4	3	1	3	3	0	2	3

Oceania

American Samoa (US)	•		•	•			•
Australia†	•			•			•
Cook Islands (New Zealand)	•						

(continued)

TABLE A.1. Continued

Country by region	Life sentences	Irreducible LWOP	LWOP	LWP	Symbolic LWP	No life	Life as ultimate penalty*
Oceania Continued							
Fiji	•		•	•			•
Guam	•			•			•
Kiribati	•			•			•
Marshall Islands	•			•			•
Micronesia	•			•			•
Nauru	•		•	•			•*
New Zealand	•			•			•
Northern Mariana (USA)	•			•			•
Palau	•						•
Papua New Guinea	•						•*
Samoa/Western Samoa	•			•			•
Solomon Islands	•		•	•			•
Timor-Leste						•	•
Tonga	•			•			•*
Tuvalu	•		•				•
Vanuatu	•		•	•			•
Total: 19	18	0	5	16	0	1	19(3*)
South America							
Argentina	•		•	•			•
Bolivia						•	
Brazil						•	
Chile	•			•			•
Colombia						•	
Ecuador						•	

336

Country							
Guyana	•						•*
Paraguay	•					•	
Peru			•			•	
Suriname	•					•	
Uruguay	•					•	•*
Venezuela	•					•	
Total: 12	5	0	2	5	0	7	5(2*)
Overall totals: 216	183	7	63	135	10	35	149(51*)

International Tribunals

ECCC—Extraordinary Chambers in the Courts of Cambodia	•						
ICC—International Criminal Court	•						
ICTR—International Criminal Tribunal for Rwanda	•						
ICTY—International Criminal Tribunal for the Former Yugoslavia	•						
Special Court for Sierra Leone						•	

Source: Data collected by authors.

*The "life as ultimate penalty" column lists those countries and territories that, on April 30, 2014, had provision for life imprisonment but were not using the death penalty, as identifed in Roger Hood and Carolyn Hoyle, *The Death Penalty: A Worldwide Perspective,* 5th ed. (Oxford, UK: Oxford University Press, 2016), Appendix 1. Following Hood and Hoyle, we have included all countries and territories that completely abolished the death penalty as well as those that had abolished it for all ordinary crimes. We have also included countries that, on April 30, 2014, were de facto abolitionist on the grounds that no executions had been carried out for at least ten years before that date or an official moratorium was in place. Countries and territories that were de facto abolitionist are marked with an *. In the few territories that were on our list but not included in the book by Hood and Hoyle, we have relied on our own research.

†These countries have federal systems in which there are different criminal jurisdictions with different provisions for life imprisonment.

Appendix B

Numbers of Life-Sentenced Prisoners

TABLE B.1. Numbers of Life-Sentenced Prisoners

Africa

Country	Life-sentenced prisoners total	Irreducible LWOP	LWOP	LWP	Symbolic LWP	No life	Life-sentenced prisoners per 100,000 of country population	Life-sentenced prisoners as a percentage of total prison population	Life-sentenced prisoners as a percentage of sentenced prison population
Angola	0					•	0.00	0.00	0.00
Burundi	733			733			6.78	8.48	17.59
Egypt	277			277			0.31	0.45	0.50
Ghana	131			131			0.49	0.92	1.10
Guinea-Bissau	0					•	0.00	0.00	0.00
Kenya	3,676		3,676				8.19	6.79	11.39
Liberia	156		0	156			3.55	9.08	53.42
Malawi	136		136				0.81	1.12	1.33
Morocco	751		751				2.21	1.03	1.92
Mozambique	0					•	0.00	0.00	0.00
Nigeria	545				545		0.31	0.86	1.20
Sao Tome e Principe	0					•	0.00	0.00	0.00
Sierra Leone	14		14				0.22	0.37	0.90
South Africa	13,190			,			22.67	7.68	10.51
South Sudan	30				30		0.25	0.40	0.73
Swaziland	4			4			0.32	0.11	0.14
Uganda	209		92		117		0.55	0.50	1.11
Total: 17	**19,852**	**0**	**4,669**	**14,491**	**692**				

Asia

	Total							
Afghanistan	0	0			•	0.00	0.00	0.00
Bangladesh	~5,000	0		~5,000		3.14	6.98	26.65
India	7,1632		71,632	•		5.53	17.39	53.66
Indonesia	423		423			0.17	0.26	0.38
Japan	1,842		1,842			1.44	2.95	3.33
Kazakhstan	122	26	96			0.70	0.25	0.29
Kyrgyzstan	286	286				4.89	2.84	3.59
Macao (China)	0				•	0.00	0.00	0.00
Nepal	2,283			2,283		8.10	13.58	33.04
South Korea (Republic of Korea)	1,288		1,288			2.57	2.38	3.91
Sri Lanka	341	341				1.65	1.72	3.16
Tajikistan	82	0	82			0.99	0.88	1.04
Thailand	3,176	3,176				4.69	1.03	1.31
Turkmenistan	0				•	0.00	0.00	0.00
Total: 14	**~86,475**	**3,829**	**75,363**	**~7,283**				

Caribbean

Antigua and Barbuda	8	8				8.79	2.42	4.49
Aruba (Neth.)	1	1				0.97	0.59	0.70
Cayman Islands (UK)	18	18				30.51	9.47	11.76
Curaçao (Neth.)	3	3				1.92	0.86	1.46

(continued)

TABLE B.1. Continued

Country	Life-sentenced prisoners total	Irreducible LWOP	LWOP	LWP	Symbolic LWOP	No life	Total life-sentenced prisoners per 100,000 country population	Life-sentenced prisoners as a percentage of total prison population	Life-sentenced prisoners as a percentage of sentenced prison population
Dominican Republic	0					•	0.00	0.00	0.00
Puerto Rico	0					•	0.00	0.00	0.00
St. Christopher and Nevis	23	0		23			41.86	6.88	9.79
Total: 7	53		18	35					
Central America									
Belize	33		33	•			9.38	2.14	3.30
Costa Rica	0					•	0.00	0.00	0.00
El Salvador	0					•	0.00	0.00	0.00
Guatemala	0					•	0.00	0.00	0.00
Nicaragua	0					•	0.00	0.00	0.00
Panama	0					•	0.00	0.00	0.00
Total: 6	33		33						
Europe									
Albania	155			155			5.36	2.85	5.92
Andorra	0					•	0.00	0.00	0.00
Armenia	102			102			3.39	2.56	3.55
Austria	114			114			1.34	1.29	1.89
Azerbaijan	266			266			2.76	1.18	1.42

Belarus	145		145		1.53	0.46	0.56
Belgium	211		211		1.88	1.60	2.44
Bosnia and Herzegovina	0			•	0.00	0.00	0.00
Bulgaria	173	>24	>46	•	2.40	2.20	2.40
Croatia	0				0.00	0.00	0.00
Cyprus	24		24		2.08	3.52	5.48
Czech Republic	48		48		0.46	0.26	0.29
Denmark	21		21		0.37	0.59	0.97
Estonia	40		40		3.04	1.35	1.70
Faroe Islands	0			•	0.00	0.00	0.00
Finland	209		209		3.81	6.75	8.51
France	466		466		0.73	0.60	0.77
Georgia (Europe)	81		81		2.01	0.79	0.91
Germany	1,953		1,953		2.42	2.97	3.58
Greece	1,017		1,017		9.24	8.47	11.45
Hungary	297	41	256		3.00	1.63	2.22
Iceland	0		0		0.00	0.00	0.00
Ireland	342		342		7.32	8.93	10.54
Italy	1,599		1,599		2.67	2.95	4.31
Kosovo	0		0		0.00	0.00	0.00
Latvia	54		54		2.71	1.12	1.57
Liechtenstein	0		0		0.00	0.00	0.00
Lithuania	118	118			4.05	1.31	1.47
Luxemburg	12		12		2.16	1.83	3.27
Macedonia	34		34		1.64	1.18	1.27

(continued)

TABLE B.1. *Continued*

Country	Life-sentenced prisoners total	Irreducible LWOP	LWOP	LWP	Symbolic LWOP	No life	Total life-sentenced prisoners per 100,000 country population	Life-sentenced prisoners as a percentage of total prison population	Life-sentenced prisoners as a percentage of sentenced prison population
Malta	12		12				2.87	2.10	2.84
Moldova	104			104			2.55	1.45	1.82
Monaco	0			0			0.00	0.00	0.00
Montenegro	0					•	0.00	0.00	0.00
Netherlands	32		32				0.19	0.32	0.59
Norway	0					•	0.00	0.00	0.00
Poland	342			342			0.89	0.44	0.51
Portugal	0					•	0.00	0.00	0.00
Romania	158			158			0.80	0.50	0.54
Russia	1,760			1,760			1.23	0.26	0.35
San Marino	0					•	0.00	0.00	0.00
Serbia	0					•	0.00	0.00	0.00
Slovakia	41		0	41			0.76	0.40	0.47
Slovenia	0			0			0.00	0.00	0.00
Spain	0			0			0.00	0.00	0.00
Sweden	144			144			1.48	2.46	3.33
Switzerland	38			38			0.46	0.55	1.01
Turkey	6,687	126		6,561			8.63	7.02	5.62
United Kingdom	8,661	50		8,611			13.41	9.09	10.96
Ukraine	1,753		1,753				3.90	1.90	2.37
Total: 50	**27,213**	**176**	**>1,980**	**>24,954**	**0**				

Middle East								
Iraq	84		84			0.24	0.18	0.31
Israel	1,214	1		1,213		15.29	6.51	10.14
Lebanon	114			114		2.03	1.90	5.61
Total: 3	1,412	1	84	1,327	0			
North America								
Bermuda	25			25		40.32	10.87	12.02
Canada	3,024			3,024		9.94	9.34	14.41
Greenland	0	•				0.00	0.00	0.00
United States	161,957	•	53,290	108,667		50.33	7.20	9.47
Total: 4	165,006	0	53,290	111,716	0			
Oceania								
Australia	1,016		>55	>495		4.30	2.84	3.75
New Zealand	526		0	526		11.28	5.87	7.48
Timor-Leste	0	•				0.00	0.00	0.00
Total: 3	1,542	0	>55	>1,021	0			
South America								
Argentina	2,453	171		2,282		5.71	3.82	7.57
Bolivia	0	•				0.00	0.00	0.00
Brazil	0	•				0.00	0.00	0.00
Chile	424			424		2.39	0.99	1.38

(*continued*)

TABLE B.1. Continued

South America

Country	Life-sentenced prisoners total	Irreducible LWOP	LWOP	LWP	Symbolic LWOP	No life	Total life-sentenced prisoners per 100,000 country population	Life-sentenced prisoners as a percentage of total prison population	Life-sentenced prisoners as a percentage of sentenced prison population
Colombia	0					•	0.00	0.00	0.00
Ecuador	0					•	0.00	0.00	0.00
Paraguay	0					•	0.00	0.00	0.00
Peru	351		•	•			1.13	0.48	0.96
Uruguay	0					•	0.00	0.00	0.00
Venezuela	0					•	0.00	0.00	0.00
Total: 10	3,228	0	171	2,706	0				
Grand total: 114	304,814	177	64,129	231,613	7,975				
Merged totals	All LWOP: 64,306	All LWP: 239,588							

International Tribunals

ECCC— Extraordinary Chambers in the Courts of Cambodia	1			1					
ICC— International Criminal Court				•					

346

ICTR—International Criminal Tribunal for Rwanda	16	16
ICTY—International Criminal Tribunal for the Former Yugoslavia	5	5
Special Court for Sierra Leone	0	•

Source: Data collected by authors; Marcelo Aebi, Mélanie Tiago, and Christine Burkhardt, *SPACE I—Council of Europe Annual Penal Statistics: Prison Populations, Survey 2014* (Strasbourg, France: Council of Europe, 2016); United Nations, Department of Economic and Social Affairs, Population Division, *World Population Prospects: The 2015 Revision, DVD Edition* (New York: United Nations, Department of Economic and Social Affairs, Population Division, 2015); World Prison Brief, http://www.prisonstudies.org/world-prison-brief-data.

Dates of recording varied slightly. We requested figures for September 1, 2014, or the nearest possible date to that. All figures are within twelve months of that date. For the United States, however, we used life-sentenced data collated in 2016 (Ashley Nellis, *Still Life: America's Increasing Use of Life and Long-Term Sentences* [Washington, D.C.: The Sentencing Project 2017], 7–9), together with national population and prison population data from 2015.

Appendix C

Persons Serving Formal Life Sentences by Offense

TABLE C.1. Persons Serving Formal Life Sentences by Offense

Country	Total	Homicide		Sex offenses		Other crimes against the person		Drugs		Crimes against property		Other*	
		Life	%	Life	%	Life	%	Life	%	Life	%	Life	%
Antigua and Barbuda	8	8	100.0		0.0		0.0		0.0		0.0		0.0
Armenia	104	104	100.0		0.0		0.0		0.0		0.0		0.0
Aruba	2	2	100.0		0.0		0.0		0.0		0		0.0
Australia†	226	198	87.6	2	0.9	4	1.8	18	8.0		0.0	4	1.8
Austria	143	141	98.6	2	1.4		0.0		0.0		0.0		0.0
Belize	33	33	100.0		0.0		0.0		0.0		0.0		0.0
Bermuda	25	25	100.0		0.0		0.0		0.0		0.0		0.0
Cayman Islands	18	17	94.4	1	5.6		0.0		0.0		0		0.0
Chile	424	84	19.8	82	19.3	241	56.8		0.0	4	0.9	13 (8)	3.1
Curaçao	3	2	66.7		0.0		0.0		0.0		0.0	1 (1)	33.3
Czech Republic	48	48	100.0		0.0		0.0		0.0		0.0		0.0
Denmark	21	21	100.0		0.0		0.0		0.0		0.0		0.0
Estonia	39	39	100.0		0.0		0.0		0.0		0.0		0.0
Finland	206	205	99.5		0.0		0.0		0.0		0.0	1	0.5
France	478	363	75.9	32	6.7	59	12.3		0.0	6	1.3	18 (18)	3.8
Georgia (Europe)	77	66	85.7		0.0		0.0	9	11.7		0.0	2	2.6
Germany‡	1,900	1,889	99.4	2	0.1	3	0.2		0.0	1	0.1	5 (4)	0.3
Ghana	131	113	86.3		0.0	18	13.7		0.0		0.0		0.0
Indonesia	422	218	51.7		0.0	2	0.5	139	32.9	6	1.4	57 (41)	13.5
Ireland	315	297	94.3		0.0		0.0		0.0		0.0	18 (18)	5.7
Israel	1,214	1,214	100.0		0.0		0.0		0.0		0.0		0.0
Kyrgyzstan	286	243	85.0	29	10.1		0.0		0.0		0.0	14	4.9

Latvia	53	53	100.0		0.0		0.0		0.0		0.0	0.0
Lebanon	138	90	65.2		0.0		0.0	14	10.1		0.0	34	24.6
Liberia	90	36	40.0	32	35.6	8	8.9	1	1.1		0.0	13	14.4
Lithuania	114	114	100.0		0.0		0.0		0.0		0.0		0.0
Luxemburg	12	12	100.0		0.0		0.0		0.0		0.0		0.0
Malta	14	14	100.0		0.0		0.0		0.0		0.0		0.0
Morocco	746	720	96.5		0.0		0.0		0.0		0.0	26 (5)	3.5
Netherlands	32	31	97.5		0.0		0.0		0.0		0.0	1	2.5
New Zealand	526	523	99.4		0.0		0.0	3	0.6		0.0		0.0
Poland	352	352	100.0		0.0		0.0		0.0		0.0		0.0
Romania	158	158	100.0		0.0		0.0		0.0		0.0		0.0
Sierra Leone	14	13	92.9		0.0		0.0		0.0		0.0	1 (1)	7.1
Sri Lanka	347	347	100.0		0.0		0.0		0.0		0.0		0.0
St. Christopher and Nevis	25	25	100.0		0.0		0.0		0.0		0.0		0.0
Swaziland	4	4	100.0		0.0		0.0		0.0		0.0		0.0
Sweden	147	147	100.0		0.0		0.0		0.0		0.0		0.0
Uganda	208	148	71.2	41	19.7	19	9.1		0.0		0.0		0.0
United Kingdom	8,567	6,511	76.0	908	10.6	855	10.0	9	0.1	141	1.6	143 (13)	1.7
Ukraine	1,753	1,753	100.0										
United States	16,1957	10,0746	63.8	23,871	15.2	22,732	14.4	3,779	2.4	3,409	2.2	3,443 (3,977)	2.2

Source: Data collected by authors. The offense categories in this appendix follow those used for the United States by Nellis, *Still Life* (Washington, D.C.: The Sentencing Project, 2017). For all other countries we have adjusted the data we collected to those used by Nellis. Several numbers vary slightly from those in Appendix B. The numbers here reflect the latest date on which a breakdown by offense was available. These dates may not be the same as those in Appendix B, which records types of life sentence.

*Information in parentheses refers to instances where no information was recorded about these offenses. The remaining offenses were specified, but do not fit in any of the previous categories.

† These data are based only on information for New South Wales, Northern Territory, Tasmania, and Victoria.

‡ This information is an approximation. Prison statistics on offenses do not distinguish between sentence lengths.

Notes

1. Debating Life

1. Michael Ignatieff, *A Just Measure of Pain: The Penitentiary in the Industrial Revolution 1750–1850* (London: Macmillan, 1978).

2. Cesare Beccaria, *On Crimes and Punishments and Other Writings*, ed. Aaron Thomas, trans. Aaron Thomas and Jeremy Parzen (Toronto: University of Toronto Press, 2008).

3. John Howard, *The State of the Prisons in England and Wales, with Preliminary Observations, and an Account of some Foreign Prisons and Hospitals* (London: Johnson, Dilly and Cadell, 1792).

4. Beccaria, *On Crimes and Punishments*, 53–54.

5. Jacques Derrida, *The Death Penalty* (Chicago, IL: University of Chicago Press, 2013), 93–94.

6. Michel Foucault, *Discipline and Punish: The Birth of the Prison* (Harmondsworth, UK: Penguin, 1977), 95.

7. John Bowring, *The Works of Jeremy Bentham*, vol. 1 (Edinburgh: William Tait, 1838–1843), 450.

8. Thorsten Sellin, "Beccaria's Substitute for the Death Penalty," in *Criminology in Perspective: Essays in Honor of Israel Drapkin*, ed. Simha Landau and Leslie Sebba (Lexington, MA: Lexington Books, 1977), 3.

9. Catherine the Great of Russia, for example, replaced capital punishment "with 333 lashes of the knout, which in practice virtually amounted to a death sentence." Roger Hood and Carolyn Hoyle, *The Death Penalty: A Worldwide Perspective* (Oxford: Oxford University Press, 2015), 491.

10. Dirk van Zyl Smit, *Taking Life Imprisonment Seriously in National and International Law* (The Hague: Kluwer Law International, 2002), 5.

11. 191 Parl Deb HC (3rd ser.) (1868) col. 1049 (UK). Mill's speech apparently undermined the movement to abolish capital punishment to such an extent that it did not recover for many years. Leon Radzinowicz and Roger Hood, *A History of English Criminal Law and Its Administration from 1750*, vol. 5 (London: Stevens and Sons, 1986), 685.

12. 191 Parl Deb HC (3rd ser.) (1868) col. 1052 (UK).

13. William Tallack, *Penological and Preventive Principles* (London: Wertheimer, Lea and Co., 1888), 15.

14. Ibid., 151–152.

15. Ibid., 160. Tallack's own solution was influenced by the practice in Portugal, where the maximum sentence for any criminal offense was then a twenty-year term of imprisonment (ibid., 162). See also Ines Horta Pinto, "Punishment in Portuguese Criminal Law: A Penal System without Life Imprisonment," in *Life Imprisonment and Human Rights*, ed. Dirk van Zyl Smit and Catherine Appleton (Oxford, UK: Hart/Bloomsbury Publishing, 2016), 289.

16. Marion Vannier, "A Right to Hope? Life Imprisonment in France," in *Life Imprisonment and Human Rights*, 193; Van Zyl Smit, *Taking Life Imprisonment Seriously*, 5.

17. Van Zyl Smit, *Taking Life Imprisonment Seriously*, 31.

18. Art. 7 of the French Penal Code of 1810; Guy Petit, "La justice en France, 1789–1939: Une étatisation modèle?," *Crime, Histoire et Sociétés* 6(1) (2002): 85–103.

19. See David J. Rothman, "Sentencing Reforms in Historical Perspective," *Crime and Delinquency* 29 (1983): 631–647, 633.

20. Van Zyl Smit, *Taking Life Imprisonment Seriously*, 32.

21. Robert Hughes, *The Fatal Shore* (London: Collins Harvill, 1987).

22. Vannier, "A Right to Hope?" 195.

23. India: Code of Criminal Procedure (Amendment) Act, 1955; Pakistan: Law Reforms Ordinance, 1972; Bangladesh: Penal Code (Amendment) Ordinance, 1985.

24. See David J. Rothman, *The Discovery of the Asylum: Social Order and Disorder in the New Republic* (Boston: Little Brown and Co., 1971).

25. Leon Radzinowicz, *History of English Criminal Law*, vol. 4 (London: Stevens and Sons, 1968).

26. See Zebulon Brockway, "The Idea of a True Prison System for a State," in *Transactions of the National Congress on Penitentiary and Reformatory Discipline Held at Cincinnati, Ohio, October 12–18, 1870*, ed. Enoch C. Wines (Albany, NY: Weed, Parsons and Co., 1871), 38; and Enoch C. Wines, "The Present Outlook of Prison Discipline in the United States," in *Transactions*, 19.

27. Wines, "The Present Outlook of Prison Discipline," 19.

28. Michele Pifferi, *Reinventing Punishment: A Comparative History of Criminology and Penology in the Nineteenth and Twentieth Centuries* (Oxford, UK: Oxford University Press, 2016).

29. Ibid.

30. Quoted in Patricia O'Brien, "The Prison on the Continent: Europe, 1865–1965," in *The Oxford History of the Prison: The Practice of Punishment in Western Society*, ed., Norval Morris and David J. Rothman (New York: Oxford University Press, 1995), 189.

31. David J. Rothman, *Conscience and Convenience: The Asylum and Its Alternatives in Progressive America* (Boston: Little, Brown and Co., 1980), 68–70; Dirk van Zyl Smit and Alessandro Corda, "American Exceptionalism in Parole Release and Supervision: A European Perspective" in *American Exceptionalism in*

Crime and Punishment, ed. Kevin R. Reitz (New York: Oxford University Press, 2017).

32. Michele Pifferi, "Individualization of Punishment and the Rule of Law: Reshaping Legality in the United States and Europe between the 19th and the 20th Century," *American Journal of Legal History* 52 (2012): 325–376.

33. Mark Pieth, *Bedingte Freiheit: Disziplinierung zwischen Gnade und Kontrolle,* (Basel, Switzerland: Helbing und Lichtenhahn, 2001).

34. Jörg Kinzig, *Die Sicherungsverwahrung auf dem Prüfstand* (Freiburg: Max-Planck-Institut für ausländisches und internationales Strafrecht, 1996), 16–22.

35. Norval Morris's careful study of Western European habitual criminal legislation in the immediate post–Second World War period revealed that most European countries adopted laws that limited the use of judicially imposed indeterminate preventive detention, to be served after the completion of a determinate sentence, to a relatively small group of dangerous offenders. More-over, they retained judicial control over the enforcement of detention and the processes of release of such offenders for longer periods than their initial determinate sentences allowed. Norval Morris, *The Habitual Criminal* (London: Longmans, 1951).

36. Foucault, *Discipline and Punish,* 74.

37. Art. 6, Déclaration des droits de l'homme et du citoyen de 1789.

38. Whitman has noted that Enlightenment concerns with human dignity had an ameliorating impact on punishment in Europe even before they were enshrined in (human rights) law. James Q. Whitman, *Harsh Justice: Criminal Punishment and the Widening Divide between America and Europe* (New York: Oxford University Press, 2003).

39. Nigel Rodley and Malcolm Pollard, *The Treatment of Prisoners under International Law,* 3rd ed. (Oxford: Oxford University Press, 2009).

40. M. Cherif Bassiouni, "Human Rights in the Context of Criminal Justice: Identifying International Procedural Protections and the Equivalent Protection in National Constitutions," *Duke Journal of Comparative and International Law* 3 (1993): 235–297, 263.

41. See William A. Schabas, *The Death Penalty as Cruel Treatment and Torture* (Boston: Northeastern University, 1996).

42. Franz Streng, *Strafrechtliche Sanktionen,* 2nd ed. (Stuttgart, Germany: Kohlhammer, 2002).

43. The United Nations Convention on the Rights of the Child (November 20, 1989), art. 37.

44. United Nations Office on Drugs and Crime, *Compendium of United Nations Standards and Norms in Crime Prevention and Criminal Justice* (New York: United Nations, 2006); Council of Europe, *Penitentiary Questions Council of Europe: Conventions, Recommendations and Resolutions* (Strasbourg, France: Council of Europe, 2009).

45. Rodley and Pollard, *The Treatment of Prisoners,* 383.

46. *Muršić v. Croatia,* ECtHR (app. 7334/13), October 20, 2016 [GC], partially dissenting opinion of Judge Pinto de Albuquerque, § 2.

47. Hood and Hoyle, *The Death Penalty,* 18.

48. Ibid.

49. Ibid., 22.

50. *Trop v. Dulles* 356 US 86, 101 (1958).

51. *Brown v. Plata,* 563 US 493, 510 (2011); Jonathan Simon, "The Second Coming of Dignity," in *The New Criminal Justice Thinking,* ed. Sharon Dolovich and Alexandra Natapoff (New York: New York University Press, 2017), 275.

52. Leon Shaskolsky Sheleff, *Ultimate Penalties* (Columbus: Ohio State University Press, 1987), ch. 5, "Imprisonment and Human Rights."

53. Address of Pope Francis to the Delegates of the International Association of Penal Law, October 23, 2014, online at w2.vatican.va/content/francesco/en /speeches/2014/october/documents/papa-francesco_20141023_associazione -internazionale-diritto-penale.html.

54. Dirk van Zyl Smit and Andrew Ashworth, "Disproportionate Sentences as Human Rights Violations," *Modern Law Review* 67 (2004): 541–560.

55. *In re Lynch,* 105 Cal. Rptr. 217 (1972).

56. This strand in US penological thought is well summarized in Francis A. Allen, *The Decline of the Rehabilitative Ideal: Penal Policy and Social Purpose* (New Haven, CT: Yale University Press, 1981).

57. For a classic contemporary account of how this challenge was articulated, see Thomas Mathiesen, *The Politics of Abolition* (London: Martin Robertson, 1974).

58. Tapio Lappi-Seppällä, "Life Imprisonment and Related Institutions in the Nordic Countries," in *Life Imprisonment and Human Rights,* 461.

59. See, for example, the decision of the South African Constitutional Court in *S v. Dodo* 2001 (3) SA 382 (CC), 403–404 (S.Afr.).

60. UN General Assembly, *Basic Principles for the Treatment of Prisoners,* A/RES 45/111, December 14, 1990; UN General Assembly, *Body of Principles for the Protection of All Persons under any Form of Detention of Imprisonment,* A/RES/43/173, December 9, 1998.

61. UN General Assembly, *United Nations Standard Minimum Rules for the Treatment of Prisoners* (the Nelson Mandela Rules), A/RES/70/175, December 17, 2015. Recognised in human rights law in *Muršić v. Croatia* October 20, 2016 [GC], § 59.

62. *Obediah Makoni v. Commissioner of Prisons & Anr,* CCZ 8/16, July 13, 2016, 12.

63. *Muršić v. Croatia,* October 20, 2016, partially dissenting opinion of Judge Pinto de Albuquerque, § 2.

64. Dirk van Zyl Smit, "Punishment and Human Rights," in *The SAGE Handbook of Punishment and Society,* ed. Jonathan Simmons and Richard Sparks (London: SAGE, 2013), 395, 406–410.

65. Dirk van Zyl Smit, "Regulation of Prison Conditions," *Crime and Justice* 39 (2010): 503–563.

66. See Chapter 8.

67. See *Khoroshenko v. Russia,* ECtHR (app. 41418/04), June 30, 2015 [GC], discussed more fully in Chapter 8.

68. See Chapter 9.

69. United Nations Office at Vienna, Crime Prevention and Criminal Justice Branch, *Life Imprisonment* (Vienna: United Nations, 1994), 17.

70. *The Recommendation, Rec (2003) 23 of the Committee of Ministers of the Council of Europe to Member States on the Management by Prison Administrations of Life Sentence and other Long-term Prisoners* (adopted October 9, 2003), replaced Resolution (76) 2 on the *Treatment of Long-term Prisoners* (adopted February 17, 1976).

71. *Kafkaris v. Cyprus,* ECtHR (app. 21906/04), February 12, 2008 [GC]; *Vinter and others v. UK,* ECtHR (apps. 66069/09, 130/10 and 3896/10), July 9, 2013 [GC]; *Khoroshenko v. Russia,* June 30, 2015; *Murray v. The Netherlands,* ECtHR (app. 10511/10), April 26, 2016 [GC].

72. European Committee for the Prevention of Torture and Inhuman or Degrading Treatment or Punishment, *25th General Report of the CPT* (Strasbourg, France: Council of Europe, 2016), CPT/Inf (2016) 10. See also Chapter 8.

73. Horst Schüler-Springorum, *Strafvollzug in Übergang* (Göttingen. Germany: Otto Schwartz, 1969); Constantijn Kelk, *Recht voor gedetineerden: een onderzoek naar die beginselen van het gevangenisrecht* (Alpen aan den Rijn, The Netherlands: Samson, 1978).

74. BVerfGE 35, 202, 236 (Ger.).

75. BVerfGE 45, 187. (Ger.)

76. Sonja Meijer, "Rehabilitation as a Positive Obligation," *European Journal of Crime, Criminal law and Criminal Justice* 25 (2017): 145–162.

77. Van Zyl Smit, *Taking Life Imprisonment Seriously,* 174.

78. Franklin E. Zimring, *The Contradictions of American Capital Punishment* (New York: Oxford University Press, 2003), 17–24.

79. Art. 27 of the Charter of the International Military Tribunal (August 8, 1945); Art. 16. Of the International Military Tribunal for the Far East Charter (IMTFE Charter), also known as the Tokyo Charter (January 19, 1946).

80. Dirk van Zyl Smit, *Taking Life Imprisonment Seriously,* 194. A prominent exception was Rudolf Hess, who was sentenced to life imprisonment by the International Military Tribunal in Nuremberg and who remained in prison until his death more than forty years later. However, it was widely recognized that the exceptionally long term he served was more the product of political expediency than carefully calculated penal policy. Norman J. W. Goda, *Tales from Spandau: Nazi Criminals and the Cold War* (Cambridge: Cambridge University Press, 2007).

81. William A. Schabas, "War Crimes, Crimes against Humanity and the Death Penalty," *Albany Law Review* 60 (1997): 733–770, 742–743.

82. UN International Law Commission, "Summary Record of the 2157th Meeting," *Yearbook of the International Law Commission* (1990), vol. 1, UN Doc A/CN.4/SER.A/1990, 50–61.

83. UN International Law Commission, "Ninth Report on the Draft Code of Crimes against the Peace and Security of Mankind," *Yearbook of the International Law Commission* (1991), vol. 2(1), A/CN.4/SER.A/1991/Add.l, 37–44, 40, § 29.

84. UN International Law Commission, "Summary Record of the 2157th Meeting," *Yearbook of the International Law Commission* (1990) vol. 1, 50.

85. Commissioner Tudela from Peru in UN International Law Commission, "Summary Record of the 2212th Meeting," *Yearbook of the International Law*

Commission (1991) vol. 1, A/CN.4/SER.A/1991, 34, § 4; See also the comments from Commissioner Barboza from Argentina in UN International Law Commission, "Summary Record of the 2209th Meeting," *Yearbook of the International Law Commission* (1991), vol. 1, 16 § 20; and those of Commissioner Rodrigues from Brazil in UN International Law Commission, "Summary Record of the 2208th Meeting," *Yearbook of the International Law Commission* (1991), vol. 1, 12, § 21.

86. Commissioner Njenga from Kenya in UN International Law Commission, "Summary Record of the 2210th Meeting," *Yearbook of the International Law Commission* (1991), vol. 1, 26, § 47.

87. Commissioner Graefrath from the German Democratic Republic in UN International Law Commission, "Summary Record of the 2208th Meeting," *Yearbook of the International Law Commission* (1991) vol. 1, 10, § 10.

88. UN International Law Commission, "Summary Record of the 2213th Meeting," *Yearbook of the International Law Commission* (1991) vol. 1, 43, § 14.

89. Ibid., 42, § 12.

90. Ibid., 43, § 14.

91. UN International Law Commission, "Summary Record of the 2210th Meeting," *Yearbook of the International Law Commission* (1991), vol. 1, 24, § 33.

92. Ibid., § 36.

93. Dirk van Zyl Smit, "International Imprisonment," *International and Comparative Law Quarterly* 54 (2005): 357–386, 366.

94. Statute of the ICTY, art. 24(1); Statute of the ICTR art. 23(1).

95. *Prosecutor v. Galić,* MICT-14–83-ES (June 23, 2015). See also Chapter 9.

96. Rome Statute, art. 77. See also Chapter 5.

97. Ibid. art. 110. See also Chapter 9.

98. *Vinter and others v. United Kingdom,* July 9, 2013, § 120; *Murray v. The Netherlands,* April 26, 2016, § 99. Hoge Raad der Nederlanden 15/00402, ECLI:NL:HR:2016:1325, July 5, 2016.

99. Protocol 6, ETS 114, April 28, 1983; Protocol 13, ETS 187, May 3, 2002.

100. Dirk Van Zyl Smit and Angelika Reichstein, "Life Imprisonment as an Alternative to the Death Penalty in a Period of Political Transition: Choices and Consequences in the Balkans and Elsewhere," in *Mapping the Penological Landscape of the Balkans: A Regional Survey on Sentencing and Imprisonment Realities in Southeast Europe,* ed. Michael Kilchling, et al (Berlin: Duncker and Humblot, 2018 forthcoming).

101. Miklós Lévay, "Constitutionalising Life Imprisonment without Parole: The Case of Hungary, in *Life Imprisonment and Human Rights,* 169.

102. Filip Vojta has pointed out that the death penalty was rarely used in the former Yugoslavia and that in the last years of its existence overall incarceration rates were low by international standards. Filip Vojta, "Life and Long-Term Imprisonment in the Countries of the Former Yugoslavia," in *Life Imprisonment and Human Rights,* 353.

103. Zimring, *The Contradictions,* 37.

104. Jamil Mujuzi, "Life Imprisonment in South Africa: Yesterday, Today and Tomorrow," *South African Journal of Criminal Justice* 22 (2009): 1–38.

105. Article 73 of the Correctional Services Act 111 of 1998.

106. Van Zyl Smit and Reichstein, "Life Imprisonment as an Alternative to the Death Penalty in a Period of Political Transition."

107. See, in general, Evi Girling, "Sites of Crossing and Death in Punishment: The Parallel Lives, Trade-Offs and Equivalencies of the Death Penalty and Life without Parole in the US," *The Howard Journal of Crime and Justice* 55 (2016): 345–361; Christopher N. J. Roberts. "Human Rights Lost: The (Re)making of an American Story," *Minnesota Journal of International Law* 26(1) (2017): 1–62.

108. See, among many accounts, David Garland, *Peculiar Institution: America's Death Penalty in an Age of Abolition* (Cambridge, MA: Harvard University Press, 2010); Zimring, *The Contradictions.*

109. *Furman v. Georgia*, 408 US 238 (1972).

110. See the explanation of the introduction of LWOP sentences in Alabama and Illinois in the early 1970s, in Note, "A Matter of Life and Death: The Effect of Life-without-Parole-statutes on Capital Punishment," *Harvard Law Review* 119 (2006): 1838–1854, 1841.

111. Christopher Seeds, "Disaggregating LWOP: Life without Parole, Capital Punishment, and Mass Incarceration in Florida, 1972–1995," *Law and Society Review* 52 (2018): 172–205.

112. Carol S. Steiker and Jordan M. Steiker, "Opening a Window or Building a Wall? The Effect of Eighth Amendment Death Penalty Law and Advocacy on Criminal Justice More Broadly," *University of Pennsylvania Journal of Constitutional Law* 11 (2008–2009): 155–205; Carol S. Steiker and Jordan M. Steiker, *Courting Death: The Supreme Court and Capital Punishment* (Cambridge, MA: Harvard University Press, 2016); Brandon L. Garrett, *End of Its Rope: How Killing the Death Penalty Can Revive Criminal Justice* (Cambridge, MA: Harvard University Press, 2017).

113. American Law Institute, *Model Penal Code: Sentencing, Proposed Final Draft* (approved May 24, 2017), 161.

114. *Solem v. Helm*, 463 US 277 (1983). See the discussion of this case and subsequent decisions in the context of restraints on imposing life imprisonment in Chapter 5.

115. *Atkins v. Virginia*, 536 US 304, 316 (2002).

116. *Roper v. Simmons*, 543 US 551, 567 (2005).

117. *Graham v. Florida*, 560 US 48, 81 (2010), quoting *Roper v. Simmons* (2005), 578.

118. S. Exec. Rep. No. 102–23 at 7 (1992).

2. Describing Life

1. The CPT's definition is similarly inclusive: It defines a life sentence as: "an indeterminate sentence imposed by a court in the immediate aftermath of a conviction for a criminal offense which requires the prisoner to be kept in prison either for the remainder of his or her natural life or until release by a judicial,

quasi-judicial, executive or administrative process which adjudges the prisoner to no longer present a risk to the public at large": European Committee for the Prevention of Torture and Inhuman or Degrading Treatment of Punishment, *25th General Report of the CPT* (Strasbourg: Council of Europe, 2016), CPT/Inf (2016) 10, § 68.

2. Algeria: Penal Code, art. 5; Djibouti: Penal Code, art. 33; Gabon: various articles of the Penal Code; Mali: Penal Code, art. 4; Guinea: Penal Code, art. 8; Monaco: Penal Code, art. 6; Rwanda: Penal Code, art. 38; Luxemburg: Penal Code, art. 7; Switzerland: Penal Code, art. 40; Benin: Penal Code, art. 7; Central African Republic: Penal Code, art. 17; Chad: Penal Code, art. 4; Comoros: Penal Code, art. 7; Burkina Faso: Penal Code, art. 9; Cameroon: various articles of the Penal Code; Côte d'Ivoire: the law replacing the death penalty; Niger: Penal Code, art. 5; Tunisia: Penal Code, art. 5; Burundi: Penal Code, art. 45; Democratic Republic of the Congo: Penal Code, art. 18.

3. Chile: Penal Code, art. 2; Peru: Penal Code, art. 29; Honduras: Penal Code, various articles; Mexico: Penal Code of Chihuahua, art. 32; Penal Code of the State of Mexico, art. 23; Penal Code of Quintana Roo, art. 22; Penal Code of Veracruz, art. 48; Penal Code of Puebla, various articles; Spain: Penal Code, art. 33.

4. Penal Code of France, art. 131-1.

5. The Penal Code of France only uses that sentence for the following offenses: treason (art. 411-2), attempts against the institutions or the territorial integrity of the Republic (art. 412-1), and leading an insurrectionist movement (art. 412-6).

6. Penal Code of Belgium, arts. 8 and 10.

7. Penal Code of Argentina, arts. 6 and 9, respectively.

8. *Mendoza and others v. Argentina,* Inter-Am. Ct. H.R. Series C No. 260, fn. 65.

9. *R v. Cornick* [2014] EWHC 3623 (QB), [2015] EMLR 9 (Eng.); Criminal Justice Act 2003, s. 277. For the history, see Nicola Padfield, *Beyond the Tariff: Human Rights and the Release of Life Sentence Prisoners* (Uffculme, UK: Willan, 2002), 8.

10. Juveniles can be sentenced to detention at the executive's pleasure in Antigua and Barbuda: Offences against the Person Act, art 3.1; Barbados: of the Juvenile Offenders Act, art. 14; Botswana: Penal Code, art. 26; Brunei Darussalam: Criminal Procedure Code, art. 238; Guyana: Criminal Law (Procedure) Act, art. 164; Kenya: Penal Code, art. 25; Malawi: Penal Code, art. 26; Malaysia: Child Act 2001, art. 97; Tanzania: Penal Code, art. 26; and Zambia: Penal Code, art. 25. In Jamaica, the Juveniles Act of 1951, s. 29(1), provided for the possibility of detention at the governor-general's pleasure; however, following the case of *Director of Public Prosecutions v. Mollison (Jamaica)* [2003] UKPC 6, [2003] 2 AC 411 (Eng.), the sentence became detention at the court's pleasure.

11. The latter appears to be most common: for example, in Barbados, the Offences against the Person Act 1994, s. 4 allows for detention in a mental hospital of persons convicted of manslaughter who suffer from an "abnormality of mind," "until Her Majesty's pleasure is known"; in Ghana, the Criminal

Procedure Code, s. 137 allows for the detention of "criminal lunatics," "until the President's pleasure shall be known."

12. See, for example, the Penal Code of Brunei Darussalam, art. 53(2), which states, "Notwithstanding the provisions of any other written law, the words 'imprisonment for life' means imprisonment for the remainder of the natural life of the person so sentenced."

13. "Reprieve Death Row, Lifers to Overcome Prison Congestion, Says Report," *Sunday Times,* April 9, 2017, http://www.sundaytimes.lk/170409/news /reprieve-death-row-lifers-to-overcome-prisons-congestion-says-report-236593 .html.

14. Human Rights Clinic, *Designed to Break You: Human Rights Violations on Texas' Death Row Austin* (Austin: University of Texas School of Law, 2017), 8.

15. Public Safety Canada, *2015 Corrections and Conditional Release Statistical Overview,* https://www.publicsafety.gc.ca/cnt/rsrcs/pblctns/ccrso-2015/index -en.aspx.

16. American Law Institute, "Model Penal Code: Sentencing, Proposed Final Draft" (approved May 24, 2017), 160.

17. WY Stat. Ann. § 6–10 (2017), see also Wyo. Const. art. 3, § 53 (2017), "Creation of Criminal Penalties Not Subject to Governor's Power to Commute."

18. Ga. Code Ann. § 17–10–16 (2017). See a brief history of the executive clemency system of Georgia on the website of the Georgia State Board of Pardons of Paroles at https://pap.georgia.gov/about. For more information on the "pardons scandal" of the 1940s, see Charles S. Bullock III, Scott E. Buchanan, and Ronald Keith Gaddie, *The Three Governors Controversy: Skullduggery, Machinations, and the Decline of Georgia's Progressive Politics* (Athens: University of Georgia Press, 2015), 38.

19. Ga. Const. art. 4, s. II § II (2017).

20. Ga. Code Ann. § 17-10-16 (2017).

21. Chihuahua: Penal Code, art. 29; Puebla: Penal Code, art. 41; Quintana Roo: Penal Code, art. 22; State of Mexico: Penal Code, art. 23; Veracruz: Penal Criminal Code, art. 18.

22. Law on the Execution of Sentences and Judicial Measures of the State of Quintana Roo, 2011, art. 92. Similarly, in the Mexican State of Puebla, the Penal Code, art. 122, mentions the possibility of executive pardon, but only for prisoners who "have provided important services to the nation or to the state," or who "deserve it for humanitarian or social reasons." It is excluded for "crimes qualified as serious," which would seem to include life offences.

23. The Constitution of Honduras, art. 245.24.

24. The Law on Pardons, 2013, art.7, lists the offenses for which pardon cannot be granted, and art. 10 excludes those mentioned in art. 7 from a humanitarian pardon.

25. The Constitution of Haiti, art. 146 read with art. 21.1.

26. See, inter alia, *Nivette v. France,* ECtHR (app. 44190/98), July 3, 2001; *Einhorn v. France,* ECtHR (app. 71555/01), October 16, 2001; *Stafford v. United Kingdom,* ECtHR (app. 73299/01), December 12, 2002; and *Wynne v. United Kingdom,* ECtHR (app. 67385/01), May 22, 2003. By that time, the

ECtHR had already decided that irreducible life sentences for children infringed against the ECHR. See Chapter 4.

27. *Kafkaris v. Cyprus,* ECtHR (app. 21906/04), February 12, 2008 [GC].

28. *Vinter and Others v. United Kingdom,* ECtHR (apps. 66069/09, 130/10 and 3896/10), July 9, 2013 [GC].

29. Crime (Sentences) Act 1997, s. 30(1).

30. Chapter 12, point 12.2.1 of Prison Service Order 4700 in HM Prison and Probation Service, *Indeterminate Sentence Manual* (London: HM Prison & Probation Service, n.d.), https://www.justice.gov.uk/offenders/psos/pso-4700 -indeterminate-sentence-manual, last modified April 5, 2017.

31. *R v. Oakes and Others* [2012] EWCA (Crim) 2435, [2013] QB 979 (Eng.). See also *R v. Bieber* [2008] EWCA Crim 1601, [2009] 1 WLR 223 (Eng.).

32. *R v. Newell; R v. McLoughlin* [2014] EWCA Crim 188, [2014] 1 WLR 3964 (Eng.).

33. *Hutchinson v. United Kingdom,* ECtHR (app. 57592/08), January 17, 2017.

34. Ibid. See the dissenting opinion of Judge Pinto de Albuquerque, with whom Judge Sajó agreed in substance.

35. Dirk van Zyl Smit and Angelika Reichstein, "Lebenslang in Europa: Die neue Rechtsprechung des Europäischen Gerichtshofs für Menschenrechte," *Forum Strafvollzug* 4 (2017): 229–234.

36. *The Sun,* January 18, 2017, https://www.thesun.co.uk/news/2640546/triple -murderer-arthur-hutchinsons-latest-appeal-against-uk-life-sentences-dismissed-by -eu-human-rights-judges/.

37. The Law on the Execution of Penalties and Security Measures, 2004, art. 107(16), provides that there shall be no conditional release "in the event of conviction to aggravated life imprisonment for committing, as part of the activities of an illegal organisation, one of the crimes included under Section Four headed Crimes Against the Security of the State, Section Five headed Crimes Against the Constitutional Order and the Functioning of this Order, and Section Six headed Crimes Against National Defence, in Part Four, Chapter Two of the Turkish Criminal Code (Law No. 5237)."

38. Constitution of Turkey, art. 104.

39. BVerfG, 2 BvR 2299/09, § 28 (Ger.).

40. *Öcalan v. Turkey (No. 2),* ECtHR (apps. 24069/03, 197/04, 6201/06 and 10464/07), March 18, 2014, § 203.

41. Ibid.

42. *Kaytan v. Turkey,* ECtHR (app. 27422/05), September 15, 2015; *Gurban v. Turkey,* ECtHR (app. 4947/04), December 15, 2015. See also İdil Aydınoğlu, *Turkiye'de Agirlastirilmiş Muebbet Olmak* [Being an aggravated life prisoner in Turkey] (Istanbul: TCPS kitapligi, 2016).

43. See Chapter 3.

44. *Schick v. Reed,* 419 US 256, 268 (1974).

45. *Harmelin v. Michigan,* 501 US 957, 1008 (1991). See also the dissenting opinion in *Solem v. Helm,* 463 US 277, 316 (1983), which claims that in practice, prisoners serving LWOP could expect to be released by their sentences being commuted.

46. *Graham v. Florida,* 560 US 48 69 (2010).

47. *Naovarath v. State,* 779 P. 2d 944, 944 (1989).

48. On the assumption that life-sentenced prisoners will never be released, see Molly M. Gill, "Clemency for Lifers: The Only Road Out Is the Road Not Taken," *Federal Sentencing Reporter* 23 (2010): 21–26. A list of all commutations by Barack Obama is available on the website of the United States Justice Department, https://www.justice.gov/pardon/obama-commutations. See also Jeffrey Crouch, "Barack Obama and the Clemency Power: Real Reform on the Way?," *Presidential Studies Quarterly* 45 (2015): 778–795; P. S. Ruckman Jr., "Federal Executive Clemency in the Administration of Barack Obama (2009–2013): A Pardon Power Report," Midwest Political Science Association Annual Meeting, Chicago, April 2013, https://ssrn.com/abstract=2234261 or http://dx.doi.org/10.2139/ssrn.2234261; Barack Obama, "The President's Role in Advancing Criminal Justice Reform," *Harvard Law Review* 130 (2017): 811–865, 835–838.

49. BVerfGE 113,154, § III.1. See generally Hans Kromrey and Christine Morgenstern, "Auslieferung bei drohender lebenslanger Freiheitsstrafe ohne Aussetzungsmöglichkeit," *Zeitschrift für Strafrechtsdogmatik* 13 (2014): 704–716.

50. Robert Johnson and Sandra McGunigall-Smith, "Life without Parole, America's Other Death Penalty," *The Prison Journal* 88 (2008): 328–346.

51. *Regina (Wellington) v. Secretary of State for the Home Department* [2008] UKHL 72, [2009] 1 A.C. 335 (HL) (Eng.).

52. *Kafkaris v. Cyprus,* February 12, 2008.

53. *Harkins and Edwards v. United Kingdom,* ECtHR (apps. 9146/07 and 32650/07), January 7, 2012; *Babar Ahmad and others v. United Kingdom,* ECtHR (apps. 24027/07, 11949/08, 36742/08, 66911/09 and 67354/09), April 10, 2012.

54. *Trabelsi v. Belgium,* ECtHR (app. 140/10), September 4, 2014.

55. Ibid., § 22.

56. Wiene van Hattum and Sonja Meijer, "An Administrative Procedure for Life Prisoners: Law and Practice of Royal Pardon in the Netherlands," in *Life Imprisonment and Human Rights,* ed. Dirk Van Zyl Smit and Catherine Appleton (Oxford: Hart/Bloomsbury Publishing, 2016).

57. Quoted in the decision of the Appeal Committee, Case 14/1296/GA of August 21, 2014.

58. HR no. S 15/00402, July 5, 2016.

59. *Vinter and Others v. United Kingdom,* July 9, 2013; *Murray v. The Netherlands,* ECtHR (app. 10511/10), April 26, 2016 [GC].

60. HR, July 5, 2016, § 3.2.

61. Ibid., § 3.3.

62. Ibid.

63. HR no. S 15/00402, December 19, 2017. This judgment also described the new procedure.

64. Wiene van Hattum, "De Hoge Raad en het reviewmechanisme," *Nederlands Juristenblad,* 64, (2018): 916–930.

65. *Harakchiev and Tolumov v. Bulgaria,* ECtHR (app. 73593/10), July 8, 2014.

66. Fundamental Law of Hungary, art. IV(2).

67. *Lazlo Magyar v. Hungary,* ECtHR (app. 73593/10), May 20, 2014.

68. *T. P. and A. T. v. Hungary,* ECtHR (apps. 37871/14 and 73986/14), October 4, 2016.

69. Miklós Lévay, "Constitutionalising Life Imprisonment without Parole: The Case of Hungary," in *Life Imprisonment and Human Rights,* 169.

70. *Matiošaitis and others v. Lithuania,* ECtHR (apps. 22662/13, 51059/13, 58823/13, 59692/13, 59700/13, 60115/13, 69425/13 and 72824/13), May 23, 2017.

71. Matthew Agius, "Prisoners Serving Life Whould Be Eligible for Parole, Court Rules in Landmark Judgment," *Malta Today,* March 22, 2018. https://www.maltatoday.com.mt/news/court_and_police/85513/prisoners_serving_life_should_be_eligible_for_parole_court_rules_in_landmark_judgment#.Wsp4vYjwbIU.

72. Andrew Dyer, "Irreducible Life Sentences: What Difference Have the European Convention on Human Rights and the United Kingdom Human Rights Act Made?" *Human Rights Law Review* 16 (2016): 541–584.

73. *Makoni v. Commissioner of Prisons and another,* CCZ 8/16, July 13, 2016.

74. Constitution of Zimbabwe, s. 112(1).

75. *Makoni v. Commissioner of Prisons,* 14.

76. Ibid, 22.

77. See the discussion of this intervention in the context of symbolic life sentences below. For the numbers of persons serving LWOP, as opposed to symbolic life, see Appendix B.

78. Penal Reform International, *The Abolition of the Death Penalty and Its Alternative Sanction in Central Asia: Kazakhstan, Kyrgyzstan and Tajikistan* (London: Penal Reform International, 2012), 11.

79. Daniel Pascoe, "Is Diya a Form of Clemency?," *Boston University International Law Journal* 34 (2016), 149–179.

80. Project questionnaire, Ghana, September 1, 2014.

81. Telephone conversation between Dirk van Zyl Smit, Kwame Frimpong, and the commissioner of prisons for Ghana, March 31, 2016.

82. See Chapter 6.

83. See Chapter 10.

84. Recommendation Rec (2003)22 of the Committee of Ministers of the Council of Europe to member states on *Conditional Release (Parole)* (adopted October 9, 2003) defines conditional release as follows: "For the purposes of this recommendation, conditional release means the early release of sentenced prisoners under individualised post-release conditions. Amnesties and pardons are not included in this definition."

85. *Prosecutor v. Kayishema and Ruzindana,* ICTR-95-1-T (May 21, 1999), ICTR-95-1-A (June 1, 2001).

86. *Prosecutor v. Renzaho,* ICTR-97-31-T (July 14, 2009), ICTR-97-31-A (April 1, 2011).

87. Esther Gumboh, "The Penalty of Life Imprisonment under International Criminal law," *African Human Rights Law Journal* 11 (2011): 75–92; Jamil Mujuzi, "Is There a Need for the ICTY to Clarify the Difference(s) between Life Imprisonment and Imprisonment for the Remainder of the Offender's Life? The

Galić and *Lukič* Decisions," *International Criminal Law Review* 10 (2010): 855–886.

88. *Prosecutor v. Galić,* MICT-14-83 (June 23, 2015). See also Chapter 9.

89. For more details on gubernatorial vetoes of parole, see Chapter 9.

90. Diarmuid Griffin and Ian O'Donnell, "Confusingly Compliant with the European Convention on Human Rights: The Release of Life Sentence Prisoners in Ireland," in *Life Imprisonment and Human Rights,* 267.

91. Penal Code of Liberia, 2008, s. 15.3.4.

92. According to World Health Organization data, published in 2015, http://www.worldlifeexpectancy.com/liberia-life-expectancy.

93. See also Chapter 6.

94. *R. v. Bourque* 2014 NBQB 237 (Can.); R. E. Brown, "A Beacon of Hope—Sunny Ways: Life-Sentenced Offenders," *Executive Exchange,* Fall 2016, 29–38.

95. See Appendix A.

96. Criminal Justice Act 1953, s. 3, as amended by the Penal Code (Amendment) Act 2003.

97. Firearms (Increased Penalties) Act 1971 (as amended 2006), § 2; Penal Code (as amended 2012), § 57.

98. *Cyril Ozuloke v. The State* (S.C. 574/64) 1965 NMLR 125 (Nigeria).

99. Prisons Act 2006, § 86(3).

100. *Attorney General v. Susan Kigula and 417 others,* criminal appeal no. 03 of 2006, [2009] UGSC 6 (Uganda).

101. *Stephen Tigo v. Uganda,* criminal appeal no. 08 of 2009, [2011] UGSC 7 (Uganda.).

102. Jamil Mujuzi, "Life Imprisonment and Human Rights in Uganda," in *Life Imprisonment and Human Rights,* 97.

103. The Penal Code 1860, amended by the Penal Code (Amendment) Ordinance 1985, § 57.

104. *Rokia Begum v. State,* 19 BLC (AD) (2014) (Bangla.).

105. Ibid., § 24.

106. The International Crimes Tribunal is a domestic war crimes tribunal in Bangladesh, which was set up in 2009 to try persons charged with crimes against humanity committed in 1971 during the Bangladesh Liberation War: Marieke Wierda and Anthony Triolo, "Resources," in *International Prosecutors,* ed., Luc Reydams, Jan Wouters, and Cedric Ryngaert (Oxford, UK: Oxford University Press, 2012).

107. *Sayedee v. Government of the People's Republic of Bangladesh,* criminal appeal nos.39–40 of 2013, SC (unreported), p. 151 of the typescript (Bangla.).

108. International Crimes (Tribunals) Act 1973, art. 20(2).

109. *Ataur Mridha @ Ataur and Hossain v. The State:* criminal appeal nos. 15–16 of 2010, SC, February 14, 2017 (unreported), p. 89 of the typescript (Bangla.).

110. See the Penal Code, 1860, amended by Law Reforms Ordinance 1972, § 57 and Pakistan Prisons Rules 1978, Rule 140(i): "Imprisonment for life will mean twenty-five years rigorous imprisonment and every life prisoner shall undergo a minimum of fifteen years substantive imprisonment."

111. Project questionnaire Pakistan, October 8, 2015.

112. Indian Penal Code, ss. 55 and 57.

113. *Gopal Vinayak Godse v. The State of Maharashtra and others* (1961), 3 SCR 440 (India).

114. See the authorities collected in *Union of India v. Sriharan alias Murugan and Others*, (2015), WP (Crl) No. 48 of 2014, §§ 50–61 (India).

115. *Swamy Shraddananda (2) alias Murali Manohar Mishra v. State of Karnataka* (2008), 13 SCC 767, § 57 (India).

116. Penal Code of Greece, arts. 105 and 106.

117. Criminal Code of Turkey, arts. 46–48.

118. Such is the case in Nepal, where life imprisonment can be accompanied by the confiscation of the convict's entire property; *Muluki Ain* (General Code of Nepal), ch. 2, nr. 7. Payment of damages to the victim is a condition for release in Lebanon. Project questionnaire, Lebanon, March 16, 2015.

119. Singapore: Penal Code: art. 301 life and a caning; art, 121 life and a fine.

120. *S v. Silulale and another*, 1999 (2) SACR 102 (SCA), 106–107 (S. Afr.). See also S. *v. Gaingob and others* (Case nos. SA 7/2008 and 8/2008) February 6, 2018, where the Supreme Court of Namibia came to the same conclusion.

121. For details on sentence duration in Central and South America, see Francisco Javier De León Villalba, "Long-term Imprisonment in Latin America," in *Life Imprisonment and Human Rights*, 329.

122. Decision on cases 5–2001/10-2001/24-2001/25-2001/34-2002/40-2002/3-2003/10-2003/11-2003/12-2003/14-2003/16-2003/19-2003/22-2003/7-2004, of December 23, 2010. Full text (in Spanish), http://escuela.fgr.gob.sv/wp-content/uploads/Leyes/Leyes-2/Sentencias_INC_Acumulas_CSJ_DICIEMBRE_2010.pdf.

123. Ibid., 111.

124. The legislature amended the Penal Code in 2012, replacing the seventy-five-year maximum fixed-term sentence with a sixty-year maximum (Law Decree No. 1009, 2012). See also the note, "Reforma Penal establece 60 años como pena máxima de prisión," on the website of the Salvadoran Legislative Assembly, February 29, 2012, http://www.asamblea.gob.sv/noticias/archivo-de-noticias/modifican-pena-maxima. This new maximum would still take any prisoner beyond the average life expectancy in El Salvador and thus would be unlikely to stand up to constitutional scrutiny from the Salvadoran court.

125. William Thomas Worster, "Between a Treaty and Not: A Case Study of the Legal Value of Diplomatic Assurances in Expulsion Cases," *Minnesota Journal of International Law* 21 (2012): 253–346.

126. *United States v. Pileggi* 703 F.3d 675 (4th Cir. 2013).

127. Constitution of Costa Rica, art. 40; Penal Code of Costa Rica, art. 51.

128. *United States v. Pileggi*, 361 Fed. Appx. 475, 479 (4th Cir. 2010). The UK courts have been less generous: see *Pham v United States* [2014] EWHC 4167 (Admin); [2015] AC 62 (Eng.) where the Queen's Bench of the High Court refused to treat a potential, very long, fixed-term sentence as de facto LWOP and therefore challengeable in the context of extradition.

129. Described in *United States v. Pileggi* 703 F.3d 675 (4th Cir. 2013). This interpretation of fifty-year sentences as de facto life sentences is not shared in a

recent decision of the Constitutional Chamber of Costa Rica. When faced with the question of whether sentences of fifty years were necessarily a violation of the constitutional prohibition on life imprisonment, the chamber declared such sentences compatible with the constitution: Decision 2015-19582 of December 16, 2015. Although the fifty-year sentence has now been formally declared constitutional, it is not without its critics, who point out that it has not had the desired effect of reducing the country's crime rates. Roy Murillo Rodríguez, "Populismo punitivo, cárcel perpetua y hacinamiento crítico en Costa Rica: Más inseguridad por menos libertad," in *Reflexiones Jurídicas frente al Populismo Penal en Costa Rica*, ed., Rosaura Chinchilla Calderón (San José, Costa Rica: Editorial Investigaciones Jurídicas S.A., 2012); "Pena máxima de 50 años no bajó la criminalidad," *La Nación*, March 3, 2014, https://goo.gl/QHQFiM.

130. *People v. Caballero*, (2012) 55 Cal. 4th 262. The decision was taken in response to the ruling of the Supreme Court in *Graham v. Florida*, 560 US 48 (2012), that imposing LWOP for a nonhomicide crime was unconstitutionally severe.

131. "La cadena perpetua existe hoy en Colombia: Minjusticia," *El Tiempo*, January 19, 2015. http://www.eltiempo.com/politica/justicia/la-cadena-perpetua -existe-hoy-en-colombia-minjusticia/15115637.

132. Constitutional Chamber of the Supreme Court of El Salvador, 5-2001/ 10-2001/24-2001/25-2001/34-2002/40-2002/3-2003/10-2003/11-2003/12-2003/ 14-2003/16-2003/19-2003/22-2003/7-2004, December 23, 2010. Full Spanish text (in Spanish), https://goo.gl/vI9Ttz.

133. Giovanna Maria Frisso, "The Abolition of Life Imprisonment in Brazil and Its Contradictions," in *Life Imprisonment and Human Rights*.

134. United States Sentencing Commission, *Life Sentences in the Federal System* (Washington, D.C.: United States Sentencing Commission, 2015), 10.

135. Ibid.

136. United States Sentencing Commission, *2015 Sourcebook of Federal Sentencing Statistics*, Appendix A, 7.

137. United States Sentencing Commission, *Life Sentences*, 15.

138. Ibid.

139. Jessica S. Henry, "Death-in-Prison Sentences. Overutilized and Underscrutinized," in *Life without Parole: America's New Death Penalty?* ed. Charles J. Ogletree and Austin Sarat (New York: New York University Press, 2012), 66.

140. For a powerful case for drawing this distinction, see Stephen J. Morse, "Protecting Liberty and Autonomy: Desert/Disease Jurisprudence," *San Diego Law Review* 48 (2011): 1077–1125.

141. Since 1965, Swedish law has had no defense of insanity. All persons who commit criminal acts, even persons with a severe mental disorder, may be convicted and sentenced by criminal courts. Those who suffer from a severe mental disorder cannot be sent to prison but instead are sentenced to serve a term of involuntary psychiatric care in a mental institution. C. Svennerlind, T. Nilsson, N. Kerekes, P. Andiné, M. Lagerkvist, A. Forsman, H. Anckarsäter, and H. Malmgren, "Mentally Disordered Criminal Offenders in the Swedish Criminal System," *International Journal of Law and Psychiatry* 33 (2010): 220–226. The Swedish approach is controversial but has not been amended. Susanna Radovica, Gerben Meynenc, and Tova Bennet, "The Case of Sweden

Compared to The Netherlands," *International Journal of Law and Psychiatry* 40 (2015): 43–49.

142. Andrew Ashworth and Lucia Zedner, *Preventive Justice* (Oxford, UK: Oxford University Press, 2014), 13; Christopher Slobogin, "Preventive Detention in Europe, the United States and Australia," in *Preventive Detention: Asking the Fundamental Questions*, ed. Patrick Keyser (Cambridge: Intersentia, 2013), 31.

143. Cal. Penal Code, §. 667 and §.1170.12 (West 1999).

144. For details on the sentence of imprisonment for public protection, including when it could be imposed and how these provisions were amended and subsequently repealed, see Andrew Ashworth, *Sentencing and Criminal Justice*, 5th ed. (Cambridge: Cambridge University Press, 2010), 231–235, and 6th ed. (Cambridge: Cambridge University Press, 2015), 326–327; Harry Annison, *Dangerous Politics: Risk, Political Vulnerability and Penal Policy* (Oxford: Oxford University Press, 2015).

145. See Catherine Appleton and Dirk van Zyl Smit, "The Paradox of Reform: Life Imprisonment in England and Wales,"in *Life Imprisonment and Human Rights*.

146. The order for lifelong restriction was introduced into Scots law by the Criminal Justice (Scotland) Act 2003. Its classification as a life sentence became apparent to the authors in informal communications with the Scots authorities.

147. Canada: Criminal Code, s. 753 (1); South Africa: Criminal Procedure Act 1977, s. 286A.

148. *R v. Lyons* [1987] 2 SCR 309 (Can.).

149. *S v. Bull & another; S v. Chavulla & others* 2002 (1) SA 535 (SCA) (S.Afr.).

150. See, for example, Public Safety Canada *2015 Corrections and Conditional Release Statistical Overview*, Table C13. https://www.publicsafety.gc.ca/cnt/rsrcs/pblctns/ccrso-2015/index-en.aspx.

151. Cynthia Calkins, Elizabeth Jeglic, Robert A. Beattey, Steve Zeidman, and Anthony D. Perillo, "Sexual Violence Legislation: A Review of Case Law and Empirical Research," *Psychology, Public Policy, and Law* 20 (2014): 443–462.

152. Ibid. The details vary across jurisdictions.

153. *Kansas v. Hendricks,* 521 US 346 (1997).

154. Stephen J. Schulhofer, "Two Systems of Social Protection: Comments on the Civil-Criminal Distinction, with Particular Reference to Sexually Violent Predators Laws," *Journal of Contemporary Legal Issues* 7 (1996): 69–96; Eric S. Janus, *Failure to Protect: America's Sexual Predator Laws and the Rise of the Preventive State* (Ithaca, N.Y.: Cornell University Press, 2006); Tamara Rice Lave and Justin McCrary, "Do Sexually Violent Predator Laws Violate Double Jeopardy or Substantive Due Process—An Empirical Inquiry," *Brooklyn Law Review* 78 (2012–2013): 1391–1439.

155. *Seling v. Young,* 531 US 250 (2001); *Kansas v. Crane,* 534 US 407 (2002); *United States v. Comstock,* 560 US 126 (2010).

156. For the UK perspective on Minnesota, see *Sullivan v. Government of United States of America* [2012] EWHC 1680 (Admin), (2012) 156(25) SJLB 31 (Eng.). For California, see *Government of United States of America v. Giese* [2015] EWHC 2733 (Admin) [2016] ACD 4 (Eng.). In a case involving New York State, *Government of United States of America v. Bowen* [2015] EWHC 1873

(Admin), [2015] All ER (D) (Eng.), the English court did allow extradition. However, in *Giese* it was strongly suggested that not enough expert testimony had been placed before the court in *Bowen*. If it had been, extradition to New York would probably have been denied too.

157. S. 13 of the Dangerous Prisoners (Sexual Offenders) Act 2003.

158. *Fardon v. Attorney-General for the State of Queensland* [2004] HCA 46.

159. *Fardon v. Australia,* CCPR/C/98/D/1629/2007, UN Human Rights Committee (HRC), 10 May 2010, http://www.refworld.org/cases,HRC,4c19e97b2 .html.

160. *Forvaring* applies only to certain serious offenses and may only be imposed "when a sentence for a specific term is deemed to be insufficient to protect life, health or freedom of others": Criminal Code 2015, § 39c. Tapio Lappi-Seppälä, "Life Imprisonment and Related Institutions in the Nordic Countries," in *Life Imprisonment and Human Rights.*

161. Denmark: Criminal Code, § 70; France: Criminal Procedure Code, arts. 706–53–13 to 706–53–22; the Netherlands: Criminal Code, art. 37a; and Sweden: Penal Code, ch. 31, s. 3.

162. Denmark: Lappi-Seppälä, "Life Imprisonment and Related Institutions in the Nordic Countries"; The Netherlands: Frans Koenraadt and Antoine Mooij, "Mentally Ill Offenders" in *Dutch Prisons,* ed. Miranda Boone and Martin Moerings (The Hague: BJu Legal Publishers, 2007).

163. Anna Coninx, "Life without Parole for Preventive Reasons? Lifelong Post-Sentence Detention in Switzerland," in *Life Imprisonment and Human Rights.*

164. *M v. Germany,* ECtHR (app. 19359/04), December 17, 2009; Kirstin Drenkhahn, Christine Morgenstern, and Dirk van Zyl Smit, "What Is in a Name? Preventive Detention in Germany in the Shadow of European Human Rights Law," *Criminal Law Review* 2012: 167–187.

165. BVerfGE 128, 326.

166. Ibid.

167. *Bergmann v. Germany,* ECtHR (app. 23279/14), January 7, 2016.

168. People on whom *Sicherungsverwahrung* is now imposed in Germany would previously have been subjected to a hospital order. See, in general, Axel Dessecker, "Constitutional Limits on Life Imprisonment and Post-Sentence Preventive Detention in Germany," in *Life Imprisonment and Human Rights.* The first empirical evidence indicates that since the recent reforms there is movement towards developing increased training opportunities for persons serving *Sicherungsverwahrung* in Germany: Axel Dessecker, "Die produktive Krise der Sicherungsverwahrung und ihre Folgen aus empirischer Sicht," in *Krise— Kriminalität—Kriminologie,* ed. Frank Neubacher und Nicole Bögelein (Mönchengladbach, Germany: Forum Verlag Godesberg, 2016).

169. Criminal Procedure Code of France, arts. 706-53-14 to 706-53-17. This provision has not been used.

170. Jill Peay, "Responsibility, Culpability and the Sentencing of Mentally Disordered Offenders: Objectives in Conflict," *Criminal Law Review* 3 (2016): 152–164.

171. Marie Gottschalk, "Sentenced to Life: Penal Reform and the Most Severe Sanctions," *Annual Review of Law and Social Science* 9 (2013): 353–382.

3. Prevalence of Life

1. Ashley Nellis, *Still Life: America's Increasing use of Life and Long-Term Sentences* (Washington: The Sentencing Project, 2017). See Appendix B.

2. United Nations, Department of Economic and Social Affairs, Population Division, *World Population Prospects: The 2015 Revision, DVD Edition* (New York: United Nations, Department of Economic and Social Affairs, Population Division, 2015); Institute for Criminal Policy Research, *World Prison Brief,* http://www.prisonstudies.org/world-prison-brief-data, as well as the data we collected ourselves.

3. See Appendix A. The UN membership of 193 states is narrower than the 216 countries and territories that form our baseline in Appendix A.

4. These countries are Chile, El Salvador, Fiji, Israel, Kazakhstan, and Peru. In addition, Brazil abolished the death penalty for ordinary crimes in 1979. However, Brazil has no life imprisonment either and has not carried out an execution since 1855. Roger Hood and Carolyn Hoyle, *The Death Penalty: A Worldwide Perspective,* 5th ed. (Oxford, UK: Oxford University Press, 2016), 506.

5. See Appendix A.

6. The relevant articles in the national constitutions are: Portugal: art. 30; Angola: art. 66; Brazil: art. 5-XLVII; Bolivia: art. 118; Cape Verde: art. 33; Colombia: art. 34; Costa Rica: art. 40; East Timor: art. 32; El Salvador: art. 27; Mozambique: art. 61; Nicaragua: art. 37; São Tomé and Príncipe: art. 37; and Venezuela: art. 44.

7. According to Amnesty International, "At least 19,094 people were believed to be under sentence of death worldwide at the end of 2014," while at least 607 executions were carried out during that year. Amnesty International, *Death Sentences and Executions 2014* (London: Amnesty International, 2015), 5–6. The total number of executions does not include China, where all relevant information is a state secret.

8. See Nellis, *Still Life,* 10.

9. Ibid., 7. See also Jessica S. Henry, Christopher Salvatore and Bai-Eyse Pug, "Virtual Life Sentences: An Exploratory Study," *The Prison Journal.* 2018: DOI: 10.1177/0032885518764915.

10. Additional data on numbers of persons serving life imprisonment in European countries were provided by the Council of Europe database, SPACE I: Marcelo Aebi, Mélanie Tiago, and Christine Burkhardt, *SPACE I—Council of Europe Annual Penal Statistics: Prison Populations, Survey 2014* (Strasbourg, France: Council of Europe, 2016).1. These data were used to check the information provided by our respondents on the workings of life imprisonment in their countries.

11. There were 18 life-sentenced prisoners on the Cayman Islands, which amounts to 30.5 per 100,000. Similarly, in Saint Christopher and Nevis, 23 life-sentenced prisoners amount to 41.9 per 100,000, and Bermuda has 25 life-sentenced prisoners, which corresponds to 40.3 per 100,000 of the country's population.

12. Sixty-seven percent of the Indian prison population was awaiting trial on December 31, 2015. World Prison Brief, *Data by Country,* http://www.prisonstudies.org/country/india.

13. For example, in Denmark the number of prisoners in post-conviction preventive detention was approximately double the number of life-sentenced prisoners: Tapio Lappi-Seppälä, "Life Imprisonment and Related Institutions in the Nordic Countries," in *Life Imprisonment and Human Rights,* ed. Dirk van Zyl Smit and Catherine Appleton (Oxford, UK: Hart Publishing, 2016).

14. Afghanistan,* Angola,* Antigua and Barbuda, Argentina, Bangladesh, Belgium, Belize, Benin,* Bhutan, Burundi, Cambodia, Chile, Colombia,* Comoros, Costa Rica,* Croatia,* Dominican Republic,* Ecuador,* El Salvador,* Equatorial Guinea, Estonia, France, Gabon, Ghana, Guatemala,* Guinea (Republic of), Hong Kong, Hungary, India, Israel, Japan, Jordan, Kazakhstan, Liberia, Madagascar, Malawi, Mali, Malta, Mauritius, Mexico, Montenegro,* Namibia, Panama,* Papua New Guinea, Peru, Philippines, Puerto Rico, Rwanda, Serbia,* South Korea (Republic of Korea), Spain, Sri Lanka, St Christopher and Nevis, Swaziland, Sweden, Thailand, Togo, Trinidad and Tobago, Turkey, Uganda, United Kingdom, United States, Uruguay,* and, Zimbabwe. The countries with asterisks have no formal life imprisonment.

15. General Law to Prevent and Punish Crimes of Kidnapping, 2010, art. 11.

16. Alaska Stat. §12.55.125 (2017). The same applies to Puerto Rico; P.R. Laws Ann. tit. 33 § 4644 (2017).

17. Axel Dessecker, *Die Vollstreckung lebenslanger Freiheitsstrafen: Dauer und Gründe der Beendigung im Jahr 2014* (Wiesbaden: Kriminologische Zentralstelle, 2016), 26.

18. Nellis, *Still Life,* 5.

19. Argentina, Armenia, Aruba, Australia, Azerbaijan, Barbados, Bolivia, Botswana, Burkina Faso, Canada, Costa Rica, Croatia, Cuba, Curaçao, Czech Republic, Denmark, Dominica, Ethiopia, France, Georgia, Germany, Greece, Greenland, Guatemala, Honduras, Italy, Jordan, Kenya, Liberia, Macedonia, Mauritius, Netherlands, New Zealand, Norway, Peru, Poland, Romania, Russia, San Marino, Serbia, Slovakia, Slovenia, Somalia, South Africa, Spain, Switzerland, Taiwan, United Kingdom, United States, and Uruguay.

20. Lappi-Seppälä, "Life Imprisonment."

21. Ibid.

22. Kriminologische Zentralstelle E.V., http://www.krimz.de/forschung/strafen/lebenslange/.

23. Data for the Rest of the World in Figures 3.3 and 3.4 include estimates for countries for which data were not available. For the named countries, most, but not all, years were available. In these instances, linear interpolation was used to estimate the relevant data points.

24. In Figure 3.4, the data were indexed to a common starting point of 1.00 for the year 2000.

25. Nellis, *Still Life.*

26. These figures build on work undertaken in Catherine Appleton and Bent Grøver, "The Pros and Cons of Life without Parole," *British Journal of Criminology* 47 (2007): 597–615.

27. Indian Penal Code 1860, ss. 45 and 53; Code of Criminal Procedure 1973, s. 432.

28. *Union of India v. Sriharan alias Murugan and Others,* WP (Crl), No. 48 of 2014, December 2, 2015 (India).

29. Tobias Smith and Su Jiang, "Making Sense of Life without Parole in China," *Punishment and Society* 21 (2018), DOI: 10.1177/1462474517739848.

30. Nellis, *Still Life.*

31. Axel Dessecker, "Constitutional Limits on Life Imprisonment and Post-Sentence Preventive Detention in Germany," in *Life Imprisonment and Human Rights*; Lappi-Seppälä, "Life Imprisonment."

32. For a brief overview of the costs of life sentences, see Appleton and Grøver, "The Pros and Cons of Life without Parole," 611; Marc Mauer, Ryan King, and Malcolm Young, *The Meaning of "Life": Long Prison Sentences in Context* (Washington, D.C.: The Sentencing Project, 2004), 25.

4. Exempt from Life

1. Malta: Penal Code, art. 40; Greece: Penal Code, art. 33.

2. Human Rights Committee, *Bronson Blessington and Matthew Elliot v. Australia,* Communication No. 1968/2010, U.N. Doc. CCPR/C/112/D/1968/2010 (2014).

3. The de facto LWOP was a product of post-sentence legislative amendments rather than of the law as it stood at the time of sentence. At the time Blessington and Elliot committed their offenses, they could apply for release after ten years. However, subsequent amendments to legislation in New South Wales made release much more unlikely. For more details, see Kate Fitz-Gibbon, "Life without Parole in Australia: Current Practices, Juvenile and Retrospective Sentencing," in *Life Imprisonment and Human Rights,* ed., Dirk Van Zyl Smit and Catherine Appleton (Oxford, UK: Hart/Bloomsbury Publishing, 2016); John L. Anderson, "The Label of Life Imprisonment in Australia: A Principled or Populist Approach to an Ultimate Sentence," *University of New South Wales Law Journal* 35(3) (2012): 747–778.

4. Human Rights Committee, *Blessington and Elliot v Australia* (2014), § 7.7.

5. Ibid., § 7.8.

6. *Vinter and Others v. United Kingdom,* ECtHR (App. nos. 66069/09, 130/10 and 3896/10), July 9, 2013 [GC]. See Chapter 2.

7. Human Rights Committee, *Blessington and Elliot v. Australia* (2014), § 7.11.

8. Fitz-Gibbon, "Life without Parole in Australia"; Andrew Dyer, "Irreducible Life Sentences: What Difference Have the European Convention on Human Rights and the United Kingdom Human Rights Act Made?," *Human Rights Law Review* 16 (2016): 541–584.

9. Committee on the Rights of the Child, *General Comment No. 10 (2007): Children's Rights in Juvenile Justice,* CRC/C/GC/10, April 25, 2007.

10. Ibid., § 77.

11. Ibid.

12. Human Rights Council, *Report of the Special Rapporteur on Torture and Other Cruel, Inhuman or Degrading Treatment or Punishment, Juan E. Méndez,* A/HRC/28/68, March 5, 2015.

13. Ibid. § 74.

14. Ibid. § 84(h).

15. Human Rights Council, *Human Rights in the Administration of Justice, Including Juvenile Justice,* A/HRC/30/L.16, September 29, 2015, § 24.

16. Inter-American Court of Human Rights, *Case of Mendoza and others v. Argentina* (2013), Series C No. 260. In an overlapping process, the Federal Court of Criminal Appeals in Argentina reached the same conclusion on August 30, 2012: that life imprisonment for children under 18 was unconstitutional. It did so by relying on the Convention on the Rights of the Child as applied in the light of the protection of children's rights in the constitution of Argentina. See *Mendoza, César Alberto y otros s / recurso de revision,* causa N° 14.087-Sala II-C.F.C.P. Summary and link to full judgment, www.crin.org/node/39316.

17. *Case of Mendoza and others. v. Argentina* (2013), § 163.

18. Ibid.

19. Ibid., § 166.

20. Ibid.

21. Ibid., § 183.

22. *V v. United Kingdom,* ECtHR (app. 24888/94), December 16, 1999 [GC].

23. Council of Europe, *European Rules for Juvenile Offenders subject to Sanctions and Measures,* (Strasbourg; Council of Europe) 35 (Commentary on Rule 2).

24. *Weeks v. United Kingdom,* ECtHR (app. no. 9787/82), March 2, 1987.

25. *V v. United Kingdom,* December 16, 1999, § 3, of the joint dissenting opinion of Judges Pastor Ridruejo, Ress, Makarczyk, Tulkens, and Butkevych.

26. *Murray v. the Netherlands,* ECtHR (app. 10511/10), April 26, 2016 [GC], § 99.

27. In France, only two children have ever been sentenced to life imprisonment. One of these life sentences was later overturned, and there is currently only one person convicted as a child who is still serving a sentence of life imprisonment as an adult. See Child Rights International Network, *Life Imprisonment of Children in the European Union* (London: CRIN, 2014), 21.

28. The Powers of Criminal Courts (Sentencing) Act 2000, s. 90, makes life sentences mandatory for murder, although technically they take the form of detention during Her Majesty's pleasure. A discretionary life sentence may also be imposed on children in England and Wales in terms of s. 91 of the same Act. Similar provisions apply in Scotland and Northern Ireland. Child Rights International Network, *Life Imprisonment of Children in the European Union,* 35–39.

29. In Cyprus, the Juvenile Offenders' Law (Cap. 157) does not apply to persons over seventeen, who can be tried and sentenced as adults; persons fourteen to sixteen years old can be sentenced to imprisonment as well, in some cases, and life imprisonment is not expressly excluded. In France, young offenders aged sixteen to eighteen can, in rare cases, get life imprisonment, if the judge assesses the special circumstances and personality of the relevant offender and concludes that life imprisonment is justified (Ordinance 45-174 of February 2, 1945, s. 20–2).

30. *Ilnseher v. Germany* (app. 10211/12 and 27505/14) February 2, 2017.

31. Prop.135 L (2010–2011), 104–5.

32. HR-2017-290-A, 10. For critique of this decision, see Linda Gröning and Hilde Švrljuga Sætre, "Child Rights and Criminal Justice: Detention of Children," in *Measuring Child Rights in Norway,* ed. Malcolm Langford, Marit Srkivenes, and Karl Søvig (Oslo: Universitetsforlaget, forthcoming 2018).

33. Hungary: Penal Code, art. 41; Bulgaria: Penal Code, art. 38-2.

34. Austria: Juvenile Justice Act (JGG), § 19; Macedonia: Penal Code, art. 35(4).

35. Serbia: Penal Code, art. 45.

36. Greece: Penal Code, art. 133 with art. 83.

37. Juvenile Justice Act, § 105.

38. Frieder Dünkel, "Juvenile Justice and Crime Policy in Europe," in *Juvenile Justice in Global Perspective,* ed. Franklin Zimring, Máximo Langer, and David Tanenhaus (New York: New York University Press, 2015).

39. "Recommendation CM/Rec (2008)11 of the Committee of Ministers to Member States on the European Rules for Juvenile Offenders Subject to Sanctions or Measures" (November 5, 2008).

40. Dünkel, "Juvenile Justice," 25.

41. Scotland and Northern Ireland, the other parts of the United Kingdom, have very different systems of child justice and are not analyzed here, although life imprisonment for children is possible in Scotland and Northern Ireland: In Scotland, children as young as twelve who commit murder can be detained "without limit of time": see Criminal Procedure (Scotland) Act 1995, art. 205.2. In Northern Ireland, children can be detained during the secretary of state's pleasure from the age of ten; see Criminal Justice (Children) (Northern Ireland) Order 1998, art. 45.1.

42. *R v. Cornick* [2015] EWCA Crim 110, [2015] 1 Cr. App. R. (S.) 69 (Eng.) (twenty years on a guilty plea). See also *R v. Taylor and Thomas* [2007] EWCA Crim 803, [2008] 1Cr App R (S) 4 (Eng.) (eighteen years after a trial); *Attorney General's Reference (No 126 of 2006)* [2007] EWCA Crim 53, [2007] 2 Cr App R (S) 59 (Eng.) (fifteen years on a guilty plea).

43. *R v. Fairweather,* (Eng.), sentencing remarks, https://www.judiciary.gov.uk /judgments/r-v-fairweather-sentencing-remarks/.

44. *R v. Cornick* [2014] EWHC 3623, [2015] E.M.L.R. 9 (QB) (Eng.).

45. Child Rights International Network, *Inhuman Sentencing: Life Imprisonment of Children around the World* (London: CRIN, 2015), 7.

46. *Centre for Child Justice v. Minister of Justice,* 2009 (2) SACR 477 (CC) (S. Afr.).

47. Anne Skelton, "Juvenile Justice in South Africa," in *Juvenile Justice,* 277.

48. Youth Criminal Justice Act SC 2002, ch. 1, s 64(1).

49. Criminal Code, art. 745.1. Moreover, a judge sentencing children to life imprisonment can impose even shorter minimum periods for younger children convicted of the same offense. For an example of how this is applied in Canada, see *R v. Ferriman,* 2006 CanLII 33472 (ONSC) (Can.).

50. *Roper v. Simmons,* 543 US 551, 568 (2005).

51. Ibid., III.B.

52. This was the case in Texas; see Note, "A Matter of Life and Death: The Effect of Life-without-Parole-Statutes on Capital Punishment," *Harvard Law*

Review 119 (2006): 1838–1854; Carol S. Steiker and Jordan M. Steiker, "Opening a Window or Building a Wall? The Effect of Eighth Amendment Death Penalty Law and Advocacy on Criminal Justice More Broadly," *University of Pennsylvania Journal of Constitutional Law* 11 (2008–2009): 155–206.

53. Kimberly P. Jordan, "Kids Are Different: Using Supreme Court Jurisprudence about Child Development to Close the Juvenile Court Doors to Minor Offenders," *Northern Kentucky Law Review* 41(2014): 187–203.

54. *Graham v. Florida,* 560 US 48 (2010).

55. *Miller v. Alabama,* 567 US 460 (2012).

56. Ibid., 472.

57. *Montgomery v. Louisiana,* 577 US _, 136 S.Ct. 718 (2016) 734.

58. John R. Mills, Anna M. Dorn and Amelia Courtney Hritz, "Juvenile Life without Parole in Law and Practice: Chronicling the Rapid Change Underway," *American Law Review* 65 (2016): 535–605, 552, and 568–571.

59. *People v. Caballero,* (2012) 55 Cal.4th 262.

60. *Diatchenko v. District Attorney* 1 N.E.3d 270, 284–85 (Mass. 2013). The Massachusetts legislature subsequently removed LWOP for juveniles from the statue book: LAWS ANN. ch. 265, § 2 (amended by H.B. 4307, 188th Gen. Ct. [Mass. 2014]).

61. *State of Iowa v. Isaiah Sweet,* 879 N.W.2d 811 (2016).

62. Lindsey E. Krause, "One Size Does Not Fit All: The Need for a Complete Abolition of Mandatory Minimum Sentences for Juveniles in Response to Roper, Graham, and Miller," *Law and Inequality* 33 (2015): 481–506.

63. American Civil Liberties Union, *False Hope; How Parole Systems Fail Youth Serving Extreme Sentences* (New York: ACLU Foundation, 2016), 35.

64. *Atwell v. Florida,* 197 So.3d 1040 (2016). Florida law still allows the imposition of LWOP on children in narrowly defined circumstances: see Florida: Penal Code, s. 921.1402.

65. See *Papon v. France* (no. 1), ECtHR (app. 64666/01), June 7, 2001; *Priebke v. Italy,* ECtHR (app. 48799/99, April 5, 2001; *Hasko v. Turkey,* ECtHR (app. 20578/05), January 17, 2012.

66. *Sawoniuk v. the United Kingdom,* ECtHR, (app. 63716/00), May 29, 2001.

67. Georgia: Penal Code, art. 51.2; Kyrgyzstan: Penal Code, art. 50.2; Mauritania: Penal Code, art. 64; and Uzbekistan: Penal Code, art. 51.

68. Belarus: Penal Code, art. 58.2.3; Kazakhstan: Penal Code, art. 48.4; Romania: Penal Code, art. 57; Russia: Penal Code, art. 57.2; Ukraine: Penal Code, art. 64.2.

69. *Khamtokhu and Aksenchik v. Russia,* ECtHR (app. nos 60367/08 and 961/11), May 13, 2014 (admissibility), § 23.

70. *Sawoniuk v. the United Kingdom,* ECtHR, (app. 63716/00), May 29, 2001.

71. South Africa: Correctional Services Act 111 of 1998 (as amended), s. 73(2). Similarly, in Burundi, the old are not excluded from life per se, but the minimum time to be served is shorter once the prisoner is over age seventy. Burundi: Penal Code, art. 127.

72. Tunisia: Criminal Procedure Code, art. 355.

73. France: Criminal Procedure Code, art. 729; Spain: Penal Code, art. 91.

74. Italy: Penitentiary Law on Home Detention, art. 47-ter.1.

75. Such is the case, for example, for persons over the age of sixty in Mauritania (Penal Code, art. 64) and for persons over the age of seventy in Madagascar (Penal Code, art. 70–71) and Benin (Penal Code, art. 70).

76. *R v. Sampford* [2014] EWCA Crim 1560, § 15 (Eng.). See also *R v. Walker* [2005] EWCA Crim 82, [2005] 2 Cr. App. R. (S.) 55 (Eng.); *R v. Archer* [2007] EWCA Crim 536, [2007] 2 Cr. App. R. (S.) 71 (Eng.); *R v. Symmons* [2009] EWCA Crim 1304 [2010], 1 Cr. App. R. (S.) 68 (Eng.); *R v. Troughton* [2012] EWCA Crim 1520 [2013] 1 Cr. App. R. (S.) 75. (Eng.)

77. *R v. Lowe,* (Eng.) sentencing. https://www.judiciary.gov.uk/wp-content /uploads/2014/10/sentencing-remarks-r-v-lowe.pdf.

78. See the sentencing statement, http://www.scotland-judiciary.org.uk/8/1338 /HMA-v-ANGUS-SINCLAIR.

79. Albania: Penal Code, art. 31; Azerbaijan: Penal Code, art. 57.2; Belarus: Penal Code, art. 58.2.2; Kazakhstan: Penal Code, art. 48.4; Kyrgyzstan: Penal Code, art. 50.2; Moldova: Penal Code, art. 71(3); Russia: Penal Code, art. 57.2; Uzbekistan: Penal Code, art. 51; Armenia: Penal Code, art. 60; Bulgaria: Penal Code, art. 38-2; Tajikistan: Penal Code, art. 58(1); and Ukraine: Penal Code, art. 64.2.

80. See, for example, the historical practices in the United Kingdom and Canada; Shani D'Cruze and Louise A. Jackson, *Women, Crime and Justice since 1660* (London: Palgrave Macmillan, 2009); Frank Murray Greenwood and Beverley Boissery, *Uncertain Justice: Canadian Women and Capital Punishment, 1754–1953* (Toronto: Dundurn Press, 2000).

81. Roy Walmsley, *World Female Imprisonment List,* 4th ed. (London: Institute for Criminal Policy Research, 2017), 2. See also Chapter 3.

82. *Khamtokhu and Aksenchik v. Russia,* ECtHR (Apps. 60367/08 and 961/11), January 24, 2017 [GC].

83. *Khamtokhu and Aksenchik v. Russia,* ECtHR (Apps. 60367/08 and 961/11), May 13, 2014 (admissibility decision).

84. Ibid., § 24.

85. Ibid.

86. Ibid., § 21.

87. *Khamtokhu and Aksenchik v. Russia,* January 24, 2017, § 82.

88. Ibid., concurring opinion of Judge Turković § 6.

89. Ibid., § 11.

5. Offenses That Carry Life

1. Albania, Algeria, Antigua and Barbuda, Argentina, Armenia, Aruba, Australia, Austria, Azerbaijan, Bahamas, Bahrain, Bangladesh, Barbados, Belarus, Belgium, Belize, Benin, Bhutan, Bolivia, Botswana, Brazil, Brunei Darussalam, Bulgaria, Burkina Faso, Burundi, Cambodia, Cameroon, Canada, Cayman Islands, Central African Republic, Chad, Chile, China, Colombia, Comoros, Côte d'Ivoire, Croatia, Cuba, Curacao, Cyprus, Czech Republic, Democratic Republic of Congo, Denmark, Djibouti, Dominica, Egypt, El Salvador, Eritrea, Estonia, Ethiopia, Fiji, Finland, France, Gabon, Gambia, Georgia, Germany, Ghana,

Greece, Guatemala, Republic of Guinea, Guyana, Haiti, Hawaii, Honduras, Hong Kong, Hungary, Iceland, India, Indonesia, Iran, Iraq, Ireland, Israel, Italy, Jamaica, Japan, Jordan, Kansas, Kazakhstan, Kenya, Kosovo, Kyrgyzstan, Laos, Latvia, Lebanon, Lesotho, Liberia, Lithuania, Luxemburg, Macedonia, Madagascar, Malawi, Malaysia, Mali, Malta, Mauritania, Mauritius, Mexico, Monaco, Mongolia, Montserrat, Morocco, Namibia, Nepal, Netherlands, New Zealand, Niger, Nigeria, Pakistan, Papua New Guinea, Peru, Philippines, Poland, Portugal, Romania, Russia, Rwanda, Senegal, Seychelles, Sierra Leone, Singapore, Slovakia, Slovenia, Somalia, South Africa, South Korea (Republic of Korea), South Sudan, Spain, Sri Lanka, St. Christopher and Nevis, Sudan, Swaziland, Sweden, Switzerland, Taiwan, Tajikistan, Tanzania, Thailand, Togo, Trinidad and Tobago, Tunisia, Turkey, Turkmenistan, Uganda, United Kingdom, Ukraine, United States, Uzbekistan, Vietnam, Zambia, and Zimbabwe. The number of offenses considered was further reduced, because in the case of federal countries (Australia, Mexico, the United Kingdom, and the United States) the offenses from the different internal jurisdictions were consolidated and counted only once, even if they appear in more than one jurisdiction within the country. For the United States we considered only state offenses from California, Florida, New York and Texas, as well as from the federal system, as indicative of the offenses for which life imprisonment may in law be imposed in the country as a whole. If all the US states had been considered, the list would have been longer, even allowing for overlaps.

2. See https://www.theguardian.com/uk/2013/mar/11/huhne-pryce-normal -sentence-crime.

3. A few offenses (23) did not seem to fit logically into any of these categories. However, they were not significant as we could not identify any persons actually sentenced to life imprisonment for having committed these offenses.

4. The only exceptions we found were Brazil and El Salvador that only have life imprisonment for military offenses other than murder, and Slovenia, where two or more murders must be committed before a life sentence can be imposed. No one was serving life imprisonment for any offense in Brazil or Slovenia, and we suspect that the situation is the same in El Salvador.

5. Among countries that provide for life imprisonment for some offenses, the following do not have life imprisonment for murder: Sierra Leone, Sri Lanka, and Sudan. In all three countries, murder is punishable by death. In some other countries, such as Brunei, Gambia, Ghana, Kenya, Malaysia, and Singapore, the death penalty is mandatory for murder, but not for attempted murder, which carries life imprisonment. These latter countries were coded as having life imprisonment for murder.

6. Such is, for instance, the case in Belgium: Penal Code, art. 518; France: Penal Code, art. 322-10; Greece: Penal Code, art. 264; Indonesia: Penal Code, art. 479f; Jordan: Penal Code, art. 372; Malta: Penal Code, art. 312; the Netherlands: Penal Code, s. 157; and Niger: Penal Code, arts. 384–385.

7. See, for example, in: Guatemala: Penal Code, art. 175; Jordan: Penal Code, art. 292; Macedonia: Penal Code, art. 188(4); Mali: Penal Code, art. 226; Peru: Penal Code, art. 173; Tajikistan: Penal Code, art. 138.3; Thailand: Penal Code, art. 27; and Vietnam: Penal Code, art. 112.

8. For example, in Cameroon: Penal Code, art. 346; India: Indian Penal Code, s. 376D; Liberia: Penal Code, art. 14.70.2; State of Mexico: Penal Code, art. 274.I; Pakistan: Penal Procedure Code, s. 376; Tanzania: Penal Code, art. 131.A.

9. That is the case, for example, in Algeria: Penal Code, art. 337; Côte d'Ivoire: Penal Code, art. 354; Egypt: Penal Code, art. 267; Haiti: Penal Code, art. 281; Mauritania: Penal Code, art. 310; Rwanda: Penal Code, art. 192.

10. See, for example, in France (Penal Code, art. 222–26), or in Djibouti (Penal Code, art. 346).

11. For example, in Madagascar, kidnapping is punishable by life imprisonment if it lasts more than a month (Penal Code, art. 342).

12. Albania, Algeria, Argentina, Austria, Bahrain, Bangladesh, Barbados, Belgium, Belize, Benin, Botswana, Brunei Darussalam, Bulgaria, Burkina Faso, Burundi, Cameroon, Canada, Central African Republic, Chad, Chile, China, Comoros, Côte d'Ivoire, Democratic Republic of Congo, Djibouti, Egypt, France, Gabon, Georgia, Germany, Ghana, Greece, Guatemala, Guinea (Republic of), Haiti, Honduras, Hong Kong, Hungary, Iceland, India, Iraq, Israel, Italy, Jamaica, Japan, Kosovo, Laos, Liberia, Luxembourg, Madagascar, Malaysia, Mali, Malta, Mauritania, Mexico, Montserrat, Morocco, Netherlands, Niger, Pakistan, Peru, Philippines, Rwanda, Senegal, Singapore, Slovakia, South Korea (Republic of Korea), St. Christopher and Nevis, Sweden, Switzerland, Taiwan, Thailand, Togo, Tunisia, Uganda, United States, Vietnam, Zimbabwe.

13. Argentina, Benin, Burkina Faso, Cameroon, Central African Republic, Chad, China, Comoros, Côte d'Ivoire, Democratic Republic of Congo, Djibouti, Gabon, Guinea (Republic of), Haiti, Israel, Japan, Kosovo, Luxemburg, Madagascar, Mauritania, Mexico, Morocco, Netherlands, Niger, South Korea (Republic of Korea), Taiwan, Togo, Tunisia, United States.

14. In Europe, Austria, Cyprus, Estonia, France, Georgia, Greece, Hungary, and Ireland have provisions for sentences of life imprisonment for drug-related offenses in their penal codes. Most of these have no one serving a life sentence for a drug offense. There is positive evidence in this regard that Austria, Estonia, France, Ireland, Luxemburg, Malta, and Romania have no such prisoners. Only in Georgia and in the United Kingdom do we have evidence of prisoners serving life imprisonment for drug offenses. See Appendix C.

15. Kidnapping carries a life sentence in: Argentina: Penal Code, art. 170; Belize: Penal Code, art. 54; Chile: Penal Code, arts. 141–142; Guatemala: Penal Code, art. 201; Honduras: Penal Code, art. 192; and Peru: Penal Code, art. 152; as do three states in Mexico, being Puebla: Penal Code, art. 302; Quintana Roo: Penal Code, art. 118;and Veracruz: Penal Code, art. 163. All of these provisions refer either to aggravated forms of kidnapping, or to kidnapping leading to death. The only example we found of a Latin American country that has a life sentence but not for kidnapping is Guyana.

16. The only relevant provision we found was in Guatemala, where Law for the Prevention of Drug Trafficking, art. 52, mentions a sentence of life imprisonment for certain drug-related offenses.

17. Castration is punishable by life imprisonment in: Algeria: Penal Code, art. 274; Benin: Penal Code, art. 316; Burkina Faso: Penal Code, art. 337; Central

African Republic: Penal Code, art. 77; Chad: Penal Code, art. 257; the Co-moros: Penal Code, art. 30; Côte d'Ivoire: Penal Code, art. 343; Gabon: Penal Code, art. 238; the Republic of Guinea: Penal Code, art. 305; Madagascar: Penal Code, art. 326; Morocco: Penal Code, art. 412, Niger: Penal Code, art. 232; Senegal: Penal Code, art. 304; and Tunisia: Penal Code, art. 221. Counterfeiting coinage is punishable by the same sentence in: Algeria: Penal Code, art. 197; Benin: Penal Code, art. 132; Burkina Faso: Penal Code, art. 250; Cameroon: Penal Code, art. 211; Central African Republic: Penal Code, art. 358; Chad: Penal Code, art. 175, the Comoros: Penal Code, art. 118; Côte d'Ivoire: Penal Code, art. 293; Gabon: Penal Code, art. 105, Republic of Guinea: Penal Code, art. 142; Madagascar: Penal Code, art. 132; Malawi: Penal Code, art. 372; Mali: Penal Code, art. 86; Mauritania: Penal Code; art. 129, Morocco: Penal Code, art. 334; Nigeria: Penal Code, art. 174; Senegal: Penal Code, art. 119; Tanzania: Penal Code, art. 354; Tunisia: Penal Code, art. 185; and Zambia: Penal Code, art. 364. The French Penal Code of 1810, which became applicable in West Africa in 1877, and which constitutes the basis for most of these texts, contains the same provisions on counterfeiting coinage (art. 132) and castration (art. 316).

18. In Slovenia, the Penal Code, art. 46, lists the offenses for which a life sentence may be imposed. The situation in Spain, which, in 2015, was the most recent European country to introduce life imprisonment, is similar. The Penal Code of Spain allows life sentences for only six offenses: certain specific forms of aggravated murder (art. 140); murder of the king or queen (art. 485); a terrorist act leading to death (art. 573 bis); murder of a foreign head of state, or other person protected under international law (art. 605); aggravated forms of genocide (art. 607); and aggravated crimes against humanity (art. 607 bis).

19. American Civil Liberties Union, *A Living Death* (New York: ACLU Foundation, 2013), 23, https://www.aclu.org/report/living-death-life-without -parole-nonviolent-offenses.

20. German Penal Code, § 38(2).

21. See Appendix B.

22. Barry Mitchell and Julian V. Roberts, *Exploring the Mandatory Life Sentence for Murder* (Oxford: Hart, 2012), 16.

23. German Penal Code, § 211(2). For a clear exposition in English of this issue in German Law, see Antje du Bois-Pedain, "Intentional Killings: The German Law," in *Homicide Law in Comparative Perspective,* ed. Jeremy Horder (Oxford, UK: Hart, 2007), 69–70.

24. According to the United Nations Office on Drugs and Crime (UNODC), in 2013, the homicide rate of the United Kingdom was 0.9 per 100,000 of popula-tion, and that of Germany was 0.8 per 100,000. UNODC statistics, https://data .unodc.org/.

25. Criminal Code of Canada, 1985, s. 231(2) and 231(8) with ss. 745(c) and 745.4.

26. Penal Code, art. 221-1.

27. Penal Code, art. 221-3. The life sentence is then mandatory, unless there are extenuating circumstances under the Penal Code, arts. 122-1 to 122-8.

28. Penal Code, art. 221-4, which includes a list of all aggravating factors.

29. Penal Code, arts. 221-4 and 132-23.

30. Such is the case, for example, in: Benin: Penal Code, art. 302; Burundi: Penal Code, art. 213; Chad: Penal Code, art. 246; Côte d'Ivoire: Penal Code; art. 343, Djibouti: Penal Code, art. 315; and Madagascar: Penal Code, art. 302. In some instances, where simple murder would carry a life sentence, the distinction between murder and assassination persists, but the more severe sentence prescribed is the death penalty. That is the case in Algeria: Penal Code, art. 261; Burkina Faso: Penal Code, art. 324; Cameroon: Penal Code, art. 276; the Central African Republic: Penal Code, art. 58; the Comoros: Penal Code, art. 286; the Democratic Republic of the Congo: Penal Code, art. 45; the Republic of Guinea: Penal Code, art. 286; Mauritania: Penal Code, art. 278; Morocco: Penal Code, art. 393; Niger: Penal Code, art. 243; and Tunisia: Penal Code, art. 201–204. In France itself, parricide and poisoning do not carry specific life sentences anymore, but the overall structure with respect to assassination remains unchanged.

31. Cal. Penal Code § 667. When this provision was introduced, in 1994, any third felony, even relatively minor ones, would automatically lead to life imprisonment. In 2012, Proposition 36 amended the provision, so that it currently requires a "serious or violent felony." See the memorandum posted in May 2016 by J. Richard Couzens and Tricia A. Bigelow, "The Amendment of the Three Strikes Sentencing Law," at http://www.courts.ca.gov/20142.htm.

32. Charles J. Ogletree and Austin Sarat, "Introduction," in *Life without Parole: America's New Death Penalty,* ed., Charles Ogletree and Austin Sarat (New York: New York University Press, 2012), 4–5.

33. Julian V. Roberts and Andrew von Hirsch, eds., *Previous Convictions at Sentencing Theoretical and Applied Perspectives,* (Oxford, UK: Hart, 2014), vi–viii.

34. Examples of countries that have special provisions dealing with the punishment of homicide, or attempted homicide, committed by convicted prisoners include Botswana: Penal Code, art. 218; Brunei: Penal Code, art. 307; Gambia: Penal Code, art. 201; the United States: 18 U.S. Code, § 1118; Ghana: Penal Code, art. 49; India: Indian Penal Code, art. 307; Malawi: Penal Code, art. 224; Uganda: Penal Code, art. 205; and Zambia: Penal Code, art. 216.

35. *Solem v. Helm,* 463 US 277 (1983).

36. Ibid., headnote.

37. *Rummel v. Estelle,* 445 US 263 (1980).

38. *Harmelin v. Michigan,* 501 US 957 (1991).

39. *Lockyer v. Andrade,* 538 US 63 (2003); *Ewing v. California,* 538 US 11 (2003).

40. Breyer J., with whom Stevens, Souter and Ginsburg, JJ, joined, dissenting in *Ewing.* See also the dissent by Souter, J, joined by Stevens, Ginsburg, and Breyer, JJ, in *Andrade.*

41. American Law Institute, "Model Penal Code: Sentencing, Proposed Final Draft" (approved May 24, 2017) 161Draft Model Penal Code, § 6.06 (2)(a).

42. Anthony Bottoms and Roger Brownsword, "Dangerousness and Rights," in *Dangerousness: Problems of Assessment and Prediction,* ed. John Hinton (London: George Allen and Unwin, 1983), 9.

43. Andrew von Hirsch and Andrew Ashworth, *Proportionate Sentencing* (Oxford, UK: Oxford University Press, 2005), ch. 4, "Extending Sentences for Dangerous Offenders? The Bottoms-Brownsword Model" 50–61, 52.

44. Ronald Dworkin, *Taking Rights Seriously,* (London: Duckworth, 1978), 11.

45. France: Criminal Procedure Code, art. 706-53-13

46. German Penal Code, § 66.

47. Greece: Penal Code, art. 90.

48. El Salvador: Penal Code, arts. 129, 149, and 150.

49. For example, in Ecuador, cumulative sentences cannot extend beyond 40 years: Penal Code, arts. 40 and 55. In Peru, the maximum fixed-term sentence, even for multiple offenses, is 35 years: Penal Code, art. 50. This maximum is 30 years in Paraguay (Law 3440/08 modifying the Penal Code, art. 38), in Venezuela (the Constitution, art. 44 and Penal Code, art. 94), and in the International Criminal Court (Statute of the International Criminal Court, art.78). In the Democratic Republic of the Congo, cumulative fixed-term sentences cannot exceed 20 years: Criminal Procedure Code, art. 27.

50. Allan Manson, "Multiple-Offense Sentencing: Looking for Pragmatism, Not a Unifying Principle," in *Sentencing Multiple Crimes,* ed. Jesper Ryber, Julian V. Roberts, and Jan W. de Keijser (New York: Oxford University Press, 2018).

51. In Finland, one person is serving a life sentence for genocide (committed in Rwanda); in the Netherlands, there is also one person serving life for multiple war crimes.

52. These figures are estimates for 2013. It is difficult to get precise figures, as offense types are not recorded by sentence length in German prison statistics. These figures are confirmed by calculations in other reports. See Axel Dessecker, *Die Vollstreckung lebenslanger Freiheitsstrafen* (Wiesbaden, Germany: Kriminologische Zentralstelle, 2016), who notes that since 1991, 96 percent of convictions leading to life imprisonment have been for murder (Penal Code, § 211).

53. There were 423 life-sentenced prisoners in Indonesia on September 1, 2014; 139 of them were serving such sentences for drug-related offenses. In addition, at least 54 people were on death row for such offenses on April 30, 2015; see Amnesty International, *Flawed Justice: Unfair Trials and the Death Penalty in Indonesia*, ASA 21/2434/2015 (London: Amnesty International, 2015), 22.

54. South Africa increased the number of life-sentenced prisoners from 408 in 1995 to 6,998 in 2006, and to almost double that number, 13,190, in 2014. See Chapter 3.

55. This information was drawn from Chris Giffard and Lukas Muntingh, *The Effect of Sentencing on the Size of the South African Prison Population* (Cape Town, South Africa: Open Society Foundation, 2006). We were unable to obtain a more recent breakdown of the overall life-sentenced prison population by offense. However, there is no reason to think that the pattern has changed, as the life-sentenced prison population has almost doubled again since 2006.

56. The eighteen countries on whom we had information on sentences of LWOP by offense for which it could be imposed were Australia, Belize, Cayman Islands, Ghana, Israel, Lebanon, Liberia, Lithuania, Malta, Morocco, Netherlands, New Zealand, Romania, Sierra Leone, Uganda, United Kingdom, Ukraine,

and the United States. Of these Belize, Israel, Lithuania, Malta, New Zealand, Romania, and Sierra Leone could impose LWOP only for homicide, and in most cases only for an aggravated form of the offense.

57. Figures calculated from Table 3, titled, "Crime of Conviction for LWOP, LWP, and Virtual Life-Sentenced Prisoners" in Ashley Nellis, *Still Life* (Washington, D.C.: The Sentencing Project, 2016), 18.

58. ACLU, *A Living Death: Life without Parole for Nonviolent Offenses* (New York: American Civil Liberties Union, 2013).

59. Craig S. Lerner, "Who's Really Sentenced to Life Without Parole?: Searching for 'Ugly Disproportionalities' in the American Criminal Justice System," *Wisconsin Law Review* 2015(5) (2015): 789–861, argues that many of the offenses regarded by the ACLU as nonviolent contain an element of violence.

6. Imposing Life

1. United Nations Office at Vienna, Crime Prevention and Criminal Justice Branch, *Life Imprisonment* (Vienna: United Nations, 1994), 16.

2. Andrew Novak, *The Global Decline of the Mandatory Death Penalty, Constitutional Jurisprudence and Legislative Reform in Africa, Asia and the Caribbean* (Farnham, UK: Ashgate, 2014).

3. In 2016, there were eighteen such states plus the District of Columbia. https://deathpenaltyinfo.org/life-without-parole#States.

4. Turkey: Criminal Code, art. 82.

5. *De Boucherville v. Government of Mauritius* [2008] UKPC 37, 25 B.H.R.C. 433.

6. For Privy Council judgments against mandatory death sentences in various jurisdictions, see *Reyes v. The Queen,* (2002) UKPC 11, (2002) 2 AC 235 (Belize); *Hughes v. The Queen,* (2002) UKPC 12, (2002) 2 AC 259 (St. Lucia); and *Fox v. The Queen,* (2002) UKPC 13, (2002) 2 AC 284 (St. Kitts and Nevis).

7. *R v. August* (Criminal Appeal 22 of 2012), Court of Appeal of Belize, November 4, 2016.

8. Constitution of Belize, ss. 6 and 7.

9. See *Reyes v. The Queen* (2002), which originated in Belize, and more generally Novak, *The Global Decline of the Mandatory Death Penalty,* ch. 4.

10. *August and Gabb v. The Queen,* 2018 CCJ 7 AJ March, 29, 2018.

11. *R v. Lichniak* [2002] UKHL 47, [2003] 1 AC 903, § 8 (Eng.).

12. BGHSt 30, 105, 109–110. (Ger.).

13. Gabrielle Kett-Straub, *Die lebenslange Freiheitsstrafe* (Tübingen, Germany: Mohr Siebeck, 2011), 89.

14. *R v. Latimer,* [2001] 1 SCR 3 (Can.). For a sociological account of the circumstances of this remarkable case, see Joane Martel, "Remorse and the Production of Truth," *Punishment and Society* 12 (2010): 414–437.

15. *R v. Morrisey,* [2000] SCC 39, [2000] 2 SCR 90 (Can.).

16. A similar justification for a mandatory life sentence for murder was adopted by the Supreme Court of Ireland in the face of an argument that it made

it impossible for a sentencing court to impose a proportionate sentence: *Lynch and Whelan v. Minister for Justice Equality and Law Reform and others* [2010] IESC 34, [2012] 1 IR 1 (Ir.).

17. These countries are the Bahamas, Bahrain, Bangladesh, Barbados, Belize, Brunei Darussalam, Chile, China, the Democratic Republic of the Congo, Egypt, Ethiopia, India, Iraq, Israel, Japan, Jamaica, Laos, Liberia, Malawi, Malaysia, Mali, Niger, Pakistan, Sri Lanka, Tajikistan, Thailand, Taiwan, Trinidad and Tobago, and the United States.

18. Chile, Liberia, Malawi, Mali, Niger, Singapore, Sri Lanka, South Sudan, Sudan, and Tajikistan.

19. Bahamas, Belize, Brunei Darussalam, India, Iraq, Malaysia, Thailand, and the United States.

20. Bahamas, Bangladesh, Belarus, Belize, Brunei Darussalam, Dominica, India, Iraq, Lebanon, Malaysia, Pakistan, Sri Lanka, St. Christopher and Nevis, Tajikistan, Thailand, and the United States.

21. *Union of India v. Sriharan alias Murugan and Others* (2015), WP (Crl), No. 48 of 2014 (India).

22. See Firearms (Increased Penalties) Act 1971, s. 7—trafficking in firearms; Penal Code, art. 121—waging war against a ruler; and various offenses under the Strategic Trade Act 2010.

23. Note, "A Matter of Life and Death" *Harvard Law Review* 119 (2006): 1838–1854; Carol S. Steiker and Jordan M. Steiker, "Opening a Window or Building a Wall? The Effect of Eighth Amendment Death Penalty Law and Advocacy on Criminal Justice More Broadly," *University of Pennsylvania Journal of Constitutional Law* 11 (2008–2009): 155–205.

24. *Simmons v. South Carolina,* 512 US 154 (1994).

25. *Ring v. Arizona,* 536 US 584 (2002).

26. Note, "A Matter of Life and Death"; Christopher Seeds, "Bifurcation Nation: American Penal Policy in Late Mass Incarceration," *Punishment and Society* 19 (2017): 590–610.

27. Such provisions can be found, among others, in the penal codes of Benin: art. 463; Burkina Faso: art. 81; Burundi: art. 34; Cameroon: art. 90; the DRC: art. 18; Gabon: art. 45; Madagascar: art. 463; Mali: art. 18; Morocco: art. 146; Niger: art. 53; Rwanda: art. 76; and Somalia: art. 119. Similar provisions can be found around the world, for instance, in the penal codes of: Bhutan: arts. 17 and 23; Vietnam: art. 46; Japan: art. 14; Laos: art. 40; Armenia: art. 64; Belgium: arts. 79 and 80; Greece: art. 83 and 84) Iraq: art. 130; and Jordan: art. 99.

28. Criminal Code, art. 36. We have been able to locate similar provisions in the Penal Codes of Benin: art. 463; the DRC: art. 8; Laos: art. 40; and Armenia: art. 64.

29. Penal Code, art. 130.

30. Greece: Penal Code, art. 83; Rwanda: Penal Code, art. 78; Cameroon: Penal Code, art. 90.

31. Penal Code, art. 14.

32. Belgium: Penal Code, art. 80; Mali: Penal Code, art. 18; Somalia: Penal Code, art. 119; Taiwan: Penal Code, art. 65; Algeria: Penal Code, art. 294; Burkina Faso: Penal Code, art. 81; Morocco: Penal Code, art. 146.

33. Penal Code, art. 121.

34. Penal Code, art. 122-1.

35. Criminal Law Amendment Act 1997, s. 51, read with Part 1 of Schedule 2 to the same act.

36. *S v. Malgas,* (2) SA 1222 (SCA) (S. Afr.) § 25.

37. *S v. Dodo* 2001 (3) SA 382 (CC) (S. Afr.).

38. Catherine Appleton and Dirk Van Zyl Smit, "The Paradox of Reform: Life Imprisonment in England and Wales," in *Life Imprisonment and Human Rights,* ed. Dirk van Zyl Smit and Catherine Appleton (Oxford, UK: Hart, 2016), 223.

39. Legal Aid, Sentencing and Punishment of Offenders Act 2012, s. 122.

40. See also the similar legislation in New Zealand: *R v Harrison* [2016] NZCA 381, [2016] 3 NZLR 602 (N.Z.).

41. Jamil Mjuzi, "Life Imprisonment and Human Rights in Uganda," in *Life Imprisonment and Human Rights*, 99–100.

42. Project questionnaire, Pakistan, October 8, 2015.

43. Statute of the International Criminal Court, art. 77.

44. Rules of Procedure and Evidence of the ICC, ch. 7, rule 145.

45. See Table 9.1 in Chapter 9.

46. Criminal Code, art. 57. The German release process is described more fully in Chapter 9.

47. BVerfGE 86, 288. (Ger.).

48. Ibid., 340–354.

49. Ibid., 354.

50. Walter Stree, "Neue Probleme der Aussetzung einer lebenslangen Freiheitstrafe," *Neue Zeitschrift für Strafrecht* 13 (1992): 464–468; Renate Elf, "Die Relativierung der lebenslangen Freiheitsstrafe für Mord durch die rechtsgestaltende Wirkung der Rechtsprechung des BVerfG und der Strafgerichte," *Neue Zeitschrift für Strafrecht* 13(1992): 468–470; Ernst Stark, "Die lebenslange Freiheitsstrafe nach der Entscheidung des BVerfG vom 3. Juni 1992," *Juristen Zeitung* 1994, 189–191.

51. N.Y. Penal Law § 70.10 with § 70.00 (2017).

52. *People v. Smart,* 100 A.D.3d 1473, 954 N.Y.S.2d 322 (2012), aff'd, 23 N.Y.3d 213, 12 N.E.3d 1061 (2014).

53. Sentencing Act 2002, as amended, art. 102: "Presumption in favour of life imprisonment for murder."

54. Ibid., art. 103.

55. Penal Code, art. 132–23. See also Martine Herzog-Evans, *Droit de l'Exécution des Peines,* 5th ed. (Paris: Dalloz, 2016), 383–384. In French courts, a mixed bench of judges and jurors takes these decisions on appeal, the procedure is sometimes challenged but reasons for adopting a particular minimum period are not required or recorded in the appellate judgments: Laurent Griffon, "La computation de la période de sûreté," *Actualité juridique pénale*, 2013, 595–596.

56. The French Penal Code, art. 221-3, limits this to murders where the victim is a minor under fifteen, where the murder was accompanied by rape, torture or barbaric acts, or to the murder of a police or military police officer, a judge, a

penitentiary officer, or any other person of public authority, if the act was committed while they were on duty or because of their public role.

57. Maria Ejchart-Dubois, Maria Niełaczna, and Aneta Wilkowska-Płóciennik, "The Right to Hope for Lifers: An Analysis of Court Judgments and Practice in Poland," in *Life Imprisonment and Human Rights,* 380–381.

58. Criminal Justice Act 1991, s. 34; *R (Anderson) v. Secretary of State for the Home Department* [2002] UKHL 46, [2003] 1 AC 837 (HL) (Eng.).

59. Criminal Justice Act 2003, Schedule 21. Andrew Ashworth, *Sentencing and Criminal Justice,* 6th ed. (Cambridge: Cambridge University Press, 2015), 124–127.

60. Barry Mitchell and Julian Roberts, *Exploring the Mandatory Life Sentence for Murder* (Oxford, UK: Hart, 2012): 44–46.

61. In the British Virgin Islands, the mandatory sentence for murder is life imprisonment: Criminal Code 1997, ss. 23 and 150. The Parole Act 1997, s. 9(2), provides that a judge sentencing a person to life imprisonment is required to state whether that person may be eligible for parole and, if so, to set a minimum period before the person may be considered for parole.

62. See *Milton and another v. The Queen (British Virgin Islands)* [2015] UKPC 42, where the Privy Council, which is the court of final instance for the British Virgin Islands, noted with gentle irony: "The courts [of the British Virgin Islands] are entitled to look for guidance to sentencing practices in other countries, but the Board would not recommend that they bind themselves too closely to the regime of a particular country, including the UK. Local judges are in the best position to assess the appropriate tariff in their jurisdiction, subject to their own statutory provisions" (§ 33).

63. Conditional Release Law, 2014, s. 14 (Cayman Islands).

64. See Appendix B; Marcelo Aebi, Mélanie Tiago and Christine Burkhardt, *SPACE I—Council of Europe Annual Penal Statistics: Prison Populations, Survey 2014* (Strasbourg, France: Council of Europe, 2016), Table 7.

65. See the Convention Rights (Compliance) (Scotland) Act 2001 (ASP 7).

66. Project questionnaire, Malta, September 1, 2014.

67. *MacKenzie v. Stanford,* Index No. 2789/15 at 1*-2*(N.Y. Sup. Ct. 2016). See also Chapter 7.

68. *August and Gabb v. The Queen,* CCJ, March, 29, 2018, § 137.

69. Penal Code, art. 50. Michelle Miao, "Two years between life and death: A critical analysis of the suspended death penalty in China," *International Journal of Law, Crime and Justice* 45 (2016): 26–43. Huang G. "Death Penalty in China after the Ninth Amendment: Legislatively Abolishing and Judicially Limiting" *Journal of Forensic Science and Criminology* 4(3) (2016): 303.

70. "Kenya Commutes Sentences of All Death Row Inmates," *The Independent,* October 25, 2016, http://www.independent.co.uk/news/world/africa/kenya-death-row-inmates-spare-live-commute-sentence-a7378751.html; Penal Reform International, *The Abolition of the Death Penalty and Its Alternative Sanction* in East Africa: Kenya and Uganda (London: Penal Reform International, 2012).

71. *Muruatetu and Mwangi v. Republic* (Petitions 15 and 15 of 2015) Supreme Court, December 14, 2017 (Kenya).

72. Andrew Novak, *Comparative Executive Clemency: The Constitutional Pardon Power and the Prerogative of Mercy in Global Perspective* (London: Routledge, 2016), 153.

73. *Schick v. Reed*, 419 US 256 (1974), discussed in Chapter 2.

74. See http://www.deathpenaltyinfo.org/clemency#process, accessed December 26, 2016.

75. *Lendore and others v. Attorney General of Trinidad and Tobago*, Civ App Nos 01, 10, 13, 14 and 19 of 2010; [2017] UKPC 25.

76. *Harmelin v. Michigan*, 501 US 957, 1008 (1991).

77. *Bordenkircher v. Hayes*, 434 US 357 (1978).

78. Bernard Harcourt, *Against Prediction: Profiling, Policing, and Punishing in an Actuarial Age* (Chicago: University of Chicago Press, 2007). In the United States, the concern is often that actuarial risk instruments reproduce racial bias in sentencing, as previous convictions become a proxy for race. It is claimed that this is not necessarily the case but that it depends on the type of instrument used: Jennifer Skeem and Christopher Lowenkamp, "Risk, Race and Recidivism: Predictive Bias and Disparate Impact," *Criminology* 54 (2016): 680–712.

79. *R v. Hodgson* [1967] 52 Cr App R 113, 114 [1968] Crim. L.R. 46 (Eng.).

80. *R v. McNee, Gunn and Russell* [2007] EWCA Crim 1529, [2008] 1 Cr App R (S) 108 [109] (Eng.).

81. For an overview, see Julian Roberts, "Listening to the Crime Victim: Evaluating Victim Input at Sentencing and Parole," *Crime and Justice* 38 (2009): 347–412.

7. Doing Life

1. See Gresham Sykes, *The Society of Captives* (Princeton, N.J.: Princeton University Press, 1958); Erving Goffman, *Asylums* (London: Penguin, 1961); Stanley Cohen and Laurie Taylor, *Psychological Survival: The Experience of Long-Term Imprisonment* (Harmondsworth, UK: Penguin Books, 1972); Timothy Flanagan, ed., *Long-Term Imprisonment: Policy, Science, and Correctional Practice* (London: Sage Publications, 1995).

2. Wilfried Rasch, "The Effects of Indeterminate Detention: A Study of Men Sentenced to Life Imprisonment," *International Journal of Law and Psychiatry"* 4 (1981): 417–431; P. Banister, F. Smith, K. Heskin, and N. Bolton, "Psychological Correlates of Long-Term Imprisonment I: Cognitive Variables," *British Journal of Criminology* 13 (1973): 312–323; P. Banister, F. Smith, K. Heskin, and N. Bolton, "Psychological Correlates of Long-Term Imprisonment II: Personality Variables," *British Journal of Criminology* 13 (1973): 323–330; Alison Liebling and Shadd Maruna "Introduction," in *The Effects of Imprisonment,* ed. Alison Liebling and Shadd Maruna (Cullompton, Devon, UK: Willan, 2005).

3. Alison Liebling, *Prisons and Their Moral Performance: A Study of Values, Quality and Prison Life* (Oxford, UK: Oxford University Press, 2004).

4. Craig Haney, "Prison Effects in the Age of Mass Incarceration," *The Prison Journal*, July 25, 2012, 1–24.

5. Craig Hemmens and James Marquart, "Straight Time: Inmate's Perceptions of Violence and Victimization in the Prison Environment," *Journal of Offender Rehabilitation* 28 (1999): 1–21; E. Gullone, T. Jones, and R. Cummins, "Coping Styles and Prison Experience as Predictors of Psychological Well-Being in Male Prisoners," *Psychiatry, Psychology and Law* 7 (2000): 170–181.

6. Haney, "Prison Effects in the Age of Mass Incarceration," 12.

7. Ibid.; Laura Gibson, John Holt, Karen Fondacaro, Tricia Tang, Thomas Powell, and Erin Turbitt, "An Examination of Antecedent Traumas and Psychiatric Co-Morbidity among Male Inmates with PTSD," *Journal of Traumatic Stress* 12 (1999): 473–484; Susan Greene, Craig Haney, and Aída Hurtado, "Cycles of Pain: Risk Factors in the Lives of Incarcerated Women and Their Children," *Prison Journal* 80 (2000): 3–23; Dorothy McClellan, David Farabee, and Ben Crouch, "Early Victimization, Drug Use, and Criminality: A Comparison of Male and Female Prisoners," *Criminal Justice and Behavior* 24 (1997): 455–476; Janet Mullings, Deborah Hartley, and James Marquart, "Exploring the Relationship between Alcohol Use, Childhood Maltreatment, and Treatment Needs among Female Prisoners," *Substance Use and Misuse* 39 (2004): 277–305; Catherine Appleton, *Life after Life Imprisonment* (Oxford, UK: Oxford University Press, 2010).

8. Adolf Vischer, *Barbed-Wire Disease: A Psychological Study of the Prisoner of War* (London: John Bale and Danielson, 1919), cited in Timothy Flanagan, "Dealing with Long-Term Confinement," *Criminal Justice and Behavior* 8 (1981): 201–222, 202; see also Avi Ohry and Zahava Solomon, "Dr Adolf Lukas Vischer (1884–1974) and 'barbed-wire disease,'" *Journal of Medical Biography*, 22 (2014): 16–18. For an early account of "mental disease" in English prisons, see also Lionel Fox, *The Modern English Prison* (London: Routledge and Kegan Paul, 1934), 108–111.

9. Max Grünhut, *Penal Reform: A Comparative Study* (Oxford, UK: Oxford University Press, 1948), cited in Dennis Chapman, *Sociology and the Stereotype of the Criminal* (London: Routledge, 1968), 231.

10. A. J. Taylor, "Social Isolation and Imprisonment," *Psychiatry* 24 (1961): 373–376, 373.

11. Cohen and Taylor, *Psychological Survival,* 115.

12. Sykes, *The Society of Captives,* xiv.

13. Goffman, *Asylums,* 16.

14. Ibid., 11.

15. Ibid., 43.

16. Ibid., 50.

17. Flanagan, "Dealing with Long-Term Confinement," 203.

18. John Irwin and Donald Cressey, "Thieves, Convicts and the Inmate Culture," *Social Problems* 10 (1962): 142–155. See also Leo Carroll, *Hacks, Blacks and Cons: Race Relations in a Maximum Security Prison* (Long Grove, Ill.: Waveland, 1974); James Jacobs "Street Gangs behind Bars," *Social Problems* 21 (1974): 395–409; John Irwin, "The Changing Social Structure of the Men's Prison," in *Corrections and Punishment,* ed. David Greenberg (Beverly Hills, Calif.: SAGE, 1977); James Jacobs, *Stateville: The Penitentiary in Mass Society* (Chicago: University of Chicago Press, 1977); and Loïc Wacquant, "Deadly

Symbiosis: When Ghetto and Prison Meet and Mesh," *Punishment and Society* 3 (2001): 95–134.

19. See John Irwin, *Prisons in Turmoil* (Boston: Little Brown, 1981).

20. Banister., Smith, Heskin, and Bolton, "Psychological Correlates of Long-Term Imprisonment I: Cognitive Variables," 312–323; K. Heskin, N. Bolton., F. Smith, and P. Banister, "Psychological Correlates of Long-Term Imprisonment III: Attitudinal Variables," *British Journal of Criminology* 14 (1974): 150–157; Robert Sapsford, "Life Sentence Prisoners: Psychological Changes during Sentence," *British Journal of Criminology* 16 (1978): 128–145; L. Bukstel and P. Kilmann, "Psychological Effects of Imprisonment on Confined Individuals," *Psychological Bulletin* 88 (1980): 469–493; Flanagan, "Dealing with Long-Term Confinement"; Nigel Walker, "The Side-Effects of Incarceration," *British Journal of Criminology* 23 (1983): 61–71.

21. Doris MacKenzie and Lynne Goodstein, "Long-term incarceration: impacts and characteristics of long-term offenders, an empirical analysis," *Criminal Justice and Behavior* 12 (1985): 395–414; J. Stephen Wormwith, "The Controversy over the Effects of Long-Term Imprisonment," *Canadian Journal of Criminology* 26 (1984): 423–437. See also Liebling and Maruna, "Introduction," 1–29.

22. Rasch, "The Effects of Indeterminate Detention," 423.

23. Monika Reed and Francis Glamser, "Aging in a Total Institution: The Case of Older Prisoners," *Gerontologist* 19 (1978): 354–360, 354.

24. Seth Goldsmith, "Jailhouse Medicine—Travesty of Justice?" *Health Services Report* 87 (1972): 767–774.

25. James Bonta and Paul Gendreau, "Reexamining the Cruel and Unusual Punishment of Prison Life," *Law and Human Behavior* 14 (1990): 347–372, 357.

26. Banister, Smith, Heskin, and Bolton, "Psychological Correlates," 312–323; Heskin, Bolton, Smith, and Banister, "Psychological Correlates," 150–157; N. Bolton, F. Smith, K. Heskin and P. Banister, "Psychological Correlates of Long-Term Imprisonment IV: A Longitudinal Analysis," *British Journal of Criminology* 16 (1976): 38–47.

27. Rasch, "The Effects of Indeterminate Detention," 423, 424.

28. Sapsford, "Life Sentence Prisoners."

29. Timothy Flanagan, "Adaptation and Adjustment among Long-Term Prisoners," in *Long-Term Imprisonment: Policy, Science, and Correctional Practice,* 111.

30. See Wormwith, "The Controversy over the Effects of Long-Term Imprisonment."

31. Mortiz Liepmann, *Die Todestrafe: Sonderabdruck aus den Verhandlungen des 31. Deutschen Juristentages* (Berlin: Gutenplan, 1912), 186.

32. BVErfGE 45 187 (Ger.).

33. See, for example, Edward Zamble, "Behaviour and Adaption in Long-Term Prison Inmates: Descriptive Longitudinal Results," *Criminal Justice and Behavior* 19 (1992): 409–425; Kenneth Adams, "Adjusting to Prison Life," *Crime and Justice* 16 (1993): 275–359; Alison Liebling, "Prison Suicide and Prisoner Coping," in *Prisons, Crime and Justice: A Review of the Research,* vol. 26, ed., Michael Tonry and Joan Petersilia (Chicago: University of Chicago Press, 1999); Liebling, *Prisons and Their Moral Performance;* Alison Liebling, Susie Hulley, and Ben Crewe, "Conceptualising and Measuring the Quality of Prison Life," in *The*

SAGE Handbook of Criminological Research Methods, ed. David Gadd, Susanne Karstedt, and Steven Messner (London: SAGE Publications, 2012).

34. Frank Porporino, "Differences in Response to Long-Term Imprisonment: Implications for the Management of Long-Term Offenders," *Prison Journal* 80 (1990): 35–36.

35. Ibid., 36.

36. Bonta and Gendreau "Reexamining," 347–372.

37. Alison Liebling, "Doing Research in Prison: Breaking the Silence?," *Theoretical Criminology* 3 (1999): 147–173, 167.

38. Ben Crewe, "Depth, Weight, Tightness: Revisiting the Pains of Imprisonment," *Punishment and Society* 13 (2011): 509–529.

39. As adopted by King and McDermott in Roy King and Kathleen McDermott, *The State of Our Prisons* (Oxford, UK: Oxford University Press, 1996), 90.

40. Alison Liebling, "Moral Performance, Inhuman and Degrading Treatment and Prison Pain," *Punishment and Society* 13 (2011): 530–550, 536.

41. Ibid., 536.

42. See especially Hans Toch, "The Long-Term Prisoner as a Long-Term Problem," in *Long-Term Imprisonment: An International Seminar;* Timothy Flanagan, "The Pains of Long-Term Imprisonment," *British Journal of Criminology* 20 (1982): 148–156; Edward Zamble and Frank Porporino, *Coping, Behavior, and Adaptation in Prison Inmates* (New York: Springer-Verlag, 1988); Barry Mitchell, *Murder and Penal Policy* (London: Palgrave Macmillan, 1990); Margaret Leigey, *The Forgotten Men: Serving a Life without Parole Sentence* (New Brunswick, N.J.: Rutgers University Press, 2015); Robert Johnson and Sandra McGunigall-Smith, "Life without Parole, America's Other Death Penalty: Notes on Life under Sentence of Death by Incarceration," *The Prison Journal* 88 (2008): 328–346; Yvonne Jewkes, "Loss, Liminality and the Life Sentence: Managing Identity through a Disrupted Lifecourse," in *The Effects of Imprisonment;* Elaine Crawley, "Institutional Thoughtlessness in Prisons and Its Impacts on the Day-to-Day Prison Lives of Elderly," *Journal of Contemporary Criminal Justice* 21 (2005): 350–363.

43. Marc Mauer, Ryan King, and Malcolm Young, *The Meaning of "Life": Long Prison Sentences in Context* (Washington, D.C.: The Sentencing Project, 2004), 15.

44. Manuela Dudeck, Kirstin Drenkhahn, Carsten Spitzer, Sven Barnow, Philipp Kuwert, Harald Freyberger, and Frieder Dünkel, "Traumatization and Mental Distress in Long-Term Prisoners in Europe," *Punishment and Society* 13 (2011): 403–423.

45. Marieke Liem and Maarten Kunst, "Is There a Recognizable Post-Incarceration Syndrome among Released 'Lifers'?," *International Journal of Law and Psychiatry* 36 (2013): 333–337, 334. Although these studies emphasized the greater prevalence of mental health illnesses among individuals serving long sentences, little is known about whether prison time leads to the development of these problems or whether it merely exacerbates a preexisiting condition: see Jason Schnittker, Michael Massoglia, and Christopher Uggen, "Out and Down: Incarceration and Psychiatric Disorders," *Journal of Health and Social Behavior* 53 (2012): 448–464. Some are undoubtedly preexisting conditions, some are

aggravated by the harshness and stress of imprisonment, and others may originate in the trauma and chronic pains generated by prison experiences: Craig Haney, "The Wages of Prison Overcrowding: Harmful Psychological Consequences and Dysfunctional Correctional Reactions," *Washington University Journal of Law and Policy* 22 (2006): 265–293.

46. John Irwin and Barbara Owen, "Harm and the Contemporary Prison," in *The Effects of Imprisonment*, 94.

47. MacKenzie and Goodstein, "Long-Term Incarceration," 409.

48. Hans Toch and Kenneth Adams, with J. Douglas Grant, *Coping: Maladaptation in Prisons* (New Brunswick, N.J.: Transaction Publishers, 1989). See also Banister, Smith, Heskin, and Bolton, "Psychological Correlates," 312–323; Timothy Flanagan, "Time-Served and Institutional Misconduct: Patterns of Involvement in Disciplinary Infractions among Long-Term and Short-Term Inmates," *Journal of Criminal Justice* 8 (1980): 357–367; Heskin, Bolton, Smith, and Banister, "Long-Term Imprisonment III: Attitudinal Variables"; Hans Toch and Kenneth Adams, *Acting Out: Maladaptive Behavior in Confinement* (Washington, D.C.: American Psychological Association, 2002); Margaret Leigey, "For the Longest Time: The Adjustment of Inmates to a Sentence of Life without Parole," *The Prison Journal* 90 (2010): 247–268; Leigey, *The Forgotten Men;* Sapsford, "Life Sentence Prisoners"; Zamble, "Behaviour and Adaption in Long-Term Prison Inmates"; Zamble and Porporino, *Coping, Behavior, and Adaptation in Prison Inmates.*

49. William Palmer, "Programming for Long-Term Inmates," in *Long-Term Imprisonment: Policy, Science, and Correctional Practice*, 220.

50. Donald Clemmer, *The Prison Community* (New York: Holt, Rinehart and Winston, 1958), 299. See also Donald Clemmer, "The Process of Prisonization," in *The Sociology of Corrections: A Book of Readings,* ed. Robert Leger and John Stratton (New York: John Wiley and Sons, 1977); Lloyd Ohlin, *Sociology and the Field of Corrections* (New York: Russell Sage Foundation, 1956); Joycelyn Pollock, "The Social World of the Prisoner," in *Prisons: Today and Tomorrow,* ed. Joycelyn Pollock (Gaithersburg, Md.: Aspen Publishers, 1997); and Wayne Gillespie, *Prisonization: Individual and Institutional Factors Affecting Inmate Conduct* (New York: LFB Scholarly Publishing, 2003).

51. Donald Clemmer, "Observations on Imprisonment as a Source of Criminality," *Journal of Criminal Law and Criminology,* 41(1950): 311–319, 316.

52. Johnson and McGunigall-Smith, "Life without parole, America's Other Death Penalty," 338.

53. Cohen and Taylor, *Psychological Survival;* Zamble, "Behaviour and Adaption in Long-Term Prison Inmates"; Appleton, *Life after Life Imprisonment.*

54. John Irwin, *The Warehouse Prison: Disposal of the New Dangerous Class* (Los Angeles, Calif.: Roxbury Publishing, 2005), 154.

55. Ibid., 166.

56. MacKenzie and Goodstein, "Long-Term Incarceration"; Brent Paterline and David Petersen, "Structural and Social Psychological Determinants of Prisonization," *Journal of Criminal Justice* 27 (1999): 427–441; Glenn Walters, "Changes in Criminal Thinking and Identity in Novice and Experienced

Inmates," *Criminal Justice and Behavior* 30 (2003): 399–421; Haney, "Prison Effects of the Age of Mass Incarceration."

57. Craig Haney, *Reforming Punishment: Psychological Limits to the Pains of Imprisonment* (Washington, D.C.: American Psychological Association, 2006).

58. See Flanagan, "Dealing with Long-Term Confinement"; Zamble, "Behaviour and Adaption in Long-Term Prison Inmates"; Jewkes, "Loss, Liminality and the Life Sentence"; Appleton, *Life after Life Imprisonment;* Marguerite Schinkel, "Punishment as Moral Communication: The Experiences of Long-Term Prisoners," 16 (2014): 578–597; Ian O'Donnell, *Prisoners, Solitude and Time* (Oxford, UK: Oxford University Press, 2014).

59. John Irwin, *Lifers: Seeking Redemption in Prison* (New York: Routledge, 2009); Robert Johnson and Ania Dobrzanska, "Mature Coping among Life-Sentenced Inmates: An Exploratory Study of Adjustment Dynamics," *Corrections Compendium* (November–December 2005): 8–38; Appleton, *Life after Life Imprisonment;* Leigey, *The Forgotten Men;* Mark Pettigrew, "Deterioration and the Long-Term Prisoner: A Descriptive Analysis of Myra Hindley," *International Journal of Prisoner Health,* 12 (2016): 115–126.

60. Ben Crewe, Susie Hulley, and Serena Wright, "Swimming with the Tide: Adapting to Long-Term Imprisonment," *Justice Quarterly* 34 (2017): 517–541, 527, 517.

61. Ruth Jamieson and Adrian Grounds, "Release and Adjustment: Perspectives from Studies of Wrongly Convicted and Politically Motivated Prisoners," in *The Effects of Imprisonment.*

62. Ibid.; John Coker and John Martin, *Licensed to Live* (Oxford, UK: Basil Blackwell, 1985); Appleton, *Life after Life Imprisonment;* Melissa Munn and Chris Bruckert, *On the Outside: From Lengthy Imprisonment to Lasting Freedom* (Vancouver, Canada: University of British Columbia Press, 2013); Marieke Liem and Maarten Kunst, "Is There a Recognizable Post-Incarceration Syndrome among Released 'Lifers'?," *International Journal of Law and Psychiatry* 36 (2013): 333–337; Marieke Liem, *After Life Imprisonment* (New York: New York University Press, 2016).

63. See Chapter 10.

64. Cohen and Taylor, *Psychological Survival,* 99.

65. Jack Abbott, *In the Belly of the Beast* (New York: Vintage Books, 1981), 44–45.

66. Quoted in Howard Zehr, *Doing Life: Reflections of Men and Women Serving Life Sentences* (Akron, Pa.: Mennonite Central Committee, 1996), 47. See also Max Rutherford and Joanna Keil, "The Stress of Helplessness," *Inside Time,* October 8, 2008, https://insidetime.org/the-stress-of-helplessness/.

67. Ibid., 58; 14; 60 and 86, respectively.

68. Tony Parker, *Life after Life; Interviews with Twelve Murderers* (London: Pan Books), 212–213.

69. Serena Wright, Ben Crewe, and Susie Hulley "Suppression, Denial, Sublimation: Defending against the Initial Pains of Very Long Life Sentences," *Theoretical Criminology* 21 (2017): 225–246, 232.

70. Quoted in Zehr, *Doing Life,* 16.

71. Ibid., 103.

72. Johnson and McGunigall-Smith, "Life without Parole: America's Other Death Penalty," 339.

73. Quoted in Zehr, *Doing Life,* 44.

74. Quoted in Johnson and McGunigall-Smith, "Life without Parole: America's Other Death Penalty," 344.

75. Jewkes, "Loss, Liminality and the Life Sentence," 366.

76. Quoted in Johnson and McGunigall-Smith, "Life without Parole: America's Other Death Penalty," 6.

77. Quoted in Parker, *Life after Life,* 163–164.

78. Johnson and Dobrzanska, "Mature Coping among Life-Sentenced Inmates," 37.

79. John McGrath, "Time," *Scottish Child,* June–July 1992, 17, cited in Vivien Stern, *A Sin Against the Future: Imprisonment in the World* (Harmondsworth, UK: Penguin Books), 186. See also Abbott, *In the Belly of the Beast.*

80. Erwin James, *A Life Inside: A Prisoner's Notebook* (London: Atlantic Books, 2005), 60.

81. Quoted in Johnson and McGunigall-Smith, "Life without Parole: America's Other Death Penalty," 338.

82. Jens Soering, *One Day in the Life of 179212: Notes from an American Prison* (New York: Lantern Books, 2012), 18.

83. Johnson and McGunigall-Smith, "Life without Parole: America's Other Death Penalty," 338.

84. Quoted in Zehr, *Doing Life,* 11.

85. Erin George, *A Woman Doing Life: Notes from a Prison for Women* (Oxford, UK: Oxford University Press, 2010), 34.

86. Quoted in Zehr, *Doing Life,* 76.

87. Ibid., 88.

88. Ibid., 71.

89. Stephanie Walker and Anne Worrall, "Life as a Woman: The Gendered Pains of Indeterminate Imprisonment," *Prison Service Journal* 132 (2000): 27–37.

90. Ben Crewe, Suzie Hulley, and Serena Wright, "The Gendered Pains of Imprisonment," *British Journal of Criminology* 57 (2017), 1359–1378, 1359.

91. Ibid., 1368.

92. Ibid.

93. Walker and Worrall, "Life as a Woman," 28. See also Marion Vannier, "Women Serving Life without the Possibility of Parole: The Different Meanings of Death as Punishment," *Howard Journal of Crime and Justice,* 55 (2016): 328–344.

94. The importance of the right to family life as part of the process of rehabilitation was confirmed in *Dickson v. United Kingdom,* ECtHR (app. 44362/04), December 4, 2007, as discussed in Chapter 8.

95. Hans Toch, *Mosaic of Despair: Human Breakdowns in Prison* (Washington, D.C.: American Psychological Association, 1992), 386.

96. Jimmy Boyle, *A Sense of Freedom* (London: Pan Books, 1977), 179.

97. O'Donnell, *Prisoners, Solitude and Time,* 223.

98. Quoted in Glenn Abraham, "Prisoners Serving Sentences of Life without Parole: A Qualitative Study and Survey" (PhD diss., University of Kentucky Doctoral Dissertations, 2011), 117.

99. Toch, *Mosaic of Despair: Human Breakdowns in Prison.* See also Flanagan, "The Pains of Long-Term Imprisonment."

100. Quoted in Zehr, *Doing Life,* 64.

101. Kenneth Hartman, ed., *Too Cruel, Not Unusual Enough: An Anthology Published by the Other Death Penalty Project* (Lancaster, Calif.: The Other Death Penalty Project, 2013), 173, 29, 125 and 147, respectively.

102. Dortell Williams, "Making Sense Out of Life without the Possibility of Parole," in *Too Cruel, Not Unusual Enough,* 43. Similarly, in recent years, scholars refer to this extreme form of punishment as, for example a "death in prison" sentence (Jessica Henry, "Death-in-Prison Sentences: Overutilized and Underscrtinized," in *Life without Parole: America's New Death Penalty?* ed. Charles Ogletree and Austin Sarat (New York: New York University Press, 2012), 66–95; or, as Sliva suggests, a "civil death for the prisoner, who is sentenced to live a shadow life within the walls of the prison and die behind bars": Shannon Sliva, "On the Meaning of Life: A Qualitative Interpretive Meta Synthesis of the Lived Experience of Life without Parole," *Journal of Social Work* 15 (2015): 498–515, 500.

103. Dina Potter, "Diplomat's Son Seeks Deportation," *Fredericksburg.com,* February 24, 2011, http://www.fredericksburg.com/local/diplomat-s-son-seeks -deportation/article_def97b13-4420-5f5d-bf08-30906fe8c290.html. Soering experienced despair despite having a large support group who continue to assert his innocence and argue for his transfer to Germany; see his website, http://www .jenssoering.com/. See also Chapter 9.

104. See also Catherine Appleton and Bent Grøver, "The Pros and Cons of Life without Parole," *British Journal of Criminology* 47 (2007): 597–615; Dirk Van Zyl Smit, Pete Weatherby, and Simon Creighton, "Whole Life Sentences and the Tide of European Human Rights Jurisprudence: What Is to Be Done?" *Human Rights Law Review* 14 (2014): 59–84.

105. Hartman, "The Five Stages of Life without the Possibility of Parole," in *Too Cruel, Not Unusual Enough,* 154.

106. Joseph Dole, "The Meaning of Life," in *Too Cruel, Not Unusual Enough,* 124.

107. Quoted in Elaine Crawley and Richard Sparks, "Is There Life after Imprisonment? How Elderly Men Talk about Imprisonment and Release," *Criminology and Criminal Justice,* 6(2006): 63–82, 74.

108. Quoted in Zehr, *Doing Life,* 73.

109. Tracie Bernardi, "Worse Than Death," in *Too Cruel, Not Unusual Enough,* 127.

110. See, for example, Johnson and McGunigall-Smith, "Life without Parole: America's Other Death Penalty"; Leigey, *The Forgotten Men;* and Sliva "On the Meaning of Life."

111. See, for example, Charlie Praphatananda, "Just a Matter of Time," in *Too Cruel, Not Unusual Enough*; Kenneth E. Hartman, "Too Cruel a Fate," *Too Cruel, Not Unusual Enough.*

112. George, *A Woman Doing Life,* 31–32.

113. See especially Vannier, "Women Serving Life without the Possibility of Parole," 333–334.

114. Leigey, *The Forgotten Men,* 127.

115. Maggie Bolger, "Offenders," in *Death, Dying and Social Differences,* ed. David Oliviere and Barbara Monroe (New York: Oxford University Press, 2004), 139. See also Ronald Aday and Azrini Wahidin, "Older Prisoners' Experiences of Death, Dying and Grief behind Bars," *Howard Journal of Crime and Justice* 55 (2016): 312–327.

116. Violet Handtke, Wiebke Bretschneider, Bernice Elger, and Tenzin Wangmo, "The Collision of Care and Punishment: Ageing Prisoners' View on Compassionate Release," *Punishment and Society* 19 (2017): 5–22, 6.

117. Ibid. See also Aday and Wahidin "Older Prisoners' Experiences of Death."

118. Patricia Prewitt, "Slow Death Row," in *Too Cruel, Not Unusual Enough,* 32. See also Joan Leslie Taylor, "Life Without the Possibility of Parole: The View from Death Row", in *Too Cruel, Not Unusual Enough,* 162.

119. Anthony Willis and Barbara Zaitzow, "Doing 'Life': A Glimpse into the Long-Term Incarceration Experience," *Laws* 4 (2015): 559–578. See also Ashley Nellis, "For Henry Montgomery—A Catch 22," February 28, 2018, https://www .themarshallproject.org/2018/02/28/for-henry-montgomery-a-catch-22.

120. Victor Hassine, *Life without Parole: Living in Prison Today,* 2nd ed. (Los Angeles, Calif.: Roxbury Publishing Company, 1999). See also Robert Johnson, and Sonia Tabiz, eds., *Life without Parole: Living and Dying in Prison Today* (New York: Oxford University Press, 2011).

121. Edward Shauer, "Book Review: *Life without Parole: Living and Dying in Prison Today* (5th ed.), by Victor Hassine, edited by Robert Johnson and Sonia Tabriz," *Southwest Journal of Criminal Justice* 8 (2011): 177–178.

122. *MacKenzie v. Stanford,* Index No. 2789/15 at 1*-2*(N.Y. Sup. Ct. 2016); "A Challenge to New York's Broken Parole Board," *New York Times,* June 13, 2016, 18; Joseph Goldstein, "Merciless End for a Long Island Cop Killer," *New York Times,* October 28, 2016.

123. For first-person experiences of solitary confinement, see Jean Casella, James Ridgeway, and Sarah Shourd, eds., *Hell Is a Very Small Place: Voices from Solitary Confinement* (New York: New Press, 2016); Marieke Liem, *After Life Imprisonment: Reentry in the Era of Mass Incarceration* (New York: New York University Press, 2016); Lorna Rhodes, *Total Confinement: Madness and Reason in the Maximum Security Prison* (Berkeley and Los Angeles, Calif.: University of California Press, 2004).

124. Sharon Shalev, *Supermax: Controlling Risk through Solitary Confinement* (Cullompton, UK: Willan: 2009).

125. For a critical summary see Craig Haney, "Mental Health Issues in Long-Term Solitary and 'Supermax' Confinement," *Crime and Delinquency,* 49 (2003): 124–156; Craig Haney and Mona Lynch, "Regulating Prisons of the Future: The Psychological Consequences of Solitary and Supermax Confinement," *New York University Review of Law and Social Change* 23 (1997): 477–570; Peter Scharff-Smith, "The Effects of Solitary Confinement on Prison Inmates: A Brief History and Review of the Literature," *Crime and Justice* 34 (2006): 441–528; Shalev, *Supermax.*

126. Haney, "Mental Health Issues in Long-Term Solitary and 'Supermax' Confinement," 130–131.

127. Jean Casella and James Ridgeway, "Introduction" in *Hell Is a Very Small Place,* 11.

128. Ibid. See also Fatos Kaba, Andrea Lewis, Sarah Glowa-Kollisch, James Hadler, David Lee, Howard Alper, Daniel Selling, Ross MacDonald, Angela Solimo, Amanda Parsons, and Homer Venters, "Solitary Confinement and Risk of Self-Harm among Jail Inmates," *American Journal of Public Health* 104 (2014): 442–447.

129. Nelson Mandela, *Long Walk to Freedom* (London: Little Brown, 1994), 494.

130. Lewis Beale, "The Agony of Solitary Confinement: It's Like Being 'Buried Alive' Prisoners Say," April 13, 2016, http://www.thedailybeast.com/articles/2016 /04/13/the-agony-of-solitary-confinement-it-s-like-being-buried-alive-prisoners-say .html. The harmful effects of penal isolation have been described in similar terms for almost two hundred years. One of the earliest, and perhaps most eloquent, critics of penal isolation can be found in Charles Dickens, *American Notes for General Circulation* (London: Penguin Classics, 2000; originally published in 1842 by Chapman and Hall), 111.

131. William Blake, "A Sentence Worse Than Death," in *Hell Is a Very Small Place,* 33.

132. O'Donnell, *Prisoners, Solitude and Time,* 109.

133. Jim Stewart and Paul Lieberman, "What Is This New Sentence That Takes away Parole?," *Student Lawyer* 11 (1982): 14–17, 16. See also Archie Bland, "Crime and Punishment: Why Throwing away the Key Doesn't Work," *Independent,* March 13, 2014, http://www.independent.co.uk/news/uk/crime/crime-and -punishment-why-throwing-away-the-key-doesnt-work-9039185.html.

134. Cited in Bland, "Crime and Punishment."

135. See Thomas Reidy, Mark Cunningham, and Joe Sorensen, "From Death to Life: Prison Behaviour of Former Death Row Inmates," *Criminal Justice and Behavior* 28 (2001): 67–82; Mark Cunningham and Jon Sorensen, "Nothing to Lose? A Comparative Examination of Prison Misconduct Rates among Life-without-Parole and Other Long-Term High-Security Inmates," *Criminal Justice and Behavior* 33 (2006): 683–705; Catherine Appleton, "Life without Parole," in *Oxford Handbooks Online* (Oxford, UK: Oxford University Press, 2015), Leigey, *The Forgotten Men.*

136. Johnson and Dobrzanska, "Mature Coping among Life-Sentenced Inmates," 36. See also Eric Cullen and Tim Newell, *Murderers and Life Imprisonment: Containment, Treatment, Safety and Risk* (Winchester, UK: Waterside Press, 1999), 78.

137. Richard Dieter, "Sentencing for Life: Americans Embrace Alternatives to the Death Penalty" (1993), https://deathpenaltyinfo.org/sentencing-life-americans -embrace-alternatives-death-penalty.

138. Ibid.

139. Johnson and Dobrzanska, "Mature Coping among Life-Sentenced Inmates," 36.

140. Leigey, *The Forgotten Men,* 130.

141. O'Donnell, *Prisoners, Solitude and Time,* 33. See also Steve Herbert, "Inside or Outside? Expanding the Narratives about Life-sentenced Prisoners," *Punishment and Society* (2017), DOI: 10.1177/1462474517737048.

142. M. C. A. Liem, Y. A. J. M. van Kuijck, and B. C. M. Raes, "Detentiebeleving van (levens)langgestraften. Een empirische pilotstudie," *Delikt en Delinkwent* 2 (2016): 10–29. We have translated the words of the Dutch-speaking prisoners.

143. Ibid., 17.

144. Ibid., 19.

145. European Committee for the Prevention of Torture and Inhuman or Degrading Punishment, *25th General Report of the CPT on Activities During the Period 1 January–31 December 2015* (Strasbourg, France: Council of Europe, 2016).

146. Penal Reform International, *The Abolition of the Death Penalty and Its Alternative Sanction in Central Asia: Kazakhstan, Kyrgyzstan and Tajikistan* (London: PRI, 2012); Penal Reform International, *Towards the Abolition of the Death Penalty and Its Alternative Sanctions in the Middle East and North Africa: Algeria, Egypt, Jordan, Lebanon, Morocco, Tunisia and Yemen* (London: PRI, 2012); Penal Reform International, *The Abolition of the Death Penalty and Its Alternative Sanction in East Africa: Kenya and Uganda* (London: PRI, 2012).

147. See Johnson and McGunigall-Smith, "Life without Parole: America's Other Death Penalty," 331; and Alison Liebling, Helen Arnold, and Christina Straub, *An Exploration of Staff-Prisoner Relationships: 12 Years On* (London: Ministry of Justice, 2011), respectively. For a discussion of the treatment of convicted terrorists in the United Kingdom, many of whom are serving life sentences, see Catherine Appleton and Clive Walker, "The Penology of Terrorism," in *Routledge Handbook of Law and Terrorism,* ed., Genevieve Lennon and Clive Walker (London: Routledge, 2015).

148. For example, Azerbaijan: CPT/Inf (2009) 28; Bulgaria: CPT/Inf (2015) 36; Cyprus: CPT/Inf (2014) 31; Georgia: CPT/Inf (2015) 42; Latvia: CPT/Inf (2014) 5; Lithuania: CPT/Inf (2014) 18; the Slovak Republic: CPT/Inf (2014) 29; and Ukraine: CPT/Inf (2015) 21.

149. *Khoroshenko v. Russia,* ECtHR (app. 41418/04), June 30, 2015 [GC].

150. Ibid.; Russian Code of Execution of Criminal Sentences 1997, arts. 126 and 127.

151. Armenia: CPT/Inf (2016) 31; Azerbaijan: CPT/Inf (2009) 28; Georgia: CPT/Inf (2015) 42; Latvia: CPT/Inf (2014) 5; Lithuania: CPT/Inf (2014) 18; Ukraine: CPT/Inf (2015) 21; Penal Reform International, *The Abolition of the Death Penalty and Its Alternative Sanction in Eastern Europe: Belarus, Russia and Ukraine* (London: PRI, 2012); Penal Reform International, *The Abolition of the Death Penalty and Its Alternative Sanction in Central Asia: Kazakhstan, Kyrgyzstan and Tajikistan.*

152. Visit to colony UK161/3 in Kostanay on April 24, 2011, by Dirk van Zyl Smit, cited in Penal Reform International, *The Abolition of the Death Penalty and Its Alternative Sanction in Central Asia,* 16.

153. Penal Reform International, *The Abolition of the Death Penalty and its Alternative Sanction in Central Asia,* 46.

154. Bulgaria: CPT/Inf (2015) 36; Moldova: CPT/Inf (2012) 3; Romania: CPT/Inf (2015) 31; Slovakia: CPT/Inf (2014) 29; and Turkey: CPT/Inf (2015) 6.

155. The Law on the Execution of Prison Sentences, s. 79(2) and Decree 368/2008 of the Ministry of Justice, s. 78(4), which introduces the rules on the

execution of prison sentences as recorded by CPT/Inf (2014) 29, § 45. The CPT report also revealed that the standard regime in the Slovak Republic, may be mitigated "by means of an internal differentiation ('D2 regime'). Inmates classified as D2 may benefit from certain privileges, such as the possibility to move in a restricted area outside their cells, to associate with other D2 prisoners, to have contact visits, to participate in group activities (organised for life-sentenced prisoners), and to participate in selected activities organised for prisoners not sentenced to life": CPT/Inf (2014) 29, § 45.

156. Execution of Punishments and Pre-Trial Detention Act 2009, § 197(1).

157. See, for example, Armenia: CPT/Inf (2011) 24; CPT/Inf (2015) 10; and Ukraine: CPT/Inf (2015) 21; CPT/Inf (2017) 15.

158. Alison Liebling, Helen Arnold, and Christina Straub, *An Exploration of Staff-Prisoner Relationships at Whitemoor: 12 Years on* (London: Ministry of Justice, 2011), 28.

159. Ibid.

160. For example, service dogs have been used to escort life-sentenced prisoners within prisons in Ukraine. CPT/Inf (2015) 21, § 48.

161. Olena Ashenko and Vadym Chovgan, *Ukranian Penitentiary Legislation in the Light of the Standards of the UN and Council of Europe Anti-Torture Committees* (Kharkiv, Ukraine: Prava Ludny, 2014), 116.

162. Weisberg and colleagues reported in 2011 that 75 percent of life-sentenced prisoners in California were classified as "low risk" by the California Static Risk Assessment instrument, a figure that is starkly different from that of the general prisoner population, where 28 percent were classified as low risk. Robert Weisberg, Debbie Mukamal, and Jordan Segall, *Life in Limbo: An Examination of Parole Release for Prisoners Serving Life Sentences with the Possibility of Parole in California* (Stanford, Calif.: Stanford Criminal Justice Center, 2011), 16. Similarly, Toch and Adams studied disciplinary records of thousands of prisoners from New York State and found that long-term prisoners consistently had lower infraction rates than other prisoners. Toch and Adams, *Acting Out: Maladaptive Behavior in Confinement.*

163. Flanagan, "Dealing with Long-Term Confinement"; Toch and Adams, *Acting Out: Maladaptive Behavior in Confinement*; Johnson and Dobranska "Mature coping among life-Sentenced Inmates"; Johnson and McGunigall-Smith, "Life without Parole: America's Other Death Penalty."

164. Turkey: Penal Code, § 47. See also Chapter 2.

165. Penal Reform International, *The Abolition of the Death Penalty and Its Alternative Sanction in Eastern Europe*, 21.

166. Ibid.

167. Ukraine: CPT/Inf (2011) 29, § 90.

168. Different names exist for these units and facilities, such as "maximum security units, supermaximum prisons, special housing units or intensive management units." Rhodes, *Total Confinement*, 23–24.

169. Ibid., 406–407.

170. Liem, *After Life Imprisonment*, 75.

171. Penal Reform International, *The Abolition of the Death Penalty and Its Alternative Sanction in Central Asia*, 46.

172. Execution of Punishments and Pre-Trial Detention Act 2009, s. 61(1). The three regimes applicable in prisons in Bulgaria are, the "special regime," the "severe regime," and the "general regime."

173. Ibid., s. 198(1).

174. Section 71(3), which was inserted in December 2012 and came into effect on January 1, 2013, provided that persons sentenced to life imprisonment with or without commutation and placed under the "severe regime" were likewise to be kept in constantly locked cells and under heightened supervision unless it was possible, in compliance with the requirements of s. 198(2), to house them with the general prison population. According to the explanatory note to that amendment, the new provision was necessary to fend off legal challenges brought by life prisoners to their being kept constantly under lock and key, even though their regime had been changed from "special" to "severe."

175. CPT/Inf (2015) 31, § 71. In Romania, the CPT found that some prisoners were subject to handcuffing during any movement outside their cell, based on individual assessments. But it was unclear how such assessments were reconsidered or how prisoners could appeal such decisions. Ibid., § 76. Furthermore, in one prison, women prisoners who were subject to the high-security regime were subject to closed visits (through a glass partition) and to systematic strip searches before and after visits. Ibid., § 104. Conjugal visits were sometimes permitted for some male prisoners who were subject to the high-security regime, but never for females. Ibid., § 106.

176. *Khoroshenko v. Russia,* ECtHR (app. 41418/04), June 30, 2015 [GC].

177. For example, Armenia: CPT/Inf (2016) 31; Azerbaijan: CPT/Inf (2009) 28; Bulgaria: CPT/Inf (2015) 12; Cyprus: CPT/Inf (2014) 31; Malta: CPT/Inf (2013) 12; Romania: CPT/Inf (2015) 31; Ukraine: CPT/Inf (2015) 21.

178. Bulgaria: CPT/Inf (2015) 12, § 86.

179. Mark Franchetti, "Killing Time," *Sunday Times Magazine,* October 12, 2014, 41.

180. Rachael Stokes, "A Fate Worse Than Death? The Problems with Life Imprisonment as an Alternative to the Death Penalty," in *Against the Death Penalty: International Initiatives and Implications,* ed. Jon Yorke (Farnham, UK: Ashgate Publishing, 2008).

181. Ibid., 288.

182. Penal Reform International has highlighted that "dozens" of life-sentenced prisoners have died from such illnesses or by committing suicide, and that "some who had been kept in single cells for a long time had lost the ability to move around unaided" (Penal Reform International, *The Abolition of the Death Penalty and Its Alternative Sanction in Central Asia,* 32).

183. K. Abdymen, "Central Asia, Abolition Close but Spectre of Death Remains," *IPS News,* September 24, 2007, cited in Stokes, "A Fate Worse Than Death?," 288.

184. Penal Reform International, *Towards the Abolition of the Death Penalty and Its Alternative Sanctions in the Middle East and North Africa: Algeria, Egypt, Jordan, Lebanon, Morocco, Tunisia and Yemen,* 9.

185. Penal Reform International, *The Abolition of the Death Penalty and Its Alternative Sanction in East Africa: Kenya and Uganda,* 7.

186. Armenia: CPT/Inf (2015) 10, § 20.

187. Ibid.

188. Penal Reform International, *The Abolition of the Death Penalty and Its Alternative Sanction in Central Asia,* 46.

189. Law on the Execution of Sentences and Security Measures, s.25

190. *Khoroshenko v. Russia,* ECtHR (app. 41418/04), June 30, 2015 [GC].

191. Ibid., § 37.

192. Ibid., § 51.

193. Ibid., § 54. Under the ordinary regime, the situation improves marginally, to three short-term and three long-term visits per year, with an increase to four short-term and four long-term visits per year under the facilitated regime. See also Chapter 8.

194. Human Rights Watch, *Against All Odds: Prison Conditions for Youth Offenders Serving Life without Parole Sentences in the United States* (New York: Human Rights Watch, 2012), 21. The report draws on research conducted by Human Rights Watch from 2004 to 2011, including face-to-face interviews and correspondence with 560 individuals serving LWOP for crimes committed as children across eleven different US jurisdictions.

195. Penal Reform International, *The Abolition of the Death Penalty and Its Alternative Sanction in Central Asia,* 33.

196. Human Rights Watch, *Against All Odds,* 32.

197. Ukraine: CPT/Inf (2011) 29, § 90.

198. Penal Reform International, *The Abolition of the Death Penalty and Its Alternative Sanction in Eastern Europe,* 21.

199. Ibid., 35.

200. Kristin Drenkhahn, "Activities of the ECtHR," in *Long-Term Imprisonment and Human Rights,* ed. Kirsten Drenkhahn, Manuela Dudeck, and Frieder Dünkel (London: Routledge, 2014), 55.

201. Cyprus: CPT/Inf (2014) 31, § 65.

202. Malta: CPT/Inf (2013) 12, § 26.

203. Maria Ejchart-Dubois, Maria Nielaczna, and Aneta Wilkowska-Plociennik, "The Right to Hope for Lifers" in *Life Imprisonment and Human Rights,* ed. Dirk Van Zyl Smit and Catherine Appleton (London: Hart, 2016), 384.

204. *Roodal v. The State of Trinidad and Tobago*[2003] UKPC 78, [2005] 1 A.C. 328 (PC)

205. Peter Hodgkinson, Seema Kandelia, and S. Lina Gyllensten, "Capital Punishment: A Review and Critique of Abolition Strategies," in *Against the Death Penalty: International Initiatives and Implications.*

206. India: Penal Code, art. 53; Lebanon: Penal Code, art. 56; Jordan: Penal Code, art. 18; Japan: Penal Code, art. 10; Benin: Penal Code, art. 7; the Central African Republic: Penal Code, art. 17; Chad: the Criminal Procedure Code, art. 502; Côte d'Ivoire: Criminal Procedure Code, art. 689; Madagascar: Law 2014–035 on the abolition of the death penalty, art. 2; and Mauritania: Penal Code, art. 7.

207. The ill-treatment that was highlighted in the report by the CPT consisted of "punches, kicks and blows with truncheons, as well as sexual abuse using a truncheon." CPT/Inf (2009) 28, § 11. More recently in Ukraine, the CPT received "credible allegations of physical ill treatment (consisting mainly of

punches and kicks) of life-sentenced prisoners by some of the custodial staff." CPT/Inf (2017) 15, § 6.

208. Azerbaijan: CPT/Inf (2009) 28, § 8. See also Ukraine: CPT/Inf (2017) 15.

209. European Committee for the Prevention of Torture and Inhuman or Degrading Treatment or Punishment, *25th General Report of the CPT on Activities during the Period 1 January–31 December 2015*, 71.

210. Ibid., 72.

211. Ibid.

212. Dirk Van Zyl Smit, "Abolishing Life Imprisonment?" *Punishment and Society* 3 (2001): 299–306; Appleton and Grøver "Pros and Cons," 597–615.

213. See Chapter 1.

8. Implementing Life Well

1. *Khoroshenko v. Russia,* ECtHR (app. 41418/04), June 30, 2015 [GC].

2. Council of Europe, Recommendation Rec (2006)2 of the Committee of Ministers to Member States on the European Prison Rules (January 11, 2006).

3. Council of Europe, Recommendation Rec (2003)23 of the Committee of Ministers to Member States on the Management by Prison Administrations of Life-Sentence and Other Long-Term Prisoners (October 9, 2003).

4. For background of the CPT and its impact on the debate about life imprisonment, see Chapter 1.

5. *Khoroshenko v. Russia,* June 30, 2015, §§ 81–84.

6. For details of the relevant UN instruments, see Chapter 1.

7. Rule 61(A) of the ICTY's Rules Governing the Detention of Persons Awaiting Trial or Appeal before the Tribunal or Otherwise Detained on the Authority of the Tribunal (July 21, 2005); *Oscar Elías Biscet and others v. Cuba Rep.* Inter. Am. Ct. H.R., 67/06, Case 12.476, October 1, 2006, § 236.

8. *Khoroshenko v. Russia,* June 30, 2015, § 121.

9. United Nations Crime Prevention and Criminal Justice Branch, *Life Imprisonment* (Vienna: United Nations, 1994), § 20.

10. Council of Europe, Recommendation on the Management by Prison Administrations of life-Sentence and Other Long-Term Prisoners, § 2.

11. United Nations Crime Prevention and Criminal Justice Branch, *Life Imprisonment*, § 37.

12. Council of Europe, Recommendation on the Management by Prison Administrations of Life-Sentence and Other Long-Term Prisoners. See also Nigel Newcommen, "Managing the Penal Consequences of Replacing the Death Penalty in Europe," in *Managing Effective Alternatives to Capital Punishment*, ed. Nicola Browne and Seema Kandelia (London: Centre for Capital Punishment Studies, 2005).

13. Ibid.

14. Council of Europe, Recommendation on the Management by Prison Administrations of Life Sentence and Other Long-Term Prisoners, § 4.

15. Ibid., § 5.

16. Ibid., § 6.

17. Ibid., § 7.

18. Ibid., § 8.

19. CPT/Inf (2016)10, § 74.

20. Ibid., § 75.

21. Ibid., § 79.

22. Ibid.

23. Ibid.

24. Ibid.

25. Ibid.

26. *Murray v. the Netherlands,* ECtHR (app. 10511/10), April 26, 2016 [GC]. See also the discussion of the *Murray* case in Chapter 9.

27. United Nations Crime Prevention and Criminal Justice Branch, *Life Imprisonment,* § 71.

28. CPT/Inf (2016)10, §§ 73 and 76.

29. Council of Europe, Recommendation on the Management by Prison Administrations of Life-Sentence and Other Long-Term Prisoners, § 7; CPT/Inf (2016)10, § 74.

30. Council of Europe, Recommendation on the Management by Prison Administrations of Life-Sentence and Other Long-Term Prisoners, § 10; European Prison Rules, Rule 105; United Nations Crime Prevention and Criminal Justice Branch, *Life Imprisonment,* § 71; United Nations Standard Minimum Rules for the Treatment of Prisoners (the Mandela Rules), May 21, 2015, E/CN.15/2015/L.6/Rev.1, Rules 96–103.

31. *Öcalan v. Turkey (No.2),* ECtHR (apps. 24069/03, 197/04, 6201/06 and 10464/07), March 18, 2014.

32. *Harakchiev and Tolumov v. Bulgaria,* ECtHR (apps. 5018/11 and 61199/12), July 8, 2014.

33. TOSLO-2015-107496-3, 13 (Oslo district court), http://www.domstol.no /contentassets/9082215b86804731af6ddc9691116cf3/15-107496tvi-otir-dom -20042016breivik.pdf. Breivik's application was overturned by the Supreme Court of Norway, but he has applied to the ECtHR for the matter to be reconsidered. See Agence France-Presse, "Anders Breivik Not Treated Inhumanely, Appeals Court Rules," *The Guardian,* March 1, 2017, https://www.theguardian.com /world/2017/mar/01/anders-breivik-not-treated-inhumanely-appeals-court-rules; "Anders Breivik: Mass Murderer to Take Ill Treatment Claim to European Court of Human Rights," *The Independent,* June 8, 2017, http://www.independent.co .uk/News/world/europe/norway-anders-behring-breivik-appeal-european-court -human-rights-prison-isolation-neo-nazi-beliefs-a7779186.html.

34. *Khoroshenko v. Russia,* June 30, 2015.

35. "Constitutional Court Allows Life-Sentence Prisoners to Have One Long Prison Visit a Year" *Russian Legal Information Agency,* November 17, 2016, http://rapsinews.com/legislation_news/20161117/277158837.html.

36. *Dickson v. United Kingdom,* ECtHR (app. 44362/04), December 4, 2007 [GC]. The case was brought by both Dickson and his wife and raised interesting questions about the impact of life sentences on family members of life prisoners.

37. Ibid., § 28.

38. *Vinter and others v. United Kingdom,* ECtHR (apps. 66069/09, 130/10 and 3896/10), July 9, 2013 [GC].

39. *Khoroshenko v. Russia,* June 30, 2015 (joint concurring opinion of Judges Pinto de Albuquerque and Turković), § 10.

40. United Nations Crime Prevention and Criminal Justice Branch, *Life Imprisonment,* § 38–42.

41. *European Prison Rules,* Rule 103.8.

42. Council of Europe, *Recommendation on the Management by Prison Administrations of Life-Sentence and Other Long-Term Prisoners,* § 2.

43. CPT/Inf (2016)10, § 77.

44. *Murray v. the Netherlands,* April 26, 2016 (partly concurring opinion of Judge Pinto de Albuquerque, internal references omitted), § 2.

45. Wiene van Hattum, "Van gratie naar herbeoordeling: Over de verkorting van de levenslange gevangenisstraf," *Delikt en Delinkwent* 47 (2017): 239–260.

46. *R (James, Lee and Wells) v. Secretary of State for Justice* [2009] UKHL 22, [2010] 1 AC 553 (Eng.).

47. Ibid. On IPP sentences generally, see Chapter 2.

48. *James, Lee and Wells v. United Kingdom,* ECtHR (apps. 25119/09, 57715/09 and 57877/09), September 18, 2012.

49. *R (on the applications of Haney, Kaiyam, and Massey) v. The Secretary of State for Justice* [2014] UKSC 66, [2015] A.C. 1344 (Eng.)

50. *Rangelov v. Germany,* ECtHR (app. 5123/07), March 22, 2012.

51. Federal Constitution of Switzerland: art. 123a.

52. For a wider discussion, see Anna Coninx, "Life without Parole for Preventive Reasons? Lifelong Post-Sentence Detention in Switzerland," in *Life Imprisonment and Human Rights,* ed. Dirk van Zyl Smit and Catherine Appleton (Oxford, UK: Hart/Bloomsbury Publishing, 2016), 435–460.

53. *Kansas v. Hendricks,* 521 US 346 (1997).

54. Christopher Slobogin, "Preventive Detention in Europe the United States and Australia," in *Preventive Detention: Asking the Fundamental Questions,* ed. Patrick Keyser (Cambridge: Intersentia, 2013), 31–54.

55. Human Rights Committee, *Miller and Carroll v. New Zealand,* Communication No. 2502/2014, U.N. Doc. CCPR/C/112/D/2502/2014 (2017), para. 8.5.

56. Council of Europe, Recommendation Rec (1982)17 of the Committee of Ministers to Member States Concerning Custody and Treatment of Dangerous Prisoners (September 24, 1982), §§ 1–3.

57. Ibid., §§ 5, 7–8. See also Council of Europe, Recommendation Rec (2014)3 of the Committee of Ministers to Member States Concerning Dangerous Offenders (February 19, 2014).

58. CPT/Inf (2016)10, 41.

59. United Nations Office on Drugs and Crime, *Handbook on the Management of High-Risk Prisoners* (New York: United Nations, 2016), 10.

60. In the United Kingdom there have been examples of some high-security prisons that were designed to deliver a liberal, relaxed regime specifically to individuals serving life sentences or long-term imprisonment. See Anthony Bottoms, Richard Sparks, and Will Hay, *Prisons and the Problem of Order*

(Oxford, UK: Oxford University Press, 1996); Peter Whatmore, "Barlinnie Special Unit: An Insider's View," in *Problems of Long-Term Imprisonment*, ed. Anthony Bottoms and Roy Light (Aldershot, UK: Gower, 1987); Jimmy Boyle, *The Pain of Confinement* (London: Canongate, 1984).

61. Andrew Coyle, "Replacing the Death Penalty: The Vexed Issue of Alternatives," in *Capital Punishment: Strategies to Abolition*, ed. Peter Hodgkinson and William Schabas (Cambridge: Cambridge University Press, 2004), 110.

62. See the section on prisoner movement in Department of Corrections, *Prison Operations Manual*, http://www.corrections.govt.nz/resources/policy_and _legislation/Prison-Operations-Manual/Movement.html.

63. See the section on security classification, http://www.corrections.govt.nz /resources/policy_and_legislation/Prison-Operations-Manual/Movement/M.02 -Security-classification/M.02-5.html.

64. HM Prison Service, *Lifer Manual* (London: HM Prison Service, 2008), § 8.2.

65. See Neil Stone, *Life Sentences*, 2nd ed. (Crayford, Kent, UK: Shaw and Sons, 2008), 39–40.

66. Kirstin Drenkhahn, "Sentence Planning," in *Long-Term Imprisonment and Human Rights*, ed. Kirsten Drenkhahn, Manuela Dudeck, and Frieder Dünkel (London: Routledge, 2014), 291.

67. Ibid., 293.

68. Stone, *Life Sentences*, 38.

69. See, for example, Tapio Lappi-Seppälä, "Imprisonment and Penal Policy in Finland," in *Long-Term Imprisonment and Human Rights*, 144.

70. Drenkhahn, Dudeck, and Dünkel, eds., *Long-term Imprisonment and Human Rights*.

71. The Prison Act 1976, s. 13, now applicable in terms of legislation of the individual federal states. Axel Dessecker, "Constitutional Limits on Life Imprisonment and Post-Sentence Preventive Detention in Germany," in *Life Imprisonment and Human Rights*, 420.

72. BVerfGE, 64, 261 (Ger.).

73. Dirk van Zyl Smit, "Leave of Absence for West German Prisoners: Legal Principle and administrative Practice," *British Journal of Criminology* 28 (1988): 1–18.

74. Dessecker, "Constitutional Limits on Life Imprisonment and Post-Sentence Preventive Detention in Germany," 420.

75. European Prison Rules, Rule 4.

76. Ram Subramanian and Alison Shames, *Sentencing and Prison Practices in Germany and the Netherlands: Implications for the United States* (New York: Vera Institute of Justice, 2013); Federal Office of Justice, *The Execution of Sentences and Measures in Switzerland: An Overview of the System and Execution of Sentences and Measures in Switzerland for Adults and Juveniles* (Berne: Federal Department of Justice and Police, 2010); Doris Schartmueller, "Life Imprisonment in Scandinavia: The Ultimate Punishment in the Penal Environments of Denmark, Finland and Sweden" (PhD diss., Northern Arizona University, 2015).

77. The leading ECtHR decision recognizing prisoners' right to vote, *Hirst v. United Kingdom (No.2)*, ECtHR (appl.74025/0), October 6, 2005, [GC],

concerned a life-sentenced prisoner but did not turn on that point. On the contrary, while the Grand Chamber ruled that a blanket ban on all prisoners voting infringed the ECHR, it left open the possibility that certain classes of prisoners, including presumably those serving life sentences, could be excluded from voting. In *Scoppola v. Italy (No. 3)*, ECtHR (app. 126/05), May 22, 2012 [GC], the Grand Chamber upheld a lifelong prohibition on the right of a life-sentenced prisoners to vote. The only amelioration in Italian law was that, three years after his release, the former life-sentenced prisoner could apply to have the right to vote reinstated.

78. Denmark Ministry of Justice, *A Programme of Principles for Prison and Probation Work in Denmark* (Copenhagen: Department of Prisons and Proba-tion, 1994), 10. See also Anette Storgaard, "Denmark," in *Long-Term Imprison-ment and Human Rights*, 106–118.

79. Gleeds, *Rehabilitation by Design: Influencing Offender Behaviour* (London: Gleeds Consultancy, 2016); Nicholas Turner and Jeremy Travis, "What We Learned from German Prisons," *New York Times*, August 6, 2015; Katherine Leonard, "Reform the Prison, Then the Prisoner"; *New York Times*, May 31, 2017.

80. Jessica Jacobson and Helen Fair, *Connections: A Review of Learning from the Winston Churchill Memorial Trust Prison Reform Fellowships* (London: Prison Reform Trust, 2016), 9.

81. For example, at San Quentin prison in California various gardening projects have been set up to encourage prisoners to train in landscape gardening and cultivate their own food as part of the rehabilitation process. Eliza Barclay, "Prison Gardens Help Prisoners Grow Their Own Food—and Skills," *The Salt*, January 12, 2014, http://www.npr.org/sections/thesalt/2014/01/12/261397333 /prison-gardens-help-inmates-grow-their-own-food-and-skills. Similarly, in England, Springhill prison's lottery-funded farms and gardens project has "offered prisoners solid training in a number of significant occupations." See HM Chief Inspector of Prisons, *Report on an Unannounced Short Follow-Up Inspection of HMP Spring Hill, 5–7 March 2012* (London: Her Majesty's Inspectorate of Prisons, 2012), 13.

82. John Irwin, *Lifers: Seeking Redemption in Prison* (New York: Routledge, 2009), 84–86.

83. Ibid.; Catherine Appleton, *Life after Life Imprisonment* (Oxford, UK: Oxford University Press, 2010); Margaret Leigey, *The Forgotten Men: Serving a Life without Parole Sentence* (New Brunswick, N.J.: Rutgers University Press, 2015); Marieka Liem, *After Life Imprisonment: Reentry in the Era of Mass Incarceration* (New York: New York University Press, 2016).

84. See Norman Bishop, "Prisoner Participation in Prison Management," *Champ Pénal/Penal Field* 3 (2006): 1–11.

85. See Alexandra Topping, "A Newspaper, not a Screws' Paper," *The Guardian*, May 7, 2008, https://www.theguardian.com/society/2008/may/07 /prisonsandprobation.insidetime; Miranda Sawyer, "Inside Tracks: Life at the UK's Prison Radio Station," *The Guardian*, January 28, 2017, https://www .theguardian.com/society/2017/jan/28/national-prison-radio-brixton-styal-inside -tracks.

86. Alisa Stevens, *Offender Rehabilitation and Therapeutic Communities: Enabling Change the TC Way* (London: Routledge, 2013); HM Prison Service, *Prison Service Order 2400 Democratic Therapeutic Communities* (London: HM Prison Service, 2004).

87. See Elaine Genders and Elaine Player, *Grendon: Study of a Therapeutic Community* (Oxford, UK: Oxford University Press, 2001); Ursula Smartt, *Grendon Tales: Stories from a Therapeutic Community* (Winchester, UK: Waterside Press, 2001); Richard Shuker and Elizabeth Sullivan, *Grendon and the Emergence of Forensic Therapeutic Communities: Developments in Research and Practice* (Chichester, UK: John Wiley and Sons, 2010); Stevens, *Offender Rehabilitation and Therapeutic Communities.*

88. *Khoroshenko v. Russia,* June 30, 2015, § 84.

89. Unsupervised family visits are acknowledged by several national reports in Dirk van Zyl Smit and Frieder Dünkel, *Imprisonment Today and Tomorrow: International Perspectives on Prisoners' Rights and Prison Conditions,* 2nd ed. (The Hague: Kluwer, 2001); Penal Reform International, *The Abolition of the Death Penalty and Its Alternative Sanction in Central Asia: Kazakhstan, Kyrgyzstan and Tajikistan* (London: PRI, 2012).

90. Geordon Omand, "Conjugal Visits Increase Success of Prisoner Rehabilitation: Mission Warden," *Canadian Press,* February 1, 2017, http://bc.ctvnews.ca /conjugal-visits-increase-success-of-prisoner-rehabilitation-mission-warden-1 .3266458.

91. Susan Phillips, *Video Visits for Children Whose Parents Are Incarcerated: In Whose Best Interest?* (Washington, D.C.: The Sentencing Project, 2012).

92. Rick Ruddell, Ian Broom and Matthew Young, "Creating Hope for Life-Sentenced Offenders," *Journal of Offender Rehabilitation* 49 (2010): 324–341, 330. See also R. E. "Bob" Brown, "A Beacon of Hope—Sunny Ways: Life-Sentenced Offenders," *Executive Exchange,* Fall 2016, 29–38. However, the federal government canceled funding to the LifeLine program in 2012: CBC News, "Prison Rehab Program Axed due to Budget Cuts," April 16, 2012, http://www.cbc.ca/news/canada/prison-rehab-program-axed-due-to-budget-cuts-1 .1179484.

93. Penal Reform International, *Making Law and Policy That Works: A Handbook for Law and Policy Makers on Reforming Criminal Justice and Penal Legislation, Policy and Practice* (London: Penal Reform International, 2010). See also www.kris.a.se.

94. See, for example, Shadd Maruna, *Making Good: How Ex-Convicts Reform and Rebuild Their Lives* (Washington, D.C.: American Psychological Association, 2001); Stephen Farrall and Adam Calverley, *Understanding Desistance from Crime: Theoretical Directions in Resettlement and Rehabilitation* (Maidenhead, UK: Open University Press, 2006); and Fergus McNeill, "A Desistance Paradigm for Offender Management," *Criminology and Criminal Justice* 6 (2006): 39–62. See also Chapter 10.

95. Penal Reform International, *Alternatives to the Death Penalty Information Pack,* 2nd ed. (London: Penal Reform International, 2015), 57.

96. Kirstin Drenkhahn, Manuela Dudeck, and Frieder Dünkel, "Conclusion," in Drenkhahn, Dudeck and Dünkel, eds., *Long-Term Imprisonment and Human*

Rights, 377. For an interesting recent relationship between a university and a high-security prison in England, see Carrie Braithwaite, "Prisoners at High Security Prison Enroll at Leeds Beckett University," February 6, 2017, http://www .leedsbeckett.ac.uk/news/0217-prisoners-at-high-security-prison-enrol-at-leeds -beckett-university/.

97. Schartmueller, *Life Imprisonment in Scandinavia.*

98. John Howard Society of Alberta, *Life Imprisonment* (Edmonton, Canada: John Howard Society of Alberta) available at http://www.johnhoward.ab.ca/pub /old/C40.htm#disc.

99. Eric Cullen and Tim Newell, *Murderers and Life Imprisonment: Containment, Treatment, Safety and Risk* (Winchester, UK: Waterside Press, 1999), 101.

100. *R (on the applications of Haney, Kaiyam, and Massey) v. The Secretary of State for Justice* [2014] (Eng.).

101. For further information, see http://www.osborneny.org/programs.cfm ?programID=19.

102. Irwin, *Lifers;* Appleton, *Life after Life Imprisonment;* Leigey, *The Forgotten Men;* Liem, *After Life Imprisonment.*

103. Kirstin Drenkhahn, "Leisure Time," in *Long-term Imprisonment and Human Rights,* 332.

104. http://norlam.md/libview.php?l= en&idc=96&id=892#.WWjPOoTyuYn. See also Victor Drosu and Nadejda Burciu, *Life Imprisonment and Release on Parole in the Republic of Moldova* (Chişinău, Moldova: Norwegian Mission for the Rule of Law Advisers to Moldova, 2017).

105. John Irwin, *Lifers: Seeking Redemption in Prison* (New York: Routledge, 2009), 68. See also Robert Johnson and Ania Dobrzanska, "Mature Coping among Life-Sentenced Inmates: An Exploratory Study of Adjustment Dynamics," *Corrections Compendium,* November–December 2005, 8–38.

106. Margaret Leigey, *The Forgotten Men: Serving a Life without Parole Sentence* (New Brunswick, N.J.: Rutgers University Press, 2015), 106.

107. Anthony Willis and Barbara Zaitzow, "Doing 'Life': A Glimpse into the Long-Term Incarceration Experience," *Laws* 4 (2015): 559–578, 561. See also K. C. *Carceral, Behind A Convict's Eyes: Doing Time in a Modern Prison* (Belmont, Calif.: Wadsworth, 2003).

108. K. Auty, A. Copel, and A. Liebling, "A Systematic Review and Meta-Analysis of Yoga and Mindfulness Meditation in Prison: Effects on Psychological Well-Being and Behavioural Functioning," *International Journal of Offender Therapy and Comparative Criminology* 61(6) (2017): 689–710.

109. Robert Booth, "Britain's Most Dangerous Prisoners to Get Meditation Lessons," *The Guardian,* October 18, 2015, https://www.theguardian.com/society /2015/oct/19/britains-most-dangerous-prisoners-to-get-meditation-lessons.

110. See https://prisonyoga.org/; http://www.liberationprisonyoga.com/who -we-are/and https://mic.com/articles/111976/meet-the-woman-changing-the -prison-experience-one-yoga-mat-at-a-time#.DTAnR6gWL, respectively.

111. Sannyasi Janaki, "Benefits of Yoga for Prisoners," *Yoga Magazine of the Bihar School of Yoga, 1999,* http://www.yogamag.net/archives/1999/fnov99 /bnygpris.shtml.

112. HM Inspectorate of Probation and HM Inspectorate of Prisons, *A Joint Inspection of Life Sentence Prisoners* (London: HMIP, 2013), 35.

113. Schartmueller, *Life Imprisonment in Scandinavia*, 238.

9. Release from Life

1. See the discussion of release in the context of the European approach to irreducible LWOP in Chapter 2.

2. BVerfGE 45 187, 246 (Ger.). Cf. also 252 and 254–256.

3. *Vinter and Others v. United Kingdom,* ECtHR (apps. 66069/09, 130/10 and 3896/10), July 9, 2013 [GC]. The later decisions are summarized in *Matiošaitis and others v. Lithuania* ECtHR (apps. 22662/13, 51059/13, 58823/13, 59692/13, 59700/13, 60115/13, 69425/13 and 72824/13), May 23, 2017.

4. *Murray v. The Netherlands,* ECtHR (app. 10511/10), April 26, 2016 [GC], partly concurring opinion of Judge Pinto de Albuquerque, § 13. Words in quotation marks are from the judgment of the Court.

5. *Hutchinson v. United Kingdom,* ECtHR (app. 57592/08), January 17, 2017.

6. Recommendation Rec (2003) 22 of the Committee of Ministers to Member States on conditional release (parole) (September 24, 2003), § 3.

7. Ibid., § 4.a.

8. See most recently Rules, 4, 87, and 90 of the UN General Assembly, *United Nations Standard Minimum Rules for the Treatment of Prisoners* (the Nelson Mandela Rules), A/RES/70/175, December 17, 2015.

9. United Nations Office at Vienna, Crime Prevention and Criminal Justice Branch, *Life Imprisonment* (Vienna: United Nations, 1994), 18. Emphasis added.

10. German Penal Code, § 57a, which was introduced on December 8, 1981, and amended on December 22, 2006.

11. Austria: Prison Act, § 152; Belgium: Penal Code, art. 30 § 1; Finland: Penal Code, ch. 2(c), s. 10; France: Penal Code, art. 730; Greece: Penal Code, art. 730; Germany: Penal Code, § 57a; Italy: Presidential Decree 431/76, art. 94bis; Spain: Penal Code, art. 92; and Sweden: Act on the Commutation of Life Sentences 2006.

12. Albania: Penal Code, arts. 65 and 65a; Armenia: Penal Code, art. 76; Azerbaijan: Penal Code, art. 57.3; Belarus: Penal Code, ch. 4, art. 58; Bulgaria: Penal Procedure Code, art. 450; Czech Republic: Penal Code, § 61; Estonia: Penal Code, § 77; Latvia: Criminal Law, s. 61(4); Macedonia: Penal Code, art. 36; Moldova: Penal Code, art. 91; Poland: Penal Code, art. 77 §1; Romania: Criminal Code, art. 99; Russia: Penal Code, art. 79; and Slovakia: Penal Code, s. 68.

13. Such is the case in: Kazakhstan: Penal Code, art. 72; and Turkmenistan: Criminal Executive Code, art. 167 and Criminal Procedure Code, art. 478.4.

14. Ethiopia: Penal Code, art. 202; Nigeria: Administration of Criminal Justice Act 2015, s. 468(1); and Tunisia: Criminal Procedure Code, art. 342 *bis*. The procedure in Tunisia is very similar to that in France, except that it involves a specialist judge for the execution of sentences rather than a specialist court. The Central African Republic also has a French-style judge for the execution of sentences, but the final decision is taken by the minister of justice.

15. Argentina: Penal Code, art. 14; Peru: Penal Execution Code, art. 55.

16. Regulation issued by the Supreme Court of the PRC, published June 1, 2014; Michelle Miao, "Two Years between Life and Death: A Critical Analysis of the Suspended Death Penalty in China," *International Journal of Law, Crime and Justice* 45 (2015): 26–43.

17. Russia: Penal Code, art. 79(5).

18. *Harakchiev and Tolumov v. Bulgaria*, ECtHR (app. 15018/11 and 61199/12), July 8, 2014, § 71.

19. Ethiopia: Criminal Code, 2005, art. 202(1); Nigeria: Administration of Criminal Justice Act, 2015, s. 468(1).

20. 18 U.S.C. 3582(c)(1)(A)(ii). See the somewhat cynical comment of the Aikins LJ in *Shaw v. United States* [2014] EWHC 4654 (Admin), [2015] A.C.D. 63 (Eng.), § 35, that in the light of these clear provisions a person facing extradition and a possible life sentence in the United States would know what to do to secure his release.

21. Inspector General of the US Department of Justice, *The Impact of an Aging Inmate Population on the Federal Bureau of Prisons* (Washington, D.C.: Office of the Inspector General US Department of Justice, 2015), https://oig.justice.gov /reports/2015/e1505.pdf.

22. Sonja Snacken, Kristel Beyens, and Marie-Aude Beernaert, "Belgium," in *Release from Prison: European policy and Practice*, ed. Nicola Padfield, Dirk van Zyl Smit, and Frieder Dünkel (Uffculme, UK: Willan, 2010), 70; Sonja Snacken, Ineke Casier, Caroline Devynck, and Diete Humblet, "Life Imprisonment in Belgium: Current Human Rights Challenges," in *Life Imprisonment and Human Rights,* ed. Dirk van Zyl Smit and Catherine Appleton (Oxford, UK: Hart, 2016).

23. *Bodein v. France*, ECtHR (app. 40014/10), November 13, 2014.

24. Kim Reuflet "France," in *Release from Prison.*

25. Axel Dessecker, "Constitutional Limits on Life Imprisonment and Post-Sentence Preventive Detention in Germany," in *Life Imprisonment and Human Rights.*

26. Ibid.

27. Ibid.

28. BVerfG, 2 BvR 2009/08 of April 30, 2009 (Ger.) discussed in Dirk van Zyl Smit, "Release from Life Imprisonment. A Comparative Note on the Role of Pre-release Decision Making in England and Germany" in *Fervet Opus; Liber Amicorum Anton van Kalmthout,* ed. Marc Groenhuijsen, Tijs Kooijmans, and Theo de Roos (Apeldoorn, The Netherlands: Maklu, 2010).

29. Dessecker, "Constitutional Limits," ch 4.

30. Frieder Dünkel, "Kommentierung zu §§ 55–57b StGB," in *Nomos Kommentar zum Strafgeseztbuch,* ed. Urs Kindhäuser, Ulfrid Neumann, and Ullrich Paeffgen, 4th ed. (Baden-Baden, Germany: Nomos, 2103).

31. *Prosecutor v. Galić*, MICT-14–83-ES (June 23, 2015).

32. Rules of Procedure and Evidence of the International Criminal Court, UN Doc. PCNICC/2000/1/Add.1 (2000), Rule 223.

33. The Organic Prison Law Reform (Law 354 of 1975), art. 4-bis, as modified by Law 356 of 1992 (Italy).

34. See the discussion of the position of the so-called *ergastolo ostativo* by Paulo Pinto de Albuquerque, "Life Imprisonment and the European Right to Hope," *Rivista AIC* (2/2015) http://www.rivistaaic.it/life-imprisonment-and-the -european-right-to-hope.html. See also Carmelo Musumeci and Andrea Pugiotto, *Gliergastolani senza scampo. Fenomenologia e criticità costituzionali dell'ergastolo ostativo* (Naples, Italy: Editoriale Scientifica, 2016).

35. Argentina: Criminal Code, art. 13; Peru: Code on the Execution of Sentences, art. 59A.

36. *Vinter v. United Kingdom,* July 9, 2013, § 120; *Hutchinson v. United Kingdom,* January 17, 2017, § 47.

37. Bermuda: Parole Board Act, 2001 and Criminal Code Act 1907, art. 700; Canada: Corrections and Conditional Release Act 1992, art. 107(1); Chile: Law Decree no 321 of 1925 Establishing Conditional Release for Convicts, art. 4; Cyprus: Prisons (Amendment) Law 2009, art. 14A(1); England and Wales: Criminal Justice Act 1991, s. 32; Jamaica: Parole Act, 1978, as amended in 2010, art. 4(d); Kosovo: Criminal Code, art. 94.4 read with Law 04/L-149 on the Execution of Penal Sanctions, art. 122; Liberia: Criminal Procedure Code, § 35.4; Papua New Guinea: Parole Act 1991, art. 7; New Zealand: Parole Act 2002, art. 28; Scotland: Prisoners and Criminal Proceedings Act (Scotland) 1993, s. 20. In Australia see: Australian Capital Territory: Crimes [Sentence Administration] Act 2005, ch. 7; Northern Territory: Parole Act, as in force at 5 August 2016, art. 5; Queensland: Corrective Services Act 2006, ch. 5; South Australia: Correctional Services Act 1982, s. 67; Tasmania: of the Corrections Act 1997, s. 72; and Victoria: Corrections Act 1986, division 5). In the Northern Territory, Tasmania and Victoria, this does not apply to prisoners sentenced to LWOP. In Western Australia, life-sentenced prisoners can only be paroled by the Governor; see Sentence Administration Act 2003, s. 25.

38. See, in general, Edward E. Rhine, Joan Petersilia, and Kevin R. Reitz, "The Future of Parole Release," *Crime and Justice* 46 (2017): 279–338.

39. In Botswana, the minister of home affairs reviews all recommendations for parole but in the case of life imprisonment a decision to grant parole has to be confirmed in writing by the President of Botswana: Prisons Act of Botswana Act 18 2006, s. 87

40. See also the due process criteria set by the Caribbean Court of Justice for a parole board responsible for the release of life-sentenced prisoners in *August and Gabb v. The Queen,* 2018 CCJ 7 AJ March, 29, 2018.

41. *Weeks v. United Kingdom,* ECtHR (app. 9787/82), March 2, 1987, § 61.

42. *R v. Brooke and others* [2008] EWCA Civ 2, [2008] 1 W.L.R. 823 (Eng.).

43. Catherine Appleton and Dirk van Zyl Smit, "The Paradox of Reform: Life Imprisonment in England and Wales," in *Life Imprisonment and Human Rights.*

44. *The Queen on the application of (1) DSD and NBV and others,* [2018] EWHC 694 (Admin) (UK).

45. Dirk van Zyl Smit, *Taking Life Imprisonment Seriously in National and International Law* (The Hague: Kluwer Law International, 2002), ch. 2. The key case is *Stafford v. United Kingdom,* ECtHR (app. 73299/01) December 12, 2002, followed and applied by the House of Lords in *R (Anderson) v. Secretary of State for the Home Department* [2002] UKHL 46, [2003] 1 AC 837 (HL) (Eng.).

46. Crime (Sentences) Act 1997 (as amended by the Criminal Justice Act 2003), s. 28(6).

47. The development was summarized and taken further by the UK Supreme Court in *Osborn v. The Parole Board,* [2013] UKSC 61, [2014] A.C. 1115 (Eng.). See also Nicola Padfield, "Life Sentences in Law and Practice," *Prison Service Journal,* 217 (January 2015): 21–26.

48. *Kafkaris v. Cyprus (No 2),* ECtHR (app. 9644/09), June 21, 2011 (admissibility). For examples of where the standard set for the United Kingdom in the *Stafford* case was held to be irrelevant, see *Streicher v. Germany,* ECtHR (app. 40384/04) February, 10, 2009; and *Meixner v. Germany,* ECtHR (app. 26958/07), November, 3, 2009 (admissibility).

49. "Harry Roberts: Police Killer Released from Prison," *BBC,* November 12, 2014, http://www.bbc.com/news/uk-england-london-30016319. For critical comments, see, for example, John Shammas, "Harry Roberts: Vile Triple Police Killer Pictured out and about Enjoying Freedom Following Controversial Prison Release," *Daily Mirror,* June 8, 2015, http://www.mirror.co.uk/news/uk-news /harry-roberts-vile-triple-police-5843861.

50. Snacken, Beyens, and Beernaert, " Life imprisonment in Belgium," 241.

51. Nicola Padfield, "England and Wales," in *Release from Prison;* Dirk Van Zyl Smit, Pete Weatherby, and Simon Creighton, "Whole Life Sentences and the Tide of European Human Rights Jurisprudence: What Is to Be Done?" *Human Rights Law Review* 14 (2014): 59–84, 82.

52. Bronwyn Naylor and Johannes Schmidt, "Do Prisoners Have a Right to Fairness before the Parole Board?" *Sydney Law Review* 32 (2010): 437–469.

53. *R v. Bourque,* 2014 NBQB 237 (CanLII), [2014] NBJ 295 (QL).

54. Human Rights Committee, *Miller and Carroll v. New Zealand,* Communication No. 2502/2014, U.N. Doc. CCPR/C/112/D/2502/2014 (2017).

55. Ashley Nellis, *Still Life: America's Increasing Use of Life and Long-Term Sentences* (Washington, D.C.: The Sentencing Project, 2016).

56. Kevin Reitz, "Dominant Discretionary Decision-Making: Discretionary Prison Release Systems in the U.S. A Comparative Framework," in *Offender Release and Supervision: The Role of Courts and the Use of Discretion,* ed. Martine Herzog-Evans (Oisterwijk, The Netherlands: Wolf Legal Publishers, 2014), 81–108.

57. Rhine, Petersilia, and Reitz, "The Future of Parole Release."

58. American Civil Liberties Union, *False Hope: How Parole Systems Fail Youth Serving Extreme Sentences* (New York: ACLU Foundation, 2016); The Sentencing Project, *Delaying a Second Chance: The Declining Prospects for Parole on Life Sentences* (Washington, D.C.: The Sentencing Project, 2017). For a further overview focused on juvenile life imprisonment, see Chapter 4 and also Sarah French Russell, "Review for Release: Juvenile Offenders, State Parole Practices, and the Eighth Amendment," *Indiana Law Journal* 89 (2014): 373–440.

59. *Greenholtz v. Inmates of the Nebraska Penal and Correctional Complex,* 442 US 1 (1979). See also *Swarthout v. Cooke,* 562 US 216 (2011).

60. *California Department of Corrections v. Morales* 514 US 499 (1995); *Garner v. Jones* 529 US 244 (2000).

61. The original letter from Muse is reproduced at http://j.b5z.net/i/u /2108258/f/Parole2012/Brief_von_William_Muse_an_C._Straesser_-_31.Aug .2012.pdf.

62. For the background to this case, see "Judith Clark, Getaway Driver in Deadly Brink's Heist, Is Denied Parole," *New York Times,* April 22, 2017; "'I Want to Live It Out,' Says Brink's Heist Driver after Denied Parole," *New York Times,* May 3, 2017.

63. *In re Lawrence* (2008) 44 Cal.4th 1181; Kate Hatheway, "Creating a Meaningful Opportunity of Review: Challenging the Politicization of Parole for Life-Sentenced Prisoners" *American Criminal Law Review* 54 (2017) 601–625.

64. *Morrisey v. Brewer,* 408 US 471, 477 (1972).

65. Benin: Criminal Procedure Code, art. 811; Burkina Faso: Criminal Procedure Code, art. 690; Burundi: Criminal Procedure Code, art. 131; Central African Republic: Criminal Procedure Code, art. 427; Chad: Criminal Procedure Code, art. 503; Côte d'Ivoire: Criminal Procedure Code, art. 690; Democratic Republic of Congo: Penal Code, art. 38; Madagascar: Criminal Procedure Code, art. 575; Mali: See the minister of justice's website, http://demarchesadministratives.gouv.ml /demarches/afficher/Liberation-conditionnelle-demande, but there are no specific provisions; Mauritania: Criminal Procedure Code, art. 654; Niger: Criminal Procedure Code, art. 672; the Republic of Guinea: Criminal Procedure Code, art. 786; and Rwanda: Criminal Procedure Code, art. 247.

66. *Kafkaris v. Cyprus,* ECtHR (app. 21906/04), February 12, 2008 [GC].

67. *Makoni v. Commissioner of Prisons and Minister of Justice Legal and Parliamentary Affairs,* CCZ 8/16, July 13, 2016, 27.

68. Regulation 119A and 119B of the Prisons (Amendment) Regulations of 1998.

69. For details and further references, see Diarmuid Griffin and Ian O'Donnell, "Confusingly Compliant with the European Convention on Human Rights: the Release of Life Sentence Prisoners in Ireland," in *Life Imprisonment and Human Rights.*

70. *Lynch and Whelan v. Minister for Justice Equality and Law Reform* [2010] IESC 34; *Lynch and Whelan v. Ireland,* ECtHR (apps. 70495/10 and 74565/10) July 8, 2014.

71. *Lynch and Whelan v. Ireland,* July 8, 2014.

72. Quoted in *Lynch and Whelan v. Ireland,* July 8, 2014, § 9.

73. Diarmuid Griffin, *Killing Time: Life Imprisonment and Parole in Ireland* (Cham, Switzerland: Palgrave Macmillan, 2018).

74. See Chapter 10.

75. *Lynch and Whelan v. Ireland,* July 8, 2014, § 19.

76. *Lynch and Whelan v. Minister for Justice Equality and Law Reform,* quoted in *Lynch and Whelan v. Ireland,* July 8, 2014 § 11.

77. For example, in the Netherlands. See Wiene van Hattum and Sonja Meijer, "An Administrative Procedure for Life Prisoners," in *Life Imprisonment and Human Rights.*

78. *Solem v. Helm* 463 US 277, 300–301 (1983); citations omitted.

79. Andrew Novak, *Comparative Executive Clemency: The Constitutional Pardon Power and the Prerogative of Mercy in Global Perspective* (London: Routledge, 2016), 5 (United States), 11 (Germany).

80. Hinke Piersma, *De drie van Breda: Duitse oorlogsmisdadigers in Nederlandse gevangenschap 1945–1989* (Amsterdam: Balans, 2005).

81. See Chapter 2.

82. Novak, *Comparative Executive Clemency.*

83. Art 6(4) of the International Covenant on Civil and Political Rights (December 16, 1966).

84. Act CCXL of 2013, s. 46/F as amended from January 1, 2015.

85. *T.P. and A.T. v. Hungary,* ECtHR (apps. 37871/14 and 73986/14), October 4, 2016.

86. *Trabelsi v. Belgium,* September 4, 2014, § 137.

87. Barack Obama, "The President's Role in Advancing Criminal Justice Reform," *Harvard Law Review* 130 (2017): 811–865, 835–838.

88. Ibid., 837. Obama specifies that that they earned their chance by obtaining a General Education Diploma, taking vocational programming to learn skills for future employment, or addressing the substance abuse that so often led to their criminal conduct.

89. Jing Cao, "Commuting Life without Parole Sentences: The Need for Reason and Justice over Politics: (SJ.D. Diss., Fordham University, New York, 2015), 87.

90. Correctional Services Act 1998, s. 75(1)(c) (S. Afr.).

91. Canadian Criminal Code, ss. 753, 761.

92. Criminal Procedure Act, 1977, s. 286A.

93. Belgium: Law on the Court for the Implementation of Sentences 2007, art 4; France: Criminal Procedure Code, art. 706–53–13; Germany: Penal Code, § 67e.

94. "Confining sex offenders after prison release is constitutional, Minn. court rules" *Washington Post,* January 3, 2017.

95. *Karsjens v. Piper* 845 F.3d. 394 (2017). See also *Kansas v. Hendricks* 521 US 346, 366 (1997).

96. Human Rights Committee, *Miller and Carroll v. New Zealand,* (2017), § 8.5.

97. The Republic of Trinidad and Tobago Inspector of Prisons, *2012 Report,* http://www.inspectorofprisonstt.com/report2012/, §77.

98. Griffin and O'Donnell, "Confusingly Compliant."

99. Law on the Execution of Penalties and Security Measures, 2004, art 107.

100. Marc Mauer, Ryan S. King, and Malcolm C. Young. *The Meaning of "Life": Long Prison Sentences in Context* (Washington, D.C.: The Sentencing Project, 2004), 12.

101. Axel Dessecker, "Wie lange dauert lebenslange Freiheitstrafe?" *Monatsschrift für Kriminologie und Strafrechtsreform* 95 (2012): 82–92.

102. Eric Cullen and Tim Newell, *Murderers and Life Imprisonment* (Winchester, UK: Waterside Press, 1999), 21; Ministry of Justice, personal communication with authors, February 10, 2015.

103. Roger Hood and Stephen Shute, with Aidan Wilcox, *The Parole System at Work: A Study of Risk-Based Decision-Making* (London: Home Office, 2000), 81 and xvii. See also Roger Hood, Stephen Shute, Martina Feilzer, and Aidan Wilcox, "Sex Offenders Emerging from Long-Term Imprisonment: A Study of Their Long-Term Reconviction Rates and Parole Board Members' Judgment of Their Risk," *British Journal of Criminology,* 42 (2002): 371–294.

104. Padfield, "Life Sentences in Law and Practice," 23.

105. The comparison may be slightly exaggerated because the minimum terms here apply to mandatory life sentences while those for discretionary life sentences may be slightly shorter. However, this is unlikely to change the outcome.

106. Doris Schartmueller, "Too Dangerous to Get Out? The Use of Individualized Release Mechanisms for Lifetime Incarcerated Offenders in Sweden," *Criminal Justice Policy Review* 25 (2014): 407–431.

107. Dessecker, "Wie lange dauert lebenslange Freiheitstrafe?"; Hartmut-Michael Weber, *Die Abschaffung der lebenslangen Freiheitsstrafe* (Baden-Baden, Germany: Nomos, 1999) 59.

108. American Law Institute, *Model Penal Code: Sentencing, Proposed Final Draft* (approved May 24, 2017).

109. *R v. Secretary of State for the Home Department, Ex parte Doody* [1994] 1 AC 531 (HL) (Eng.).

110. Jeremy Isard, "Under the Cloak of Brain Science: Risk Assessments, Parole, and the Powerful Guise of Objectivity," *California Law Review* 105 (2017): 1223–1255.

111. Diarmuid Griffin and Ian O'Donnell, "The Life Sentence and Parole," *British Journal of Criminology* 52 (2012): 611–629.

112. Netanel Dagan and Dana Segev, "Retributive Whisper: Communicative Elements in Parole," *Law & Social Inquiry* 40 (2015): 611–630; Julian Roberts, "Listening to the Crime Victim: Evaluating Victim Input at Sentencing and Parole," *Crime and Justice* 38 (2009): 347–412.

113. See the concurring opinion of Judge Bratza in *Kafkaris v. Cyprus*, ECtHR February 12, 2008 [GC]. This opinion was not followed in *Kafkaris v. Cyprus (No 2)*, ECtHR, June 21, 2011. For why Judge Bratza's approach should be followed, see Van Zyl Smit et al., "Whole Life Sentences and the Tide of European Human Rights Jurisprudence," 16–19.

10. Life after Life

1. For two recent exceptions, see Catherine Appleton, *Life after Life Imprisonment* (Oxford, UK: Oxford University Press, 2010), a study of 138 released discretionary life-sentenced prisoners in England and Wales; and Marieke Liem, *After Life Imprisonment* (New York: New York University Press, 2016), a study that follows up sixty-eight released life-sentenced prisoners in the state of Massachusetts.

2. This is often the case for released prisoners subject to informal life sentences, that is, post-conviction indefinite preventive detention. See, for example, prisoners sentenced to imprisonment for public protection in England and Wales, discussed in Chapter 2.

3. United Nations Office Crime Prevention and Criminal Justice Branch, *Life Imprisonment* (Vienna: United Nations, 1994), § 71.

4. Ibid., § 66.

5. Ibid.

6. Council of Europe, Recommendation Rec(2003)23 of the Committee of Ministers to Member States on the Management by Prison Administrations of Life-Sentence and Other Long-Term Prisoners (October 9, 2003).

7. Council of Europe, Recommendation Rec(2003)22 of the Committee of Ministers to Member States on Conditional Release (Parole) (September 24, 2003), § 3.

8. Ibid., § 11.

9. Recommendation CM/Rec (2017) 3 of the Committee of Ministers on the European Rules on community sanctions and measures (March 22, 2017).

10. These were Albania, Algeria, Argentina, Armenia, Aruba, Australia, Austria, Azerbaijan, Bahamas, Bahrain, Bangladesh, Belgium, Benin, Bermuda, Botswana, Burkina Faso, Burundi, Cambodia, Canada, Cayman Islands, Central African Republic, Chad, Chile, China, Côte d'Ivoire, Cuba, Curaçao, Cyprus, Czech Republic, Democratic Republic of Congo, Denmark, Djibouti, Eritrea, Estonia, Finland, France, Georgia, Germany, Greece, Guinea, Guyana, Hungary, Indonesia, Ireland, Israel, Italy, Jamaica, Japan, Kazakhstan, Kosovo, Kyrgyzstan, Latvia, Lebanon, Liberia, Lithuania, Luxemburg, Macedonia, Madagascar, Mali, Mauritania, Monaco, Montserrat, Morocco, Netherlands, New Zealand, Niger, Pakistan, Papua New Guinea, Peru, Poland, Romania, Rwanda, Senegal, Serbia, Slovenia, Spain, St. Christopher and Nevis, Sweden, Switzerland, Thailand, Tunisia, Turkey, and the United Kingdom.

11. Project questionnaire for Bangladesh, May 1, 2014.

12. Appleton, *Life after Life Imprisonment,* 82–83.

13. The Parole Board of the Northern Territory, for example, may impose any of the following additional conditions if they were deemed necessary to either support the ex-prisoner on their release or to prevent them from committing further offences while on parole: not consume or purchase alcohol; breath testing and urinalysis; no contact, directly or indirectly, with a victim or other specified person; reside at a specified community or outstation; participate in and complete an assessment / treatment / counselling regime (residential or sessional attendance) such as alcohol programs, domestic violence programs, sex offender programs, psychiatric treatment; not consume a dangerous drug or abuse a prescribed substance that is lawfully obtained; not to engage in conduct that might lead to a domestic violence order being made; and an accommodation curfew. Northern Territories: Parole Act 1971.

Similarly, in Queensland, a parole order may contain additional conditions the board considers necessary, such as: a condition about the parolee's place of residence; employment or participation in a particular program; a condition imposing a curfew for the parolee; and, a condition requiring the parolee to give a test sample. Queensland Correctional Services Act 1982.

14. Information on release conditions from the United States was not derived from our primary data collection. Secondary sources were employed, including Joan Petersilia, *When Prisoners Come Home: Parole and Prisoner Reentry* (Oxford, UK: Oxford University Press, 2003); for California, http://www.cdcr.ca .gov/Parole/Parole_Conditions/index.html; for New York, http://www.doccs.ny .gov/Parole_Handbook.html#h3_7; and for New Jersey, http://www.state.nj.us /parole/docs/AdultParoleHandbook.pdf (Appendix 9).

15. Switzerland: Penal Code, art. 94; Monaco: Penal Code, art. 409, read together with ordonnance no. 4.035 du 17 mai 1968 sur la libération conditionnelle; Peru: Penal Code, art. 58.

16. Petersilia, *When Prisoners Come Home*, 105.

17. Ibid. See also Jeremy Travis, "Invisible Punishment: An Instrument of Social Exclusion," in *Invisible Punishment: The Collateral Consequences of Mass Imprisonment*, ed. Marc Mauer and Meda Chesney-Lind (Washington, D.C.: New Press, 2002).

18. Argentina, Australia, Bahamas, Bermuda, Canada, Chile, Cyprus, France, Germany, Gibraltar, Guernsey, India, Ireland, Isle of Man, Jamaica, Jersey, Kenya, Maldives, Malta, New Zealand, Nigeria, the Pitcairn Islands, Portugal, South Africa, South Korea, Spain, Taiwan, Trinidad and Tobago, and the United Kingdom. See Office of Sex Offender Sentencing, Monitoring, Apprehending, Registering, and Tracking (SMART), *Global Survey of Sex Offender Registration and Notification Systems* (Washington DC: US Department of Justice SMART, 2016), https://smart.gov/pdfs/global-survey-2016-final.pdf; John Pratt, "Risk control, rights and legitimacy in the limited liability state," *British Journal of Criminology* 57 (2017): 1322–1339.

19. Ministry of Justice National Offender Management Service, *MAPPA Guidance 2012* (Version 4.1, updated December 2016) (London: National Offender Management Service Offender Management and Public Protection Group, 2016), § 6.48.

20. Ibid.

21. Malcolm Feeley and Jonathan Simon, "Actuarial Justice: The Emerging New Criminal Law," in *The Futures of Criminology*, ed. David Nelken (London: Sage, 1994); David Garland, *The Culture of Crime Control: Crime and Social Order in Contemporary Society* (Oxford, UK: Oxford University Press, 2001); John Pratt, David Brown, Mark Brown, Simon Hallsworth, and Wayne Morrison, eds., *The New Punitiveness: Trends, Theories, Perspectives* (Uffculme, UK: Willan Publishing, 2005).

22. Malcolm Feeley and Jonathan Simon, "The New Penology: Notes on the Emerging Strategy of Corrections and Its Implications," *Criminology* 30 (1992): 449–474. See also Jonathan Simon, *Poor Discipline: Parole and the Social Control of the Underclass, 1890–1990* (Chicago, IL: University of Chicago Press, 1993), 203; Jonathan Simon, "Managing the Monstrous: Sex Offenders and the New Penology," *Psychology, Public Policy and Law* 4(1998): 452–467; Jonathan Simon and Malcolm Feeley, "True Crime: The New Penology and Public Discourse on Crime," in *Punishment as Social Control: Essays in Honor of Sheldon Messinger*, ed. Thomas Blomberg and Stanley Cohen (New York: Aldine de Gruyter, 1995).

23. Petersilia, *When Prisoners Come Home*, 90. See also James Austin and John Irwin, *It's about Time: America's Imprisonment Binge*, 4th ed. (Belmont, Calif.: Cengage Learning, 2012).

24. See, for example, Anne-Marie McAlinden, "The Governance of Sexual Offending across Europe: Penal Policies, Political Economies and the Institution-alization of Risk," *Punishment and Society* 14 (2012): 166–192.

25. Appleton, *Life after Life Imprisonment*.

26. Research examining the recidivism rates of released life-sentenced prisoners has generally been limited. Existing studies on this topic often have methodolog-ical shortcomings due to short follow-up periods, small samples, selection effects, and a lack of control variables: Lila Kazemian and Jeremy Travis, "Imperative for

Inclusion of Long Termers and Lifers in Research and Policy," *Criminology and Public Policy* 14 (2015): 355–395. For an overview of previous research findings, see Marieke Liem, Margaret A. Zahn, and Lisa Tichavsky, "Criminal Recidivism among Homicide Offenders," *Journal of Interpersonal Violence,* 29 (2014): 2630–2651.

27. Marc Mauer, Ryan King, and Malcolm Young, *The Meaning of "Life": Long Prison Sentences in Context* (Washington, D.C.: The Sentencing Project, 2004), 23.

28. California Department of Corrections and Rehabilitation, *Lifer Parolee Recidivism Report* (Sacramento: California Department of Corrections and Rehabilitation, 2013), 5.

29. Robert Weisberg, Debbie Mukamal, and Jordan Segall, *Life in Limbo: An Examination of Parole Release for Prisoners Serving Life Sentences with the Possibility of Parole in California* (Stanford, Calif.: University of Stanford, Stanford Criminal Justice Center, 2011), 17.

30. Kimberley Keyser, *2011 Inmate Releases: Three-Year Post Release Follow-Up* (Albany: New York State Community Corrections and Community Supervision, 2012), 9.

31. Liem, Zahn, and Tichavsky, "Criminal Recidivism among Homicide Offenders," 2643.

32. Stål Bjørkly and Leif Wagge, "Killing Again: A Review of Research on Recidivistic Single-Victim Homicide," *International Journal of Forensic Mental Health* 4 (2005): 99–106.

33. Mauer, King and Young, *The Meaning of "Life,"* 23.

34. The National Parole Board, *Offenders Serving a Life Sentence for Murder: A Statistical Overview* (Canada: National Parole Board, 2002), 12. See also Correctional Service Canada, "Forum on Corrections Research: Recidivism among Homicide Offenders" 4 (1992) ,http://www.csc-scc.gc.ca/research/forum /e042/e042c-eng.shtml; Jesse Cale, Darryl Plecas, Irwin M. Cohen, and Stephanie Fortier, "An Exploratory Analysis of Factors Associated with Repeat Homicide in Canada," *Homicide Studies,* 14 (2010): 159–180.

35. Parole Board of Canada, *Performance Monitoring Report 2014–2015* (Canada: Parole Board of Canada, 2015), 51.

36. Ibid.

37. HMI Probation and HMI Prisons, *A Joint Inspection of Life Sentence Prisoners* (London: Criminal Justice Joint Inspection, 2013), 6.

38. Barry Mitchell and Julian Roberts, *Exploring the Mandatory Life Sentence for Murder* (Oxford, UK: Hart Publishing, 2012), 60–61.

39. G. Matthew Snodgrass, Arjan A. J. Blokland, Amelia Haviland, Paul Nieuwbeerta, and Daniel S. Nagin, "Does the Time Cause the Crime? An Examination of the Relationship between Time Served and Reoffending in the Netherlands," *Criminology,* 49 (2011): 1149–1194, 1167.

40. Shasta Holland, Kym Pointon and Stuart Ross, *Who Returns to Prison? Patterns of Recidivism among Prisoners Released from Custody in Victoria in 2002–03,* Corrections Research Paper No 1 (Victoria: Department of Justice, 2007), 10. See also Barbara Thompson, *Recidivism in NSW: General Study,* Research Publication No 31 (New South Wales: Department of Corrective Services, May 1995), 29–30.

41. Roderic Broadhurst, Ross Maller, Max Maller, and Brigitte Bouhours "The Recidivism of Homicide Offenders in Western Australia," *Australia and New Zealand Journal of Criminology,* (2017): 8, DOI: 10.1177/0004865817722393. See also Wai-Yin Wan and Don Weatherburn "Violent Criminal Careers: A Retrospective Longitudinal Study," *New South Wales Bureau of Crime Statistics and Research Crime and Justice Bulletin* 198 (2016): 1–12.

42. Joakim Sturup and Per Lindqvist, "Homicide Offenders 32 Years Later—A Swedish Population-based Study on Recidivism," *Criminal Behaviour and Mental Health,* 24 (2014): 5–17. See also Markku Eronen, Panu Hakola and Jari Tiihonen, "Factors Associated with Homicide Recidivism in a 13-Year Sample of Homicide Offenders in Finland," *Psychiatric Services* 47 (1996): 403–406.

43. Mauer, King and Young, *The Meaning of "Life,"* 24.

44. Matthew Durose, Alexia Cooper, and Howard Snyder, *Recidivism of Prisoners Released in 30 States in 2005: Patterns from 2005 to 2010* (Washington, D.C.: US Bureau of Justice Statistics, 2014).

45. See Mark Cunningham and Thomas Reidy, "Integrating Base Rate Data in Violence Risk Assessments at Capital Sentencing," *Behavioral Sciences and the Law* 16 (1998): 71–95; James Marquart and Jonathan Sorensen, "A National Study of the *Furman*-Commuted Inmates: Assessing the Threat to Society from Capital Offenders," in *The Death Penalty in America: Current Controversies,* ed. Hugo Bedau (Oxford, UK: Oxford University Press, 1997).

46. Marquart and Sorensen, "A National Study of the *Furman*-Commuted Inmates: Assessing the Threat to Society from Capital Offenders," 174.

47. Ibid.

48. Ibid., 172.

49. See also UK Home Office, *Life Licencees: Reconviction and Recall by the End of 1995: England and Wales* (London: Home Office, 1997); UK Home Office, *Reconvictions of Prisoners Discharged from Prison in 1993, England and Wales* London: Home Office, 1997); Robert Weisberg, Debbie Mukamal and Jordan Segall, *Life in Limbo;* California Department of Corrections and Rehabilitation, *Lifer Parolee Recidivism Report;* R. E. "Bob" Brown, "A Beacon of Hope—Sunny ways: Life Sentenced Offenders," *Executive Exchange,* Fall 2016, 29–38.

50. Hugo Bedau, "Recidivism, Parole, and Deterrence," in *The Death Penalty in America,* 3rd ed., ed. Hugo Bedau (Oxford, UK: Oxford University Press, 1982), 175–180.

51. For classic work on the significance of the age-crime relationship, see Sheldon Glueck and Eleanor Glueck, *Juvenile Delinquents Grown Up* (New York: Commonwealth Fund, 1940). See also Travis Hirschi and Michael Gottfredson, "Age and the Explanation of Crime," *American Journal of Sociology* 89 (1983): 552–584; Walter Gove, "The Effect of Age and Gender on Deviant Behavior: A Biopsychosocial Perspective," in *Gender and the Life Course,* ed. Alice Rossi (New York: Aldine, 1985); and Neal Shover, *Great Pretenders: Pursuits and Careers of Persistent Thieves* (Boulder, Colo.: Westview Press, 1996). For a more recently developed age-graded theory of social bonds or informal social control as an explanation of desistance, see Robert Sampson and John Laub, *Crime in the Making: Pathways and Turning Points through Life* (Cambridge,

Mass.: Harvard University Press, 1993); John Laub and Robert Sampson, *Shared Beginnings, Divergent Lives: Delinquent Boys to Age 70* (Cambridge, Mass.: Harvard University Press, 2003); Stephen Farrall, Ben Hunter, Gilly Sharpe, and Adam Calverley, *Criminal Careers in Transition: The Social Context of Desistance from Crime* (Oxford, UK: Oxford University Press, 2014).

52. See, for example, Ros Burnett, *The Dynamics of Recidivism* (Oxford, UK: Centre for Criminological Research, University of Oxford, 1992); Shadd Maruna, *Making Good: How Ex-Convicts Reform and Rebuild Their Lives* (Washington, D.C.: American Psychological Association, 2001); Peggy Giordano, Stephen Cernkovich, and Jennifer Rudolph, "Gender, Crime and Desistance: Toward a Theory of Cognitive Transformation," *American Journal of Sociology* 197 (2002): 990–1064; and Ray Paternoster and Shawn Bushway, "Desistance and the 'Feared Self': Toward an Identity Theory of Criminal Desistance," *Journal of Criminal Law and Criminology* 99 (2009): 1103–1156. For critical discussion on the subjective and social changes related to desistance, see Thomas LeBel, Ros Burnett, Shadd Maruna, and Shawn Bushway, "The 'Chicken and Egg' of Subjective and Social Factors in Desistance from Crime," *European Journal of Criminology* 5 (2008): 130–158.

53. John Coker and John Martin, *Licensed to Live* (Oxford, UK: Basil Blackwell, 1985), 231.

54. Appleton, *Life after Life Imprisonment.* On the importance of a therapeutic relationship in supporting desistance from crime, see also Ros Burnett and Fergus McNeill, "The Place of the Officer-Offender Relationship in Assisting Offenders to Desist from Crime," *Probation Journal* 52 (2005): 221–242; and Daniel Martin, John Garske, and M. Katherine Davis, "Relation of the Therapeutic Alliance with Outcome and Other Variables: A Meta-Analytic Review," *Journal of Consulting and Clinical Psychology* 68 (2000): 438–450.

55. Melissa Munn and Chris Bruckert, *On the Outside: From Lengthy Imprisonment to Lasting Freedom* (Vancouver, Canada: University of British Columbia Press, 2013). See also Melissa Munn, "Living in the Aftermath: The Impact of Lengthy Incarceration on Post-Carceral Success," *Howard Journal of Criminal Justice* 50 (2011): 233–246.

56. Munn and Bruckert, *On the Outside,* 93.

57. Ibid., 169.

58. Munn, "Living in the Aftermath," 241. See also Sabine Heinlein, *Among Murderers: Life after Prison* (Berkeley: University of California Press); and Nancy Mullane, *Life after Murder: Five Men in Search of Redemption* (New York: Public Affairs, 2012).

59. Liem, *After Life Imprisonment.* See also Marieke Liem, "Desistance after Life Imprisonment," in *New Perspectives on Desistance: Theoretical and Empirical Developments,* ed. Esther F. J. C. van Ginneken and Emily Luise Hart (London: Palgrave Macmillan, 2017).

60. Liem, *After Life Imprisonment,* 203.

61. See Stephen Farrall, Gilly Sharpe, Ben Hunter, and Adam Calverley, "Theorizing Structural and Individual-Level Processes in Desistance and Persistence: Outlining an Integrated Perspective," *Australian and New Zealand Journal of Criminology* 44 (2011): 218–234; Joanna Shapland, Stephen Farrall, and

Anthony Bottoms, *Global Perspectives on Desistance: Reviewing What We Know and Looking to the Future* (Abingdon, UK: Routledge, 2016).

62. See Alison Liebling, "Moral Performance, Inhuman and Degrading Treatment and Prison Pain," *Punishment and Society* 13 (2011): 530–550. For a review of the role prisons can play in supporting desistance, see Anne Owers, Paul Leighton, Clodach McGrory, Fergus McNeill, and Phil Wheatley, *Review of the Northern Ireland Prison Service* (Belfast: Prisons Review Team, 2011).

63. John Irwin, *Lifers: Seeking Redemption in Prison* (New York: Routledge, 2009). Irwin interviewed seventeen incarcerated men who were serving sentences of twenty years or more in San Quentin prison in California. He found that most life-sentenced prisoners changed drastically during the course of their sentence. The men experienced a process of "awakening," which became the point at which they understood that there has been something fundamentally wrong with their former behavior and that their actions had led them to their current situation.

64. See Trish McCulloch, "Probation, Social Context and Desistance: Retracing the Relationship," *Probation Journal* 52 (2005): 8–22; Fergus McNeill, "A desistance paradigm for offender management," *Criminology and Criminal Justice* 6 (2006): 39–62.

65. For insight on some of the difficulties of release after LWOP, see Jessica Earnshaw, "Life after Life without Parole," *The Marshall Project*, June 13, 2017, https://www.themarshallproject.org/2017/06/13/life-after-life-without-parole?utm_medium= email&utm_campaign= newsletter&utm_source= opening-statement &utm_term= newsletter-20170613-776#.NSgSziWEV.

66. Appleton, *Life after Life Imprisonment,* 217.

67. United Nations Office Crime Prevention and Criminal Justice Branch, *Life Imprisonment,* 64.

68. In the United Kingdom, release conditions are referred to as the "life license," since it remains in place for the rest of the individual's lifetime. However, the supervision requirement of the license may be lifted: normally after a minimum of four continuous trouble-free years, or ten in the case of a sex offender. Life-sentenced prisoners, however, remain liable to recall even if license conditions have been removed. See Appleton, *Life after Life Imprisonment,* 180.

69. Justice, *Sentenced to Life: Reform of the Law and Procedure for Those Sentenced to Life Imprisonment* (London: Justice, 1996), 75.

70. United Nations Office Crime Prevention and Criminal Justice Branch, *Life Imprisonment,* § 64.

71. Council of Europe, Recommendation Rec(2003)22 on Conditional Release (parole), § 30; Council of Europe, Recommendation CM/Rec (2017) 3 of the Committee of Ministers on the European Rules on Community Sanctions and Measures (March 22, 2017).

72. Council of Europe, Recommendation Rec(2003)22 on Conditional Release (parole), § 32.

73. Ibid., § 33.

74. Council of Europe, Recommendation Rec(2003)23 on the Management by Prison Administrations of Life-Sentence and Other Long-Term Prisoners, § 34. See also Recommendation CM/Rec (2017) 3 of the Committee of Ministers on the European Rules on Community Sanctions and Measures (March 22, 2017).

75. For example, Council of Europe, Recommendation Rec (2006)2 of the Committee of Ministers to Member States on the European Prison Rules (January 11, 2006).

76. *Stafford v. United Kingdom,* ECtHR (app. 46295/99), May 28, 2002 [GC].

77. *Morrissey v. Brewer,* 408 US 471 (1972); *Gagnon v. Scarpelli,* 411 U.S. 778 (1973). For discussion of the limits of the due process rights of prisoners facing recall, see Dirk van Zyl Smit and Alessandro Corda, "American Exceptionalism in Parole Release and Supervision: A European Perspective" in *American Exceptionalism in Crime and Punishment,* ed, Kevin R. Reitz (New York: Oxford University Press, 2017).

78. Human Rights Committee, *Miller and Carroll v. New Zealand,* Communication No. 2502/2014, U.N. Doc. CCPR/C/112/D/2502/2014 (2017).

79. Albania, Algeria, Argentina, Armenia, Aruba, Australia, Austria, Azerbaijan, Bahamas, Bahrain, Bangladesh, Belgium, Benin, Bermuda, Bhutan, Botswana, Burkina Faso, Burundi, Cambodia, Canada, Cayman Islands, Central African Republic, Chad, Chile, China, Côte d'Ivoire, Cuba, Curaçao, Cyprus, Democratic Republic of Congo, Denmark, Djibouti, Egypt, Eritrea, Estonia, Finland, France, Georgia, Germany, Greece, Guinea, Guyana, Hungary, Indonesia, Ireland, Israel, Italy, Jamaica, Japan, Kosovo, Latvia, Lebanon, Liberia, Luxemburg, Macedonia, Madagascar, Mali, Mauritania, Monaco, Montserrat, Morocco, New Zealand, Niger, Pakistan, Papua New Guinea, Peru, Poland, Romania, Rwanda, Senegal, Serbia, Slovenia, Spain, Sweden, Switzerland, Thailand, Tunisia, Turkey, and the United Kingdom. While many respondents outlined the procedures of recall, only Canada, England and Wales, Ireland, New Zealand, and Poland provided statistical information on the number of life-sentenced prisoners recalled to prison in 2014.

80. Project questionnaire for the Czech Republic, September 1, 2014; project questionnaire for Belarus, March, 1, 2013; project questionnaire for Bangladesh, May 1, 2014.

81. Albania, Algeria, Argentina, Armenia, Aruba, Australia, Austria, Azerbaijan, Bahamas, Bahrain, Belgium, Benin, Bermuda, Bhutan, Botswana, Burkina Faso, Burundi, Cambodia, Canada, Central African Republic, Chad, Chile, China, Côte d'Ivoire, Cuba, Curaçao, Cyprus, Democratic Republic of Congo, Denmark, Djibouti, Eritrea, France, Georgia (Europe), Germany, Greece, Guinea, Guyana, Indonesia, Ireland, Israel, Italy, Jamaica, Japan, Latvia, Liberia, Luxemburg, Macedonia, Madagascar, Mali, Mauritania, Monaco, Montserrat, New Zealand, Niger, Pakistan, Papua New Guinea, Peru, Poland, Romania, Rwanda, Senegal, Spain, Sweden, Switzerland, Thailand, Tunisia, Turkey, and the United Kingdom.

82. Slovenia: Criminal Code, art. 89(1). See also Katja Šugman Stubbs and Matjaž Ambrož, "Recalling Conditionally Released Prisoners in Slovenia," *European Journal of Probation* 4 (2012): 99–111; Katja Šugman Stubbs and Matjaž Ambrož, "Slovenia," in *Release from Prison: European Policy and Practice,* ed. Nicola Padfield, Dirk van Zyl Smit, and Frieder Dünkel (Devon, UK: Willan Publishing, 2010).

83. Slovenia: Criminal Code, art. 88(8). See also Stubbs and Ambrož, "Slovenia."

84. Germany: Penal Code, art. 56f.

85. Bahamas, Belgium, Benin, Burkina Faso, Burundi, Central Africa Republic, Chad, Chile, Côte d'Ivoire, Cuba, Democratic of Congo, Eritrea, France, Madagascar, Mali, Mauritania, Monaco, New Zealand, Niger, Rwanda, Senegal, Spain, and the United Kingdom.

86. Benin, Cuba, the United Kingdom, France, and Canada respectively.

87. Cuba: Penal Code, art. 58.

88. These were Egypt, Estonia, Finland, Hungary, Kosovo, Lebanon, Morocco, and Serbia.

89. See Tapio Lappi-Seppälä, "Life Imprisonment and Related Institutions in the Nordic Countries," in *Life Imprisonment and Human Rights,* ed. Dirk van Zyl Smit and Catherine Appleton (London: Hart, 2016).

90. For example, Algeria, Benin, Burkino Faso, Burundi, Chad, Côte d'Ivoire, Congo, Guinea, Madagascar, Mauritania, Niger, Rwanda, and Senegal.

91. Burundi: Criminal Code, art. 131.

92. For critical analysis of the recall system in England and Wales, see Justice, *Sentenced for Life;* Nigel Stone, *A Companion Guide to Life Sentences,* 2nd ed. (Crayford, UK: Shaw and Sons, 2008); Nicola Padfield, "Parole and Early Release: the Criminal Justice and Immigration Act 2008 Changes in Context," *Criminal Law Review* (2009): 116–187; Nicola Padfield, "Recalling Conditionally Released Prisoners in England and Wales," *European Journal of Probation* 4 (2012): 34–45; Appleton, *Life after Life Imprisonment.*

93. See Karin Bruckmüller, with assistance from Katrin Forsner, "Recalling Conditionally Released Prisoners in Austria," *European Journal of Probation* 4 (2012): 6–18; Ineke Pruin, "Recalling Conditionally Released Prisoners in Germany," *European Journal of Probation* 4 (2012): 63–72; Nicola Padfield and Alison Liebling, with Helen Arnold, *An Exploration of Decision-Making at Discretionary Lifer Panels* (London: Home Office, 2000); Nicola Padfield, "Editorial," *European Journal of Probation* 4 (2012): 1–5.

94. See Kim Reuflet, "France," in *Release from Prison;* Martine Herzog-Evans, "Non-Compliance in France: A Human Approach and a Hair Splitting Legal System," *European Journal of Probation* 4 (2012): 46–62.

95. Liem, *After Life Imprisonment,* 175.

96. Justice, *Sentenced to Life;* Appleton, *Life after Life Imprisonment;* Liem, *After Life Imprisonment.*

97. Switzerland: Penal Code, art. 89.

98. Austria: Penal Code, art. 48(1). See also Karin Bruckmüller and Veronika Hofinger, "Austria" in *Release from Prison;* Bruckmüller, with assistance from Forsner, "Recalling Conditionally released prisoners in Austria." For some innovative responses to parole and probation violations in the United States, see Madeline M. Carter, ed., *Responding to Parole and Probation Violations: A Handbook to Guide Local Policy Development* (Washington, D.C.: US Department of Justice National Institute of Corrections, 2001); Peggy Burke, *Policy-Driven Responses to Probation and Parole Violations* (Washington, D.C.: US Department of Justice National Institute of Corrections, 1997).

99. Capital Territory, Australia: Crimes (Sentence Administration) Act 2005, s. 309.

100. South Australia: Correctional Services Act 1982, s. 68(2a).

101. Liem, *After Life Imprisonment,* 175–176.

102. During the year 2002–2003, thirty life-sentenced prisoners were recalled to prison, compared to 178 recalled in 2006–2007; see Appleton, *Life after Life Imprisonment,* 170. See also Parole Board, *Parole Board for England and Wales Annual Report and Accounts 2006–2007* (London: Stationary Office, 2007).

103. Appleton, *Life after Life Imprisonment,* 177.

104. Project questionnaire for the England and Wales, September 1, 2014.

105. Russell Webster, "IPPs, Recalls and the Future of Parole," October 25, 2017, http://www.russellwebster.com/martin-jones2.

11. Rethinking Life

1. Jacques Derrida, *The Death Penalty, Volume 1.* (Chicago, Ill.: University of Chicago Press, 2013), 93–94; Amy Swiftin, "Mastery over the Time of the Other: The Death Penalty and Life in Prison without Parole." *Law Critique.* 27 (2016): 171–186.

2. BVerfGE 45 187 at 245 (Ger.).

3. *Vinter and others v. United Kingdom,* ECtHR (apps. 66069/09, 130/10 and 3896/10), July 9, 2013 [GC]; *Khoroshenko v. Russia,* ECtHR (app. 41418/04), June 30, 2015 [GC]; *Dickson v. United Kingdom,* ECtHR (app. 44362/04), December 4, 2007 [GC]; *Hirst v. United Kingdom (2),* ECtHR (app. 74025/01), October 6, 2005 [GC].

4. *Vinter and others v. United Kingdom,* July 9, 2013, § 114, emphasis added.

5. Ibid., Concurring opinion of Judge Power-Forde.

6. See *R v. August* (Criminal Appeal 22 of 2012) Court of Appeal of Belize 4 November 2016 (Belize); *S v. Tcoeib* (SA 4/93) [1996] NASC 1; 1996 (1) SACR 390, (NmS), (Namibia); *De Boucherville v. The Government of Mauritius* [2008] UKPC 37, 25 B.H.R.C. 433; and *Makoni v. Commissioner of Prisons,* CCZ 8/16, July 13, 2016 (Zimbabwe).

7. *Prosecutor v. Galić,* MICT-14–83-ES (June 23, 2015), §§ 19–22.

8. These recent developments add extra weight to arguments for the abolition of LWOP that we have advanced previously. Catherine Appleton and Bent Grøver, "The Pros and Cons of Life without Parole," *British Journal of Criminology* 47 (2007): 597–615; Dirk van Zyl Smit, "Life Imprisonment: Recent Issues in National and International Law," *International Journal of Law and Psychiatry* 29 (2006): 405–421.

9. Michael Tonry, "Equality and Human Dignity," *Crime and Justice* 45 (2016): 459–496.

10. Jonathan Simon "Dignity and Risk" in *Life without Parole: America's New Death Penalty?* ed. Charles J. Ogletree and Austin Sarat (New York: New York University Press, 2012).

11. Joshua Kleinfeld, "Two Cultures of Punishment," *Stanford Law Review* 68 (2016): 933–1036.

12. Ibid., 950.

13. Craig S. Lerner, "Life without Parole as a Conflicted Punishment," *Wake Forest Law Review* 48 (2013): 1101–1173. See also Paul Cassell, "In Defense of

the Death Penalty," in *Debating the Death Penalty: Should America Have Capital Punishment?*, ed. Hugo Bedau and Paul Cassell (Oxford, UK: Oxford University Press, 2004).

14. Lerner, "Life without Parole as a Conflicted Punishment," 1170.

15. Ibid., 1171.

16. For an exposition of the controversial amendment, see Anna Connix, "Life without Parole for Preventive Reasons? Lifelong Post-Sentence Detention in Switzerland," in *Life Imprisonment and Human Rights*, ed. Dirk van Zyl Smit and Catherine Appleton (London: Hart, 2016), 439–443.

17. For an overview of LWOP as an alternative to the death penalty, see Roger Hood and Carolyn Hoyle, *The Death Penalty: A Worldwide Perspective*, 5th ed. (Oxford, UK: Oxford University Press, 2015), 478–484.

18. American Law Institute, "Model Penal Code: Sentencing, Proposed Final Draft" (approved May 24, 2017), 161.

19. Ibid.

20. Ibid.

21. Ibid.

22. *R (Ralston Wellington) v. Secretary of State for the Home Department* [2007] EWHC 1109 (Admin) (Eng.), § 39 (iv).

23. Sentencing Remarks of Mr. Justice Openshaw, in *R v Stephen Port*, Central Criminal Court, in London, November 25, 2016: "The sentence therefore upon the counts of murder is a sentence of life imprisonment; I decline to set a minimum term; the result is a whole life sentence and the defendant will die in prison" (https://www.judiciary.gov.uk/judgments/sentencing-remarks-of-mr-justice -openshaw-r-v-stephen-port/). See also the sentencing remarks in *R v. Halliwell* (https://www.judiciary.gov.uk/wp-content/uploads/2016/09/r-v-halliwell-sentencing -remarks.pdf) and *R v. Dennehy* (https://www.judiciary.gov.uk/wp-content /uploads/JCO/Documents/Judgments/the-queen-v-dennehy-sentencing-remarks -28022014.pdf).

24. See the procedure for dealing with consecutive fixed-term sentences in South Africa discussed in Chapter 9.

25. Rachel E. Barkow, "Life without Parole and the Hope for Real Sentencing Reform," in *Life without Parole: America's New Death Penalty?*, 211.

26. Marie Gottschalk, "No Way Out? Politics and the Hope for Real Sentencing Reform," in *Life without Parole: America's New Death Penalty?*, 227.

27. Diário da Câmara dos Senhores Deputados (Journal of the Sessions of the Chamber of Deputies) 1884: 1022–1023, quoted and translated in Ines Horta Pinto, "Punishment in Portuguese Criminal Law: A Penal System without Life Imprisonment," in *Life Imprisonment and Human Rights*, 292.

28. Ibid.

29. Paulo Pinto de Albuquerque, *Direito Prisional Português e Europeu* (Coimbra: Coimbra Editora, 2006).

30. Portugal: art. 30; Angola: art. 66; Brazil: art. 5-XLVII; Bolivia: art. 118; Cape Verde: art. 33; Colombia: art. 34; Costa Rica: art. 40; East Timor: art. 32; El Salvador: art. 27; Mozambique: art. 61; Nicaragua: art. 37; São Tomé and Príncipe: art. 37; and Venezuela: art. 44.

31. Constitution of the Portuguese Republic, 7th revision, [2005], art. 30.

32. Bolivia: art. 118; Nicaragua: art. 37; Venezuela: art. 44.

33. Colombian Constitutional Court, decision C-397/10 of May 25, 2010. Full text (in Spanish), http://www.corteconstitucional.gov.co/relatoria/2010/C -397–10.htm.

34. There appears to be an ongoing effort to introduce the life sentence in Colombia, with a succession of, so far unsuccessful, attempts in 2011, 2013, and as recently as 2015. "Se hundió el referendo de prisión perpetua," *El Espectador,* September 13, 2011, http://www.elespectador.com/noticias/politica/se-hundio-el -referendo-de-prision-perpetua-articulo-298975; "Proponen cadena perpetua revisable contra violadores de menores de edad," *El Espectador,* July 31, 2013, http://www.elespectador.com/noticias/politica/proponen-cadena-perpetua -revisable-contra-violadores-de-articulo-437110; "Revive proyecto para establ-ecer la cadena perpetua en Colombia," *El Espectador,* February 19, 2015, http://www.elespectador.com/noticias/politica/revive-proyecto-establecer-cadena -perpetua-colombia-articulo-545062; "Se revive debate por cadena perpetua para violadores de niños," *El Tiempo,* September 20, 2015, http://www.eltiempo.com /politica/congreso/cadena-perpetua-para-violadores/16382007.

35. "Observaciones de la Comisión Asesora para el Diseño de la Política Criminal del Estado Colombiano, a la Iniciativa sobre la Imposición de Cadena Perpetua a Ciertos Delitos Realizados contra Menores," https://de.scribd.com/doc /61527060/2011-CADENA-PERPETUA-FINAL4, 35. See also "Comisión asesora de política criminal vuelve trizas proyecto de cadena perpetua," *La silla vacia,* August 2, 2011, http://lasillavacia.com/historia/comision-asesora-de-politica -criminal-vuelve-trizas-proyecto-de-cadena-perpetua-26323.

36. Constitution of Mexico, art. 22.

37. Supreme Court of Justice of Mexico, P./J. 126/2001 and P./J. 127/2001 of October 1, 2001, *Semanario Judicial de la Federación y su Gaceta* XIV (October 2001), Novena Época, Pleno, 14 and 15.

38. Rodrigo Labardini, "Life imprisonment and extradition: historical development, international context, and the current situation in Mexico and the United States," *Southwestern Journal of Law and Trade in the Americas* 11 (2005): 1–108; Ydalia Pérez Fernández Ceja, "El cambio de Jurisprudencia de la Suprema Corte de Justicia de la Nación," *Revista Jurídica Online* (Facultad de Jurisprudencia, Universidad Católica de Santiago de Guayaquil, México), 631–667.

39. Supreme Court of Justice of Mexico, *Acción de inconstitucionalidad 20/2003,* decision of September 6, 2005, in Spanish, https://www.scjn.gob.mx /Transparencia/Epocas/HistoricoInformacionOtorgadaParticulares/Pleno/2003/ai -20–2003-pleno.pdf; P./J. 1/2006 and P./J. 2/2006 of May 1, 2006, *Semanario Judicial de la Federación y su Gaceta,* Novena Época XXIII (February 2006), 5, 6. See also Pérez Fernández Ceja, "El cambio de Jurisprudencia"; María del Pilar Espinosa Torres, "La cadena perpetua. Una pena sin sentido. La prisión vitalicia en Veracruz," *Letras jurídicas: revista de los investigadores del Instituto de Investigaciones Jurídicas U. V.* 26 (2012): 4.

40. Chihuahua: Penal Code, art. 29; Puebla: Penal Code, art. 41; Quintana Roo: Penal Code, art. 22; State of Mexico: Penal Code, art. 23; Veracruz: Penal Code, art. 48.

41. If such majority is not reached, "the rulings pronounced by the Supreme Court of Justice shall have effect only on the particular case in question.": Constitution of Mexico, art. 105.

42. "Correa rechaza implantar cadena perpetua en Ecuador," *El Universo,* June 24, 2007, http://www.eluniverso.com/2007/06/24/0001/8/B3973D3FD47B4 F3DBDC1DD854188B4AA.html.

43. In Slovenia, the life sentence was introduced in art. 46-2 of the new Penal Code of 2008: Filip Vojta, "Life and Long-Term Imprisonment in the Countries of the Former Yugoslavia," in *Life Imprisonment and Human Rights.* In Spain, Organic Law 1/2015 of March 30, 2015 modified art. 36-1 of the Spanish Criminal Code. See also Julián Carlos Ríos Martín, *Life Imprisonment in Spain: An Inhuman and Unlawful Punishment,* www.statewatch.org/analyses/no-259 -life-imprisonment-in-Spain.pdf.

44. BVErfGE 45, 187 (Ger.).

45. The earlier German arguments are comprehensively spelled out in Hartmut-Michael Weber, *Die Abschaffung der lebenslangen Freiheitsstrafe* (Baden-Baden, Germany: Nomos, 1996). For recent academic arguments favoring the abolition of life imprisonment in Germany, see Katrin Höffler and Johannes Kaspar, "Plädoyer für die Abschaffung der lebenslangen Freiheitsstrafe," *Goltdammer's Archiv für Strafrecht* 162 (2015): 453–462; Tonio Walter, "Vom Beruf des Gesetzgebers zur Gesetzgebung: zur Reform der Tötungsdelikte und gegen Fischer et al. in NStZ 2014, 9," *Neue Zeitschrift für Strafrecht* 34 (2014): 368–376. The major inquiry conducted by the German federal government into the reform of homicide law in 2014 considered the desirability of retaining life imprisonment and concluded, by a majority of fourteen votes to zero, with four abstentions, that it should remain as a punishment for serious homicide. *Abschlussbericht der Expertengruppe zur Reform der Tötungsdelikte (§§ 211—213, 57a StGB),* June 2015, 53–54, http://www.bmjv.de/SharedDocs/Downloads/DE /Artikel/Abschlussbericht_Experten_Toetungsdelikte.pdf;jsessionid=64509F1F56 C2F6A05EA0F968D10C646B.1_cid324?__blob= publicationFile&v=2; Thomas Uwer and Jasper von Schlieffen, *Abschaffung der lebenslangen Ftreiheitsstrafe* (Berlin: Policy Paper der Strafverteidigervereinigungen, 2016).

46. *S v. Tcoeib* (SA 4/93) [1996] NASC 1; 1996 (1) SACR 390 (NmS) (Namibia). This case gives a full account of the reasoning in *S* v. *Xehemia Tjijo* (High Court of Namibia, 4/9/91. Unreported), where the argument that life imprisonment was unconstitutional was upheld.

47. *Öcalan v. Turkey (No. 2),* (Apps 24069/03, 197/04, 6201/06 and 10464/07), March 18, 2014, minority opinion of Judge Pinto de Albuquerque, §§ 7, 9–10.

48. *Khamtokhu and Aksenchik v. Russia,* ECtHR (Apps. 60367/08 and 961/11), January 24, 2017 [GC]. Dissenting opinion of Judge Pinto de Albuquerque.

49. Ibid., § 32.

50. Address of Pope Francis to the Delegates of the International Association of Penal Law, October 23, 2014, w2.vatican.va/content/francesco/en/speeches /2014/october/documents/papa-francesco_20141023_associazione-internazionale -diritto-penale.html; Meritxell Abellán Almenara and Dirk van Zyl Smit, "Human Dignity and Life Imprisonment: The Pope Enters the Debate," *Human Rights Law Review* 15 (2015): 369–376.

51. See Chapter 8.

52. Tapio Lappi-Seppälä, "Life Imprisonment and Related Institutions in the Nordic Countries," in *Life Imprisonment and Human Rights.*

53. Walter, "Vom Beruf des Gesetzgebers zur Gesetzgebung."

54. Marc Mauer, *A Proposal to Reduce Time Served in Federal Prison,* Testimony to Charles Colson Task Force on Federal Corrections, March 11, 2015 (Washington, D.C.: The Sentencing Project, 2015) 4, http://sentencingproject.org/wp-content/uploads/2015/09/Colson-Task-Force-Testimony-Mar-2015.pdf.

55. *Öcalan v. Turkey (No. 2),* March 18, 2014, Dissenting opinion of Judge Pinto de Albuquerque, § 5 footnote 12.

56. Ibid., § 6.

57. Ibid., § 6.

58. Andrew von Hirsch and Andrew Ashworth, *Proportionate Sentencing* (Oxford, UK: Oxford University Press, 2005) 52. See also Chapter 5.

59. "Breivik Convicted to Permanent Detention," http://www.domstol.no/no/Enkelt-domstol/22–7/Nyheter-om-227-saken/Breivik-convicted-to-permanent-detention. See also Catherine Appleton, "Lone Wolf Terrorism in Norway," *International Journal of Human Rights* 18 (2014) 127–142.

60. Marc Mauer and Ashley Nellis, "The Impact of Life Imprisonment on Criminal Justice Reform in the United States," in *Life Imprisonment and Human Rights.*

61. *S v. Dodo* 2001 (3) SA 382 (CC), 403–404 (S. Afr.).

62. Hugo Adam Bedau, "Imprisonment vs. Death: Does Avoiding Schwarzschild's Paradox Lead to Sheleff's Dilemma," *Albany Law Review* 54 (1989–1990): 481–495; Penal Reform International, *Prison Reform Briefing* 1 (2007) 1–12. On life imprisonment from the perspective of a suitable replacement for the death penalty, see Hood and Hoyle, *Death Penalty,* ch. 11; Appleton and Grøver, "The Pros and Cons of Life without Parole."

63. The UN Model Treaty on Extradition (GA Res. 45/116," as amended by res. 52/88) art. 4 (b), provides that extradition may be refused: "If the offence for which extradition is requested carries the death penalty under the law of the requesting State, unless that State gives such assurance as the requested State considers sufficient that the death penalty will not be imposed or, if imposed, will not be carried out." Footnote 9 to this Article provides that: "Some countries may wish to apply the same restriction to the imposition of a life, or indeterminate sentence."

64. OAS TS, No. 60, February 25, 1981, s. 9 (emphasis added).

65. This agreement applies with treaty status to the MERCOSUR states, that is Argentina, Brazil, Uruguay, and Venezuela, as well as to Bolivia, Chile, and Ecuador: CMC 14/98. Extended pursuant to CMC 15/98.

66. Sala Plena Auto Supremo: 157A/2010 EXP. N°: 609/2009 FECHA: 21 de mayo de 2010.

67. OJ C 313 of June 23, 1996.

68. Ines Horta Pinto, "Punishment in Portuguese Criminal Law: A Penal System without Life Imprisonment," in *Life Imprisonment and Human Rights.*

69. Article 5.2 of the European Union Council Framework Decision of June 13, 2002, on the European Arrest Warrant and Surrender Procedures between Member States, 2002/584/JHA.

70. *Trabelsi v. Belgium,* ECtHR (app. 140/10), September 4, 2014.

71. Podcast of the Grand Chamber case of *Harkins v. United Kingdom,* January 11, 2017, http://www.echr.coe.int/Pages/home.aspx?p= hearings&w=715 3714_11012017&language= lang&c=&py=2017. In the end the Grand Chamber concluded that the case before it was not admissible as the facts had not changed since the ECtHR had decided it in 2012: *Harkins and Edwards v. the United Kingdom,* ECtHR (apps. 9146/07 and 32650/07), January 7, 2012. That decision remained final, notwithstanding the subsequent development of the law in *Vinter.* See *Harkins v. United Kingdom,* ECtHR (app. 71537/14), June 15, 2017 [GC] (admissibility decision).

72. European Committee for the Prevention of Torture, *25th General Report of the CPT* (Strasbourg, France: Council of Europe, 2016), CPT/Inf (2016), 10.

73. United Nations Office at Vienna, Crime Prevention and Criminal Justice Branch, *Life Imprisonment* (Vienna: United Nations, 1994).

74. UN General Assembly, "United Nations Standard Minimum Rules for the Treatment of Prisoners (the Nelson Mandela Rules)," A/RES/70/175, December 17, 2015.

75. Lila Kazemian and Jeremy Travis, "Imperative for Inclusion of Long Termers and Lifers in Research and Policy," *Criminology and Public Policy* 14 (2015): 355–395.

Acknowledgments

This book is based largely on material collected in the course of our Life Imprisonment Worldwide Research Project, which was funded by a generous grant from the Leverhulme Trust (RPG-2013–369). We are grateful for the "no strings" approach of the Trust, which gave us time and resources to assemble a research team, to collect a wide range of materials, and generally to develop our ideas freely from February 2014 to February 2017.

The School of Law at the University of Nottingham provided a supportive base throughout the project. It also provided additional funding for Catherine Appleton during the writing stage.

Other institutions played important parts too:

- The Max Planck Society gave us both research fellowships to enable us to work in 2014 in the superb library of the Max Planck Institute for Foreign and International Criminal Law in Freiburg im Breisgau.
- The Oñati International Institute for the Sociology of Law in Spain enabled us to hold a workshop in April 2015 for an international group of scholars interested in life imprisonment. The twenty-two papers presented at the workshop, an invaluable source of information for this book, have been published separately as *Life Imprisonment and Human Rights,* ed. Dirk van Zyl Smit and Catherine Appleton (Oxford: Hart/Bloomsbury Publishing, 2016).
- For the spring semester of 2017, Dirk van Zyl Smit was a visiting Global Law Professor at the School of Law at New York University, which made available its cornucopia of resources to him during the final writing period.

A global project such as this one depends on individuals around the world being prepared to provide information, and many were. We are deeply grateful to all who helped in this way, both officials providing "hard" data and private individuals who supplemented the information we obtained from official sources. When we came to the end of our project, we sent them all a short summary of what we had found. We hope that they will see this book as a further fruit of their contribution to knowledge about life imprisonment worldwide.

Some individuals went far beyond providing us with data. First among many are the researchers who worked for the project on a full-time basis. Special thanks go to Meritxell Abellán Almenara, Georgie Benford, Angelika Reichstein, and Vicky Vouleli. Not only did they do the hard work of collating data, but they also engaged fully with the study as a whole. It was a privilege to write at least one joint paper with each of them and thus to develop many of the ideas that are now incorporated in this book. As our research instruments were available in all the UN languages, they often required translation, as did many of the other materials we collected. All translations were undertaken or checked by the authors or other members of the primary research team.

We also had the advantage of having Joe Sempik as part-time consultant for much of the project. His calm approach to what were for us complex statistical issues made a significant contribution to the research team. In the final two months of writing, Ricky Röntsch worked tirelessly to check our work and put it into proper style.

From the beginning of the project and throughout the writing of this book, we were supported by an advisory panel of Alison Hannah, Roger Hood, Tapio Lappi-Seppälä, and Marc Mauer. They were always available to give advice and to comment on earlier drafts of the book. We are very grateful for their encouragement and support.

At the initial stage, when we were designing our primary data collection instrument, we were greatly assisted by Axel Dessecker, who had conducted similar surveys of life imprisonment in Germany on behalf of the Kriminologische Zentralstelle in Wiesbaden. Roy Walmsley, who, over many years, has built up the World Prison Brief into the leading database of national prisoner numbers, provided sage advice on collecting data worldwide. Our own database largely followed the division of regions and countries (including independent territories) adopted by the World Prison Brief. We chose to do this in order to facilitate comparisons between what we found about life imprisonment and imprisonment generally.

As our ideas developed, a number of scholars proved valuable critiques of them. In 2014, Jonathan Simon was the respondent to the first presentation of our research at the annual meeting of the American Society of Criminology in San Francisco. In 2015, Leslie Sebba and Miklós Lévay joined us for a special session on life imprisonment at the annual meeting of the European Society of Criminology in Porto, Portugal. We learned a great deal from both these sessions as well as from visiting scholars to the Life Imprisonment Worldwide Project in Nottingham, UK. Particular thanks are due to John Anderson, Javier de León Villalba, and Beatriz López Lorca, who spent longer periods with us and taught us much that we would otherwise not have known.

In New York, Jim Jacobs organized a group of scholars to read an early version of our manuscript and to spend a day working thorough it with us. We are very thankful to him and to Alessandro Corda, David Garland, Judy Greene, Margaret Leigey, Ashley Nellis, Daniel Pascoe, and Christopher Seeds. In addition, two anonymous reviewers provided very helpful feedback on a later version of the manuscript.

For expert guidance, insight, and support, we are particularly grateful to our editors at Harvard University Press, Thomas LeBien and Kathleen Drummy, and also to Angela Piliouras and her colleagues at Westchester Publishing Services. Sincere thanks must also go to Isabelle Lewis for her meticulous mapmaking.

Finally, we wish to thank our partners, Betine van Zyl Smit and Bent Grøver, together with our families, for their continued support and encouragement. Special thanks go to Betine, who painstakingly read each chapter draft, and to Bent for the many hours spent working with our data, carrying out statistical analyses that went far beyond our expectations. We are deeply indebted to both of them.

Index

Wines, Enoch, 8
women, 122–124, 183–184
work programs, 229

yoga programs, 231
youth justice. *See* children,
   rights of

Yugoslavia: international criminal
   tribunal, 26–28, 61–62, 240; successor
   states to, 29

Zimbabwe: clemency, 58; life without
   parole, 57–58; release mechanisms,
   257. *See also* Africa